August 8–9, 2015
Los Angeles, CA, USA

I0031383

**Association for
Computing Machinery**

*Advancing Computing as a Science & Profession*

# SUI'15

Proceedings of the 3rd ACM Symposium on
**Spatial User Interaction**

*Sponsored by:*
**ACM SIGGRAPH and SIGCHI**

*Supported by:*
**University of Wyoming, University of Hamburg,
Simon Fraser University and the University of Southern California**

**Association for
Computing Machinery**

*Advancing Computing as a Science & Profession*

**The Association for Computing Machinery**
**2 Penn Plaza, Suite 701**
**New York, New York 10121-0701**

**Notice to Past Authors of ACM-Published Articles**
ACM intends to create a complete electronic archive of all articles and/or other material previously published by ACM. If you have written a work that has been previously published by ACM in any journal or conference proceedings prior to 1978, or any SIG Newsletter at any time, and you do NOT want this work to appear in the ACM Digital Library, please inform permissions@acm.org, stating the title of the work, the author(s), and where and when published.

**ISBN:** 978-1-4503-3703-8 (Digital)

**ISBN:** 978-1-4503-3886-8 (Print)


Additional copies may be ordered prepaid from:

**ACM Order Department**
PO Box 30777
New York, NY 10087-0777, USA

Phone: 1-800-342-6626 (USA and Canada)
+1-212-626-0500 (Global)
Fax: +1-212-944-1318
E-mail: acmhelp@acm.org
Hours of Operation: 8:30 am – 4:30 pm ET

Printed in the USA

# SUI 2015 Chairs' Welcome

It is our great pleasure to welcome you to the third *ACM Symposium on Spatial User Interaction*. This event focuses on the user interface challenges that appear when users interact in the space where the flat, two-dimensional, digital world meets the volumetric, physical, three-dimensional (3D) space we live in. The symposium considers both spatial input as well as output, with an emphasis on the issues around the interaction between humans and systems. Due to the advances in 3D technologies, spatial interaction is now more relevant than ever. Powerful graphics engines and high-resolution screens are now ubiquitous in everyday devices, such as tablets and mobile phones. Moreover, new forms of input, such as multi-touch, finger and body tracking technologies are now easily available, and more and more commercial 3D systems with spatial interaction capabilities exist, many priced at the consumer level. However, the challenges, limitations, and advantages of leveraging this third dimension in human-computer interfaces are still not yet fully understood. These questions will only become more relevant as these emerging technologies continue to cross the barrier towards wide adoption.

The call for papers attracted 48 submissions from Asia, Europe, Australia, and North and South America in all areas of Spatial User Interaction research. The international program committee consisting of 19 experts in the topic areas and the three program chairs handled the review process. Eight submissions were reviewed by the program chairs and rejected without further review due to being incomplete, insufficient quality, or inappropriate for the symposium topic. All other submissions received at least four detailed reviews, two from members of the international program committee and two or more from external reviewers. The reviewing process was double-blind, with the authors' identities visible only to the program chairs and the primary program committee member assigned to the paper. In the end, the program committee accepted 17 papers (10 long, 7 short), corresponding to an overall acceptance rate of 35%. Additionally, 11 posters complement the program and appear in the proceedings. Furthermore, three research demonstrations were accepted and will be presented at the symposium. We also encourage attendees to attend the keynote talk, *TRANSFORM: Beyond Tangible Bits, Towards Radical Atoms*, presented by Hiroshi Ishii from the MIT Media Lab.

Organizing SUI 2015 was a team effort. First, we would like to thank the authors for providing the technical content of the program, along with the members of the international program committee and the external reviewers. In particular, we would like to acknowledge Robert Teather and Kyla McMullen for organizing the posters and demos, Timofey Grechkin for assisting with local arrangements, and Bireswar Laha for managing registrations. James Stewart from Precision Conference Solutions assisted by providing and maintaining the reviewing system, and Lisa Tolles from Sheridan Communications helped greatly to create the proceedings. Additionally, our institutions, the University of Wyoming, the University of Hamburg, Simon Fraser University, and the University of Southern California supported us in this endeavor. Finally, we thank the sponsoring organizations, the ACM Special Interest Groups on Graphics and Human-Computer Interaction (SIGGRAPH, SIGCHI) for co-sponsoring this event. We hope that you will find our program interesting, and that SUI 2015 will inspire you to discuss and share ideas with other researchers and practitioners of spatial user interaction from institutions around the world.

**Amy Banic**
*SUI 2015 General Chair*

**Evan Suma, Frank Steinicke, Wolfgang Stuerzlinger**
*SUI 2015 Program Chairs*

# Table of Contents

## Session: Motion and Embodiment

## Posters

# Demonstrations

# SUI 2015 Symposium Organization

**General Chair:** Amy Banic *(University of Wyoming, USA)*

**Program Chairs:** Evan Suma *(University of Southern California, USA)*
Frank Steinicke *(University of Hamburg, Germany)*
Wolfgang Stuerzlinger *(Simon Fraser University, Canada)*

**Posters Chairs:** Robert Teather *(McMaster University, Canada)*
Alec Moore *(University of Texas at Dallas, USA)*

**Demos Chairs:** Kyla McMullen *(University of Florida, USA)*
Isaac Cho *(University of North Carolina at Charlotte, USA)*

**Local Arrangements Chair:** Timofey Grechkin *(University of Southern California, USA)*

**Registration Chair:** Bireswar Laha *(Stanford University, USA)*

**Awards Chair:** Gerd Bruder *(University of Hamburg, Germany)*

**Webmaster:** Rajiv Khadka *(University of Wyoming, USA)*

**Graphic Designer:** Shelby Piche *(University of Wyoming, USA)*

**Steering Committee:** Evan Suma *(University of Southern California, USA)*
Frank Steinicke *(University of Hamburg, Germany)*
Wolfgang Stuerzlinger *(Simon Fraser University, Canada)*

**Program Committee:** Fernando Argelaguet Sanz *(Inria Rennes, France)*
Gerd Bruder *(University of Hamburg, Germany)*
Isaac Cho *(University of North Carolina at Charlotte, USA)*
Pablo Figueroa *(Universidad de los Andes, Colombia)*
Victoria Interrante *(University of Minnesota, USA)*
Kyle Johnsen *(University of Georgia, USA)*
Dan Keefe *(University of Minnesota, USA)*
Tobias Isenberg *(Inria Saclay, France)*
Bireswar Laha *(Stanford University, USA)*
Manfred Lau *(Lancaster University, UK)*
Robert Lindeman *(Worcester Polytechnic Institute, USA)*
Ryan McMahan *(University of Texas at Dallas, USA)*
Rolf Nordahl *(Aalborg University Copenhagen, Denmark)*
Christian Sandor *(Nara Institute of Science and Technology, Japan)*
Stefania Serafin *(Aalborg University Copenhagen, Denmark)*
Kazuki Takashima *(Tohoku University, Japan)*
Robert Teather *(McMaster University, Canada)*

**Additional reviewers:**

| | |
|---|---|
| Acevedo Feliz, Daniel | Kruijff, Ernst |
| Andujar, Carlos | Krum, David |
| Anslow, Craig | Kulshreshth, Arun |
| Arif, Ahmed | Kyritsis, Markos |
| Bailey, Reynold | Lewis Brooks, Anthony |
| Banic, Amy | Leyrer, Markus |
| Bennett, Terrell | lv, Zhihan |
| Bolte, Benjamin | MacKenzie, Scott |
| Bringoux, Lionel | Martinez Plasencia, Diego |
| Brooks, Eva Petersson | Miller, Wesley |
| Burrell, Andrew | Min, Chulhong |
| Chaudhuri, Abon | Nabiyouni, Mahdi |
| Chen, Jian | Neustaedter, Carman |
| Chen, Xiang | Nguyen, Huyen |
| Chu, Sharon Lynn | Nillson, Niels |
| Daiber, Florian | Nittala, Aditya |
| de Barros, Paulo | Oda, Ohan |
| Dey, Arindam | Palleis, Henri |
| Ebhrahimi, Elham | Quarles, John |
| Ens, Barrett | Raedle, Roman |
| Erkut, Cumhur | Ragan, Eric |
| Ferwerda, Bruce | Shizuki, Buntarou |
| Forbes, Angus | Stellmach, Sophie |
| Funke, Steve | Takahashi, Shin |
| Geigel, Joe | Tatzgern, Markus |
| Gellersen, Hans | Wacharamanotham, Chat |
| Grubert, Jens | Wang, Jack |
| Guo, Bin | Wang, Jia |
| Hasan, Khalad | Wartell, Zachary |
| Hodgson, Eric | Whitton, Mary |
| Jackson, Bret | Willett, Wesley |
| Jones, J. Adam | Yamane, Katsu |
| Kalwar, Santosh | Yanagida, Yasuyuki |
| Kohli, Luv | Yoon, Sang Ho |
| Kopper, Regis | Zhang, Yunbo |
| Korsgaard, Dannie | Zhang, Yupeng |

**Sponsors:** ACM**SIGGRAPH**   SIGCHI

# TRANSFORM: Beyond Tangible Bits, Towards Radical Atoms

Hiroshi Ishii
MIT Media Lab
75 Amherst Street
Cambridge, MA 02139 USA
ishii@media.mit.edu

## Abstract

Whereas today's mainstream Human Computer Interaction (HCI) research addresses functional concerns - the needs of users, practical applications, and usability evaluation - Tangible Bits and Radical Atoms are driven by vision. This is because today's technologies will become obsolete in one year, and today's applications will be replaced in 10 years, but true visions, we believe, can last longer than 100 years.

Tangible Bits seeks to realize seamless interfaces between humans, digital information, and the physical environment by giving physical form to digital information, making bits directly manipulable and perceptible. Our goal is to invent new design media, taking advantage of the richness of human senses and skills as developed through our lifetime of interaction with the physical world as well as the computational reflection enabled by real-time sensing and digital feedback.

Radical Atoms takes a leap beyond Tangible Bits by assuming a hypothetical generation of materials that can change form and properties dynamically and computationally, becoming as reconfigurable as pixels on a screen. Radical Atoms is the future material that can transform its shape, conform to constraints, and inform the users of their affordances. Radical Atoms is a vision for the future of human-material interaction, in which all digital information has a tangible manifestation for interactions.

I present the trajectory of our vision-driven design research from Tangible Bits towards Radical Atoms, and a variety of design projects presented and exhibited in arts, design, and science communities in the past 20 years.

## ACM Classification Keywords

H.5.2. Information interfaces and presentation: User Interfaces.

**Author Keywords:** Tangible Bits; Tangible User Interfaces; TUI; Radical Atoms; Transformable Materials; Programmable Materials; Shape-Changing Interfaces; Arts; Design; Trans-Disciplinary.

*SUI 2015,* August 8–9, 2015, Los Angeles, California, USA.
ACM 978-1-4503-3703-8/15/08.
http://dx.doi.org/10.1145/2788940.2788958

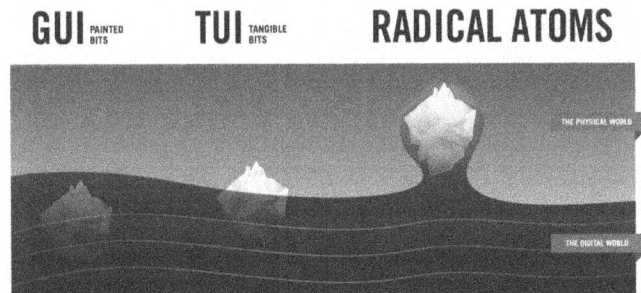

**GUI** PAINTED BITS    **TUI** TANGIBLE BITS    **RADICAL ATOMS**

## Short Bio

Hiroshi Ishii is a Jerome B. Wiesner Professor of Media Arts and Sciences at the MIT Media Lab. He was named Associate Director at the Media Lab in May 2008. He is the director of the Tangible Media Group that he founded and directs to pursue new visions of Human Computer Interaction (HCI): "Tangible Bits" and "Radical Atoms."

Prof. Ishii and his team have presented their vision of "Tangible Bits" and "Radical Atoms" at a variety of academic, design, and artistic venues (including ACM SIGCHI, SIGGRAPH, Cooper Hewitt Design Museum, Milano Design Week, Cannes Lions Festival, Aspen Ideas Festival, Industrial Design Society of America, AIGA, Ars Electronica, Centre Pompidou, and Victoria and Albert Museum, NTT ICC) emphasizing that the development of vision requires the rigors of both scientific and artistic review. Prof. Ishii was elected to CHI Academy by ACM SIGCHI in 2006.

Prior to joining the MIT Media Lab from 1988-1994, Prof. Ishii led a CSCW research group at NTT Human Interface Laboratories Japan, where his team invented TeamWorkStation and ClearBoard. Prof. Ishii was a visiting assistant professor at the University of Toronto, Canada from 1993-1994. He has received several degrees in engineering, including a B.E. degree in electronic engineering, M.E. and Ph.D. degrees in computer engineering from Hokkaido University, Japan, in 1978, 1980, and 1992, respectively.

Photo Credit: Junichi Otsuki

# Comparison of Device-Based, One and Two-Handed 7DOF Manipulation Techniques

Jinbo Feng
Charlotte Visualization Center
UNC Charlotte
9201 University Blvd.
Charlotte, NC, USA
jfeng3@uncc.edu

Isaac Cho
Charlotte Visualization Center
UNC Charlotte
9201 University Blvd.
Charlotte, NC, USA
icho1@uncc.edu

Zachary Wartell
Charlotte Visualization Center
UNC Charlotte
9201 University Blvd.
Charlotte, NC, USA
zwartell@uncc.edu

## ABSTRACT

We evaluate three bimanual 7 degree-of-freedom (7DOF) object manipulation techniques that use a pair of precision grasped isotonic devices called buttonballs. 7DOF manipulation means changing position, orientation and scale. We compare the techniques in a (stereo) Fish-tank Virtual Reality (VR) system. The user study displays multiple randomly located boxes of different sizes and the user must dock (i.e. align) each target box with an objective box at the screen center. Comparing task completion times shows that in cases where target and objective boxes are the same size, all three techniques perform equivalently. When the sizes differ--requiring a scale change--two of the technique's, Spindle+Wheel and a minor variant of Grab-and-Scale perform similarly, and are both faster than the third technique, One-Hand+Scale. We compare and contrast our results with other work including free-hand versus held device input and also with 7DOF object manipulation versus 7DOF view manipulation.

## Categories and Subject Descriptors

H.5.2 [**Information interfaces and presentation**]: User Interfaces –*Method devices and strategies.*

## General Terms

Performance, Design, Human Factors

## Keywords

3D vision, 7 Degree-of-Freedom, virtual reality, Fish tank VR, virtual object manipulation

## 1. INTRODUCTION

Many interaction techniques have been developed for 3D manipulation and navigation [1]. Among others, these involve single and bi-manual 2D input devices, multi-touch, 6 degree-of-freedom (6DOF) isotonic tracked held devices (or "props") and 3D tracked hands and fingers using various technologies. Common 3D interactions are 6DOF manipulation and navigation. However, 7 degree-of-freedom (7DOF) interaction is important as well. For object manipulation, this means including position, orientation plus scale. For navigation, this means treating view

*SUI 2015*, August 8–9, 2015, Los Angeles, California, USA.
Copyright 2015 © ACM 978-1-4503-3703-8/15/08...$15.00.
http://dx.doi.org/10.1145/2788940.2788942

scale as a separate $7^{th}$ DOF [15]. The latter becomes important in multi-scale virtual environments that use technology that makes differing view scales discernible, in which case the view scale parameter value can strongly effect usability [22] [15].

For 3D user interfaces, besides the various application requirements that influence the choice of input devices, a key issue is the mapping from the input device's DOF's to the manipulated object's DOF's. Depending on the device technology and mapping design, this might allow all object 7DOF's to be manipulated simultaneously or might allow only a subset of the 7DOF's to be manipulated at a given time using different input modes.

In a docking task, the user must align a target 3D object with an objective object [25]. A common object shape is a tetrahedron. In 6DOF docking the target and object are the same size, while in the 7DOF docking they differ in size.

For a 6DOF docking task Masliah et al. [10] find that users tend to allocate their control to the rotational and translational DOF's separately and switch control between the rotating and translating. With training, allocation of control within the translational and rotational subsets increases at a faster rate than across all 6 DOF's together. Their results suggest that the simultaneous manipulation of all DOF's does not necessary lead to the fastest completion time.

This paper evaluates 3 input techniques using isotonic 6DOF devices [25] for a 7DOF object manipulation task, i.e. manipulating the Euclidean DOF's, xyz+yaw,pitch,roll, plus scale. Our goal is to compare a technique that always engages all 7DOF against a technique where the user can choose whether to engage only pose or to engage pose and scale together. We refer to the former as "simultaneous 7DOF" and the latter as "separated 6DOF+Scale". Our study is performed in a stereo Fish-Tank virtual reality (VR) [23] (*also* Desktop VR [6]) environment with precision-grasped, 6DOF button balls. We perform a user study with 12 participants comparing the performance among the following three techniques:

- One-Hand+Scale [23] [15] – an uni-manual, separated 6DOF with Scale technique
- Spindle+Wheel [4] – a bi-manual, simultaneous 7DOF technique
- "One-Handed with Two-Handed Scaling" [5] – a bi-manual, separated 6DOF+Scale technique. (Note this technique is a minor variant of Grab-and-Scale [5]).

Our choice of these 3 techniques is discussed in Section 2.

The study's manipulation tasks include conditions that both require and do <u>not</u> require scale adjustment. Overall, we find that when users do not have to change scale, all three techniques performed equivalently. If users do have to scale, Spindle+Wheel and Grab-and-Scale perform similarly, but better than One-Hand+Scale. Some of these results are consistent with our detailed hypothesis and prior related work [9] [12] [4]; others are not. We compare and contrast our results to the others. We discuss result differences between 7DOF object manipulation versus 7DOF travel (i.e. view manipulation) and discuss free-hand [12] versus held device input and conclude with some guidelines.

## 2. BACKGROUND

7DOF interaction can control object manipulation, i.e. location $(x,y,z)$, orientation (yaw, roll, pitch) and scale. 7DOF interaction also occurs in multi-scale virtual environments where the view scale factor is discernible as a $7^{th}$ degree-of-freedom due to stereo parallax, head-coupled display's motion parallax and direct 3D manipulation [24] [22] [15]. Extensive multi-scale VE's require dynamic adjustment to this $7^{th}$ view DOF. This study is limited to a 7DOF object manipulation task rather than a 7DOF travel task. But any position control 7DOF object manipulation technique can be adapted to 7DOF travel with the scene-in-hand metaphor [2].

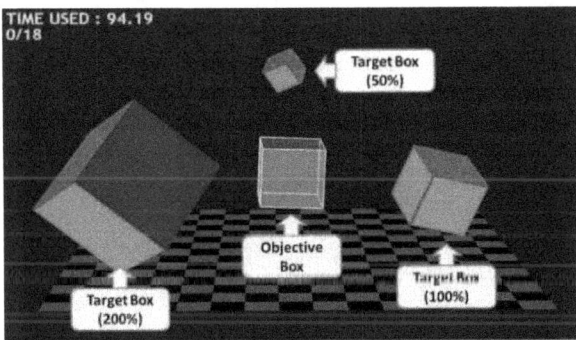

**Figure 1: Screen capture of virtual environment displayed on desktop VR system in the experiment. The white frame objective box locates in the screen center with red frame target boxes around**

A standard protocol for comparing object manipulation techniques is having users repeatedly perform a "docking" task [25]. As brief review, we introduce our experiment's particular 7DOF docking protocol. (Section 3 fully details our protocol and system hardware). Our virtual environment contains target boxes with 3 different fixed sizes at random locations in each trial. An objective box appears at fixed size at the screen center a random orientation in each trial (Figure 1). The user's task is to select each target box and manipulate it to align with the objective box. Like colored faces must be matched.

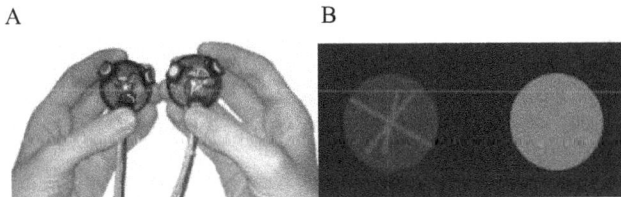

**Figure 2: (A) Button balls and (B) corresponding spherical cursors; left cursor is blue and right is pink.**

In our experiment, the user holds isotonic input devices, in particular 6DOF tracked buttonballs [16] [25] [20] (Figure 2A). Each buttonball has a corresponding (stereoscopic) 3D cursor in the virtual environment (Figure 2B).

Next, we review prior interaction techniques suitable for 7DOF manipulation and present a simplified taxonomy. Our experiment only compares position control techniques therefore the review is limited to position control. It is outside our scope to review the pluses and minuses of position, rate, and acceleration control [2]. Our review is organized based on the 3 interaction techniques that we use in our experiment.

When discussing bimanual techniques, we use Guiard's Kinematic Chain Theory terminology [7]. For brevity, the rest of this document assumes the user is right handed. In the actual user studies, the roles of the cursors would be reversed for a left handed user.

### 2.1 Hand+Fingers vs Held Devices

Isotonic 6DOF input can be controlled by either 6DOF held devices or by hand and fingers tracking (abbreviated *hand+fingers*) [2]. Hand and finger tracking can be implemented in multiple ways. 6DOF tracked "data gloves" track the hand's 6DOF pose and detect each individual finger's phalange's pose. 6DOF tracked pinch gloves track the hand's 6DOF pose and detect combinations of finger pinches. Cordless marker based tracking is possible [13] as well as "free hand" tracking that requires no markers [21].

Hand+fingers and held devices each have advantages and disadvantages. The ideal hand+finger tracking implementation is a free-hand one and the ideal held device tracking is completely untethered (no wires) with no obtrusive markers sticking out of the device on stalks, etc. With current technology, achieving these ideals involve compromises on tracking precision, tracking volume, and occlusion.

Mochring and Frochlich [13] present an extensive study comparing a close-to-ideal free-hand implementation to a close-to-ideal held-device implementation used for several uni-manual docking tasks. The same tracking technology by A.R.T. GmbH is used over all conditions. Their general conclusion is:

> "finger based interaction is generally preferred if the functionality and ergonomics of manually manipulated virtual artifacts has to be assessed. However, controller-based interaction is often faster and more robust"

The passive-haptic feedback of held devices appears beneficial. Of course, some application domains require free hand 3D input such as surgeons in an operating room.

### 2.2 A Simplified Taxonomy

There are many uni-manual and bi-manual techniques suitable for 7DOF manipulation. Many have been formally evaluated. We will compare results of our study to the result of other studies. To help compare and contrast the range of techniques, Table 1 (next page) presents a taxonomy. Techniques grouped in a single row use the same mapping of input DOF's to the manipulated object DOF's. The *Original* column indicates the earliest usage of the mapping. The *H* column indicates the number of hands used. The *DOF* column indicates the number of DOF's available, denoted '*e+s*' where *e* are the number Euclidean DOF's and *s* indicates number of scale DOF's. The *Free-Hand* and *Held Device* column separate techniques that use free-hand tracking from those that use held devices. The *C.* column encodes various classifications (*C.* abbreviates "**Classification**"). '–' means the technique cannot simultaneously adjust scale and pose, while + means the technique can simultenously adjust pose and scale. '*' means a single button/pinch engages all supported DOF's at once. '**' means that a two button/pinch's in sequence are needed to engage pose and scale. The first button/pinch engages pose and a second button/pinch engages scale (while the pose adjustment remains engaged). Potentially, by requiring two button/pinch's the '+,**' class techniques may operate slightly slower than the '+,*' class techniques. 'A' vs 'S' indicate whether a bimanual technique is symmetric or asymmetric [7]. As we review prior work, we will discuss each row of the table.

## 2.3 One-Handed with Scale (OH)

| | Original | H | DOF | C. | Free-Hand | Held Device |
|---|---|---|---|---|---|---|
| 1 | One-Hand w/ Scale [15] [23] | 1 | 6,1 | -,** | | **OH** |
| 2 | 5DOF+Scale [9] (glove) | 2 | 5+1 | +,* S | Handle-Bar [17] | TC[1] [20] Spindle [4] [14][2] |
| 3 | Spindle+Wheel [4] | 2 | 6+1 | +,* ≈S | | **Spindle+Wheel** |
| 4 | Grab-and-Scale [5] (glove) | 2 | 6+1 | +,** A | 6DOF-Hand [12] | **OTS** HIM [20] |
| 5 | Air TRS [12] (free hand) | 2 | 5+1 | +,** A | | |
| 6 | 3DOF-Hand [12] (free hand) | 2 | 6+1 | +,** A | | |

**Legend**:

+ can scale simultaneously,  − cannot scale simultaneously
* scale always enabled, ** scale engaged with 2nd pinch or button
S symmetric, A asymmetric (Guiard classification [7])
Conditions in our experiment are **Bold**

**Table 1: Rows are techniques with the same DOF mapping. However, within a row the input technology and scale engagement conditions may vary.**

Our experiment includes a one-handed isotonic technique, called "One-Handed with Scale technique" (abbreviated OH). OH works as follows. For translation and rotation, the user presses and holds the selection button after placing the cursor inside the target box [23] [15]. Then the box movement has been attached to the cursor and with the cursor center as the rotation center. To scale the target box, the user places the cursor inside the box and presses and holds a second scaling button. To scale up and down, the user moves the cursor hand toward or away from the screen. Scaling is controlled by rate control. Prior work suggests for this one-hand 7DOF technique users prefer rate control for scale compared to position control [4].

Within the taxonomy, the One-Hand with Scale (OH) appears in Table 1, row 1. 6DOF pose and scale cannot perform simultaneously and use two buttons, hence OH is '6,1' and '-,**'. OH is not bimanual and has no symmetric/asymmetric Guiard classification.

## 2.4 Spindle+Wheel (S+W)
Our experiment's first two-handed manipulation condition is Spindle+Wheel [4]. Spindle+Wheel extends prior work [9] [5] [14] by allowing all 7DOF to be manipulated simultaneously with one button.

Figure 3A shows the Spindle+Wheel visual feedback. A thin orange cylinder, the "spindle", is drawn between the two cursors [14] with a small red sphere at the mid-point. The "wheel" [4] is a disc on the right cursor indicating the plane of rotation for the pitch rotation.

To select an object, the user places the spindle's center inside the target object and presses and holds the select button on the left button ball. This engages object manipulation [14] which works as follows and is illustrated in Figure 3B. Rotating one hand about the other while keeping their distance constant, rotates the selected box in yaw and roll, moving the hands closer or farther apart scales the box, while translating the hands rigidly translates the object [9]. Figure 3B illustrates the difference between Spindle+Wheel and the earlier Mapes and Moshell's 5DOF+Scale technique (re-used by Spindle [14]). The 5DOF+Scale technique provides all the illustrated DOF's except the ability to pitch -- the green arc with arrow in Figure 3B. Spindle+Wheel supports pitch by spinning or twisting the right button ball with the fingers around wheel axis. This rotates the selected object around the spindle axis [4].

Cho and Wartell demonstrate that Spindle+Wheel yields faster completion times than the 5DOF+Scale approach for a 7DOF docking task [4]. Spindle+Wheel is "mostly" symmetric in that all but the pitch DOF are bimanually symmetric.

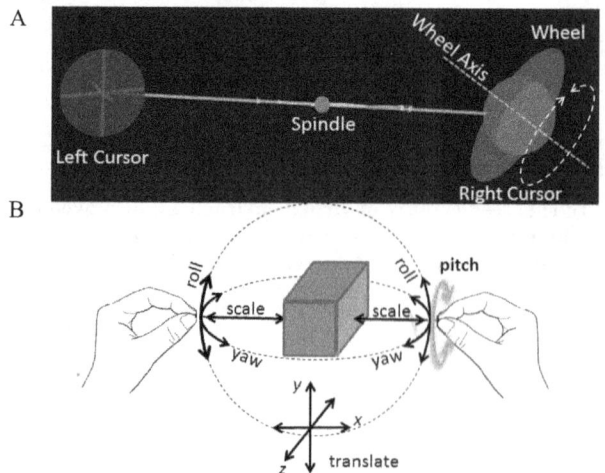

**Figure 3: Spindle+Wheel condition. (A) Spindle+Wheel's visual feedback. (B) Bimanual DOF's of Mapes and Moshell "5DOF+Scale" technique [9] versus "Spindle+Wheel" [4] which adds pitch (green).**

5DOF+Scale and Spindle appear in Table 1, row 2. All row 2 techniques are 5+1 DOF, engage all DOF's at once with one button/pinch ('+,*') and are symmetric ('S'). Spindle+Wheel in row 3. Song et al. [17] present a free-hand "Handle-Bar". By our observation Handle-bar replicates 5DOF+Scale [9] with nearly identical visual feedback of Spindle [14]. (Song et al. do not mention the replication).

---

[1] TC ('Two-Corners') is actually 5+3 (separate xyz scales), but a 5+1 variant is possible

[2] Original Spindle uses power grip SpaceGrips [13]

## 2.5 One-Handed with Two-Hand Scaling (OTS)

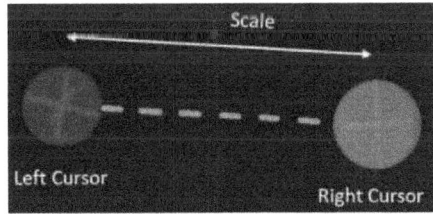

**Figure 4: Graphical representation in scaling manipulation**

Masliah et al.'s [10] result suggests a possible advantage to separating scale control into a separate second mode. This motivates evaluating a third technique called "One-Handed with Two-Hand Scaling" (OTS). In OTS, the left hand button ball operates the same as the One-Hand technique (OH) for translation and rotation by pressing a left cursor button. Additionally pressing a right cursor button engages scaling. In OTS, scale-mode displays a dotted green line between the two cursors (Figure 4). The scale is adjusted based on any ensuing change in distance between the cursors; this is similar to Spindle+Wheel.

The DOF mapping of OTS is the same a Culter et. al's bi-manual "Grab-and-Scale" (Table 1, row 4), but Grab-and-Scale uses tracked pinch gloves while OTS uses buttonballs. Also, unlike Grab-and-Scale, OTS also includes the deliberate translation offset between input device and cursor to counter fatigue [16]. OTS also essentially uses the same 7DOF mapping as the Hand-in-Middle (HIM) technique [20] and uses equivalent input devices, however, the target task differs.

We will compare and contrast our study's results to Mendes et al.'s [12] user study. So we briefly review their techniques and relate them to the ones we evaluate. Mendes et al. [12] present a bimanual free-hand technique called "6-DOF Hand" (Table 1, row 4). By our observation, 6-DOF Hand is the same as Grab-and-Scale but uses free hand tracking instead of tracked gloves. Hence, 6-DOF Hand and OTS differ in that OTS has an offset and uses buttonballs and two buttons, while 6-DOF-Hand is free-hand with two pinch gestures but no offset.

Mendes et al. [12] also present "Air TRS" (Table 1 row 5). Like 5DOF+Scale, Air TRS controls 5+1 DOF's, xyz-yaw-roll+scale, but while 5DOF+Scale is symmetric, Air TRS is asymmetric. In particular the center of scale and rotation is always the left hand. Air TRS appears to be a hybrid of 5DOF+Scale and Grab-and-Scale.

Mendes et al. also present 3DOF-Hand. It provides simultaneous 7DOF. Scaling works as in 5DOF+Scale. Translation is controlled by the initiating (left) hand but rotation is controlled by mapping the secondary hand's orientation directly to the selected object (rotation gain is 1).

## 3. EXPERIMENT

Section 2 introduced our experiment's protocol as part of a review of docking experimental protocols. Now we present our experimental design in detail.

The virtual environment is displayed in a stereoscopic, Fish-tank VR configuration [23]. The environment has a checker-board ground-plane (Figure 1). It is 40 cm square with half appearing behind the display surface and half appearing in front. In the center of the screen is a translucent box, the Objective Box, of fixed size and at a random orientation per trial. Each face has a different color. This cube's pose remains stationary relative to the display screen during target box manipulation. At each trial, three target boxes

with 50%, 100% and 200% of the objective box's size appear at random locations and orientations on the ground-plane. The user must select the target boxes one by one and align the target cube with the objective cube. Like colored faces must match. This requires object rotation, translation, and scaling to match the sizes.

When the distance between the target cube's corresponding vertices is within a tolerance (0.84 cm) of the objective cube's vertices, the frame of the cube turns green. If the target box is selected and kept green for 0.8 seconds [25], it will disappear and a success sound will be played indicating one docking operation is complete. The user then proceeds to dock the next target box. After docking the three target boxes, one trial has been completed and the system automatically generates three new target boxes for the next trial.

Once for each user (at the start of her session), the user holds the button balls and rests her elbows on the chair's arms and the experimenter sets a translational offset that places the 3D cursors in the center of the screen. This is designed to maximize the degree to which the user rests her elbows during interaction [16].

As mentioned, we evaluate three technique conditions with buttonballs devices: One-Hand with Scale (OH), Spindle+Wheel (S+W) and One-Hand with Two-Handed Scaling (OTS) crossed with 3 box sizes (50%, 100% and 200%). We also ported Spindle+Wheel to a free-hand implementation but the tracking results of commodity systems were not robust enough to perform a useful free-hand versus held-device comparison. (We discuss the specific difficulties encountered in Section 5.4).

Our experiment is within subjects. Participants perform all 3 techniques and encounter all box sizes. For each technique condition, there are two blocks: a training block followed by a 6 trials of experiment block (18 dockings total). Presentation order of manipulation technique condition was counter-balanced between participants. All participants successfully finished the study in 80 minutes.

The system hardware uses Nvidia 3D Vision glasses with Nvidia Quadro 2000 and a 120Hz 22" LCD monitor. The position of button balls and user's head are tracked by a Polhemus Fastrak. Software is written in OpenSceneGraph, VRPN [19] and an in-house C++ integration API [18].

Twelve unpaid students from the Computer Science and Computer Engineering departments with little or no experience using 3D computer graphic applications participated in the study. Participants were required to tell the distance differences of different boxes in the scene and distinguish the colors of the box frames and faces.

Our hypotheses are:

- **H1:** For 100% box size, OTS and OH will outperform S+W because S+W always engages scale and for the 100% box size which adds extra mental and physical effort to avoid changing the box size.
- **H2:** For the 50% and 200%, OTS and S+W will perform faster than OH because they allow simultaneous control of scale, while OH requires switching between 6DOF and Scale mode.
- **H3:** For the 50% and 200%, S+W will perform faster than OTS because it only requires engaging a single button to engage scale, while OTS requires the user alternatively engage and disengage the secondary scale button.
- **H4:** Overall, completion times for the 100% box will be faster than for the 50% and 200% percent cases due to the lack of need to scale.

- **H5:** Overall box sizes, OTS and S+W will outperform OH, because from **H3** they should dominate the scaling sconditions and our protocol has 2 scaling conditions and 1 non-scaling condition.

# 4. RESULTS

We next present our quantitative and subjective results. All significant results are $p=0.05$.

## 4.1 Quantitative Results

We use a 3×3 repeated measures ANOVA and use interaction technique presentation order as the between-subjects factor. Manipulation technique condition has value set {*One-handed (OH), Spindle+Wheel (S+W), One-handed with Two-handed Scale (OTS)*} and target box size has value set {*50%, 100%, 200%*}. These two variables are manipulated within participants.

There is a significant interaction effect on task completion time $(F(4,44)=9.486, p<.001, \eta_p^2=.463)$. Hence we examine the simple effects for each box size.

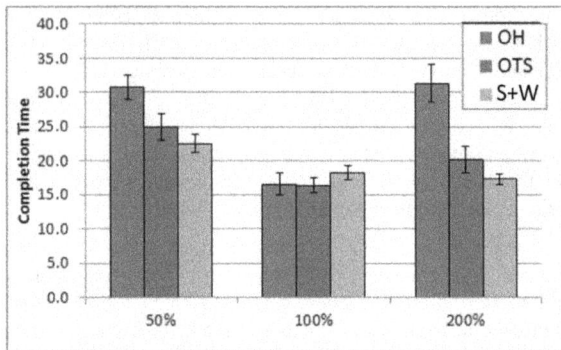

**Figure 5:** Completion time for different box sizes: 50%, 100% and 200% by different manipulation techniques

There is a significant simple effect for 50% box size $(F(2,22)=10.908, p<.005, \eta_p^2=.498)$. LSD comparisons show OTS (M=24.99, SD=6.72, $p<.005$) and S+W (M=22.56, SD=4.52, $p<.005$) has faster completion time than OH (M=30.76, SD=6.09). This partially confirms **H2** (for sub-case 50%). However the prediction that S+W is faster than OTS for 50% (**H3**) is not supported.

There is also a simple effect on 200% box size $(F(2,22)=18.883, p<.001, \eta_p^2=.632)$. LSD comparison show OTS (M=20.2, SD=6.71, $p<.005$) and S+W (M=17.34, SD=2.62, $p<.001$) has faster completion time than OH (M=31.33, SD=9.36). This completes confirmation of **H2**. Again, however the prediction that S+W is faster than OTS for 200% (**H3**) is not supported.

The simple effect of 100% box is not significant. This is surprising as it fails to support **H1**, that OTS and OH will outperform S+W. Section 5.1 elaborates on possible reasons for this in context of differing results found by others for Spindle+Wheel for 7DOF travel.

For the main effects, there exists significant difference among different box sizes $(F(2,22)=30.074, p<.001, \eta_p^2=.732)$. LSD comparisons show that 100% box size (M=17.1, SD=4.27) has faster completion time than 50% (M=26.1, SD=6.38, $p<.001$) and 200% box size (M=22.9, SD=8.7, $p<.001$). This confirms **H4**.

In addition, 200% box size has faster completion time than 50% box size $(p<.05)$. This was unexpected, however, it corroborates Cho and Wartell's [4] study of bi-manual, 7DOF navigation. They suggest users found it easier to bring hands together (scale down)

than to brings hands apart (scale up) from an initial parallel position. Section 5.2 elaborates on this issue.

Finally, there is a significant main effect on task completion time for interaction techniques $(F(2,22)=16.195, p<.001, \eta_p^2=.596)$. The LSD comparisons indicate that the completion time of both OTS (M=21.2, SD=7.33, $p<.005$) and S+W (M=21.85, SD=5.06, $p<.001$) are faster than OH (M=27.08, SD=8.82). This confirms **H5**.

## 4.2 Subjective Results

When asked which interaction technique (OH vs. S+W) is better for rotation, six participants answered S+W and the other half answered OH. Eight answered OH is better than S+W for translation, 3 answered both are equivalent, and one answered S+W. When asked which technique is better for scaling, four answered OTS, three rated S+W, three rated OH, one answered OH and OTS are equivalent, and one answered S+W and OTS are equivalent.

Regarding the question about which technique is most intuitive, five answered OTS, four answered S+W, two answered OH and one rated OH and OTS equivalent.

Overall, seven of twelve participants preferred the OTS, three rated S+W and one rated OTS and S+W equivalent. Participants rated arm fatigue after finishing the experiment for each interaction condition (on a 7-point Likert scale, 1 *no fatigue* to 7 *very painful*). There is no significant main effect on arm fatigue rate for interaction condition $(\chi^2(2)=.054)$, rates were OH=1.96, OTS=2.0 and S+W=2.04.

# 5. DISCUSSION

In this section, we compare our results to other related studies and hypothesize reasons for differences.

## 5.1 Compare to Spindle+Wheel for 7DOF Travel

**H1** predicted for 100% box size that both OTS and OH will outperform S+W because S+W always engages scale and in the 100% box size this requires additional physical and mental efforts to maintain a constant scale factor. However, the results do not support **H1** (i.e. OTS, OH and S+W perform the same). In contrast, Cho and Wartell found that OH and a modified Spindle+Wheel (that separated scale with a secondary button) both <u>did</u> perform faster than Spindle+Wheel for trials where scale change was not needed. However, their experiment explores 7DOF <u>travel</u>, adapting Spindle+Wheel using the scene-in-hand metaphor, not 7DOF object manipulation. This may explain the differing outcomes as follows.

Our manipulation task requires a selection step; the manipulation cannot be engaged until the cursor is <u>inside</u> a target box. For Cho and Wartell's 7DOF travel, the travel user interaction is engaged immediately upon button press <u>without</u> requiring the cursor to be inside the target. In the 100% case, their average completion times were 10.6s, 12.1s and 15.5s for OH, SWS, and S+W respectively. For us, in the 100% case, the averages are 16.4s, 16.5s and 17.34s for OTS, OH and S+W. The increase may be explained by the extra time required to move the cursor to the target box for a selection step. Possibly on average this adds an equal increment across all three conditions, leading to a lesser overall percentage difference between interaction techniques and hence lack of significant performance difference between OTS and S+W for 100%. Perhaps repeating our experiment, but as a 7DOF travel task, would find OTS performs better than S+W for the 100% box size.

## 5.2 200% vs 50% Box Size

The 200% box size has faster completion times than 50% box size for bimanual conditions. This corroborates Cho and Wartell's

[4] study of bi-manual 7DOF travel. They suggest that in bi-manual tasks users found it easier to scale down (bring hands together) than to scale up (brings hands apart).

We add a literature review on shoulder range-of-motion that is insightful. McCully et al. [11] study the range-of-motion (ROM) of shoulder rotation in healthy adults. "Shoulder rotation" is the anatomical adjustment that swings the lower arm at the elbow as shown in Figure 6A (next page). McCully et al. examine ROM for internal and external rotation directions when the shoulder is held at 4 different alignments. Figure 6A, B and C sketch three of their tested positions and show the mean ROMs. Internal rotations are positive and external rotations are negative. Figure 6D is our estimate of the typical internal and external rotation limits when the elbow is resting on a chair arm or table in our experiment. This is based on our anecdotal observations in our experiment and interpolating McCully et al.'s results for our typical shoulder alignment. We observe the external ("outward") rotation range is more limited than internal ("inward") rotation range which is consistent with the ROM literature. As the shoulder alignment grows farther away from being aligned with the Y-axis – where the ROM is greatest – the external rotation limit decreases. We find that in bimanual interaction in seated Fish-Tank VR, shoulder alignment ranges between situation A, B and D. In our 3D user interface, scaling up requires bringing the hands apart (external rotation) which is less comfortable than bringing them together (internal rotation) to scale down. We suspect these anatomical issues explain both our and other researchers' observation that bimanually scaling up a small object is slightly slower than scaling down a large object because the range limits cause more clutching in the former.

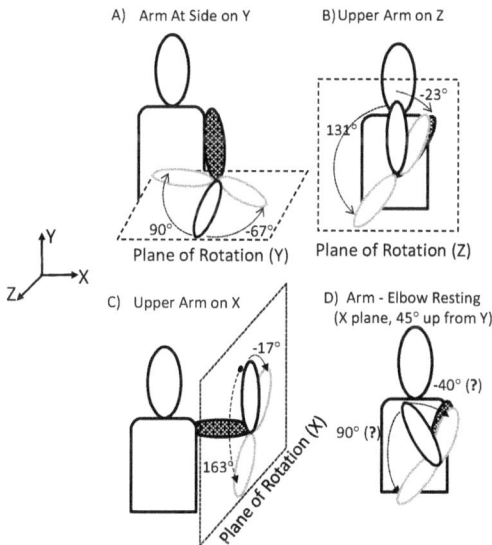

Figure 6: (A), (B) and (C) are shoulder rotation limits (internal >0; external < 0) for healthy adults with upper arms at various positions [11]. (D) is our estimate of the comfortable ROM when the elbow rests on a table as in our Fish-Tank VR environment – this is based on our observations and interpolating results of [11].

## 5.3 Compare to Prior Free-Hand Techniques

Next, we compare our results to Mendes et al. Both our and their virtual environment neither simulates gravity nor prevents object collision. Mendes et al. do not have a translation offset between the hand and the cursor; they use a horizontal stereo, head-tracked display (*aka* Responsive Workbench) and the user stands. All our conditions include a translation offset to reduce fatigue [16]; the screen is vertical, and the user sits.

Mendes et al.'s 6DOF-Hand, Air TRS and Handle-Bar techniques' relation to Grab-and-Scale and 5DOF+Scale are reviewed in Table 1 and Sections 2.4 and 2.5. A primary difference between Mendes et al.'s and our study's techniques is their use of free-hand tracking versus our use of buttonballs.

Mendes et al.'s Task #1 is a 2DOF task requiring 2D translation (dropping a ball into a solid cube with a bored out cylinder hole). In this case, 3DOF-Hand, 6DOF-Hand, Air TRS and Handle-Bar did not significantly differ; moreover the first 3 techniques only engage one hand for this task. Compare this to our 100% box trials (a 6DOF task) where OH, S+W and OTS did not significantly differ. A commonality across both their results and ours is that two-handed and one-handed techniques performed similarly when the tasks require manipulating less than or equal 6 DOF's.

Next, we compare Mendes et al.'s Task #2 to our 50% and 200% conditions (both tasks require scale adjustment). Mendes et al.'s Task #2 docks a donut into a donut shaped hole bored out of a face of a cube. Translation and size change is required but not rotation. Handle-Bar is faster than the others which performed similarly (6DOF-Hand, Air TRS, 3DOF Hand). In our 50% and 200% conditions scale change is required (7DOF). OTS and S+W perform similarly, but outperform OH. Note, Handle-Bar always simultaneously engages scale (one pinch) while 6DOF-Hand, Air TRS and 3DOF-Hand require a second pinch to engage scale. Again, scale is required for Task #2.

In our task, Spindle+Wheel, which always engages scale ('+,*'), is not faster than OTS, where scaling requires a secondary button ('+,**'). In Mendes et al's Task #2, their technique, which always engage scale ('+,*'), is faster than those that require a secondary scale engagement pinch ('+,**'). A possible hypothesis is that requiring a secondary scale engagement button ('+,**) slows performance compared to class '+,*', but due to ceiling effects it is not measurable for a more complex task, such as our Translate+Rotate+Scale, but is measurable for simpler (faster) tasks, such as Translate+Scale (Mendes et al.'s Task #2).

Next, we compare Mendes et al.'s Task #3 with our 50% and 200% conditions (both are full 7DOF). Mendes et al.'s Task #3 requires docking a half-cylinder into a half-cylinder shaped hole bored out of a cube. This is a 7DOF task but the half-cylinder can fit one of two ways, whereas our 7DOF task requires matching all like color faces – i.e. it can "fit" only one way. They find Handle-Bar and 6DOF-Hand perform similarly, but outperform Air TRS. Handle-Bar always engages scale ('+,*') while 6DOF-Hand and Air TRS require a secondary pinch ('+,**'). It does not appear the presence/absence of a secondary scale pinch alone can explain the time difference. Our 50% and 200% conditions also show no performance difference between the technique that always engages scale, Spindle+Wheel ('+,*' ; ≈Handle-Bar) and the technique that requires a secondary button/pinch to engage scale, OTS ('+,**' ; ≈6DOF-Hand). This suggests that for 7DOF object docking, the presence/absence of a required secondary scale button/pinch does not significantly affect completion time for either free-hand or held devices.

In both our and Mendes et al.'s results the Mapes-Moshell's 5DOF+Scaled derived rotation methods (Handle-Bar, Spindle+Wheel) completion time is not significantly different from the Grab-and-Scale derived methods (6DOF-Hand, OTS). [1]For rotation, Mendes et al. report that users prefer 6DOF-Hand over Handle-Bar. Similarly, our users overall preference are 7/12 preferred OTS compared to 3/12 for S+W. In both cases, more users prefer the bimanual technique where only one hand controls rotation (Table 1, row 4) over the bimanual technique where both hands control rotation (Table 1, row 2 & row 3). Mapes and Moshell's indicate their users preferred bi-manual rotation (5DOF+Scale) over a one-handed rotation [23], but they do not cite specific questionnaire results.

In Task #3, Mendes et al. suggest Handle-Bar outperforms 3DOF-Hand and Air TRS not because of different DOF mappings, but because the selection point (Handle-Bar/Spindle center) is not occluded by the user's hands. But Handle-Bar and 6DOF-Hand do not perform significantly different and 6DOF-Hand <u>does</u> have the occlusion issue. In our case, however, due to the translation offset none of our conditions co-locate the buttonball (and hence hand) with the 3D cursors and we still find Spindle+Wheel (≈Handle-Bar) performs similarly to OTS (≈6DOF-Hand). These results suggest the need to investigate whether adding translation offset versus no offset as an additional factor across all conditions would change the outcomes.

## 5.4 Free-Hand Spindle+Wheel

As mentioned in Section 3 we ported Spindle+Wheel to a free-hand implementation in our Fish-Tank VR. The user forms a U-shape with her index finger and thumb of the dominant hand to engage the pitch operation. The degree of pitch rotation comes from computing a line between the index finger tip and thumb tip and tracking the rotation of this line around the between-hand axis. Unfortunately, a Kinect + 3Gears' software implementation could not track the index and thumb robustly enough for a formal comparison against buttonball Spindle+Wheel.

We ported this interface to the Leap Motion as well and piloted a comparison of the buttonball versus free-hand Spindle+Wheel [3]. Unfortunately, the Leap Motion while better, but it is still not robust enough for formal evaluation. The U-gesture recognition rate was still significantly less than the "100% recognition rate" of a button press in the buttonball condition. We found roughly 75% recognition rate by the Leap Motion. (Others formally evaluating the Leap Motion found gesture recognition rates insufficient as well and resorted to substituting a second hand to press a keyboard key to engage their interaction techniques [2]). The tracking volume of the Leap Motion is also limited compared to the buttonballs' Polhemus. For buttonball Spindle+Wheel moving a buttonball by 1 cm moves the cursor by 1 cm. Free-hand Spindle+Wheel used the same C/D ratio. While performing the docking task it is fairly common to lose tracking while performing maneuvers equivalent to those with the buttonball because the hands exit the Leap's tracking volume. A user strategy of dividing attention between the docking task on the screen and keeping one's hands constrained in the Leap Motion tracking volume proved impractical. Using a different C/D ratio would change the distance the user maintains between her hands which alters the angular 'leverage' available when performing roll and yaw rotations. These issues prevented a fair comparison free-hand versus buttonball Spindle+Wheel. In the following section we will discuss our future plan.

## 5.5 Implications for Design and Future Work

Let, $T_1 \equiv T_2$, denote that the task completion time for techniques $T_1$ and $T_2$ are not significantly different and $T_1 > T_2$ denote $T_1$ performs <u>better</u> than $T_2$ (statistically significantly faster). Then we have the following for isotonic control (row $x$ refers to Table 1):

(i)   7DOF object docking:                          [12]
            Handle-Bar ≡ 6DOF-Hand
      (free hand, row 2) ≡ (free hand, row 4)
(ii)  7DOF travel docking:                          [4]
      Spindle+Wheel > Spindle
      (held device, row 3) > (held device, row 2)
(iii) 7DOF object docking:                   (*this paper*)
            Spindle+Wheel ≡ OTS
      (held device, row 3) ≡ (held device, row 4)
(iv)  6DOF object docking:                          [13]
            held device > free hand

Our literature review and result (iv) leaves the possibility of an interaction effect of hand+fingers versus held device implementation of a given bimanual technique and our Section 5.1 results indicate travel and object manipulation tasks that use the <u>same</u> DOF mappings can differ in performance outcomes. This suggests the following 4-way 7DOF experiment should be done:

> **EX1:** {Grab-and-Scale, Spindle+Wheel}×
> {hand+fingers, held device}×
> {travel, object manipulation}×
> {*multiple scale factors*}

From the issues we encounter and discussed in Section 5.4, experiment **EX1** must be done with a robust marker based tracking to allow proper and fair comparison between hand+finger and held device techniques [13].

1.  Completion Time:
    a.  Grab-and-Scale ≡ Spindle+Wheel    (*this paper*)
    b.  Grab-and-Scale ≡ Spindle          [12]
2.  "Average" user subjective preference-wise:
    a.  Grab-and-Scale > Spindle+Wheel    (*this paper*)
    b.  Grab-and-Scale > Spindler

Because (2) is an individual preference, the best general isotonic 7DOF manipulation guideline is:

> **G1:** If satisfying each individual user's preference is of high importance to the interface designer, give the user the option of Spindle+Wheel or Grab-and-Scale derived methods; otherwise use Grab-and-Scale.

Finally Section 5.2, suggests the following expectation for any bimanual isotonic technique that uses the scale technique derived from 5DOF+Scale:

> **G2:** A seated user is likely to be slightly slower at scaling up than scaling down.

> Potentially a designer could choose a slightly higher gain factor for scaling up to combat this.

## 6. CONCLUSION

This paper evaluated 3 input techniques using isotonic 6DOF devices for a 7DOF manipulation task. Overall, we found that when users do not have to scale, all three techniques performed equivalently. If users do have to scale, Spindle+Wheel and One-Handed-with-Two-Hand-Scaling perform better than One-Hand with Scale but similarly to each other. Some users preferred one bimanual technique over the other. Similarities with Mendes et al.'s results lead to a tentative guideline, **G1**, for 7DOF bimanual isotonic interaction. However, our comparison with several other prior suggests several possible interaction effects which indicate need for the further experiment, **EX1**. We plan to perform this experiment and within its context to also analyze the distribution of users' allocation of the different 7DOF's [8].

# 7. ACKNOWLEDGEMENTS

This work was supported in part by grant W911NF0910241 (PN55836MA) from The U.S. Army Research Office.

# REFERENCES

1   Bowman, Doug A., Kruijff, Ernst, LaViola, Joseph J., and Poupyrev, Ivan. *3D User Interfaces: Theory and Practice*. Addison Wesley, 2005.

2   Brown, Michelle A., Stuerzlinger, Wolfgang, and Filho, E. J. Mendon\c. The Performance of Un-instrumented In-air Pointing. In *Proceedings of the 2014 Graphics Interface Conference* (Toronto, Ont., Canada, Canada 2014), Canadian Information Processing Society, 59-66.

3   Cho, Isaac. *Bimanual Stereoscopic Interaction for 3D Visualization*. University of North Carolina at Charlotte, Charlotte, NC, USA, 2013.

4   Cho, Isaac. and Wartell, Zachary. Evaluation of a Bimanual Simultaneous 7DOF Interaction Technique in Virtual Environments. (Arles, France 2015), 3D User Interfaces (3DUI), 2015 IEEE Symposium on.

5   Cutler, Lawrence D., Froehlich, Bernd, and Hanrahan, Pat. Two-handed direct manipulation on the responsive workbench. In *Proceedings of the 1997 symposium on Interactive 3D graphics* ( 1997), ACM Press, 107--ff.

6   Deering, Michael. High resolution virtual reality. *ACM SIGGRAPH Computer Graphics*, 26, 2 (1992), 195-202.

7   Guiard, Yves. Asymmetric Division of Labor in Human Skilled Bimanual Action: The Kinematic Chain as a Model. *Journal of Motor Behavior*, 19 (1987), 486-517.

8   Jacob, Robert J. K., Sibert, Linda E., McFarlane, Daniel C., and Mullen, Jr., M. Preston. Integrality and Separability of Input Devices. *ACM Trans. Comput.-Hum. Interact.*, 1, 1 (March 1994), 3-26.

9   Mapes, Daniel P. and Moshell, J. Michael. A Two Handed Interface for Object Manipulation in Virtual Environments. *Presence*, 4, 4 (1995), 403-416.

10  Masliah, Maurice R and Milgram, Paul. Measuring the allocation of control in a 6 degree-of-freedom docking experiment. ( 2000), Proceedings of the SIGCHI conference on Human Factors in Computing Systems.

11  McCully, Sean P., Kumar, Naveen, Lazarus, Mark D., and Karduna, Andrew R. Internal and external rotation of the shoulder: Effects of plane, end-range determination, and scapular motion. *Journal of Shoulder and Elbow Surgery* , 14, 6 (2005), 602-610.

12  Mendes, Daniel and Fonseca, Fernando and Araujo, Bruno and Ferreira, Alfredo and Jorge, Joaquim. Mid-air interactions above stereoscopic interactive tables. ( 2014), 3D User Interfaces (3DUI), 2014 IEEE Symposium on.

13  Moehring, M. and Froehlich, B. Effective manipulation of virtual objects within arm's reach. In *Virtual Reality Conference (VR), 2011 IEEE* ( 2011), 131-138.

14  Paul Mlyniec, Jason Jerald, Arun Yoganandan F. Jacob Seagull Fernando Toledo Udo Schultheis. Studies in Health Technology and Informatics. IOS Press, 2011.

15  Robinett, Warren and Holloway, Richard. Implementation of flying, scaling and grabbing in virtual worlds. In *Proceedings of the 1992 symposium on Interactive 3D graphics* ( 1992), ACM Press, 189-192.

16  Shaw, Chris and Green, Mark. Two-handed polygonal surface design. In *Proceedings of the 7th annual ACM symposium on User interface software and technology* ( 1994), 205-212.

17  Song, Peng, Goh, Wooi Boon, Hutama, William, Fu, Chi-Wing, and Liu, Xiaopei. A handle bar metaphor for virtual object manipulation with mid-air interaction. In *Proceedings of the SIGCHI Conference on Human Factors in Computing Systems* ( 2012), 1297-1306.

18  Suma, Evan. osgVirtualEnvironment. http://sourceforge.net/projects/osgve/

19  Taylor II, Russell M., Hudson, Thomas C., Seeger, Adam, Weber, Hans, Juliano, Jeffrey, and Helser, Aron T. VRPN: a device-independent, network-transparent VR peripheral system. In *Proceedings of the ACM symposium on Virtual reality software and technology* (New York, NY, USA 2001), ACM, 55-61.

20  Ulinski, Amy, Zanbaka, Catherine, Wartell, Zachary, Goolkasian, Paula, and Hodges, Larry F. Two handed selection techniques for volumetric data. In *3D User Interfaces, 2007. 3DUI'07. IEEE Symposium on* ( 2007).

21  Wang, Robert, Paris, Sylvain, and Popovic, Jovan. 6D hands: markerless hand-tracking for computer aided design. In *Proceedings of the 24th annual ACM symposium on User interface software and technology* (New York, NY, USA 2011), ACM, 549-558.

22  Ware, Colin, Gobrecht, Cyril, and Paton, Mark Andrew. Dynamic Adjustment of Stereo Display Parameters. *IEEE Transactions on Systems, Man and Cybernetics Part A: Systems and Humans*, 28, 1 (January 1998), 56-65.

23  Ware, Colin and Jessome, Danny R. Using the bat: A six-dimensional mouse for object placement. *Computer Graphics and Applications, IEEE*, 8, 6 (1988), 65-70.

24  Wartell, Zachary, Hodges, Larry, and Ribarsky, William. Third-Person Navigation of Whole-Planet Terrain in a Head-Tracked Stereoscopic Environment. In *Proceedings of IEEE Virtual Reality '99 Conference* ( March 1999), IEEE Computer Society Press, 141-148.

25  Zhai, Shumin. Investigation of feel for 6DOF inputs: isometric and elastic rate control for manipulation in 3D environments. In *Proceedings of the Human Factors and Ergonomics Society Annual Meeting* ( 1993), 323-327.

# Factors Affecting Mouse-Based 3D Selection in Desktop VR Systems

Robert J. Teather
Dept. of Computing & Software
McMaster University
Hamilton, ON, Canada
teather@mcmaster.ca

Wolfgang Stuerzlinger
School of Interactive Arts + Technology (SIAT)
Simon Fraser University
Vancouver, BC, Canada
w.s@sfu.ca

## ABSTRACT

We present two experiments on mouse-based point selection in a desktop virtual reality system using stereo display and head-tracking. To address potential issues of using a mouse cursor with stereo display, we also evaluate the impact of using a one-eyed (mono) cursor. While a one-eyed cursor visualization eliminates depth conflicts, recent work suggests it offers worse performance than stereo cursors, possibly due to eye discomfort. Our results indicate that presenting the cursor in stereo significantly reduces performance for targets at different depths. The one-eyed cursor eliminates this effect, offering better performance than both screen-plane and geometry-sliding cursors visualized in stereo. However, it also performed slightly worse than stereo cursors in situations *without* depth conflicts. Our study suggests that this difference is not due exclusively to the relative transparency of such a cursor, hence eye fatigue or similar may be responsible.

## Categories and Subject Descriptors

H.5.2 [Information Interfaces and Presentation]: User Interfaces – input devices, interaction styles.

## Keywords

Mouse cursors, stereo 3D display, head-tracking.

## 1. INTRODUCTION

Despite falling costs and advances in 3D trackers, the mouse remains the predominant input device for interacting with 3D content. Stereo displays are becoming more common and are effective for visualizing 3D scenes. Low-cost trackers (e.g., Kinect, Wiimote) enable head-tracking, which offers the possibility of head-based viewpoint control, leaving the mouse free for other operations. There is thus interest in using the mouse with so-called "desktop" VR systems – small scale VR systems using stereo display and head-tracking for improved depth cues when interacting with 3D content. Recent work has suggested that there are benefits to stereo (and other) depth cues in otherwise 2D experiences, such as desktop 3D design [4], gaming [9, 15] and general point selection [17]. To this end, researchers have studied best practices in mouse-based input on stereo displays [12, 17, 19]. The potential benefits of head-tracking with mouse-based interaction are comparatively underexplored.

SUI '15, August 08 - 09, 2015, Los Angeles, CA, USA
Copyright is held by the owner/author(s). Publication rights licensed to ACM.
ACM 978-1-4503-3703-8/15/08…$15.00
DOI: http://dx.doi.org/10.1145/2788940.2788946

A major problem with using a standard (system) mouse cursor in stereo scenes is that the cursor is presented to both eyes with 0 disparity, yet occludes geometry behind it – even geometry closer to the viewer than the cursor. This yields a mismatch between the perceived cursor depth and that of the occluded geometry. Another problem is double vision (diplopia), caused by aligning the cursor with a feature at a different depth. A simple solution is to display the cursor to only one eye, but recent work suggests this may offer worse performance than 3D cursors [12].

We present two experiments investigating how several factors influence mouse-based selection performance on desktop VR systems. These factors include the presence of stereo display, head-tracking, cursor movement (screen-plane vs. "sliding"), and cursor visualization (stereo, one-eyed, or transparent). The first experiment focuses on depth cues in mouse-based systems. There are two aspects to this experiment. First, we evaluate the effects of common techniques for improving depth perception (e.g., stereo and head-tracking) on mouse-based selection. Second, we examine the one-eyed cursor to quantify potential negative effects previously reported [12]. The main contribution of this experiment is a more systematic investigation of these factors than in previous work [12, 17], which primarily focused on various cursor or interaction styles. The second experiment extends this to assess if differences with a one-eyed cursor may be due to its apparent transparency. Since it is shown to only one eye, it appears effectively 50% transparent compared to a stereo cursor. The study also investigates the relative performance of so-called "sliding" cursors [17] compared to screen-based cursors.

Our experiments fix the screen-based cursor at zero depth/parallax. Note that this choice for the cursor depth is an intentionally sub-optimal one. Previous work [12] shows benefits for matching the parallax of the cursor to the geometry – this motivates our use of the sliding cursor in the second experiment. Yet, numerous real-world stereo systems get this wrong in practice. For example, many games on the Nintendo 3DS mismatch parallax between the cursor and targets. Games using automatic stereo conversion (e.g., NVidia 3D Vision) suffer from the same problem, especially when using the Windows system cursor at zero parallax. Hence, we argue for the need of studies like this, which further analyze the negative impact of what researchers might consider "sloppy" stereo.

We isolate cursor visualization to eliminate these other potentially confounding effects. To isolate this factor, the one-eyed cursor is compared in both stereo *and* mono scene visualizations. The idea of comparing one-eyed and stereo cursors in a mono display scene may initially seem odd. However, our "mono" display actually shows the scene in stereo, but using the same position for both eyes (i.e., 0 disparity). Hence we compare one-eyed and stereo cursors, across screen-plane and sliding techniques in situations where depth should not matter. This allows us to isolate any negative effects (e.g., discomfort, eye fatigue) of the one-eyed cursor from its benefits (e.g., elimination of depth cue conflicts), allowing us to get at the heart of the possible negative effects of the one-eyed cursor.

## 2. RELATED WORK

Numerous studies have evaluated 3D trackers as input devices [1]. Studies comparing fish tank VR setups to more immersive systems such as CAVEs [6] or head-mounted displays [11] typically report superior performance with fish tank systems. While fish tank systems often use 3D trackers, they are well suited for mouse-based input due to their desktop-like nature. Moreover, despite numerous available tracker-based 3D selection techniques, mouse input offers better performance if target occlusion is impossible or easily resolved [3, 17].

Head-tracking helps to resolve occlusions and is often used in fish tank VR for head motion parallax cues [2, 6, 11, 20]. Results of experiments on head-tracking tend to be mixed. Some work indicates that head-tracking has a stronger effect than stereo [2], while other work indicates the opposite [20]. We investigate head-tracking to quantify any benefits it offers for mouse-based input. Our rationale is that if head-tracking improves (or at least does not harm) performance, it may be useful in mouse-based systems with target occlusion issues; the user can simply move their head quickly and easily resolve occlusions, without requiring mode changes to use of the mouse for viewpoint control.

Recent work on mouse-based 3D selection [17] showed the benefits of Ware's one-eyed cursor [21] with screen-based cursors. However, one-eyed cursors may cause greater eye strain; recent work instead proposed the use of specialized stereo cursors [12] and found that these offered better performance than the one-eyed cursor. The authors concluded that using more carefully designed stereo cursors, rather than displaying them in the screen plane, can overcome this eyestrain. However, it is difficult to directly compare these results to other 2D pointing techniques. One reason is that the authors do not report common metrics, such as pointing throughput or error rates, and use a non-standard experimental method. Our study aims to add to this body of knowledge by re-evaluating the one-eyed cursor in situations where depth is irrelevant. The objective is to assess any negative impacts of the one-eyed cursor in isolation from situations where it is beneficial, such as when selecting targets at greater depths.

### 2.1 Fitts' law and Point Selection Tasks

We use a 3D version of the ISO 9241-9 standard [8] based on Fitts' law [7]. The predictive form of Fitts' law is:

$$MT = a + b \cdot ID, \quad \text{where} \quad ID = \log_2\left(\frac{A}{W} + 1\right) \quad (1)$$

$MT$ is movement time and $a$ and $b$ are derived by linear regression. $ID$ is the index of difficulty (in bits). $A$ is the distance to the target (amplitude), and $W$ is the target size. ISO 9241-9 [8] recommends a standardized pointing task (Figure 4) and using *throughput* ($TP$) as a primary measure:

$$TP = \frac{\log_2\left(\frac{A_e}{W_e} + 1\right)}{MT}, \quad \text{where} \quad W_e = 4.133 \cdot SD_x \quad (2)$$

$MT$ is average movement time, and $A_e$ (effective amplitude) is the average *actual* movement distance for a given condition. $W_e$ (effective width) is 4.133 standard deviations of the selection coordinates along the target approach vector ($SD_x$). This adjusts

the error rate to 4%. Throughput has been shown to be consistent despite the inherent speed-accuracy tradeoff in point selection tasks [10]. In contrast, movement time and error rate vary due to the speed-accuracy tradeoff. The main advantage of throughput is its comparative consistency between studies; consequently, it is recommended for inclusion in the analysis of pointing techniques and devices [14]. A 3D extension has been used for 3D pointing experiments [5, 17].

## 3. ISSUES WITH 2D SELECTION IN VR

This section details the main issues in using a 2D input device (e.g., a mouse) in selecting 3D targets. While these issues most commonly arise in desktop or "fish-tank" VR systems (where a mouse is a convenient input device), the same issues apply in other VR systems as well.

### 3.1 Stereo Viewing and Diplopia

When selecting a feature displayed at a different depth from the cursor on stereo systems, diplopia (i.e., double vision) occurs. Converging the eyes on the cursor produces two images of the feature. Conversely, converging the eyes on the feature yields two cursor images (Figure 1). The effect becomes more pronounced the greater the depth difference between the cursor and the target. This has been shown to impact 3D selection [17]. A simple solution is to show the cursor only to one eye [21]. While this eliminates the negative impact of diplopia [17], recent work [12] suggests that so-called "one-eyed cursors" may induce greater eye fatigue and may thus perform worse than stereo cursors.

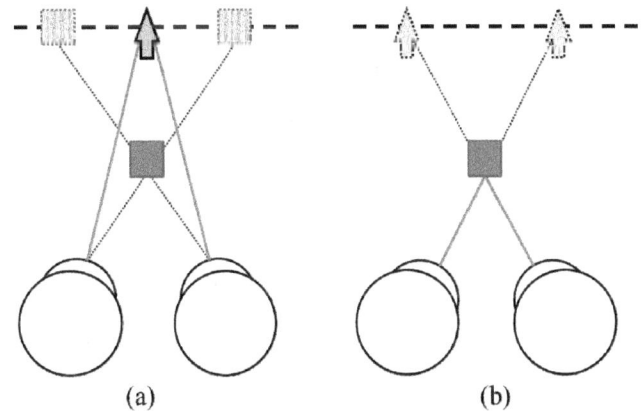

Figure 1. Double-vision. (a) Eyes converging on the cursor. (b) Eyes converging on the feature (a box). The dashed line represents the screen plane.

#### 3.1.1 Sliding vs. Screen-Plane Cursors

Diplopia most commonly occurs with screen-plane cursors [17]. A cursor drawn in the screen-plane (the default position) will generally be presented at a different depth from scene geometry behind it. There are two possible solutions to this problem using different cursor styles. The first simply draws an otherwise normal screen-plane cursor in stereo using the disparity of the surface behind it [12]. The other (which we study) draws the cursor as a 3D object in the scene, and is hence subject to perspective transforms [16, 18]. The cursor is drawn on the foremost visible surface along a ray from the eye position to the screen-plane cursor (which is not shown). Such cursors appear to "slide" along the geometry, hence we refer to them as sliding cursors. An example of sliding cursor motion is depicted in Figure 2.

Initially, one might expect that sliding cursors cannot be occluded, as they are by definition sliding on the visible geometry. Yet, this

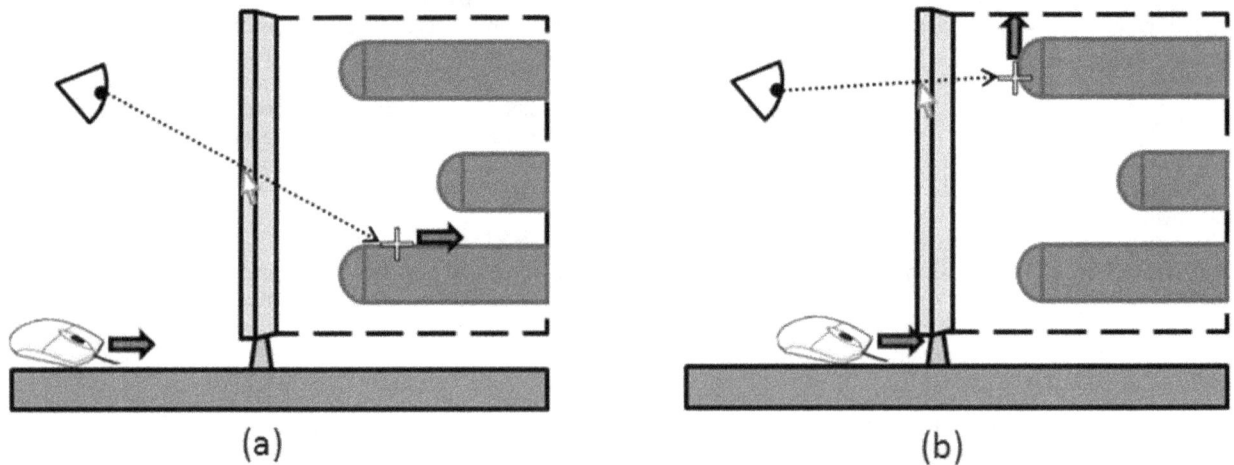

**Figure 2. Sliding cursor motion. Dashed box indicates the extents of the virtual scene behind the display (gray box). Blue cylinders represent targets. (a) The position of the cursor (the yellow "+") is determined by the intersection of the eye-mouse ray and the scene. (b) Moving the mouse forward moves the cursor along the manifold of the scene, corresponding to upward motion of the true cursor (which is hidden).**

is not completely true, as there are situations when the cursor is visible only from one eye, but not the other. For example, consider a box with one of the side faces aligned with the view direction and straight in front of the viewer. Then the sliding cursor degenerates to a one-eyed cursor. Another issue occurs when the system uses visibility from the virtual "cyclopean" eye in the middle between the two real eyes for determining the sliding cursor position. With this approach, the cursor can even disappear completely, for example, when there is a narrow hole aligned with the view direction straight in front of the viewer. If the cursor is in a hole, it can be invisible from both eyes.

In contrast, screen-plane cursors are the more "traditional" cursors that reside in the screen plane and do not move in depth. Typically, these use the ray from the eye to the cursor for selecting objects in the scene. A straightforward implementation of a stereo screen-plane cursor can be occluded by content displayed (stereoscopically) in front of the screen. An alternative approach is to displays a stereo cursor "on top" of the scene, i.e., in a plane that is closer to the viewer than everything visible in the scene. The camera near plane may be a good candidate, except that this plane may be too close to the viewer for comfortable stereo fusion. Alternatively, the depth buffer can be disabled while drawing the cursor [17]. This ensures that the cursor always occludes the scene geometry, even if the cursor appears in the screen plane. This is the option used in recent work [16] using a one-eyed cursor that was only visible to the dominant eye and moved in the screen plane.

## 3.2 Transparency vs. One-Eyed Cursor

A final issue investigated in our study is the relative difference due to the visualization of the cursor. Drawing the cursor to only one eye was originally proposed by Ware [21] and has long been used as a simple means of visualizing a 2D cursor in a stereo 3D environment. Recent work [12] suggests that there may be an inherent disadvantage to such a visualization. In particular, a one-eyed cursor may induce greater eye fatigue than a stereo cursor. We investigate this concern further. One issue is that a one-eyed cursor is effectively displayed transparently – since it is only visible to one eye, its opacity is 50% that of a standard stereo cursor. It is unclear if the impact of cursor transparency may be

stronger than the one-eyed visualization. Hence our second experiment includes a transparent visualization (of an otherwise stereo cursor) to investigate the possibility that this transparency rather than eye fatigue is responsible for performance costs.

## 4. EXPERIMENT 1

The first experiment focused on depth cues issues in mouse-based selection in desktop VR. To this end, we decided to study the influence of stereo display, head-tracking, and cursor visualization (one-eyed vs. stereoscopic) on pointing performance. Stereo display and head-tracking provide additional depth cues, e.g., convergence, stereopsis, and motion parallax. We include the cursor visualization comparison as the one-eyed cursor is necessary for selecting targets away from the screen surface, but may yield (slightly) negative effects [12]. Finally, the experiment also included targets displayed both "in front of" and "behind" the screen surface. This yields both positive and negative parallax situations, and would elicit effects due to stereo display coupled with the cursor visualization.

## 4.1 Participants

Sixteen participants took part in the study. Their ages ranged from 19 to 39 with a mean age of 23.75 years ($SD = 5.13$ years). Nine were female. All but two were right-handed, but all used the mouse regularly with their right hand. All participants had normal or corrected-to-normal vision, and were able to see in stereo. This was assessed by showing them our stereo stimulus (a target at 10 cm away from the screen) and asking them to touch where they perceived it to be. Prospective participants who could not find (roughly) the true 3D position of the target were disqualified. All participants were right-eye dominant, determined by a simple thumb occlusion test.

Participant gaming experience was also assessed, as gamers tend to perform better in 3D tasks [13]. Their responses for four game types – mouse & keyboard PC games, console games using a controller, spatial games (using devices such as a Wiimote or Kinect), and mobile games – are summarized in Figure 3. A score of "5" indicates playing every day, while a score of 1 indicates never playing. In general, participants were not regular gamers, indicating at most a score of "several times per month" at most.

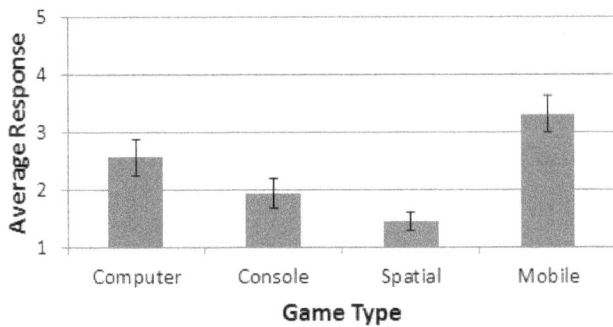

Figure 3. Average gaming experience of participants for
Experiment 1. Error bars show ±1 SE.

## 4.2 Apparatus

The experiment was conducted on an Intel i5-based PC running Windows 7. The PC had a quad-core 3.4 GHz CPU and 16 GB of RAM. An NVidia Quadro 4400 was used with 3DVision Pro glasses for stereo. Software developed in C++ and OpenGL depicted the inside of a wooden crate with target spheres supported on wooden cylinders. See Figure 4. Targets were presented in a circle parallel to the screen surface. All targets in a circle were at the same depth, but depth varied between circles.

**Figure 4. Experimental software depicting 11 targets. Arrows added to illustrate the ordering of the first four targets (not shown in the actual system).**

The software could display the scene in stereo or mono, with or without head-tracking, and with a stereo 3D or one-eyed cursor. That cursor was always shown in the screen plane, i.e., at zero parallax. In the mono view condition, the same image was presented (0 disparity) to both eyes and the stereo glasses were active to eliminate the potential confound of different brightness levels. Regardless if the scene was visualized in stereo or mono (noting again that the "mono" display actually used identical left and right eye images), the one-eyed cursor was only shown to the dominant eye, while the stereo cursor was always shown to both eyes. In our system, positive depths correspond to targets in front of the display and negative depths are behind/inside it. When head-tracking was disabled, we used a static viewpoint 65 cm in front of the screen, corresponding to a standard seated position at a desktop workstation. We used a crosshair-shaped cursor that was coloured yellow to stand out against the background. Similar to "real" cursors (e.g., the Windows system cursor), this provides a single and obvious selection hotspot (the centre of the crosshair), which is what most participants are used to.

## 4.3 Procedure

Participants were first given 20 to 30 practice trials in each condition before starting the actual experiment. They were instructed to select the red target sphere as quickly and accurately as possible, with consistent speed and accuracy. Selection required moving the cursor to the target (projection) and clicking the mouse button.

Following each selection, the target advanced according to the pattern shown in Figure 4 regardless if the target was hit or missed. Upon completing all selections in a target circle, the next circle of targets would appear with different values for target size, distance, and depth. Participants could take breaks when the top target in the circle was active (as in Figure 4), as timing began after that target. The experiment took approximately 1 hour to complete for each participant.

## 4.4 Design

The experiment used a within-subjects design with the following independent variables and levels:

*Stereo Display*: Stereo-On, Stereo-Off (i.e., mono)
*Head-Tracking*: HT-On, HT-Off
*Cursor*: STC (stereo cursor), OEC (one-eyed cursor)
*Target Size*: 0.5, 0.75, 1.0 cm
*Target Distance*: 3.5, 7.5, 9.5 cm
*Target Depth*: -10, 0, +10 cm

Stereo display, head-tracking, and cursor were counter-balanced with a Latin square. Target size, distance, and depth were selected randomly (without replacement) for each target circle. Target size and distance were not analyzed, and instead only incorporated to create a realistic distribution of task difficulties (per Fitts' law). There were 12 recorded selection trials per target circle. Thus there were $2 \times 2 \times 2 \times 3 \times 3 \times 3 \times 12 = 2592$ trials per participant (i.e., 41472 trials overall). The dependent variables were movement time (ms), error rate (% missed targets), and throughput (bits per second).

## 4.5 Results

For all dependent variables, head-tracking was not significant and also did not participate in any interaction effects. Since this factor had also very small effect, we collapse its levels (reporting only the averages of HT-on and HT-off) from here on, to help simplify the analysis. We also omit it from the figures below.

### 4.5.1 Movement Time

Movement time data were not normally distributed ($w = 0.66$, p < .01), which violates one of the prerequisites for ANOVA. Thus, we used Wobbrock's aligned rank transform [22] and performed repeated measures ANOVA on the ranks. There was a significant main effect for target depth on movement time ($F_{2,15} = 4.5$, $p < .05$). The other main effects were not significant. These results must be considered in light of the significant three-way interaction effect between stereo, target depth, and cursor ($F_{2,30} = 33.4$, $p < .00001$). See Figure 5 for movement times.

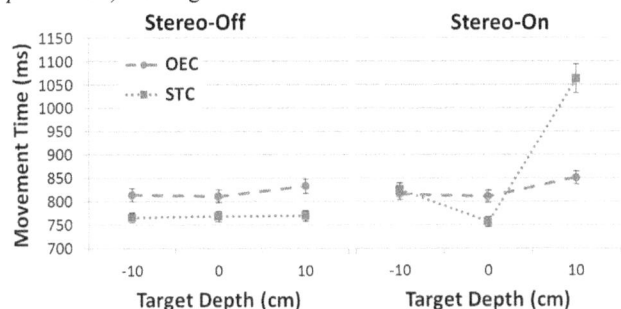

**Figure 5. Movement time by condition. Stereo conditions separated by left/right split. Error bars show ±1 SE.**

13

The two conditions with the highest movement time were both STC with stereo-on, at +10 cm target depth, significantly worse than all others. A Tukey-Kramer posthoc test revealed that no other conditions were significantly different ($p < .05$).

### 4.5.2 Error Rate
Error rate data were not normally distributed ($w = 0.75$, $p < .05$). We analyzed this non-parametrically with ART and repeated measures ANOVA on ranks. Only cursor had a significant main effect ($F_{1,15} = 8.3$, $p < .05$). Yet, the interaction of stereo display, target depth, and cursor was significant ($F_{2,30} = 8.2$, $p < .005$). The combination of stereo-on, STC and +10 cm target depth yielded higher error rates than all other conditions. See Figure 6.

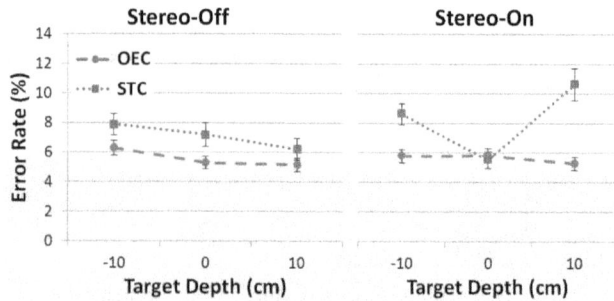

**Figure 6. Error rate by condition. Stereo conditions separated by left/right split. Error bars show ±1 SE.**

### 4.5.3 Throughput
We used a variant of "screen-projected" throughput [17]. Rather than projecting targets and selection coordinates to the screen plane, we used the intersection of the mouse ray and target plane as the selection coordinate. $A_e$ and $W_e$ were then computed normally. This effectively projects the task to the target plane and yields the same result in any plane, as throughput depends on the ratio of $A_e$ to $W_e$. Even though this is a variant, it effectively computes exactly the same value, as the relative over/undershoot of selection coordinates is invariant to the plane where throughput is computed, due to perspective projection (as long as each pair of targets is in the same plane). Note that this variant is inappropriate for scenarios involving varying depth targets. Throughput scores are summarized in Figure 7.

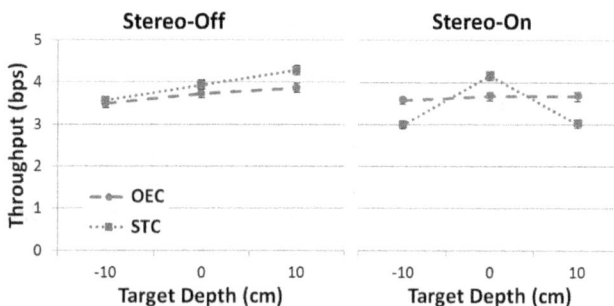

**Figure 7. Throughput by condition. Stereo conditions separated by left/right split. Error bars show ±1 SE.**

Unlike movement time and error rate, throughput data were normally distributed ($w = 0.95$, $p > .05$) and hence analyzed directly with repeated measures ANOVA. Significant main effects on throughput were found for stereo display ($F_{1,15} = 10.3$, $p < .005$) and target depth ($F_{2,15} = 16.2$, $p < .0001$). There was a significant three-way interaction between stereo, depth, and cursor ($F_{2,30} = 12.4$, $p < .001$).

This interaction is visible in the stereo-on conditions in Figure 7: the two STC 0 cm target depth conditions are significantly higher than the STC +10 cm or -10 cm target depth conditions, but not higher than the OEC conditions. The best stereo-off conditions (both STC at +10 cm target depth) were significantly higher than the stereo-on conditions at both -10 and +10 cm target depths. No other conditions were significantly different. There were no significant differences between any stereo-off conditions.

### 4.5.4 Subjective Results
We solicited qualitative results from the participants such as preferences for conditions and perceived performance in a questionnaire at the end of the study. Most participants indicated that they felt the one-eyed cursor did not affect their targeting ability (see Figure 8c) and that eye discomfort was not a concern; however, the difference in the number of participants in each response group was not significant ($\chi^2_4 = 7.1$, $p > .05$). Similarly, there was no significant difference in the number of participants in each response group for stereo scene ($\chi^2_4 = 9.0$, $p > .05$) or head-tracking ($\chi^2_4 = 5.9$, $p > .05$).

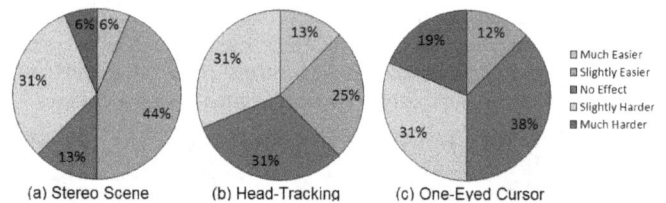

**Figure 8. Summary of participant subjective feedback for (a) stereo display, (b) head-tracking, (c) one-eyed cursor. Participants were asked about the perceived effect on targeting for each condition.**

Both in the experiment presented here and other work [17] almost all participants without VR/gaming experience were unaware of the presence of the one-eyed cursor – until questioned about it post-experiment. Thus we believe that eye discomfort and similar effects are small concerns, and that a one-eyed cursor can perform as well as a stereo cursor, contrary to previous results [12].

## 4.6 Discussion
Perhaps the most important finding of this experiment is the relatively small difference between the stereo and one-eyed cursors, contrary to previous work [12]. As suggested by Schemali and Eisemann [12], the one-eyed cursor offers *slightly* worse performance than the stereo cursor condition for conditions where depth does not matter. This includes all stereo-off conditions, and stereo-on conditions at 0 cm target depth. Yet, this effect was not significant. To further investigate this, we conducted a one-way ANOVA using *only* stereo-off conditions across both cursor conditions (stereo and one-eyed). Not only was the effect for cursor *not* significant ($F_{1,15} = 2.7$, $p = .1$), but the effect size was extremely small ($\eta^2 = .01$). The difference in throughput scores was only about 5% (3.9 bps for STC vs. 3.7 bps for OEC). Altogether, this evidence suggests little difference between the mono and stereo cursor visualization in a mono scene.

Thus, we suggest that the most important finding of this experiment is the *absence* of effects for the one-eyed cursor at zero parallax targets. While not definitive proof (since one cannot "prove the null"), this is evidence that the detrimental effects of the one-eyed cursor [12] may well be overstated. Moreover, we specifically designed our experiment to evaluate the effect of the one-eyed cursor in situations where it *should not* make a difference – if it performed worse, then this would be strong evidence of eye fatigue or discomfort as noted previously [12]. As our experiment failed to identify a significant effect and the differences in throughput are small, we take this as evidence that eye fatigue/discomfort or similar effects are small and that the one-eyed cursor is still a reasonable design choice. Nevertheless, this absence of a statistical effect partly motivates the follow-up experiment presented below. To further explore this issue, the next experiment (again) includes the one-eyed cursor in equivalent conditions to further assess its potential performance impact.

All dependent variables showed significant interactions between stereo display, cursor, and target depth. Like previous work [12, 17], this is the impact of diplopia on targets at different depths from the cursor. When presenting content at drastically different depths from a stereo cursor in a stereo scene, we expect that performance would suffer. The one-eyed cursor largely eliminates this effect, as reflected in the (mostly) flat lines across depth in Figure 5 for the OE cursor. The one-eyed cursor clearly benefits selecting targets at different depths.

Head-tracking did not significantly affect any of the dependent variables. The additional head motion parallax depth cues were not especially helpful with our effectively 2D task, even if it appeared to be 3D. It is possible that this is because participants did not move their heads much after any initial potential exploration of the capabilities of the system and the subsequent discovery of all target positions. Note that head-tracking was not necessary for individual selections. Nevertheless, since performance was also not *worse* with head-tracking, it could be useful to resolve occlusions in environments where occlusions occur frequently enough. Head-tracking also obviates explicit viewpoint mode toggling and helps mouse-based 3D interaction, which might else be hindered by occlusions.

Throughput was consistent with other ISO 9241-9 studies [17]. Previous work [12] that does not report throughput cannot be compared directly to other mouse-based pointing studies due to the speed-accuracy tradeoff inherent in point selection tasks. While the interplay of stereo display and target depth increased throughput variability, these were largely in the expected ~4 bps range. This is especially noticeable in the stereo-off conditions in Figure 7. Contrary to our expectations, performance increased slightly (but not significantly) with closer targets. This may point to a need to re-examine "projected" throughput, even though it eliminated such depth effects in previous work [17].

# 5. EXPERIMENT 2

We conducted a second experiment to further investigate these issues. This experiment study focused on the interplay between stereo viewing, cursor movement, and cursor visualization.

This experiment was also designed to isolate a previously unexplored difference between the one-eyed and stereo cursor visualizations used in Experiment 1: the effective *transparency* of the one-eyed cursor. Since it is only displayed to one eye, the cursor is effectively 50% transparent relative to the stereo cursor. This experiment thus included a 50% transparent stereo cursor to assess if transparency might have an effect in isolation from displaying the cursor to only one eye.

This experiment also included a sliding cursor [17], implemented as described earlier. The reason we included this condition is that such a cursor is always displayed at the same depth as the target. This avoids issues like stereo cue conflicts and diplopia. Previous

work identified that such cursors perform well [12] with mouse-based selection. This cursor also serves as an approximation of the approach used by modern GPUs when automatically converting 3D content to stereo 3D display. These methods display the cursor in stereo using the disparity of the surface behind it. A main difference between the GPU-based approach and the sliding cursor is that the latter is also subject to perspective and can be occluded by geometry in the scene.

## 5.1 Participants

Twelve participants took part in the study. Their ages ranged from 20 to 52 years (mean age 26, *SD* of 8.6). Three were female. All used the mouse regularly with their right hand. All participants had normal or corrected-to-normal vision, and were able to see in stereo. This was assessed in the same fashion as in Experiment 1. All participants were right-eye dominant, determined by a simple thumb occlusion test. As in Experiment 1, we assessed their gaming experience. In general, the scores here are higher than Experiment 1; participants of Experiment 2 played games slightly more regularly than those of Experiment 1.

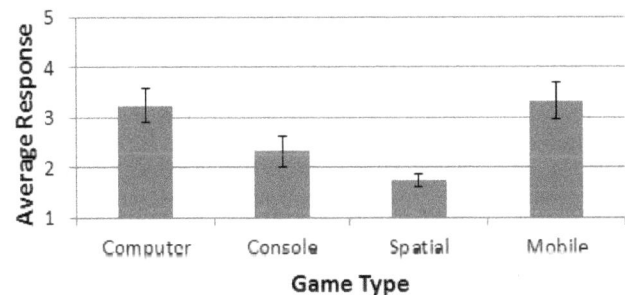

**Figure 9. Average gaming experience of participants of Experiment 2. Error bars show ±1 SE.**

## 5.2 Apparatus

Overall, the same apparatus as Experiment 1 was used. Since Experiment 1 indicated that head-tracking had a very limited (if any) effect, we used a static viewpoint in this experiment. We also added two new conditions. The first was a stereo cursor with 50% transparency. The second added a sliding cursor, as described earlier. The sliding cursor was implemented relative to a fixed head position (the "optimal" position, 65 cm from the centre of the screen) as the origin of a mouse ray. The true mouse cursor was not displayed. Instead, a 3D cursor, using the same crosshair shape as in all other conditions, was displayed the intersection point of the mouse ray and the scene. The cursor thus would effectively slide across the scene geometry.

## 5.3 Procedure and Design

The procedure was identical to that of Experiment 1, with the exception of the two newly added conditions. The experiment used a within-subjects design with the following independent variables and levels:

*Stereo Display*: Stereo-On, Stereo-Off (i.e., mono)
*Cursor*: STC, OEC, TRC
*Technique*: Screen, sliding
*Target Size*: 0.5, 1.0 cm
*Target Distance*: 3.5, 7.5, 9.5 cm
*Target Depth*: -10, 0, +10 cm

The STC and OEC cursors are the same stereo and one-eyed cursor conditions from Experiment 1. The new TRC condition was a stereo cursor displayed with 50% transparency. Technique indicated which cursor control technique was used, either in the

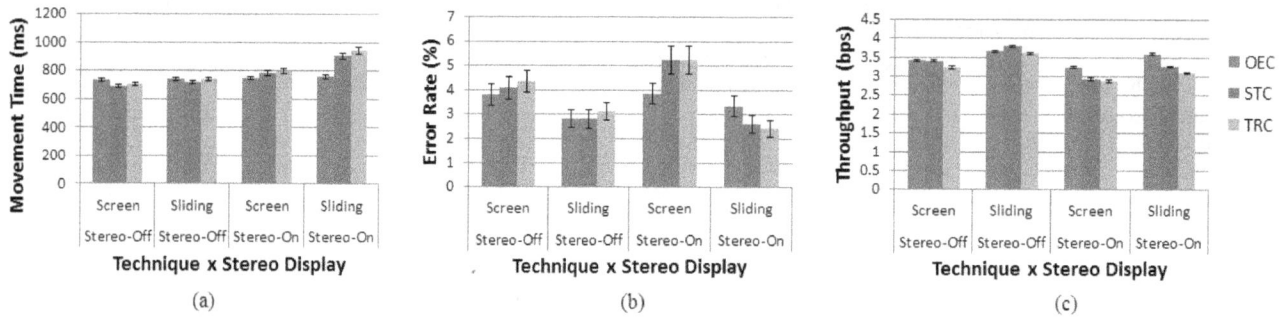

**Figure 10. Experiment 2 summary results for (a) Movement Time, (b) Error Rate, and (c) Throughput. These figures show results for each combination of cursor, technique, and stereo display. Target depth is collapsed to simplify presentation. Error bars show ±1 SE.**

screen-plane (screen) or geometry-sliding (sliding). Target size and distance were not analyzed, and instead only incorporated to create a realistic distribution of task difficulties (per Fitts' law).

The twelve combinations of stereo display, cursor, and movement were counterbalanced according to a balanced Latin square. The remaining factors (target size, distance, and depth) were presented in random order without replacement.

There were 12 recorded selection trials per target circle. Overall, there were $2 \times 3 \times 2 \times 2 \times 3 \times 3 \times 12 = 2592$ trials per participant, or 31104 trials over all twelve participants. As in experiment 1, the dependent variables were movement time (ms), error rate (% missed targets), and throughput (bits per second).

## 5.4 Results

With four independent variables of interest, results of this experiment are complex. As a result, we first present an overview/summary of the experiment results for each dependent variable in Figure 10. The figure collapses the target depth factor - i.e., it shows only the cursor, technique, and stereo display combinations, averaging across the three target depths. Figure 11 shows the same information, but in more detail, and separated across the three levels of target depth.

### 5.4.1 Movement Time

Movement time data were normally distributed ($w = 1.64$, $p > .05$), hence we analyzed results using repeated measures ANOVA. Since the experiment design used four factors (stereo display, cursor, technique, and target depth), and due to the difficulty in analyzing four-way interaction effects, we instead separate the analyses by stereo display. The remaining three factors are analyzed normally (i.e., a 3-way RM-ANOVA).

We first present an analysis excluding depth (i.e., averaging all three depths, and corresponding to the results depicted in Figure 10a). There was a significant interaction effect between stereo display, technique, and cursor ($F_{2,22} = 3.7$, $p < .05$). Tukey-Kramer multiple comparisons revealed that STC and TRC with stereo-on and the sliding cursor were significantly worse than all other conditions (which were not significantly different from each other). As in Experiment 1, results must be interpreted in light of the significant three-way interaction effect between technique, cursor, and target depth ($F_{4,44} = 5.3$, $p < .005$). The effects of diplopia at target depths away from the screen (-10 cm and +10 cm) are visible in Figure 11a for the stereo-on + screen cursor conditions. As before, the one-eyed cursor (OEC) eliminates this effect, and demonstrates fairly flat lines across target depth, as can be seen in Figure 11a. Figure 10a also depicts the consistent performance of OEC across all combinations of conditions. This

is also true for the sliding OEC combination, suggesting little difference between the sliding and screen-based techniques when the one-eyed cursor was used. However, the sliding cursor suffered with the other cursor visualizations–both TRC and STC demonstrate significantly worse performance the higher the target depth (i.e., the *closer* the target is to the viewer). In fact, the worst condition overall was the combination of a transparent sliding cursor, at +10 cm target depth, with stereo-on.

We also investigate separate main effects to help better explain the interaction effect noted above. For stereo-off conditions, there was a significant main effect for cursor ($F_{2,11} = 4.5$, $p < .05$). Tukey-Kramer posthoc analysis revealed that the OEC conditions were significantly slower than either the TRC and STC conditions ($p < .05$). This effect was more strongly pronounced for the sliding cursor conditions. See Figure 10a and Figure 11a. For stereo-on conditions, the results are more complex. There were significant main effects for technique ($F_{1,11} = 32.5$, $p < .0005$), cursor ($F_{2,11} = 6.9$, $p < .005$), and target depth ($F_{2,11} = 41.5$, $p < .0001$). This is especially noticeable in Figure 10a: the sliding cursor with stereo-on offered much worse performance with both STC and TRC than with OEC. Figure 11a highlights that this is due to the impact of different target depths, suggesting the effect is again, due to diplopia.

### 5.4.2 Error Rate

Error rates were normally distributed ($w = 3.6$, $p > .05$) hence we analyzed results using repeated measures ANOVA. As with movement time, we separated the error rate analysis by the stereo display factor. Error rates are summarized in Figure 10b, and presented in greater detail in Figure 11b.

We first analyzed error rates by averaging across target depth. Only the main effect for technique was significant ($F_{1,11} = 33.5$, $p < .0001$), with the sliding cursor globally offering lower error rates than the screen cursor. This is likely due to the high variability in error rates, particularly noticeable in Figure 11.

To analyze the effects of depth, we consider the stereo-on and stereo-off conditions separately (to avoid high-order interaction effects). For stereo-off conditions, the main effect for target depth was significant ($F_{2,11} = 3.9$, $p < .05$). Farther target depths (-10 cm) offered significantly higher error rates at about 4.1% than either of the other two target depths at 3.1% for +10 cm targets and 3.3% for 0 cm targets. The main effect for technique was also significant ($F_{2,11} = 13.5$, $p < .005$), with the sliding cursor offering better (on average) error rates than the screen cursor. No other main or interaction effects were significant for stereo-off conditions.

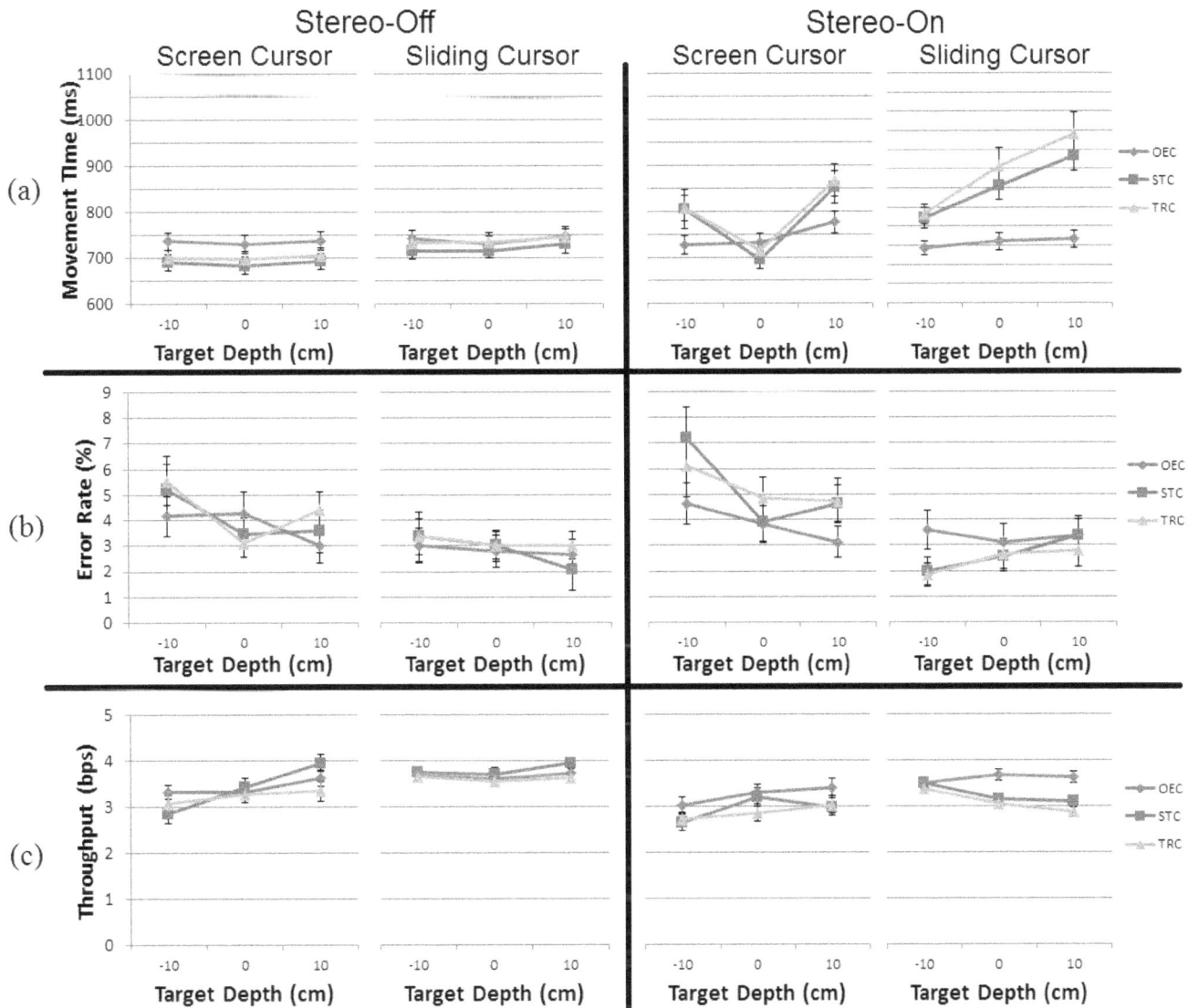

**Figure 11. Experiment 2 results for (a) Movement Time, (b) Error Rate, and (c) Throughput. The conditions on the left side are all stereo-off (mono) conditions, while the right side shows stereo-on conditions. Within these halves, the left side shows the screen-based cursor technique and the right side shows conditions using the sliding cursor technique. Error bars show ±1 SE.**

For stereo-on conditions, the only significant effect was the main effect for technique ($F_{1,11} = 21.7$, $p < .001$). Neither cursor ($F_{2,11} = 0.21$, ns), nor target depth ($F_{2,11} = 0.71$, ns) were significantly different, nor were any interaction effects. Overall, the sliding technique offered substantially better error rates than the screen-based technique, 2.8% vs. 4.8% respectively. This is likely a side effect of the slower movement time with this technique: Participants took their time to ensure careful selection, likely due to the comparative difficulty in using the technique. Note that relative absence of statistical effects for error rate is likely due to the comparatively high degree of variability in error rates (unlike movement time). For example, diplopia appeared to negatively impact error rates with the screen-based technique, particularly with the STC condition at -10 cm. However, because of the high variability, this effect was not found to be significant.

### 5.4.3 Throughput

Throughput was calculated as described earlier – using the relative over/undershoots in the target plane, rather than the screen plane. This yields the same score as a screen-space calculation [17]. Throughput scores were normally distributed ($w = 1.6$, $p > .05$) hence we analyzed results using repeated measures ANOVA. Throughput scores are summarized in Figure 10c and Figure 11c.

As with the other dependent variables, we first analyze only the "simplified" result, averaging throughput scores over target depth for each condition. See Figure 10c. Significant main effects included stereo display ($F_{1,11} = 59.7$, $p < .001$), technique ($F_{1,11} = 12.6$, $p < .005$), and cursor ($F_{2,11} = 9.6$, $p < .001$). However, the technique scene/cursor interaction effect was also significant ($F_{2,22} = 4.8$, $p < .05$). Notably, the combination of stereo-on, screen cursor, and TRC was the worst performer, significantly worse (via Tukey-Kramer, $p < .05$) than all stereo-off conditions, as well as the corresponding OEC condition. The remaining conditions were not significantly different.

As with the other dependent variables, we independently analyzed stereo-on and stereo-off conditions to simplify analysis. We first report the results for stereo-off conditions. There were significant main effects for technique ($F_{1,11} = 8.3$, $p < .01$), and target depth ($F_{2,11} = 8.1$, $p < .005$). The interaction effects between technique and target depth was significant, ($F_{2,22} = 6.3$, $p < .01$), as was the interaction effect between cursor and target depth ($F_{4,44} = 2.9$, $p < .05$). These effects are largely visible in Figure 11c (depicted as crossing lines). Notably, the OEC and TRC performance was consistent across depth, while STC offered significantly higher performance with *closer* targets using the screen-based cursor. Performance was much more consistent with all cursors for the sliding cursor.

For stereo-on conditions, there were significant main effects for technique ($F_{1,11} = 12.7$, $p < .005$), and cursor ($F_{2,11} = 12.8$, $p < .0005$). On average, the one-eyed cursor (OEC) offered significantly higher throughput at 3.4 bps vs. 2.98 bps for TRC and 3.1 bps for STC. The slide technique also offered higher throughput than the screen cursor. However, there was also a significant interaction effect between technique and target depth ($F_{2,22} = 5.1$, $p < .05$). This is visible in Figure 11c. The sliding cursor performed worse with closer (+10 cm) targets, except with the OEC cursor, which was largely immune to this effect. This may be because participants tended to slide the TRC and STC cursors up the sides of target cylinders. With OEC, they were most likely unaware they were using the sliding cursor, and hence treated it like a "normal" mouse cursor (i.e., not sliding).

### 5.4.4 Subjective Results

We also solicited subjective feedback from participants about their experience with the various conditions. In particular, we asked participants if they felt the stereo display and the one eyed cursor made targeting easier or harder. A significant number of participants felt stereo display made targeting slightly harder ($\chi^2_4 = 18.8$, $p < .001$). There was no significant difference in the number of participants in each response group for the one-eyed cursor though ($\chi^2_4 = 4.7$, $p > .05$). See Figure 12.

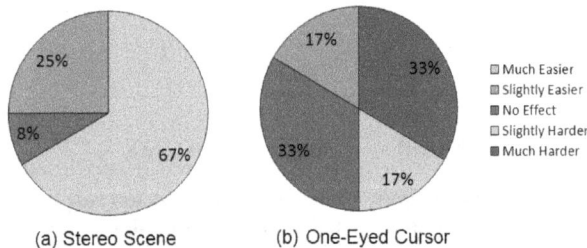

(a) Stereo Scene    (b) One-Eyed Cursor

**Figure 12. Summary of participant subjective feedback for (a) stereo vs. mono display, (b) one-eyed cursor vs. stereo cursor. Participants were asked about the perceived effect on targeting for each condition.**

We were also interested in their perceived performance with both the sliding cursor technique (compared to the screen-based technique) and whether they were aware of the difference between the one-eyed and transparent cursors. They were asked "*I found that the sliding cursor improved my targeting ability relative to the screen cursor.*" and "*I was able to tell the difference between the one-eyed and transparent cursors*". These responses were solicited on a 5-point Likert scale ranging from "Strongly Disagree" to "Strongly Agree". Figure 13 summarizes the percentage of participants in each response group. The number of participants giving each response was not significantly different for the sliding cursor ($\chi^2_4 = 3.8$, $p > .05$). Similarly, participants were unable to reliably tell the difference between the one-eyed and transparent cursors ($\chi^2_4 = 0.5$, ns) - there was a roughly equal number of participants giving each response.

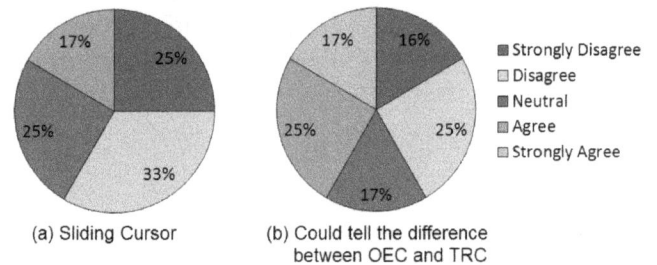

(a) Sliding Cursor    (b) Could tell the difference between OEC and TRC

**Figure 13. Subjective responses for (a) if they felt the sliding technique offered better performance than the screen technique, and (b) if they could tell the difference between TRC and OEC.**

### 5.5 Discussion

For the stereo-off conditions (i.e., mono display), the difference between the various cursor conditions was minimal. This matches the outcome of a previous comparison of the one-eyed and stereo cursors [17]. However, the combination of the one-eyed cursor and screen-plane technique showed slightly (and significantly) slower performance than the others. Note that in this condition the one-eyed cursor should have no effect *at all*; this may support previous work indicating negative aspects of the one-eyed cursor [12]. However, the difference is only significant in terms of movement time, but not in throughput. The transparent cursor also did not behave differently than the stereo cursor.

For the stereo-on conditions with the stereo cursor (STC), the sliding cursor performed worst. More interestingly, the transparent cursor performed significantly worse than the one-eyed cursor (but similar to the stereo cursor). This makes sense, as it was effectively a slightly *worse* stereo cursor. This is most noticeable at or in front of the screen – closer targets reduced performance with the sliding technique. Performance with the screen-plane cursor was worse away from the screen for the STC and TRC conditions. However, the screen plane cursor also offered worse error rates for deeper targets, potentially due to the impact of perspective - targets appeared smaller, and thus harder to select reliably [17]. This is clearly due to the effect of diplopia - as expected, this is most pronounced for targets farther from the screen, but only applies in stereo scenes. Surprisingly, the sliding cursor did much worse. This may be because participants tended to slide the cursor up the fronts of cylinders, as noted in previous work [17], despite the ability to simply move the cursor over the target (i.e., it would "pop" to the front).

It is also worth noting that the one-eyed cursor "leveled" performance across all conditions. As seen in Figure 11, the movement time and throughput lines for the OEC conditions are essentially flat across all conditions. This is an interesting result, and suggests limited differences between these conditions when the cursor is visualized in mono. Even the difference between the sliding and screen techniques was small.

Overall, and contradicting previous work, the one-eyed cursor performed well in situations where it was expected to – i.e., to eliminate negative impact of stereo cue conflicts in the stereo-on conditions. However, our study provides additional evidence that this visualization may yield some fatigue or similar effects, as previously suggested [12]. The cursor performed comparatively (slightly) *worse* in mono scene visualization (stereo-off) than stereo cursors – a condition where the benefits of the cursor are isolated from any potential negative impact it may have. However, we note that this is an unusual and unrealistic combination that would be rarely, if ever, used in practice. Thus, we can still overall recommend the one-eyed cursor as a reasonable design choice in desktop 3D systems. Ultimately, the OEC moving in either the screen-plane or sliding on geometry offered better performance than all other options in terms of movement time and throughput for common user interface setups, such as stereo display.

# 6. CONCLUSION

We presented two experiments on issues in on mouse-based 3D selection in desktop VR systems. The first experiment investigated stereo, head-tracking, and target depth. The study included the one-eyed cursor, to mitigate the negative effects of stereo conflicts commonly observed with mouse cursors in stereo 3D displays. The second experiment investigated if any negative effects of the one-eyed cursor may be due to its comparative transparency, while also comparing a screen-based and geometry-sliding cursor. Overall results confirm that presenting the cursor in stereo significantly impacts performance for different depth targets due to diplopia. The one-eyed cursor eliminates this effect, performing significantly better than any stereo cursor techniques when the scene is visualized in stereo. However, confirming previous findings, there is a small negative impact of the one-eyed cursor visualization in *mono* scenes, i.e., where its positive effects are ruled out. Consequently, it is reasonable that alternative stereo cursor presentation methods may yield better performance still. Further study on novel cursor techniques for desktop VR is still warranted.

# 7. ACKNOWLEDGEMENTS

Thanks to Brian Fisher for helpful discussion leading to the second study design, and to Eduardo Soto for help running the experiments. We also thank the anonymous reviewers for helpful suggestions to improve the final version of the paper.

# 8. REFERENCES

[1] Argelaguet, F. and Andujar, C., A survey of 3D object selection techniques for virtual environments, *Computers & Graphics*, 37, 2013, 121-136.

[2] Arthur, K. W., Booth, K. S., and Ware, C., Evaluating 3D task performance for fish tank virtual worlds, *ACM Transactions on Information Systems*, *11*, 1993, 239-265.

[3] Bérard, F., Ip, J., Benovoy, M., El-Shimy, D., Blum, J., and Cooperstock, J., Did "Minority Report" get it wrong? Superiority of the mouse over 3D input devices in a 3D placement task, in *Human-Computer Interaction – INTERACT* 2009, 400-414.

[4] Bogdan, N., Grossman, T., and Fitzmaurice, G., HybridSpace: Integrating 3D freehand input and stereo viewing into traditional desktop applications, *Proc. of the IEEE Symposium on 3D User Interfaces - 3DUI 2014*, (New York: IEEE, 2014), 51-58.

[5] Bruder, G., Steinicke, F., and Sturzlinger, W., To touch or not to touch? Comparing 2D touch and 3D mid-air interaction on stereoscopic tabletop surfaces, *Proc. of ACM Symposium on Spatial User Interaction - SUI 2013*, (New York: ACM, 2013), 9-16.

[6] Demiralp, C., Jackson, C. D., Karelitz, D. B., Zhang, S., and Laidlaw, D. H., Cave and fishtank virtual-reality displays: A qualitative and quantitative comparison, *IEEE Transactions on Visualization and Computer Graphics*, *12*, 2006, 323-330.

[7] Fitts, P. M., The information capacity of the human motor system in controlling the amplitude of movement, *Journal of Experimental Psychology*, *47*, 1954, 381-391.

[8] ISO, ISO 9241-9 Ergonomic requirements for office work with visual display terminals (VDTs) - Part 9: Requirements for non-keyboard input devices: International Standard, International Organization for Standardization, 2000.

[9] Kulshreshth, A. and LaViola Jr, J. J., Evaluating performance benefits of head tracking in modern video games, *Proc. of the ACM Symposium on Spatial User Interaction - SUI 2013*, (New York: ACM, 2013), 53-60.

[10] MacKenzie, I. S. and Isokoski, P., Fitts' throughput and the speed-accuracy tradeoff, *Proc. of the ACM Conference on Human Factors in Computing Systems - CHI 2008*, (New York: ACM, 2008), 1633-1636.

[11] Qi, W., Taylor II, R. M., Healey, C. G., and Martens, J.-B., A comparison of immersive HMD, fish tank VR and fish tank with haptics displays for volume visualization, *Proc. of the Symposium on Applied Perception in Graphics and Visualization*, (New York: ACM, 2006), 51-58.

[12] Schemali, L. and Eisemann, E., Design and evaluation of mouse cursors in a stereoscopic desktop environment, *Proc. of the IEEE Symposium on 3D User Interfaces - 3DUI 2014*, (New York: IEEE, 2014), 67-70.

[13] Smith, S. P. and Du'Mont, S., Measuring the effect of gaming experience on virtual environment navigation tasks, *Proc. of the IEEE Symposium on 3D User Interfaces - 3DUI 2009*. (New York: IEEE, 2009), 3-10.

[14] Soukoreff, R. W. and MacKenzie, I. S., Towards a standard for pointing device evaluation: Perspectives on 27 years of Fitts' law research in HCI, *International Journal of Human-Computer Studies*, *61*, 2004, 751-789.

[15] Teather, R. J. and Stuerzlinger, W., Exaggerated head motions for game viewpoint control, *Proceedings of the ACM Conference on Future Play 2008*, (New York: ACM, 2008), 240-243.

[16] Teather, R. J. and Stuerzlinger, W., Pointing at 3D targets in a stereo head-tracked virtual environment, *Proc. of the IEEE Symposium on 3D User Interfaces - 3DUI 2011*, (New York: IEEE, 2011), 87-94.

[17] Teather, R. J. and Stuerzlinger, W., Pointing at 3D target projections using one-eyed and stereo cursors, *Proc. of the ACM Conference on Human Factors in Computing Systems - CHI 2013*, (New York: ACM, 2013), 159 - 168.

[18] Teather, R. J. and Stuerzlinger, W., Visual aids in 3D point selection experiments, *Proceedings of the ACM symposium on Spatial user interaction - SUI 2014*, (New York: ACM, 2014), 127-136.

[19] Wang, G., McGuffin, M. J., Berard, F., and Cooperstock, J. R., Pop-up depth views for improving 3D target acquisition, *Proc. of Graphics Interface 2011*, (Toronto: CIPS, 2011), 41-48.

[20] Ware, C. and Franck, G., Evaluating stereo and motion cues for visualizing information nets in three dimensions, *ACM Transactions on Graphics*, *15*, 1996, 121-140.

[21] Ware, C. and Lowther, K., Selection using a one-eyed cursor in a fish tank VR environment, *ACM Transactions on Computer-Human Interaction*, *4*, 1997, 309-322.

[22] Wobbrock, J. O., Findlater, L., Gergle, D., and Higgins, J. J., The aligned rank transform for nonparametric factorial analyses using only anova procedures, *Proc. of the ACM Conference on Human Factors in Computing Systems - CHI 2011*, (New York: ACM, 2011), 143-146.

# BlowClick: A Non-Verbal Vocal Input Metaphor for Clicking

Daniel Zielasko*    Sebastian Freitag*    Dominik Rausch*    Yuen C. Law*
Benjamin Weyers*    Torsten W. Kuhlen†

*Virtual Reality Group, RWTH Aachen University
JARA – High-Performance Computing
Aachen, Germany
{zielasko, freitag, rausch, law,
weyers}@vr.rwth-aachen.de

† Jülich Supercomputing Centre,
Forschungszentrum Jülich
JARA – High Performance Computing
Jülich & Aachen, Germany
t.kuhlen@fz-juelich.de

## ABSTRACT

In contrast to the wide-spread use of 6-DOF pointing devices, free-hand user interfaces in Immersive Virtual Environments (IVE) are non-intrusive. However, for gesture interfaces, the definition of trigger signals is challenging. The use of mechanical devices, dedicated trigger gestures, or speech recognition are often used options, but each comes with its own drawbacks. In this paper, we present an alternative approach, which allows to precisely trigger events with a low latency using microphone input. In contrast to speech recognition, the user only blows into the microphone. The audio signature of such blow events can be recognized quickly and precisely. The results of a user study show that the proposed method allows to successfully complete a standard selection task and performs better than expected against a standard interaction device, the Flystick.

## Keywords

Interaction techniques; hands-free interaction; non-speech sound interaction; trigger

## Categories and Subject Descriptors

H.5.2 [**Information Interfaces and Presentation**]: User Interfaces—*Voice I/O*; I.3.7 [**Computer Graphics**]: Three-Dimensional Graphics and Realism—*Virtual reality*; J.5 [**Arts and Humanities**]: Performing Arts

## 1. INTRODUCTION

In IVEs, the most common interaction mechanism is the usage of a 6-DOF pointing device with mechanical triggers, such as a wand or the ART Flystick. While such devices offer an effective method for selection and manipulation tasks within the IVE, they may prove to be too intrusive. In recent years, advances in vision-based tracking and gesture recognition have allowed gestural interaction methods, where users are not required to wear input devices or tracking markers. However, for gesture interfaces, the definition

of trigger signals is challenging. Beside the use of dedicated mechanical devices, such as a thumb switch [7], the use of dedicated trigger gestures [3, 15], e.g., tapping in space [11], is a suitable option in line with a gestural interface. However, gesture recognition is still error-prone and suffers from per-user differences. Furthermore, performing the trigger gesture may interfere with other interaction gestures. Another alternative is speech recognition, which has the drawback of suffering from mis-recognitions and works best only if trained for individual users. For both, gesture and speech recognition, time delay from the recognition algorithm can cause further problems and introduce significant latency into the system [6], which should be avoided especially in IVEs.

The main contribution of this paper is an alternative trigger approach for hands-free interaction scenarios, which allows to precisely trigger events with low latency by blowing into a microphone. We validate the approach by comparing the performance in terms of speed and accuracy against a standard interaction device (Flystick) in a user study.

The rest of the paper is structured as follows. First, we discuss related work in terms of non-verbal vocal input (NVVI) in Section 2. Furthermore, we present our clicking metaphor in Section 3 and evaluate it against a common button trigger in Section 4. Finally, we discuss the results of the user study and point out future work in Section 5.

## 2. RELATED WORK

Non-verbal vocal input (NVVI) is a common method to enrich the interaction space of people with physical disabilities, e.g., to steer a wheelchair [4]. However, these techniques are usually very rich, as they use different combinations of voice characteristics, such as pitch and volume, and thus are not ad-hoc accessible to everybody. The *Whistling User Interface* (U³I) [14, 17], *The Vocal Joystick* [5] and the approach of Chanjaradwichai et al. [2] are recent examples for NVVI interfaces that allow motor-impaired people to use native desktop applications. In case of disabilities, the gain in interaction possibilities usually compansates for the time needed for learning.

Patel and Abowd [13] propose an interface, called *Blowable User Interface* (BLUI), which allows the user to trigger a localized click in a desktop or laptop environment by blowing. They classify the air pressure signatures of the signals recorded by a fixed-positioned microphone and assign them to 1 of 9 cells on the screen. The drawback of this design is that it requires a meaningful and fixed placement of the microphone and a calibration phase for the classifier. Furthermore, a click is not performed until the user first selects a widget by blowing and than blows harder for about one second.

**Figure 1: Experimental setup in the CAVE using a standard Fitt's law task (here T3) according to ISO 9241-400:2007.**

This brings the latency in regions of speech recognition, which we want to avoid.

Igarashi et al. [8] stated that using non-verbal characteristics of voice also could be beneficial as an interaction technique in virtual environments. Zielasko et al. [19] used an extended blowing metaphor to trigger tones out of bottles in a IVE using an HMD with a gestural interface and the fingers as pointing devices.

# 3. BLOWCLICK

The idea of BlowClick is to realize a trigger by blowing into a microphone, which may already be part of the setting when also using speech recognition and therefore should neither disturb the latter nor exclude talking to other users. Therefore, the user's breath is captured by a microphone and the current signal frame is condensed to a single strength value. This value is exponentially smoothed over time to reduce jitter. If it lies over a given threshold, the BlowClick's device state is changed to *is triggered*. When it falls below the threshold again, it is changed back to *is not triggered*. To avoid triggers caused by speaking in a normal volume, we measured the values produced by speaking in advance and set the threshold above that. With the used microphone (see below) the threshold for the averaged sample frame was 6,10% of the maximum amplitude.

For the implementation of BlowClick, we used OpenAL as audio framework. Using a buffer size of 1378 samples and a sample rate of 40kHz results in a delay of 30ms, with a neglectable processing time of a few microseconds. This meets the above defined latency requirement, because it is under the recommended threshold of 100ms [12].

# 4. USER STUDY

For validation, we conducted a quantitative user study to compare the performance of the proposed method in terms of speed and accuracy against a standard interaction device (Flystick). The use case of the proposed method lies outside the scope in which a Flystick is applicable, e.g., in a hands-free scenario, but a comparison with an established interaction device nevertheless is helpful. In advance we formulate the following hypotheses:

**H1** It is possible to reasonably solve selection tasks with the BlowClick metaphor.

**H2** The standard interaction device outperforms the Blow-Click metaphor with respect to speed and accuracy.

**H3** Blowing feels more exhausting then pressing a button as trigger.

## 4.1 Participants

18 subjects (3 female and 15 male, ages M = 28.9, SD = 5.51) participated in the study. They were unpaid and all had prior experience with IVEs. All of our participants had normal or corrected-to vision. The experiment took about 20 minutes per participant, of which 10 minutes were spent in an IVE (a 5-sided CAVE) and the rest with the introduction and completing the questionnaires. The duration of the experiment was determined in a pre-study revealing that participants get exhausted by holding the Flystick. In the experiment a head-tracked stereoscopic view was provided.

## 4.2 Design

We used a $3 \times 4 \times 21$ within-subject experimental design (3 device conditions and 4 levels of difficulty each with 21 trials). The following three device conditions appeared in counter-balanced order, following a latin squares design:

**CF** Flystick button as trigger, Flystick as pointing device

**BF** Blowing as trigger, Flystick as pointing device

**BH** Blowing as trigger, hand as pointing device

### 4.2.1 Apparatus

To track the hand, we use a light weight tracking target by ART that was strapped to the back of the hand. As Flystick, we used the Flystick2 by ART. During the whole experiment the participants wore a wireless microphone, a Sennheiser EW 300 G2 with a Sennheiser ME 3 as actual sensor. The windscreen of the microphone was removed. The threshold used to trigger a click with the microphone was identical for all participants. We added the hybrid device combination BF to the experimental design to be able to examine possible influences of the type of pointing device.

### 4.2.2 Procedure

For each device condition, 4 Fitts' Law selection tasks with increasing difficulty, designed according to ISO 9241-400:2007 [9, 16] had to be performed (see Figure 1). We measured the time between each successful selection and the total number of clicks performed during the task. Furthermore, we defined an error as a click not leading to a selection, this also includes false positives invoked by sneezing, coughing or screaming, in case of the blowing trigger. The participants were asked to prioritize accuracy over speed. As pointing feedback a simple ray was drawn, starting from the tip of the used device. No extended selection strategy was used. Each task consisted of 21 spheres arranged in a circle with a radius of 0.75m and placed 2.625m in front of the user, with the restriction to hold position in the center of the CAVE. The projection plane of the spheres lay exactly on the CAVE's back wall to exclude any effects of distance estimation [1] and reduce possible effects of target distance, as i.e. reported by [18].

The current target sphere was colored in green (see Figure 1), the currently focused, if any, in blue and all others in white. While a button was pressed, a sphere switched its color from blue to white. The sphere size varied from an easy first task (**T1**) with radius 0.1m over a second task (**T2**) with radius 0.075m and a third task (**T3**) with a radius of 0.05m, to a very difficult last task (**T4**) with a radius of 0.025m. Each of the three device combinations was introduced by a simple training task with 11 spheres of radius 0.15m and no time restriction. Additionally, the participants were told that they can take a break between the different device conditions and between the tasks.

Before the experiment, each participant filled out a demographic questionnaire and was orally briefed about the task. They had no further explanation how to use BlowClick, than "by blowing into

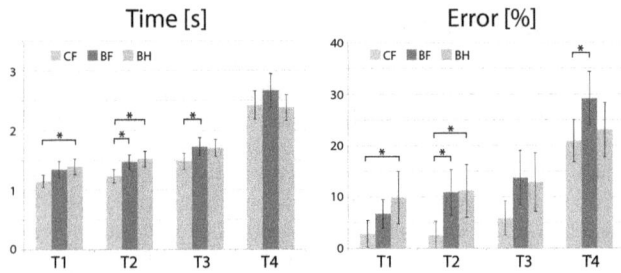

Figure 2: Left: mean time between successful selections in T1-T4, right: clicks not leading to a selection in T1-T4. Error bars show the 95% confidence intervals.

Table 1: P-values and effects for the time and the rate of error, between the different devices.

| Task | | Time | | Error | |
|------|------|------|------|------|------|
| | | effect [s] | p-value | effect [%] | p-value |
| T1 | CF - BF | -.197 | .065 | -3.823 | .388 |
| | CF - BH | -.245 | **.015*** | -6.999 | **.020*** |
| | BF - BH | -.048 | 1.000 | -3.176 | .618 |
| T2 | CF - BF | -.233 | **.018*** | -8.241 | **.016*** |
| | CF - BH | -.285 | **.003*** | -8.588 | **.011*** |
| | BF - BH | -.052 | 1.000 | -.347 | 1.000 |
| T3 | CF - BF | -.242 | **.043*** | -7.881 | .058 |
| | CF - BH | -.223 | .070 | -6.990 | .110 |
| | BF - BH | .019 | 1.000 | .891 | 1.000 |
| T4 | CF - BF | -.243 | .423 | -8.206 | **.047*** |
| | CF - BH | .043 | 1.000 | -2.126 | 1.000 |
| | BF - BH | .286 | .254 | 6.080 | .208 |

* .05 level of significance

the microphone". After performing the tasks, the participants were asked to fill out a qualitative questionnaire regarding the subjective usefulness and a device comparison (see Figure 3 and 4), and write down freetext comments.

## 4.3 Results

We averaged the time between successful selections over all 21 trials for each participant and further averaged these results per task (see Figure 2 left). Furthermore we set the number of errors in relation to the number of total clicks triggered in every task and averaged them over all participants (see Figure 2 right). Table 1 lists p-values and effects for the time and the rate of error, within task difficulties, between the different devices. As expected, the time and error increases with the difficulty of the tasks. However, the data only partially supports hypothesis H2. On the one hand, within the easier tasks T1 and T2, the classic button trigger significantly outperforms both blowing device combinations in 6 out of 8 cases (see Figure 2 and Table 1), regarding time and error, but on the other hand, in the more difficult tasks T3 and T4, only in 2 out of 8 cases. When significantly better, the effect of the standard technique does not show more than 20% increased speed and less than 8% fewer errors. This supports our main hypothesis H1, that it is possible to reasonably solve triggering tasks with the BlowClick metaphor. We did not find any interesting intra-task results.

Figure 3, 4 and Table 2 show the results of the post-study questionnaires. First of all, the results for Q5 also subjectively support H1. Question Q9, Q10 and Q12 show that in case of perceived speed, precision and overall success, the participants had no clear favorite out of standard trigger and blowing, which does not support H2. Question Q2 and Q11 clearly support H3 that blowing is exhausting, even if we do not see any effects over time in the

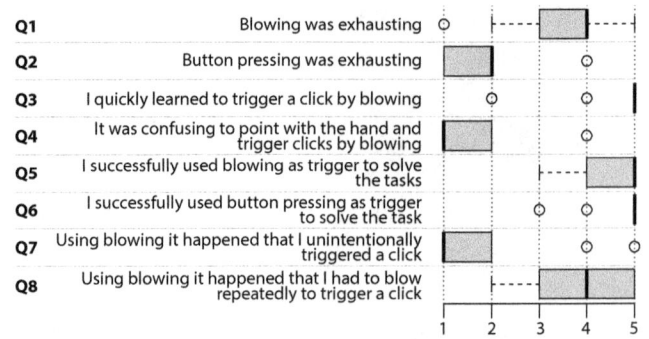

Figure 3: Results of a 5 point Likert scale questionnaire.

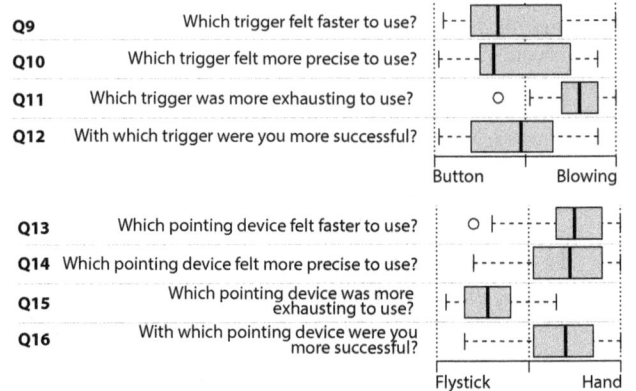

Figure 4: Results of a comparison questionnaire, inspired by NASA TLX.

data. As a spin-off result, it is interesting to notice that participants clearly preferred the hand over the Flystick as pointing device in combination with BlowClick (Q13-Q16).

## 5. DISCUSSION & FUTURE WORK

The results show that BlowClick as a metaphor for triggering, in selection tasks is a suitable solution. Additionally, it performs better than expected compared to a standard device. In the future, we want to investigate whether these results are repeatable in common application scenarios for IVEs, where the focus does not exclusively lie on the selection method. The results show also that the blowing was perceived as exhausting, which can be a problem in practice. However, the chosen experimental setup, with the goal to blow about a hundred times in a few minutes, does not sufficiently represents all real use cases. Additionally, we observed and

Table 2: Mean (M) and standard derivation (SD) for the questionnaires from Figure 3, scaling discrete from 1 to 5 and Figure 4, scaling from 0 to 20 in .5 steps.

| | M | SD | | M | SD |
|------|------|------|------|------|------|
| Q1 | 3.67 | 1.19 | Q9 | 8.11 | 6.22 |
| Q2 | 2.11 | 1.13 | Q10 | 8.11 | 5.73 |
| Q3 | 4.67 | 0.77 | Q11 | 15.14 | 3.53 |
| Q4 | 1.56 | 0.78 | Q12 | 8.47 | 5.68 |
| Q5 | 4.56 | 0.62 | Q13 | 13.97 | 4.57 |
| Q6 | 4.72 | 0.57 | Q14 | 13.39 | 5.31 |
| Q7 | 1.61 | 1.14 | Q15 | 5.19 | 3.83 |
| Q8 | 3.72 | 1.13 | Q16 | 12.78 | 5.28 |

got reported that a part of the participants spent much less effort to trigger a click by blowing than others. They relatively quickly found a way to blow directly into the microphone in a way that needs less effort and especially was possible to perform decoupled from their normal breathing rhythm. However, nearly all participants reported that they were able to quickly learn to trigger a click by blowing (Q3). Thus, it will be interesting to investigate the effects in a longitudinal study. Furthermore, we are convinced that the observed speed and error rate with the BlowClick metaphor can be further reduced. One possibility is to add a visual or auditory feedback that reveals how far away the current amount of blowing is away from triggering a click, w.r.t. the threshold. We are confident that this would reveal the reason why an intended click did not happen and additionally could give confidence to the user that a click did not happen not because of the blowing, but the pointing. We sometimes observed that participants increased the amount of blowing more and more when a series of errors happened, when the reason for that actually was not the blowing. Second, the underlying framework for the study triggered a click event on a sphere only when the *trigger down* and *trigger up* event both happened while focusing the sphere. While this is a valid method to evaluate a click, some participants reported that this was confusing to them or even led to a lot of errors, because they already aimed for the next target and only then noticed that the last sphere had not been selected. This fact influenced both trigger methods, but the influence should have been stronger with the blowing, as its duration was normally longer and so the probability that the sphere was already left was higher. Additionally, Isokoski [10] noted that there are significant differences in the performance of a computer mouse just with respect to the actual button event evaluated as trigger. Possible solutions for further investigations are, to better prepare the participants, give a clearer visual or auditory feedback that a click was performed, or that it just disappears due to the learning in a longitudinal study. Finally we want to improve the blow detection by trying to even better decide if the current audio signal originates from speech or blowing, e.g., by considering the amount of signal clipping. This would further increase the usability in many use cases.

# 6. CONCLUSION

In this paper, we presented a low-latency approach to precisely trigger events by blowing into a microphone. The results of the performed user study show that the proposed method allows to complete a standard selection task and performs better than expected against a standard interaction device.

# 7. REFERENCES

[1] G. Bruder, F. A. Sanz, A.-H. Olivier, and A. Lécuyer. Distance Estimation in Large Immersive Projection Systems, Revisited. *In Proc. of IEEE Virtual Reality*, pages 27–32, 2015.

[2] S. Chanjaradwichai, P. Punyabukkana, and A. Suchato. Design and Evaluation of a Non-Verbal Voice-Controlled Cursor for Point-And-Click Tasks. *In Proc. of International Convention on Rehabilitation Engineering & Assistive Technology*, pages 48:1–48:4, 2010.

[3] A. Choumane, G. Casiez, and L. Grisoni. Buttonless Clicking: Intuitive Select and Pick-Release Through Gesture Analysis. *In Proc. of IEEE Virtual Reality*, pages 67–70, 2010.

[4] L. Fehr, W. E. Langbein, and S. B. Skaar. Adequacy of Power Wheelchair Control Interfaces for Persons with Severe Disabilities: A Clinical Survey. *Journal of Rehabilitation Research and Development*, 37(3):353–360, 2000.

[5] S. Harada, J. Landay, and J. Malkin. The Vocal Joystick: Evaluation of Voice-Based Cursor Control Techniques. *In Proc. of International ACM SIGACCESS Conference on Computers and Accessibility*, pages 197–204, 2006.

[6] S. Harada, J. O. Wobbrock, and J. A. Landay. Voice Games: Investigation Into the Use of Non-speech Voice Input for Making Computer Games More Accessible. *In Proc. of IFIP International Conference on Human-Computer Interaction*, pages 11–29, 2011.

[7] B. Hentschel, J. Künne, I. Assenmacher, and T. Kuhlen. Evaluation of a Hands-Free 3D Interaction Device for Virtual Environments. *Virtuelle und Erweiterte Realität: Workshop der GI-Fachgruppe VR/AR*, pages 149–156, 2015.

[8] T. Igarashi and J. F. Hughes. Voice as Sound: Using Non-Verbal Voice Input for Interactive Control. *In Proc. of ACM Symposium on User Interface Software and Technology*, 3(2):155–156, 2001.

[9] ISO. *Ergonomics of Human-system Interaction: Principles and requirements for physical input devices (ISO 9241-400:2007, IDT)*. International Organisation for Standardisation, 2007.

[10] P. Isokoski. Variability of Throughput in Pointing Device Tests: Button- Up or Button-Down? *In Proc. of ACM NordiCHI*, pages 68–77, 2006.

[11] Y. Jang, S.-T. Noh, H. J. Chang, T.-K. Kim, and W. Woo. 3D Finger CAPE: Clicking Action and Position Estimation under Self-Occlusions in Egocentric Viewpoint. *IEEE Transactions on Visualization and Computer Graphics*, 21(4):501–510, 2015.

[12] J. Nielsen. *Usability Engineering*. Morgan Kaufmann Publishers Inc., 1993.

[13] S. N. Patel and G. D. Abowd. BLUI: Low-Cost Localized Blowable User Interfaces. *In Proc. of ACM Symposium on User Interface Software and Technology*, pages 217–220, 2007.

[14] O. Poláček, A. J. Sporka, and P. Slavík. A Comparative Study of Pitch-Based Gestures in Nonverbal Vocal Interaction. *IEEE Transactions on Systems, Man and Cybernetics*, 42(6):1567–1571, 2012.

[15] J. Segen and S. Kumar. Shadow Gestures: 3D Hand Pose Estimation Using a Single Camera. *In Proc. of IEEE Computer Society Conference on Computer Vision and Pattern Recognition*, 1:479–485, 1999.

[16] R. W. Soukoreff and I. S. MacKenzie. Towards a Standard for Pointing Device Evaluation, Perspectives on 27 Years of Fitts' Law Research in HCI. *International Journal of Human Computer Studies*, 61(6):751–789, 2004.

[17] A. J. Sporka, S. H. Kurniawan, and P. Slavik. Whistling User Interface ($U^3I$). *ERCIM Workshop on User Interfaces for All*, 3196:472–478, 2004.

[18] R. J. Teather and W. Stuerzlinger. Pointing at 3D Target Projections with One-eyed and Stereo Cursors. *Proc. ACM CHI*, pages 159–168, 2013.

[19] D. Zielasko, D. Rausch, Y. C. Law, T. C. Knott, S. Pick, S. Porsche, J. Herber, J. Hummel, and T. W. Kuhlen. Cirque des Bouteilles: The Art of Blowing on Bottles. *In Proc. of IEEE Symposium on 3D User Interfaces*, pages 209–210, 2015.

# Evaluating Mid-air List Interaction for Spatial Audio Interfaces

Christina Dicke
Quality and Usability Lab, Telekom Innovation
Laboratories, TU Berlin
Berlin, Germany
christina.dicke@ixds.com

Jörg Müller
Department of Computer Science, Aarhus
University
Aarhus, Denmark
joerg.mueller@acm.org

## ABSTRACT

Selecting items from lists is a common task in many applications. For wearable devices where no display is available, list selection can be challenging. To explore potential solutions we present four user studies evaluating mid-air gestures to interact with lists in an eyes-free interface. We found that a spatialized audio list in the shape of a 110 degree arc angled towards the dominant hand was a comfortable and usable layout for most users. A selection takes less than 10.6 seconds on average and error rates are below 4% when users locate and select an item in an unknown, unordered list of 20 items. For lists of 10 items the mean selection time is 5.5 seconds or less, and error rates drop below 1.4%. We compared monophonic to binaural playback of feedback sounds (musicons) and found no statistical difference for task completion times or error rates between the conditions. We also implemented and evaluated a music player application to showcase spatial audio list selection in an applied scenario.

## Keywords

Auditory Display, Mid-air Gestures, List Selection, Direct Manipulation

## Categories and Subject Descriptors

H.5.2. [**Information Interfaces and Presentation (e.g., HCI)**]: User Interfaces—*Interaction styles*

## 1. INTRODUCTION

Selecting items from lists is a common task in many applications, for example, people use menus to navigate through options, select names from contact lists, or create and share their personal playlists. Selecting an item from a list usually involves browsing the list and then selecting one or several items. Browsing and selecting requires a representation of the list, like a visual display, and some form of user interaction, such as using a scrollbar with a mouse or a swipe gesture on a touchscreen.

*SUI'15*, August 8–9, 2015, Los Angeles, CA, USA.
Copyright is held by the owner/author(s). Publication rights licensed to ACM.
ACM 978-1-4503-3703-8/15/08 ...$15.00.
DOI: http://dx.doi.org/10.1145/2788940.2788945 .

Although this form of list presentation and interaction is general, and will work in almost any traditional task situation, it is not always optimal. Scenarios–in which the device is too small for a usable visual display, where the visual display has a very low resolution, or the input capabilities are limited–are poorly supported by traditional list interaction techniques. With the spread of wearable technology and the accompanying miniaturization of I/O capabilities, traditional list selection may become slow and frustrating.

A number of eyes-free solutions have been proposed to compensate for insufficient display space. Hardware buttons, headphone cable switches or small touch-sensitive areas simplify quick interactions with a small device, such as a watch or music player, but only a reduced set of discrete interactions is supported by these methods. Cord input [32] can provide continuous input through touch location, twisting, bending and pulling but is error-prone and may not always be accessible. Complex interaction can be accomplished with speech recognition [35, 30], which offers direct, hands-free user input. But speech-recognition is still suboptimal in noisy environments or in the presence of multiple speakers.

Gestural input on or with a device is an alternative [27, 41, 36, 16, 26] and touch gestures–abstract mappings of discrete commands–can extend the number and complexity of executable functions beyond a simple switch interface. However, touch gestures cannot efficiently support tasks that require direct and continuous feedback like changing scrolling speeds for navigating through and interacting with large lists. Users either have to skip through the list step-by-step or memorize a unique gesture mapped to that function, thereby increasing cognitive load. Furthermore, touch gestures still require a physical device that is touched, held or otherwise stabilized in an accessible position, and errors may arise due to aging or clogged devices, or fumbled access through clothing.

Gustafson et al [15] proposed imaginary interfaces, a free-hand spatial interaction technique that gives users direct access to an invisible display. Spatial memory can aid orientation and enable quick access to items even after an extended period of time. The drawback here is that users have to rely on their visual short-term memory and do not receive any kind of feedback. For unknown or long lists, efficient interaction is difficult to achieve without a continuous spatial representation of the list's items and state.

To address the difficulties of the limited interaction capabilities of wearable technology–and the resultant issues of scalability, efficiency and accuracy–we conducted three user studies to investigate direct spatial manipulation for list selection facilitated by an auditory display. Because the system was controlled by mid-air gestures, miniaturization of physical input and visual output capabilities did not impact the user interaction. Furthermore, taking advantage of kinesthetic and spatial memory effects quickened the interaction, making it useful for both microinteractions [4], and for

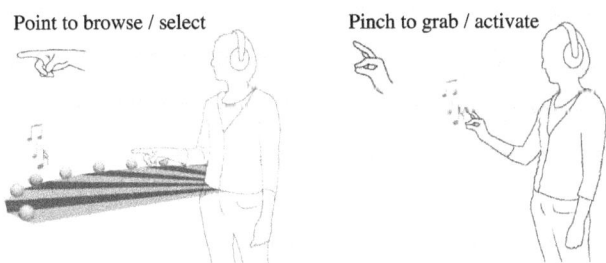

Point to browse / select          Pinch to grab / activate

Figure 1: List selection with lists arranged in an arc centred on the user. By pointing at items users can browse the list and select items (Left). Once a song is found it can be activated through a pinching gesture (Right).

more complex tasks like copying, pasting, and multiple or ranged selection.

## 2. STUDIES OVERVIEW

### 2.1 Study 1: Physical constraints, angle, location, distance

We verified the basic physical constraints of interacting with a spatial display using mid-air gestures. We assessed the range, location, and distance of such a display, as perceived by users who varied widely in what they found comfortable. Different preferences for distance lead some users to over- or undershoot a target for which spatial positions were fixed. Thus, we thus changed the grab-to-select gesture to a point-to-select gesture. Based on our findings, for the next two studies we implemented an arc-shaped list that began at 11 o'clock and ended at 3 o'clock.

### 2.2 Study 2A and 2B: Impact of list length and playback type

The second study revealed the effect of list length on users' speed and accuracy. We tested users on a list of 10 items and on one double that size. Error rates were marginal even for lists with 20 items (3.8%). Mean selection times were 5.5 seconds for 10-item lists and 10.6 seconds for 20-item lists. To measure the effect of sound rendering, we compared binaurally rendered to monaurally rendered playback for 10-item lists. Both conditions showed a strong learning effect but there were no differences in task completion times or error rates. Spatial memory and the learning effect were probably facilitated by the physical pointing gesture rather than the binaural rendering. Although both conditions were equally efficient, participants tended to find the binaural condition easier to use.

### 2.3 Study 3: Evaluation in an applied context

For the final study we built a music player to serve as an example application for a list selection task. We compared a version of the music player that is rotationally fixed to the world against one that is user-fixed. We also explored a way to scroll through and obtain an overview of lists of 60 items and to adjust the volume by continuous horizontal movement of the hand. In general, participants liked the player and its direct and physical interaction style. All participants could successfully scroll through the list and manipulate items. Participants liked the user-centred display but preferred if the display did not rotate to follow their head.

## 3. RELATED WORK

Our review of previous work will focus on two main subjects: work in the general field of gestural interaction–particularly using mid-air gestures–and 3D auditory displays that utilize gestures for user interaction.

### 3.1 Gesture-based Interaction

In an exploratory study, Wolf et al. [39] investigated how users would spontaneously interact with a spatial auditory display. Users were given a dummy device and encouraged to perform any gesture of their choosing, on or with the device, to solve 20 typical tasks, including item selection and manipulation. Wolf et al. observed that participants created gestures through associations with other known interaction techniques or analogies from other domains. These ranged from discrete one-dimensional gestures performed on the device to continuous three-dimensional gestures and combinations thereof. For interacting with spatial auditory displays they recommend small combinable gesture sets, gesture inversions for do- and undo-commands, and preferred discreet minimalistic gestures over expressive ones.

Marentakis & Brewster [20] evaluated three different gestures for browsing and selecting in a 3D soundscape. Participants used either their head, hand or a touch tablet. Eight sound sources were positioned at a distance of 2 meters on a 360 degree ring around a user's head and could be selected by turning their head towards the source, pointing at the source or browsing with a pen on the tablet. Marentakis & Brewster found that the tablet condition was significantly more accurate than the other two techniques. They observed that a significant number of participants tried to point without turning their bodies, which influenced the accuracy of the browsing and selection process. Motion Marking Menus, proposed by Oakley and Park [25], are a gestural menu technique based on rotations of a handheld device around a single axis over a 90 degree range. A user can select items from a marking menu by tapping on a touchscreen or pressing a button. Oakley and Parker found that a menu system containing 19 commands gave optimal performance and was well suited to kinesthetic and eyes-free interaction.

Gustafson et al. [15] introduced imaginary interfaces, a free-hand spatial interaction technique that allows users to create their own imaginary interfaces. Relying on visual short-term memory and a reference frame given by users' own non-dominant hands, invisible objects can be drawn and pointed at in 2D space. In three studies, Gustafson et al. showed that participants could create and annotate simple drawings, and point at locations, without requiring any feedback. They recommended exploiting visual or kinesthetic features, such as the reference hands' finger length, to support users' memory of objects' positions.

Ashbrook et al. [3] use a finger worn ring to control up to eight choices in a menu. A user can turn the ring and by means of a magnetic field sensor the ring's rotations around the finger can be mapped to elements in a list. A selection is made by moving the ring along the finger. Although this technique has a high social acceptability the list size is restricted to 8 elements.

ShoeSense, proposed by Bailly et al. [5], is an eyes-free interaction technique for mobile devices. A shoe-mounted depth-camera is used to recognize hand-gestures, such as a radial pinch, a finger-count, or a triangle formed between the right hand and left arm. ShoeSense can be used to control an eyes-free application by mapping gestures to operations. Participants found gestures required low physical and mental demand. Although gestures had a high social acceptability in general, interviews revealed that such acceptability varied with the user's location.

## 3.2 Spatial Auditory Displays

Pirhonen et al. [27] developed the TouchPlayer, a hip-worn mobile music player controlled by gestures performed on the touchscreen of a PDA. One-dimensional discrete gestures executed with one finger were mapped to the player's functions, like a sweep across to skip to the next track. Compared to a standard visual interface, the TouchPlayer significantly reduced workload and task completion times without impacting error rates. However, menu navigation or item selection were not supported and the PDA had to be worn on a belt.

PocketMenu [26] was similar to TouchPlayer in that it utilized a touch-enabled device to control a music player. A limited number of menu items were laid out along the screen's border and could be selected by a swipe gesture towards the screen's center. Users received vibro-tactile and synthesized speech feedback. PocketMenu supported discrete and continuous input, e.g. for volume adjustment.

Dicke et al. [12] built a user-centred spatial sound display for navigating between multiple sounds. The auditory display consisted of three virtual rings at different distances, on which sound streams were positioned. Users could perform discrete two-dimensional gestures with a mobile phone to rotate rings, move sources between rings, or focus on a source. Dicke et al. showed that users could quickly navigate between a limited number of sources by performing flick and pan gestures with a device.

Building on [12] Dicke et al. proposed Foogue [13], a spatial auditory display concept supporting item selection and manipulation. User interaction is supported through a combination of discrete and continuous two-dimensional gestures performed with and on a touch-enabled device. Foogue has two modes, menu mode and listening mode. In menu mode users can navigate through hierarchical structures and select single or multiple items, which are to be displayed as players in listening mode. These players can be moved freely by point-move-release gestures in an egocentric, two-dimensional, 360 degrees space. Foogue offers many solutions to the challenge of designing a mobile music player, however, it remained a design concept and was never evaluated in a user study.

Kajastila & Lokki [17] compared three methods for controlling circularly and rectangularly arranged auditory and visual menus. The circular display presented twelve spatially arranged items (numbers) spread evenly on a virtual circle surrounding a user's head. Users could make a selection by either rotating their hand or moving it towards a number. Kajastila & Lokki found that free-hand gestures were fast and accurate and that smaller circular gestures were preferred over spacious circular gestures, as they reduced effort and time. By using hand-rotation in mid-air, they overcame the necessity of holding a physical device for selecting from short lists.

Müller et al. [24] developed an interactive system to "touch", grab and manipulate sounds in mid-air. They could show that users can locate, walk towards and touch spatially rendered sounds with a high accuracy and without any visual feedback.

## 4. CONTRIBUTION

We present four user studies exploring a direct manipulation approach utilizing mid-air gestures to interact with spatialized lists in an auditory display. In the first three studies we investigated the physical constraints of spatialized lists in order to define a physiologically adequate display angle, and we looked at the effects of list length and sound rendering on selection time and error rate. To validate this work in the context of a real application, we developed a music player controlled by mid-air gestures for the fourth study. Aside from a general evaluation of the player, we also used it to learn about participants' preferences with regard to navigating a list of 60 items. We believe some of our findings are independent of the display's modality and could generally contribute to the design of gesture-based interactions, for example in three-dimensional, immersive environments like games, or in exploring interface alternatives for visually impaired users.

## 5. DESIGN SPACE OF LISTS IN AUDITORY DISPLAYS

Cockburn et al. [10] systematically described the design space for gestural interaction with and without visual feedback in a framework for air pointing. Taking this work into consideration, in this section we discuss the properties that we believe are essential to the design of spatialized lists and list-selection.

### 5.1 Representation

Efficiently representing a list that contains more than a dozen items is a challenge in auditory display design. Due to the temporal nature of sound, playback time linearly increases with the number of items in a list, and therefore the time a listener needs to find an item. To reduce this display time, researchers have proposed several solutions. For lists of sound files the most obvious solution is not to play the file itself but a much shorter handle or abstract representation. This has been done in the form of earcons [9], spearcons [38] or musicons [21]. The benefit of these methods is the reduction of playback time while maintaining a fair degree of intelligibility. Playing files or handles synchronously or with onset intervals has been explored as an additional solution [9, 34, 14] but is limited due to masking effects.

### 5.2 Display dimensionality

Although lists are one-dimensional, the way they are presented to a user is not necessarily limited to one dimension. Display dimensionality is distinct from the rendering technique as it refers to the layout of the display and not to how sounds are played to users. Examples of one-dimensional displays include the iPod Nano's VoiceOver feature and Audio Bubbles [22]. Examples of 2D displays include a multi-party conference [12] and interacting with an in-vehicle menu [34]. Examples of 3D displays include accessing a music collection [31] and outdoor navigation [37] or the audio progress bar [11]

### 5.3 Rendering

Independent of the display's dimensionality, the sound itself can be reproduced in varying dimensions. It can be rendered binaurally — coming from a position located outside of a listener's head —, with directionality, as in stereophonic sound, or monaurally, i.e. located inside a listener's head.

### 5.4 Scrolling

In visual displays, there are many well-established techniques for helping users to access long or structured lists, including sectioning, pagination, hierarchization, and zooming. There are only few such methods developed for auditory displays. [31] used a strong physical metaphor in which a music collection is divided into navigable rooms. [41, 17] built auditory menus in the style of a Marking Menu to access items in a hierarchically structured list.

### 5.5 Overview

An overview of items in a list (or of one's position there) should be readily available and easily processable. Again, the temporal nature of sound makes this a challenge. Researchers have addressed this, for example [8] in the context of hierarchical menus and [18] complex data sets.

## 5.6 Interaction

Different interaction styles and paradigms have been proposed for interacting with lists. Popular solutions are gestures performed on a device [27, 41], with a device [12, 19] or with body parts [17, 20]. Interaction can be in discrete steps as in [12] or continuously as in [19]. Depending on position and dimensionality, interaction can be limited to a range [17], an area [5] or it can be ubiquitous [12].

## 5.7 Location

Most mobile auditory displays play audio relative to a user's height at face level [31, 27, 20, 41, 12]. A likely reason for this is that usually headphones are used to display 3D sound, which naturally positions sources at head-height. A display could also be anchored at other body parts such as shoulders, hands or feet.

## 5.8 Translation

Translation refers to how a display reacts to movement. If it is fixed on a user (egocentric) it will move when the user moves. If it is fixed on a location independent of a user (world-fixed or exocentric), a user can move towards it or away from it. World-fixed displays with absolute positioning are popular for way-finding and navigational tasks [19].

## 5.9 Rotation

Rotation refers to how a display reacts to a user's rotational movements. For example, if a display is user-fixed and the user turns their head the display also rotates. This is often the case in displays that use headphones and do not compensate for head movements.

## 6. GESTURAL INTERACTION DESIGN OVERVIEW

We overcome the need for display and interaction space on a device by choosing mid-air gestures. Enabling users to mimic how they would naturally interact with physical objects draws on their already available implicit knowledge of the movement ("knowing how") and offers a mental model that is easily accessible and learnable ("knowing what") (cf. [2]). For the design of our list-selection approach we focused on optimizing gestures for ease of use and not reflecting the limitations of the current state of technology. Aspects contributing to the usability of free-hand gestures as summarized by Baudel & Beaudouin-Lafon [6] were taken into account as well as factors impacting the joy of use and social acceptability. In particular, we focused on these factors:

1. **Physiological Adequacy**: Gestures should be simple to perform, require minimal muscle stress and effort, and be designed for repetitive use.

2. **Contextual Adequacy**: Interaction should be intuitive, easily discoverable and sensible in the context of the application. Logical consistency within the gesture set should be maintained, for example by gesture reversion for do/undo-commands as recommended by [39].

3. **Social Acceptability**: Gestures should be socially acceptability to encourage adoption of gestures. Rico & Brewster [29] conducted studies on the social acceptability of device and body based gestures performed in the wild. They found that location and audience have a significant impact on users' willingness to perform gestures. Subtle imitations of everyday gestures, like shaking or tapping, were rated more acceptable in public than large or noticeable gestures, like a shoulder or nose tap. Besides social factors, the ease with which gestures can be performed had an impact on ratings. Physically uncomfortable gestures, such as head nodding, foot tapping, and wrist rotation were rated lower than easy to perform gestures. Montero et al. [23] found users' acceptance for performing a gesture in public places was influenced by whether they thought bystanders were able to interpret the intention of the gesture. Yi et al. [40] found that social respect and avoiding interruption to social activities are important user motivations for using eyes-free interaction.

Using mid-air gestures moves the interaction towards the *expressive* end of the scale defined by Reeves et al. [28] in their classification of public interfaces. Following their definition we used *suspenseful* gestures: the manipulation is obvious but as the effect is displayed aurally it is only revealed to the user wearing the headphones and not the bystanders. We chose self-explanatory gestures for our study, which are based on everyday life's physical interactions and allowed for subtle and expressive gestures to address issues of social acceptability.

## 7. STUDY 1: PHYSICAL CONSTRAINTS, ANGLE, LOCATION, DISTANCE

In this first exploratory study, we verified the basic spatial constraints of the interface. While its position in space is already restricted by human anatomy, i.e. by where it is comfortable to reach, we took a closer look at participants' subjective perception of where they would want the interface to be. Specifically, we addressed these research questions:

- RQ1: What is perceived as a comfortable angular window size for pointing at sources in space?

- RQ2: What is the preferred location for this window?

- RQ3: What is the preferred distance from hand to body for spatial pointing?

## 7.1 Experimental design

Participants were first introduced to the concept of the "point and select" interaction style of the list. They had 5 to 10 minutes to familiarize themselves with an example list of 180 degree angular range starting at -90 degrees. We started measurements once participants found their "comfort zone" and stopped measuring after four repetitions. Dependent variables for this study were *angle size*, *angle position*, and *radius*, i.e. distance from the center of the hand to the center of the head.

## 7.2 Task

Participants demonstrated their preferred shape and position of the list. They pinched (touched thumb and index finger) where they would want the list to start, circumscribed the range with their hand at a comfortable distance from their body, and then pinched again where they would want it to end.

## 7.3 Participants

We recruited 16 right-handed participants from our institutions' database (5 male). They were between 25 and 68 years old (mean age 36 years) and received a small compensation for their time.

## 7.4 Technical Setup

For all experiments we used an Optitrack [1] optical tracking system with 16 cameras for high-precision localization of participants' head and hand positions. These were received in a Processing [2] sketch from where sound positions were controlled. Via a Pure Data [3] patch, sound control events were routed to the Sound Scape Renderer [1] (SSR) [4] for binaural rendering. HRTFs measured in a small studio room as described in [7] were applied to make the rendering slightly echoic. Participants wore AKG K601 reference headphones with compensation filters applied and also a custom made glove. Optical markers were sewn onto the glove and a pinch of thumb and index finger was wirelessly transmitted and recognised by the Processing sketch.

## 7.5 Results and discussion

As shown in Fig. 2, participants varied strongly in all three aspects measured. Some were comfortable extending their arms almost completely and circumscribed nearly 180 degrees (p2, p4, and p10), but others preferred a very narrow frontal range (p11, p13, and p18). Most participants started their movement at approx. 11 o'clock (-15.39 degrees). The mean angle range was 105.32 degrees and most participants ended between 2 and 4 o'clock. We could observe a similar variance in hand-to-head distance. The shortest distance was 0.27 meters and the longest 0.66 meters with a mean of 0.55 meters.

An overlay of all 16 datasets is shown in Fig. 3. The head position is marked by the two grey lines crossing at (0.0,0.0). The black dashed line shows the overall mean angular hand-to-head distance. Given that arm lengths varied between participants and acknowledging that the average arm length of a human correlates with their height, we assumed an impact of gender on the results. As women are usually smaller and hence have a shorter arm length, we hypothesized that shorter distances were preferred by female participants. We found that this is not the case. Interestingly, both very small and close ranges and large and more distant ranges were circumscribed by female participants. Data from male participants is shown as p01, p03, p09, p16, and p17 in Fig. 2.

Concluding from the results, subjective preference seemed to be the strongest influence on the users' comfort with their chosen *angle size*, *angle position*, and *radius*. However, age or physical health may also have an influence but were not evaluated in this study. The high variance in the results seem to dispel a notion that we influenced participants by priming them with a 180 degree angle. Overall, an angle of approx. 110 degrees starting at -30 degrees and ending at 90 degrees seemed an acceptable compromise.

We took another important learning from this first study: as we saw such a strong variance in what was perceived as a comfortable hand position for pointing at objects in mid-air, we changed the initial design from a "touch the source to select" style to a "point at the source to select" style. While in the initial approach the hand position $(h_x, h_y)$ had to be in a certain radius around a source's position $(s_x, s_y)$ to initiate a selection, the new approach registers a selection based on whether the hands' position is in a isosceles triangle with the adjacent centered on an item position and of length c:

$$c = \sqrt[2]{2r^2(1 - \cos\phi)}$$

where $\phi$ is the total angle divided by the number of items to be displayed and $r$ is the distance from head to source. This improved

[1] http://www.naturalpoint.com/optitrack
[2] http://processing.org
[3] http://puredata.info
[4] http://www.tu-berlin.de/?id=ssr

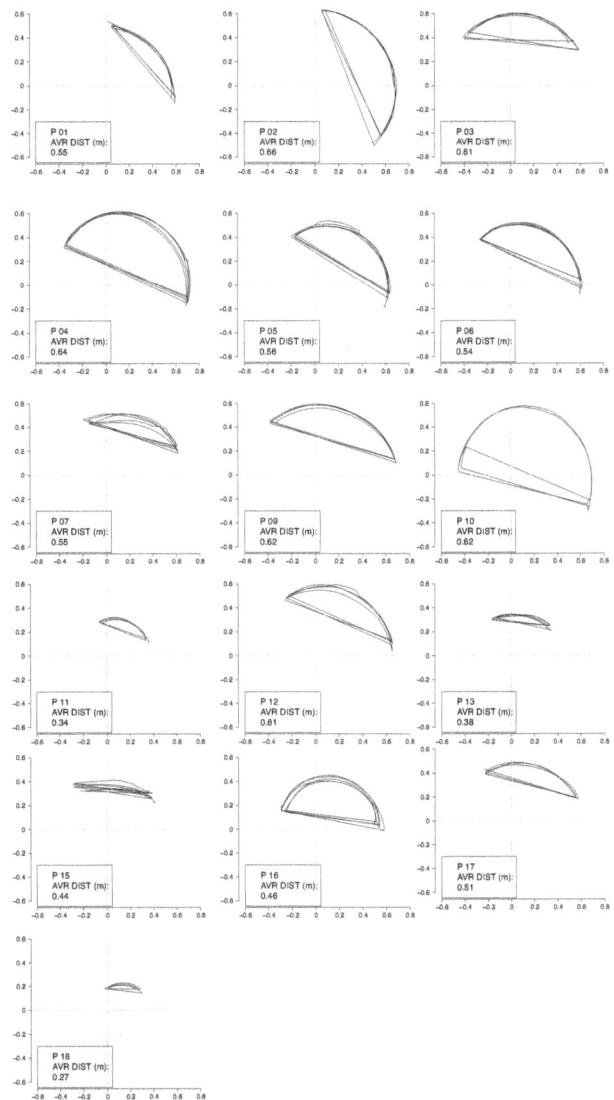

**Figure 2: Individual angles circumscribed by right-handed participants (head at 0,0). Variations in preferred head to hand distance and start- and end- positions are apparent. On average, participants covered a range of 105.32 degrees and started at -15.39 degrees. The mean distance between hand and head was 0.55 meters.**

design is illustrated in Fig. 4. The new approach is also robust against overshooting and it supports both minimal pointing gestures performed very close to the body and expressive gestures in which the arm is fully extended. As a secondary benefit, it could be used as a rapid scanning method when the hand is held close. When the arm is fully extended, angles are increased and the selection could be 'fine tuned'.

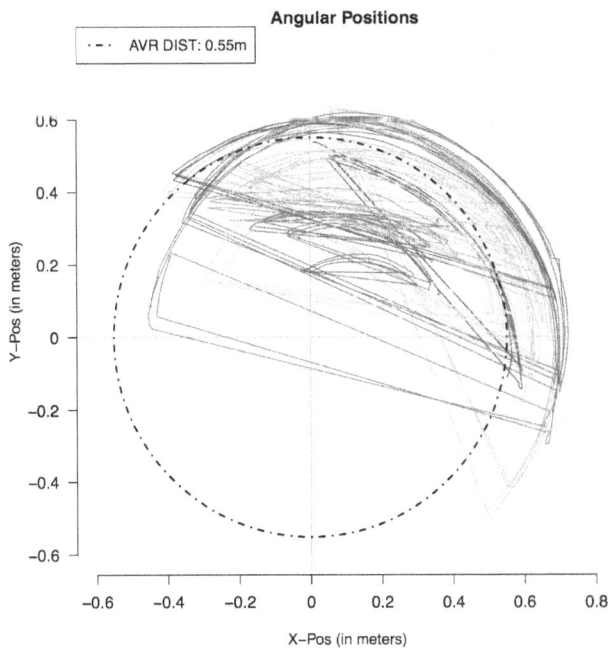

**Figure 3: An overlay all angles circumscribed by participants. On average participants started at -15.39 degrees and covered a range of 105.32 degrees. The mean distance between hand and head (at 0,0) was 0.55 meters.**

# 8. STUDY 2A: IMPACT OF PLAYBACK TYPE

The purpose of this study was to get a thorough understanding of how long on average it takes to select an item, how error prone this is, and how these two aspects are influenced by the playback type. The research question addressed in this study was:

RQ: What is the impact of the sound rendering (monophonic vs. binaural/spatial) on task completion time and error rate?

## 8.1 Experimental design

We compared two conditions in a within-subjects design:

- Cond. 1: 10 items, monophonic playback

- Cond. 2: 10 items, binaural playback

Participants completed both conditions in a counterbalanced order to prevent learning effects. Each condition consisted of 34 trials. At the beginning of a condition 10 musicons were randomly chosen from a total of 60 musicons and added to the list. The order of items was not changed during a condition but the target musicons were randomly picked from the current list. Dependent variables were *task completion time* and *error rate*. Independent variables were the *playback type of the sources pointed at (monophonic vs. binaural)*.

Before the experiment, all participants trained until they had a correct understanding of the procedure and the functionality of the equipment (usually 4 to 5 trials). Participants wore a glove to track their hands' position and register the pinch gesture. They also wore AKG K601 reference headphones with compensation filters applied, and equipped with optical markers to track their head's position and orientation. Between conditions, participants had breaks of 5 minutes. They completed the study in 30 minutes or less.

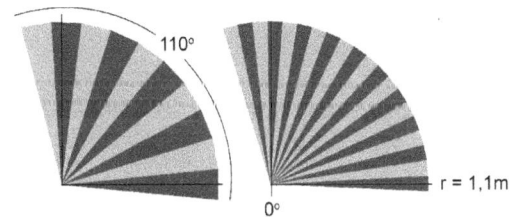

**Figure 4: An illustration of the display layout used for 10-item conditions (left) and the 20-item condition (right). Items were arranged in a 110 degree arc starting at 11 o'clock. Participants could make a selection by pointing at an item, which was displayed at a distance of 1.1 meters.**

## 8.2 Task and stimulus design

To address the research question participants had to find a song in a list of 10 songs, which were plaid to them either monophonically or binaurally with spatial rendering. For the playback of songs we chose an approach suggested by [21] and created musicons–short characteristic samples taken from popular songs–to increase recognition rates and compensate for songs with quiet beginnings. Musicons were extracted from a total of 60 popular songs, taking the most characteristic samples with a length of six seconds, such as the first six seconds of Nirvana's *Smells Like Teen Spirit* or the refrain from Joan Jett & the Blackhearts' *I love Rock 'n' Roll*.

Participants could start a trial by pressing a button on a wireless presenter held in their left hand. Each trial began with a short *beep* followed by the target musicon played monophonically. A second *beep* signaled participants to begin the task. As illustrated in Fig. 1 (Left) participants could search the list by pointing their hand or finger at an item. Based on our previous findings, items were arranged in a 110 degree arc centred on the user's position and expanding from -30 degrees to 90 degrees (as shown in Fig. 4, top view). Pointing at an item started the playback of the musicon and stopped the previous. Participants could point at any item in any order, extend their arm fully or keep their hand close to their body. Once the target item was identified, participants could pinch their fingers (as illustrated in Fig. 1, Right) and mark the item. A short feedback sound played and the timer stopped.

## 8.3 Participants

16 right-handed participants with normal hearing from our institutions' database participated in the study. These 6 men and 10 women were between 25 and 68 years old (mean age 33 years). After the study they were compensated with a € 10 voucher.

## 8.4 Results

An independent-samples t-test was conducted to compare mean task completion times in the monophonic and binaural condition. For the analysis, we removed outliers with task completion times above 60 seconds and missing values. There was no significant difference in the scores for monophonic (M=5050 msec, SD=5576 msec) and binaural (M=5479 msec, SD=5481) playback, $t(1054)=-1.161, p=.21$. We conclude that the playback type had no statistical impact on task completion times.

We found a similar distribution in error rates. Overall, error rates were very low for all conditions. In condition monophonic participants made a total of 20 errors, 21 errors in the binaural condition.

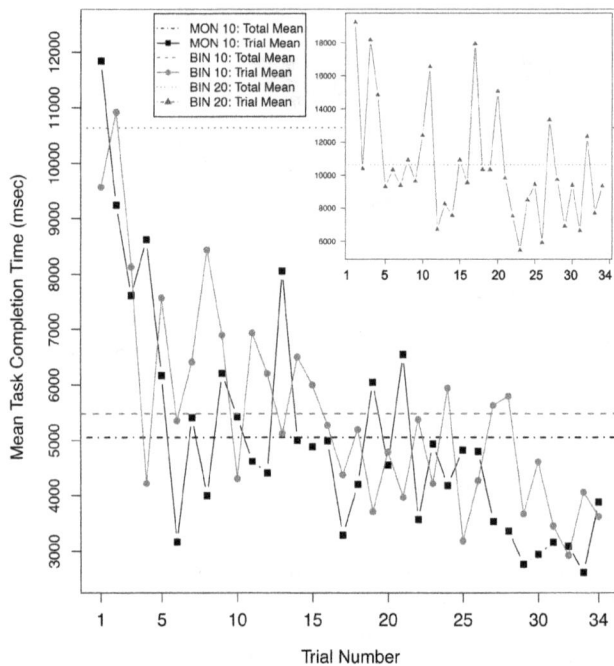

**Figure 5: Mean task completion times (horizontal lines) for all conditions by trial number starting at trial 1. The decline reveals a learning effect equally strong for binaural (10) and monophonic (10) playback and not as pronounced for binaural (20), which is rendered in the upper right corner. (Note: data points are connected for better readability although measurement is not continuous).**

## 9. STUDY 2B: IMPACT OF LIST LENGTH

In this follow-up study we were curious to learn about the impact of item numbers on task completion times and error rates. The research question addressed in this study is:

RQ: How are task completion time and error rate impacted by either 10 or 20 items in the list?

### 9.1 Experimental design

Study 2B had the same design, technical setup, number of participants and participants than study 2A, which is described in the previous section. The difference is that we compared a list of 10 items with a list of 20 items in a within-subjects design:

- Cond. 1: 10 items, binaural playback
- Cond. 2: 20 items, binaural playback

Dependent variables were *task completion time* and *error rate*. The independent variable was the *the number of items (10 vs. 20)*. Fig. 4 illustrates the different arrangement of items from a top view.

### 9.2 Results

An independent-samples t-test was conducted to compare mean task completion times in the 10 items and 20 items condition. For the analysis, we removed outliers with task completion times above 60 seconds and missing values. We found a significant difference in the scores for 10 items (M=5486 msec, SD=5485 msec) and 20 items (M=10668 msec, SD=12520), t(1038)=-8.582, p<.001. We conclude that the number of items has a statistical impact on task completion times. Participants were almost twice as fast in the 10 item condition than in the 20 item condition.

Again, error rates were low for the 10 item condition (19 errors). 60 errors were made in the 20 item condition showing a statistical difference from the 10-item condition with $\chi^2$ (1, N=1040)=31.51, p<.001) but show only a small effect size (Cramér's V=.15).

### 9.3 Discussion

Summarizing these results, we found that in most cases it took participants less than 5.5 seconds to select an item from an unordered list of 10 items. As expected, task completion times increased when the list contained 20 items to almost twice as long as in the fastest condition (monophonic, 10). As plotted in Fig. 5, over time we see a tendency for decreased task completion times for 10-item conditions, though the effect was less pronounced for the 20-item condition. Knowing where an item is in the list may help locating it faster and hence lead to faster task completion times with increasing trial numbers. We also found that playing musicons from their position in space does not decrease task completion times. If a spatial memory effect exists, i.e. participants remember where musicons are located in the list and become faster at finding, time and the physical pointing gesture are likely to have a much stronger impact than the spatialized playback. When asked about their strategy, most participants explained they memorized the position of some well known or distinct musicons. Some also mentioned *regions* they associated with a musicon, like one participant described "I knew it was somewhere close to the end so I moved my hand there first and started searching nearby".

Error rates were surprisingly low given that participants had to hold their hand at an angle smaller than 11 degrees in the 10-item conditions and 5.5 degrees in the 20-item condition.

Although no statistical difference was found between the two 10-item conditions, participants tended to find the binaural condition easier to use.

## 10. STUDY 3: EVALUATION IN AN APPLIED CONTEXT

We built a simple music player to embody what we learned about the presentation and design of lists in auditory displays. We conducted a qualitative user study to look at how participants interacted with a list in this context. We also implemented some features accessed with interactions from our design space of lists, and tested how participants used and understood these features and the underlying concepts.

### 10.1 Design and features

To design a music player, we first identified typical tasks a user should be able to perform with it. We focused on: *selecting a song*, *playing/stoping a song*, and *adjusting the song's volume*. We used the general layout of the display from studies 2A and 2B but allowed users to chose from 60 alphabetically ordered songs. These were divided into three sections of each 20 songs and arranged evenly on a 110 degree arc at a distance of 1.1m (Fig. 4, Right).

#### 10.1.1 Selecting an audio file

Sources pointed at played binaurally from their position for as long as the user's hand was in the respective angle segment (see Fig. 1, left). Touching thumb and index finger in a pinching gesture grabs the musicon, which stays at the hand's position for as long as fingers are pinched (see Fig. 1, right). Because it jumped from its original position (at a distance of 1.1 meters) to the user's hand's position its volume is now slightly increased.

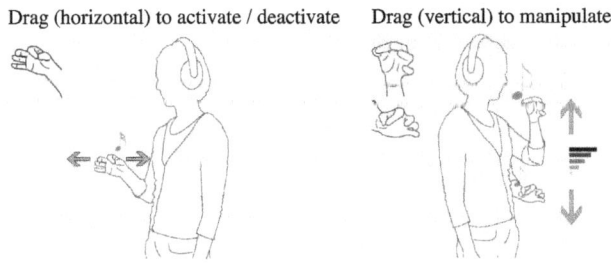

**Figure 6: Gesture: Left: Drag item horizontally to activate or deactivate. Right: Drag item vertically to change the playback volume.**

### 10.1.2 Playing and stopping an audio file

As illustrated in Fig. 6 (left), a musicon can be grabbed and pulled into a zone around the user, to play the song (in stereo). A song stops playing when it is pulled out of the play-zone.

### 10.1.3 Adjusting the volume

We implemented three different ways to change the volume. A user can: (1) grab a playing song and increase or decrease its volume by continuously moving the hand up or down and setting the volume upon release of the song (as illustrated in Fig. 6, right), (2) pinch and release fingers at different heights in the play-zone to stepwise increase or decrease the volume, (3) pull a musicon into the play-zone at a distinct height. Technically, we mapped absolute positions to absolute volume to help users associate regions of their body with loudness. A second reason we decided against a relative mapping was that without a reference point it is much easier to make harmful changes to the volume by accident.

### 10.1.4 Translation and rotation

We compared two versions: in the first, the display locked when the user's hand entered the play-zone, that is, translation remained fixed to the user but rotation was fixed to the world. In the second the display was not locked and both translation and rotation were user-fixed.

### 10.1.5 Scrolling

We implemented an approach similar to pagination to deal with a limit of around 20 items displayable in the arc. We divided a list of 60 alphabetically ordered songs into three sections. Pagination items were added at the start and end of each section. Users could page up or down by pinching this item. For example, when in section "F to P" the first item would page to songs in section "A to E" and the last would page to songs in section "R to Z".

### 10.1.6 Obtaining an overview

When a user paged to a new section, to help users gain an overview, we rapidly played all musicons consecutively for 700 msec from their spatial positions. The overview aborted when a user dropped the hand below the play-zone.

## 10.2 Experimental design and procedure

We evaluated the implementation in a qualitative user study using the thinking-aloud protocol. After we introduced participants to the player's general functionality they explored two versions–display locked and display unlocked (as described above in *Translation and rotation*)–for 10 minutes each. After the exploration period, the experimenter guided participants through each feature

and participants shared their thoughts, questions, and recommendations.

### 10.2.1 Participants

We recruited 6 right-handed participants from our institution's database (3 male). They were between 24 and 34 years old (mean age 28 years) and received a small compensation for their time.

## 10.3 Results and discussion

When asked about their mental models of the list layout participants mentioned Apple's Cover Flow or being in the center of a wheel of fortune. In general they liked the idea of being surrounded by sound. The binaural rendering added to this perception and was appreciated by all participants. Although none of the participants had prior experience with binaurally rendered sound none had problems or was irritated by the idea of grabbing and manipulating invisible sound sources.

### 10.3.1 Selecting an audio file

All participants quickly learned how to select a song. Two participants would have preferred fewer songs per section to give them better control and more accuracy when pointing. Although participants were repeatedly reminded that they could hold their hand at any height and distance most kept their arm extended and pointed slightly upwards. A reason for this might be the rendering of sources at head height. Two Participants criticised the position and angular range of the display. One would have preferred range and position similar to his field of view while the other would have liked a smaller range starting at 12 o'clock.

### 10.3.2 Playing and stopping an audio file

Participants liked the size of the play-zone (approx. 20 cm from the center of the body, above waist level) and the grab and pull gestures. All participants noticed the increase in volume when they grabbed a musicon and it was played from the position of their hand. Some participants were first irritated when they pulled the musicon into the play-zone and a "different" song started playing. This happened when participants were not familiar with the song and hence could not match the musicon to the original song. When asked about feedback sounds for the grabbing gesture participants answered that the increase in volume and the change from musicon to song when entering the play-zone was sufficient. Participants used the stop gesture without problems. One participant combined the stop gesture in one smooth motion with lowering his hands to quiet the interface.

### 10.3.3 Adjusting the volume

Participants spent most of their time exploring different ways to adjust the volume and appreciated the direct change of volume when a song was grabbed and pulled up or down. When asked whether they would prefer a horizontal pulling gesture or a knob-turning gesture over the vertical adjustment, all participants favoured the vertical movement. Stated reasons for this were the familiarity with similar horizontal controls from operating systems like Windows or Mac OS. One participant mentioned the volume adjustment should set the master volume instead of each song's individual volume.

### 10.3.4 Translation and rotation

We asked participants to explore two versions of the implementation. All participants preferred the version in which the display is locked when the hand enters the play-zone and rotation is disabled. Reasons given for this were: (1) participants liked to use their body instead of their head as reference system and found that it helped them to remember the spatial position of songs, (2) participants were keen to avoid conflicts between primary and secondary tasks in situations where orientational head movements would distract and make it difficult to target musicons, (3) participants felt more immersion in a "music space" when head rotations were compensated and physically pointing in a specific direction would always play the same song.

### 10.3.5 Scrolling

Participants could select songs from a total of 60 alphabetically ordered songs divided into three sections. Two participants initially had problems understanding the scrolling model. The main issue seemed to be the lack of analogies from similar interfaces. Two participants suggested a horizontal flicking gesture to "turn the wheel". Selecting a start or end item was the only event accompanied by a feedback sound. Most participants liked the "swooshing" sound and felt it illustrated the scrolling.

### 10.3.6 Obtaining an overview

We used rapid, successive playback of musicons to give an overview of songs in a list section. Most participants liked it as a feature but would have preferred to trigger it themselves instead of an automatic trigger when they paged to a new section. The option to interrupt the playback by lowering the hand below waist level was also appreciated. However, most participants said they would have preferred a simpler interrupt gesture like a pinch or flick gesture. All participants found playback time of 700 msec to 1000 msec sufficient

## 11. CONCLUSION

We presented four user studies exploring a direct manipulation approach utilizing mid-air gestures to interact with spatialized lists in an auditory display. We learned that a list in the shape of a 110 degree arc angled towards the dominant hand is a comfortable and usable layout for most users. We showed that a selection takes less than 11 seconds and error rates are negligible when users locate an item in an unordered list of 20 items. As an example application we implemented a music player controlled with mid-air gestures. Users found the music player to be fun to interact with and had - in general - no problems selecting a song from a list of 60 alphabetically ordered songs. Our results suggest that mid-air gestures can be an efficient way to interact with lists in auditory displays such as playlist in simple music players. Although we used high precision tracking technology in our studies we believe that tracking technology, like proposed in [33] and applied more recently in [15, 5], show good tracking approaches beyond a fixed lab setup. We believe some of our findings are independent of the display's modality (auditory or visual) and could generally contribute to the design of gesture-based interactions using lists. Interesting application areas could be devices with limited I/O capabilities, three-dimensional, immersive environments like games, or interface alternatives for visually impaired users.

## 12. REFERENCES

[1] Ahrens, J., Geier, M., and Spors, S. The soundscape renderer: A unified spatial audio reproduction framework for arbitrary rendering methods. In *Audio Engineering Society Convention 124* (May 2008).

[2] Annett, J. On knowing how to do things: a theory of motor imagery. *Brain Res Cogn Brain Res 3*, 2 (March 1996), 65–69.

[3] Ashbrook, D., Baudisch, P., and White, S. Nenya: Subtle and eyes-free mobile input with a magnetically-tracked finger ring. In *Proceedings of SIGCHI*, CHI '11, ACM (New York, NY, USA, 2011), 2043–2046.

[4] Ashbrook, D. L. *Enabling mobile microinteractions*. PhD thesis, Atlanta, GA, USA, 2010. AAI3414437.

[5] Bailly, G., Müller, J., Rohs, M., Wigdor, D., and Kratz, S. Shoesense: a new perspective on gestural interaction and wearable applications. CHI '12, ACM (2012), 1239–1248.

[6] Baudel, T., and Beaudouin-Lafon, M. Charade: remote control of objects using free-hand gestures. *Commun. ACM 36*, 7 (July 1993), 28–35.

[7] Bernschütz, B., Stade, P., and Rühl, M. A spatial audio impulse response compilation captured at the wdr broadcast studios. In *27th Tonmeistertagung âĂŞ VDT International Convention* (Cologne, Germany, 2012).

[8] Brewster, S., and Raty, V.-P. Earcons as a method of providing navigational cues in a menu hierarchy. In *In Proceedings of BCS HCI'96*, Springer (1996), 169–183.

[9] Brewster, S. A., Wright, P. C., and Edwards, A. D. N. Parallel earcons: Reducing the length of audio messages. *IJHCS 43* (1995), 153–175.

[10] Cockburn, A., Quinn, P., Gutwin, C., Ramos, G., and Looser, J. Air pointing: Design and evaluation of spatial target acquisition with and without visual feedback. *Int. J. Hum.-Comput. Stud. 69*, 6 (June 2011), 401–414.

[11] Crease, M., and Brewster, S. Making progress with sounds - the design and evaluation of an audio progress bar. In *British Computer Society* (1998), 167–177.

[12] Dicke, C., Deo, S., Billinghurst, M., Adams, N., and Lehikoinen, J. Experiments in mobile spatial audio-conferencing: key-based and gesture-based interaction. MobileHCI '08, ACM (2008), 91–100.

[13] Dicke, C., Wolf, K., and Tal, Y. Foogue: eyes-free interaction for smartphones. MobileHCI '10, ACM (2010), 455–458.

[14] Gamper, H., Dicke, C., Billinghurst, M., and Puolamäki, K. Sound sample detection and numerosity estimation using auditory display. *ACM Trans. Appl. Percept. 10*, 1 (mar 2013), 4:1–4:18.

[15] Gustafson, S., Bierwirth, D., and Baudisch, P. Imaginary interfaces: spatial interaction with empty hands and without visual feedback. UIST '10, ACM (2010), 3–12.

[16] Harrison, C., and Hudson, S, E. Abracadabra: Wireless, high-precision, and unpowered finger input for very small mobile devices. In *Proceedings of the 22nd Annual ACM Symposium on User Interface Software and Technology*, UIST '09, ACM (New York, NY, USA, 2009), 121–124.

[17] Kajastila, R., and Lokki, T. Eyes-free interaction with free-hand gestures and auditory menus. *Int. J. Hum.-Comput. Stud. 71*, 5 (may 2013), 627–640.

[18] Kildal, J., and Brewster, S. A. Non-visual overviews of complex data sets. In *CHI EA '06*, ACM (2006), 947–952.

[19] Magnusson, C., Rassmus-Gröhn, K., and Szymczak, D. Scanning angles for directional pointing. MobileHCI '10, ACM (2010), 399–400.

[20] Marentakis, G. N., and Brewster, S. A. A study on gestural interaction with a 3d audio display. In *Mobile HCI*, S. A. Brewster and M. D. Dunlop, Eds., vol. 3160 of *Lecture Notes in Computer Science*, Springer (2004), 180–191.

[21] McGee-Lennon, M., Wolters, M., McLachlan, R., Brewster, S., and Hall, C. Name that tune: musicons as reminders in the home. CHI '11, ACM (2011), 2803–2806.

[22] McGookin, D., Brewster, S., and Priego, P. Audio bubbles: Employing non-speech audio to support tourist wayfinding. HAID '09, Springer-Verlag (Berlin, Heidelberg, 2009), 41–50.

[23] Montero, C. S., Alexander, J., Marshall, M. T., and Subramanian, S. Would you do that?: understanding social acceptance of gestural interfaces. MobileHCI '10, ACM (2010), 275–278.

[24] Müller, J., Geier, M., Dicke, C., and Spors, S. The boomroom: Mid-air direct interaction with virtual sound sources. In *Proceedings of SIGCHI*, CHI '14, ACM (New York, NY, USA, 2014), 247–256.

[25] Oakley, I., and Park, J. Motion marking menus: An eyes-free approach to motion input for handheld devices. *Int. J. Hum.-Comput. Stud. 67*, 6 (June 2009), 515–532.

[26] Pielot, M., Kazakova, A., Hesselmann, T., Heuten, W., and Boll, S. Pocketmenu: non-visual menus for touch screen devices. MobileHCI '12, ACM (2012), 327–330.

[27] Pirhonen, A., Brewster, S., and Holguin, C. Gestural and audio metaphors as a means of control for mobile devices. CHI '02, ACM (2002), 291–298.

[28] Reeves, S., Benford, S., O'Malley, C., and Fraser, M. Designing the spectator experience. CHI '05, ACM (2005), 741–750.

[29] Rico, J., and Brewster, S. Usable gestures for mobile interfaces: evaluating social acceptability. CHI '10, ACM (2010), 887–896.

[30] Sawhney, N., and Schmandt, C. Nomadic radio: speech and audio interaction for contextual messaging in nomadic environments. *ACM Trans. Comput.-Hum. Interact. 7*, 3 (Sept. 2000), 353–383.

[31] Schmandt, C. Audio hallway: a virtual acoustic environment for browsing. UIST '98, ACM (1998), 163–170.

[32] Schwarz, J., Harrison, C., Hudson, S., and Mankoff, J. Cord input: An intuitive, high-accuracy, multi-degree-of-freedom input method for mobile devices. In *Proceedings of SIGCHI*, CHI '10, ACM (New York, NY, USA, 2010), 1657–1660.

[33] Segen, J., and Kumar, S. Gesture vr: vision-based 3d hand interace for spatial interaction. In *Proceedings of the sixth ACM international conference on Multimedia*, ACM (1998), 455–464.

[34] Sodnik, J., Dicke, C., Tomažič, S., and Billinghurst, M. A user study of auditory versus visual interfaces for use while driving. *IJHCS 66*, 5 (2008), 318–332.

[35] Stifelman, L. J., Arons, B., Schmandt, C., and Hulteen, E. A. Voicenotes: a speech interface for a hand-held voice notetaker. CHI '93, ACM (1993), 179–186.

[36] Strachan, S., Murray-Smith, R., and O'Modhrain, S. Bodyspace: inferring body pose for natural control of a music player. CHI EA '07, ACM (2007), 2001–2006.

[37] Vazquez-Alvarez, Y., Oakley, I., and Brewster, S. A. Auditory display design for exploration in mobile audio-augmented reality. *Personal Ubiquitous Comput. 16*, 8 (Dec. 2012), 987–999.

[38] Walker, B. N., Nance, A., and Lindsay, J. Spearcons: Speech-based earcons improve navigation performance in auditory menus. ICAD '06 (London, UK, 2006), 63–68.

[39] Wolf, K., Dicke, C., and Grasset, R. Touching the void: gestures for auditory interfaces. TEI '11, ACM (2011), 305–308.

[40] Yi, B., Cao, X., Fjeld, M., and Zhao, S. Exploring user motivations for eyes-free interaction on mobile devices. In *Proceedings of SIGCHI*, CHI '12, ACM (New York, NY, USA, 2012), 2789–2792.

[41] Zhao, S., Dragicevic, P., Chignell, M., Balakrishnan, R., and Baudisch, P. Earpod: eyes-free menu selection using touch input and reactive audio feedback. CHI '07, ACM (2007), 1395–1404.

# Models for Rested Touchless Gestural Interaction

Darren Guinness
Dept of Computer Science Baylor University
Waco, TX 76798 USA
darren_guinness@baylor.edu

Alvin Jude
Ericsson Research
200 Holger Way
San Jose, CA, 95134
alvin.jude.hari.haran@ericsson.com

G. Michael Poor
Dept of Computer Science Baylor University
Waco, TX 76798 USA
michael_poor@baylor.edu

Ashley Dover
Dept of Computer Science Baylor University
Waco, TX 76798 USA
ashley_therriault@baylor.edu

## ABSTRACT

Touchless mid-air gestural interaction has gained mainstream attention with the emergence of off-the-shelf commodity devices such as the Leap Motion and the Xbox Kinect. One of the issues with this form of interaction is fatigue, a problem colloquially known as the "Gorilla Arm Syndrome." However, by allowing interaction from a rested position, whereby the elbow is rested on a surface, this problem can be limited in its effect. In this paper we evaluate 3 possible methods for performing touchless mid-air gestural interaction from a rested position: a basic rested interaction, a simple calibrated interaction which models palm positions onto a hyperplane, and a more complex calibration which models the arm's interaction space using the angles of the forearm as input. The results of this work found that the two modeled interactions conform to Fitts's law and also demonstrated that implementing a simple model can improve interaction by improving performance and accuracy.

## Keywords

Fitts; Pointing Device; Gestural Interaction; Fatigue;

## CCS Concepts

•**Human-centered computing** → **Gestural input;** *Interaction paradigms;* Pointing devices;

## 1. INTRODUCTION

Touchless gestural interaction has achieved mainstream popularity over the last decade with the production of commercial off-the-shelf components like the Xbox Kinect and Leap Motion. Traditionally, gestural recognition has been the focus of research, while implementations have focused on coarse gestural recognition such as shape identification. However, commodity gestural recognition hardware has become increasingly more precise, with devices in

*SUI '15 Aug 8–9, 2015, Los Angeles, CA, USA*

© 2015 Copyright held by the owner/author(s). Publication rights licensed to ACM.
ISBN 978-1-4503-3703-8/15/08. . . $15.00

DOI: http://dx.doi.org/10.1145/2788940.2788948

some cases demonstrated to be accurate up to a sub-millimeter level [16] with low latency [6]. Due to these advances, researchers have started looking at gestures not simply for coarse actions, but for more fine use cases such as cursor navigation [20, 6, 32, 34].

The most common implementations of gestural input involve the user holding their arms out in mid-air. This mode of interaction results in arm and shoulder fatigue [38, 40, 17] commonly referred to as "Gorilla Arm Syndrome" [7]. This will need to be addressed before gestures can be accepted as a ubiquitous mode of interaction. Brown et al identified a simple way to address this problem by allowing the user to rest the elbow on a surface [6]. However, this simple solution may result in an interaction that is non-intuitive to the user, because it gives very little consideration to the actual mechanics of the human arm. In order to address this, Jude et al introduced a potential improvement called Personal Space [20] which used a calibration step to first map the user's input space.

In both aforementioned approaches, fatigue is addressed by performing gestural interaction from a rested position. However, they make separate but related claims: Brown et al [6] stated that fatigue is addressed simply by resting the elbow, while Jude et al [20] claimed that fatigue was addressed by modeling the user's input space from a rested position.

In this paper, we seek to investigate both approaches further, using standard evaluation methodologies provided by the ISO 9241-9 documentation. We aim to identify whether differences in performance exist between gestural interactions by using 3 different strategies: (1) a completely unmodeled approach, (2) the simple model introduced by Jude et al [20] which models palm positions onto a hyperplane, and (3) a more complex model introduced here, which models the interaction space with no loss of information, using the angles of the forearm as input. We also aim to identify whether learning is present in these gestural interfaces through the use of a longitudinal design, as current works that use only one session have not found learning [6, 34, 1].

For this study, the following two hypotheses were identified:

**H1** Users will learn gestural interaction over time, allowing for an improvement in performance.
**H2** An interaction with a model of the interaction space will perform better than an interaction which does not model the space.

The following metrics were collected to compare interactions: performance, accuracy, and subjective user feedback. Each of these metrics will be further explained within the following sections.

## 2. RELATED WORKS

### 2.1 Gestural Interaction

Gestural Interaction is a technique that leverages gestures from the body to interact with a computer. This type of interaction technique has been studied for over 3 decades since Richard Bolt's first implementation in "Put-That-There" [5]. Gestural interaction implementations are typically divided into two different types: (1) those that require the user to wear gloves, devices or specific markers and (2) touchless gestural interaction. The latter leverages the "Come As You Are" design principle [39], which states that users should not be required to wear devices or specific markers to interact with a system [40].

Recent devices such as the Xbox Kinect, Leap Motion, and Myo Armband have gained popularity amongst researchers, with some capable of sub-millimeter accuracy in static situations [16]. These devices have demonstrated the potential use of gestural interfaces in medical professions that require sterile environments [40, 29, 4], as an accessibility device for those with impairments [2, 15], and in mixed reality environments with head mounted displays [12]. These applications demonstrate the usefulness of gestural interaction, but more work is still needed before its ubiquitous adoption.

#### 2.1.1 Gestural Fatigue

The standard method of using gestures involves users holding their arms up to the display for long periods of time. This has been known to cause a fatigue problem referred to as the "Gorilla Arm Syndrome" [42, 7, 40] and is considered to be a "known limitation" [38] of gestural interaction. Segen and Kumar stated that fatigue is one of the biggest issues with gestures after prolonged interaction [36].

A simple method of overcoming this issue is to allow users to rest their elbows on a chair armrest [14, 36]. Brown et al implemented this method to perform cursor navigation in an experiment with 2 possible modes of input: the whole hand and finger pointing. Jude et al implemented a very similar approach to the previous whereby cursor navigation was done with the whole hand, but the user's input space was first modeled during a calibration stage [20]. All these approaches make the same claim: performing gestural interaction from a rested position results in a more comfortable interaction and reduces the fatigue inherent to gestural interaction.

We accept the premise of the research above and attempt to further the knowledge in the area by investigating the effects of modeled versus unmodeled interactions.

#### 2.1.2 Gestural Pointing

Recent touchless gestural pointing has been implemented in one of two general pointing methods. The first method, known as "ray pointing," is a popular approach used by many designers when implementing gestural interaction [6, 25, 3, 18]. Ray pointing uses ray casting to determine where the user is pointing [18]. This method has been demonstrated to be rapid but inaccurate [8].

Conversely, 'whole hand pointing', directly maps the 2D movements of the hand (by dropping 1 dimension) to the 2D cursor on screen [6]. The user can then move their hand or finger within this navigation space to move the cursor on screen. This method, implemented by [8, 6, 20], has been shown to be both rapid and accurate, even without visual feedback [8].

Our paper uses 'whole hand pointing' for the *Unmodeled* and *Hyperplanar* approaches. The *Spherical* approach combines both methods described above.

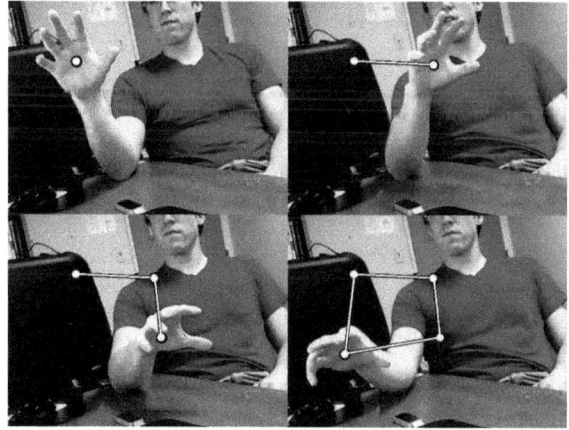

**Figure 1: User calibrating their space taken from [20] with permission. This method of calibration was used for both the *Hyperplanar* and *Spherical* models.**

#### 2.1.3 Gestural Selection

Brown found that the finger tap gesture, which was considered the closest gesture to a mouse selection, performed inadequately for use in their experiment [6]. To combat this, [6] implemented a bimanual selection method, where users used their other hand to press the space bar when the cursor was over the target. Other researchers [17, 20, 34] used a 'hover-select' or 'dwell' method which required the user to hover over the target for between 250 and 1500 milliseconds. This was the method we chose to implement in our own experiment.

### 2.2 Learning Effects

Schmidt and Lee indicated that while we cannot directly observe learning, we can measure and report performance improvements, from which we can infer learning [35]. New pointing devices are expected to demonstrate performance improvements over time, making a one day study less descriptive of the performance of the device. To account for these improvements, researchers have run longitudinal studies, performing analysis on the data when no performance improvements were found [26]. This approach was used in our experiment in line with H1 over 3 days, based on results from our pilot which showed no significant improvements after day 3.

A simple method to report performance improvements would be to calculate the difference between means of throughput between both rounds. Researchers have shown that a better way to measure performance increase is with effect size [19] measured in Cohen's *d* [10], a practice which has recently been encouraged for use in the HCI community [21]. This metric represents the difference of the mean between 2 groups over the standard deviation:

$$\text{EffectSize} = \frac{\overline{x_1} - \overline{x_2}}{s} \qquad (1)$$

In our experiment, we measure the difference in performance between days to indicate performance gained.

Researchers have indicated that random-order practice, otherwise known as Distributed Practice (e.g. A-B-C, B-C-A, C-A-B), generally benefits motor learning more than block order practice, known as massed practice (A-A-A, B-B-B, C-C-C) [24, 23]. A 3x3x3 balanced Latin cube design was used in our experiment, making the distributed practice approach trivial.

## 2.3 Pointing Device Evaluation

Since the focus of the paper is primarily gestural interaction, general pointing device evaluation related works will not be thoroughly reviewed. A brief explanation of the metrics is provided below, but we highly recommend the following works [13, 26, 37] for a more detailed read.

### 2.3.1 Fitts's Law

Fitts's law describes the relationship between Movement Time, distance, and accuracy for people in rapid motor tasks [37]. If an pointing interaction conforms to Fitts's law, it can be used as a predictive model used in user interface design [37]. To investigate whether an interface conforms to Fitts's law, a linear regression is performed over movement times (MT) on the corresponding effective Index of Difficulty conditions. The result is a regression equation which takes the form:

$$MT = a + b \times IDe \qquad (2)$$

where $a$ is the intercept term, $b$ is the slope of the regression line and $IDe$ is the index of difficulty.

The intercept $a$ is desired to be near zero, and if positive is ideally below 400ms [37]. Once the regression has been performed, the *coefficient of determination* ($R^2$), or "goodness of fit", is typically reported as it signifies the strength of the association between the IDe and MT [32]. $R^2$ is typically described as the degree to which the regression model explains the variation of the data, and the higher the $R^2$, the better the fit [27]. E.g., if $R^2 = .9$, this would mean that the regression line explains 90% of the variation.

The *linear correlation coefficient (R)* measures the strength and direction of the linear relationship between IDe and MT [32]. When there is no linear correlation or a weak linear correlation, $R$ is close to 0. A correlation is described as strong if $R > 0.8$ and weak when $R < 0.5$ [32].

### 2.3.2 Performance

We measure Index of Difficulty (IDe) using an adjusted Shannon formulation:

$$ID_e = log_2 \left( \frac{D_e}{W_e} + 1 \right) \qquad (3)$$

This formula has been adjusted to use the distance between the starting point of the cursor and the ending point, known as effective distance ($D_e$). Width has also been updated to use effective width ($W_e$), which utilizes the idea that the endpoints are normally distributed. We also have updated effective width ($W_e$) to use the standard deviation of both x and y. We use this to compute bivariate throughput, which has been demonstrated to have higher explanatory power [41]. Using the above formulation of *IDe*, we measure performance, or throughput, as:

$$\text{Throughput} = \frac{ID_e}{MT} \qquad (4)$$

### 2.3.3 Accuracy Measures

Apart from performance measured in throughput, we also measure the accuracy of each interaction. The accuracy measures introduced by Mackenzie et al [26] include Target Re-entry (TRE), Task Axis Crossing (TAC), Movement Direction Change (MDC), Orthogonal Direction Change (ODC), Movement Variability (MV), Movement Error (ME), and Movement Offset (MO). Each accuracy metric characterizes a difference between the optimal path of the cursor and the actual path.

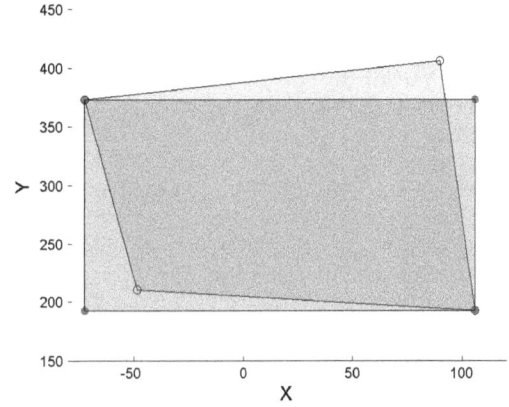

**Figure 2: A front view of the Unmodeled (blue plane) and Hyperplanar (grey plane) interaction space. Both axis denotes interaction space measured in millimeters.**

## 3. INTERACTION DESIGN

The interactions in this experiment were used specifically to test the hypotheses of this research. Therefore, we used an unmodeled interaction described by Brown et al [6], a simple model introduced by Jude et al [20], and a more complex model which we introduced for this experiment. We also built 3 angled stands $(30, 36, 44°)$ with Legos, to hold the Leap on a tilted incline as recommended by the previous authors [20].

### 3.1 Unmodeled Gestural Interaction

In this interaction, the space is constructed using two diagonal points from the calibration as shown in Figure 2. This model was replicated from [6], which drops the Z dimension and only uses X and Y for input into the source matrix. The points were chosen such that each screen boundary could be obtained without lifting the elbows from the table. We identify this approach as the *Unmodeled* interaction.

### 3.2 Rested & Calibrated Interaction – Hyperplanar Model

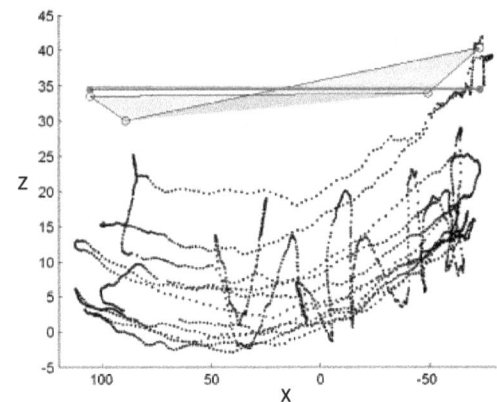

**Figure 3: A top view of the Unmodeled (red plane) and Hyperplanar (grey hyperplane) with tracked hand movement (black points). Both axis denotes interaction space measured in millimeters.**

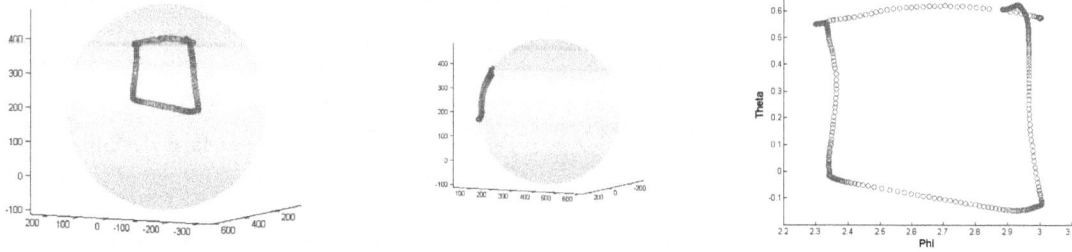

**Figure 4: L-R: (1) Front view of *Spherical model*, (2) side view of the *Spherical* interaction, (3) plotting the angles $(\theta, \phi)$ which is essentially a quadrangle.**

The intuition behind this interaction is that the unmodeled interaction creates a space that does not map well to the interaction space. The example in figure 2 shows how it could be difficult for the user to hit the bottom left of the interaction space. By first modeling the interaction space, this interaction allows the users to be able to easily reach all corners of the screen from a rested position.

This interaction was originally referred to as a "planar" interaction. We however believe the term "hyperplanar" is more descriptive as as there is no guarantee that the 4 calibrated points in 3D lie on the same plane. This is better illustrated in figure 3.

We also note that despite the *Hyperplanar* approach being closer to the interaction space, it is not as accurate as it could be. The black dots in figure 3 show the actual interaction, which indicates some information loss, despite all 3 dimensions (X, Y, Z) in cartessian space used to build the model.

### 3.3 Rested & Calibrated Interaction – Spherical Model

The *Spherical* model introduced here is based on 2 intuitions. The first is that the movement of the hand from a rested position forms a part of a sphere, as shown in Figure 4. And second, that controlling an inherently 2-dimensional interface such as a monitor will be easier if the input itself is based on 2 dimensions. We built the *Spherical* model on both these intuitions. The interaction itself uses a spherical coordinate system with the azimuth ($\theta$), mapped to medial and lateral shoulder rotation, and zenith ($\phi$), mapped to elbow flexion and extension [28], of the forearm as input, making it 2-dimensional. This translation equates to a feature reduction from 3 features (X, Y, Z) to 2 ($\theta, \phi$) and a constant radius ($r$) with no loss of information. In contrast, other interactions that perform a reduction in dimensions generally do so by eliminating one dimension, generally Z or depth.

When performing the transformation from the input to the corresponding output, this feature reduction effectively removes one linearly independent column from the matrix, which causes a loss of precision as the matrix is now further from full rank [31]. To account for this we incorporate a plane-to-plane homography, otherwise known as a projective transformation with homogeneous estimation, which projects a 3rd dimension into a 2D image. We use this 3rd dimension to preserve rank during the transformation. The transformation also provides solutions to both determined and overly-determined systems of linear equations with a bounded error [11].

Although the input required is the azimuth ($\theta$) and zenith ($\phi$) of the forearm, these values were not directly obtainable from our input device, the Leap Motion controller. We did not consider using a different device that did have these values as it would be an unfair experiment, where there would be interaction with the input

device. We therefore used the provided input by the Leap Motion controller, which is the X, Y, and Z positions of the palm in Cartesian coordinates, and transformed it to corresponding $\theta$, $\phi$ and a static $r$. We measured the length of participants' forearms as radius $r$. The center of the interaction sphere is fixed and marked on the table surface, and the users are expected to position their elbow on this exact point throughout the experiment. Given these inputs, we were able to translate the coordinates in X, Y and Z to $\theta$ and $\phi$. We then used $\theta$ and $\phi$ as input and the screen coordinates $x$ and $y$ as the intended output. We observed that using this coordinate system produces a model that closer represents the user's input, including being able to account for the curvature in the input, which was not achievable in the *Hyperplanar* model.

## 4. EXPERIMENTAL DESIGN

### 4.1 Participants

15 participants (M=9, F=6) between 19-27 years of age (mean = 20.6) took part in the experiment. All participants were students from a local university. Two participants self-reported as ambidextrous, but all elected to use their right hand for all interactions. All but 3 participants had used gestural interfaces before. Previously used gestural interfaces were limited to the Wii, Kinect, and/or PlayStation Move. Participants were compensated for their time.

### 4.2 Apparatus

All testing was conducted in a lab setting on a 30-inch Dell monitor set to 2560 x 1600 resolution. The Leap Motion Controller was used to recognize the hand position for the gestural navigation. The computer used an Intel i7-3820 CPU with 8 cores clocked at 3.6 GHz, with 32 GB RAM and ran Windows 7. The 36 degree stand was used in all cases except for 2 participants with longer forearms, for which the 30 degree stand was chosen.

### 4.3 Task

The ISO 9241-9 ring-of-circles task implementation from [41] was used to evaluate the performance of each interaction. This software was modified such that a 250 millisecond hover is used for selection. The task utilized 4 amplitudes {256, 512, 1024, 1408} and 3 target widths {64, 96, 128 } for 10 unique IDs ranging from 1.52-4.58 bits. Target amplitude and widths were identified from current literature [6] and extensive piloting. As we were using a large display, piloting revealed that a target width of 64px was the smallest target that was able to be selected by participants. The first 3 trials of each condition were taken as practice since this was the default in the software used.

## 4.4 Design

We used a 3x3x3 balanced Latin cube design with 3 interaction styles over 3 days and 3 orders. Each day included 1 session which lasted roughly 1 hour and was split into 2 rounds. In each round, participants would use all of the three interactions based on the Latin cube ordering. Participants were not told that they were using different interaction models.

## 4.5 Procedure

Participants were required to watch a video detailing the interaction and calibration method before they began trials on the first day. After the video, the calibration stage would begin. Once calibrated, participants were asked to test the interaction. A recalibration was allowed until they were pleased with the interaction. After which, participants were asked to watch a video detailing the ring-of-circles task. They then performed the task using the three gestural models. Participants were encouraged to take notes on the interaction they just used after each task, for ranking purposes. This was repeated until all 6 tasks (3 interactions × 2 rounds) were evaluated. Participants were then asked to rank the interactions from best to worst. These steps were repeated exactly every day of the experiment, with the videos only shown on day 1.

Only 1 calibration (see Figure 1) was performed each day at the beginning of the experiment to control for differing calibrations. Each model was then dynamically computed from the original source input points. All gestural interactions were performed with an off-the-shelf Leap Motion controller.

## 5. RESULTS

Analysis of our results was done to investigate 5 main aspects of each interaction: (1) Performance Improvement, (2) Conformance to the Fitts's Model, (3) Performance, (4) Accuracy, and (5) Subjective User Feedback. Metrics from (2), (3), and (4) were measured per trial across all participants per day. In each ring-of-circles task there were 23 trials (3 practice) in each of the 4 amplitude × 3 width conditions, which meant that there was a total of $20 \times 4 \times 3 = 240$ trials per task per participant. We incorporated 2 rounds with 15 participants, for a total of $240 \times 2$ rounds $\times 15$ participants $= 7200$ trials per interaction per day. In each analysis, the assumption of Sphericity was violated, thus a Greenhouse-Geisser ($p_{GG}$) epsilon correction was used to determine significance. Post-hoc tests were administered if $p_{GG} < .05$ using the MATLAB 'Bonferroni Method', which uses critical values from the t-distribution after an adjustment for multiple comparisons is made. We report the effect size of the Repeated Measures ANOVA as $\eta_p^2$ which is interpreted (0.01 = small, 0.06 = medium, 0.14 = large) as determined by Cohen [9, 33]. We report pairwise effect size, as measured by Cohen's d and fall back on Cohen's own guidelines for practical significance (0.2 = small, 0.5 = medium, 0.8 = large), as there are no domain-specific guidelines for pointing device evaluation.

## 5.1 Daily Improvement

We measure daily improvement as the difference in bivariate throughput between days in order to check for learning effects. These values are shown in Table 1, and all interactions were found to have statistical difference between days. The *Unmodeled* interaction showed a significant difference in performance between days ($F(2, 14370) = 3573$, $p_{GG} < .001$, $\eta_p^2 = 0.33$), as did the *Hyperplanar* interaction ($F(2, 14370) = 2786$, $p_{GG} < .001$, $\eta_p^2 = 0.28$) and the *Spherical* interaction ($F(2, 14370) = 2437$, $p_{GG} < .001$, $\eta_p^2 = 0.25$). The post-hoc test showed all interactions demonstrated significance between all days ($p < .001$).

|   | Unmodeled | | | Hyperplanar | | | Spherical | | |
|---|---|---|---|---|---|---|---|---|---|
|   | $\bar{x}$ | $\sigma$ | $d$ | $\bar{x}$ | $\sigma$ | $d$ | $\bar{x}$ | $\sigma$ | $d$ |
| 1 | 2.35 | .38 | - | 2.44 | .43 | - | 2.32 | .40 | - |
| 2 | 2.69 | .48 | .77 | 2.74 | .40 | .74 | 2.61 | .39 | .74 |
| 3 | 2.79 | .44 | .23 | 2.82 | .41 | .18 | 2.67 | .38 | .15 |

Table 1: Mean ($\bar{x}$) and standard deviation ($\sigma$) of bivariate throughput for each device across days 1-3. The corresponding $d$ values indicate difference in performance from the previous day measured with Cohen's d.

Due to these differences, we perform the full analysis of the interactions for performance, accuracy, and subjective feedback on data from day 3 only, while days 1 and 2 are considered practice. Therefore, all metrics reported in this paper is from day 3 of the experiment, unless stated otherwise.

## 5.2 Fitts's Regression

|   | Unmodeled | Hyperplanar | Spherical |
|---|---|---|---|
| Intercept | 585.9 | 79.9 | 16.3 |
| Slope | 155.5 | 295.7 | 331.5 |
| $R^2$ | 0.018 | 0.738 | 0.758 |
| $R$ | 0.418 | 0.859 | 0.870 |

Table 2: Metrics for Fitts's regression of each interaction.

A Fitts's law model for each interaction was built by regressing the mean movement times (MT) on the corresponding effective Index of Difficulty conditions. The result is a regression equation in the form of Equation 2.

The results for each day and interaction are shown in Table 2, while a visualization of the data from day 3 can be seen in figure 5. The plots show that the modeled approaches are better explained by Fitts's law than the unmodeled approach. Additionally, Table 4 shows that the two modeled approaches consistently improve their fit between days, while the unmodeled approach does not.

## 5.3 Performance

The speed (specifically the Movement Time) of each interaction is considered a naive metric [37], but is reported nonetheless as we consider it a good description of each interaction. A better metric to use is throughput, and specifically bivariate throughput [41].

### 5.3.1 Movement Time

|   | Unmodeled | | Hyperplanar | | Spherical | |
|---|---|---|---|---|---|---|
|   | Mean | Stdev | Mean | Stdev | Mean | Stdev |
| 3 | **1073.6** | 495.39 | **1063.4** | 481.89 | 1110.4 | 538.24 |

Table 3: Mean and standard deviation of movement time per trial for each interaction in milliseconds. Smaller values are better.

A repeated measures ANOVA showed a significant difference in movement time, which was adjusted for dwell time, between interactions ($F(2, 14370) = 18.619$, $p_{GG} < .001$, $\eta_p^2 = 0.003$). The post-hoc test found that the *Unmodeled* interaction had significantly lower movement time than the *Spherical* interaction ($p <.001$, $d = 0.07$). The post-hoc test also showed that *Hyperplanar* interaction had significantly lower movement time than the *Spherical* ($p <.001$ $d = 0.09$).

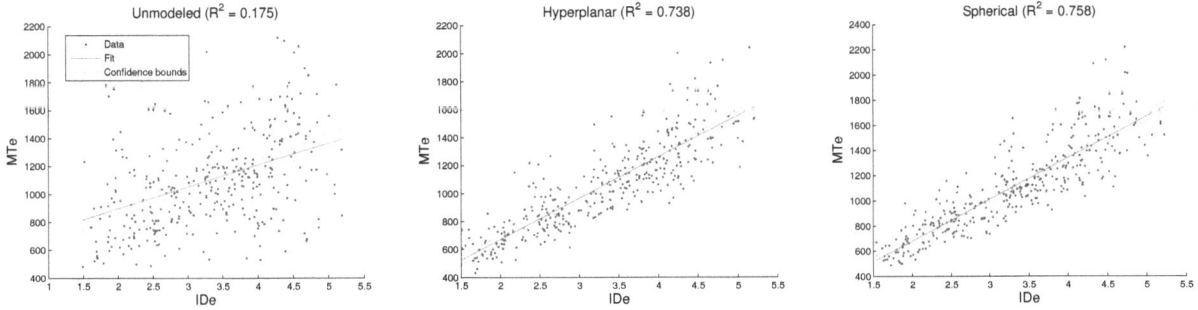

**Figure 5: Mean movement time of all participants from day 3 as a function of effective Index of Difficulty (IDe), with computed Fitts's regression lines**

| | Unmodeled | | | | Hyperplanar | | | | Spherical | | | |
|---|---|---|---|---|---|---|---|---|---|---|---|---|
| | Intercept | Slope | $R^2$ | $R$ | Intercept | Slope | $R^2$ | $R$ | Intercept | Slope | $R^2$ | $R$ |
| 1 | 453.05 | 248.18 | 0.31 | 0.56 | 113.29 | 334.08 | 0.63 | 0.79 | 18.97 | 381.91 | 0.65 | 0.81 |
| 2 | 785.04 | 108.17 | 0.07 | 0.26 | 59.47 | 308.46 | 0.73 | 0.86 | 38.62 | 332.73 | 0.71 | 0.84 |
| 3 | 585.86 | 155.53 | 0.18 | 0.42 | 79.86 | 295.67 | 0.74 | 0.86 | 16.30 | 331.50 | 0.76 | 0.87 |

**Table 4: Intercept, slope, coefficient of determination ($R^2$) and correlation coefficient ($R$) of all 3 interactions over all 3 days.**

### 5.3.2 Bivariate Throughput

A repeated measures ANOVA showed a significant difference in performance between interactions measured with bivariate throughput ($F(2, 14370) = 369.81$, $p_{GG} < .001$, $\eta_p^2 = 0.05$). A post-hoc test showed the *Hyperplanar* interaction had higher bivariate throughput than both the *Unmodeled* ($p < .005$, $d = .05$) and *Spherical* ($p < .001$, $d = 0.35$) interactions. The post-hoc test also showed that the *Unmodeled* interaction had higher bivariate throughput than the *Spherical* interaction ($p < .001$, $d = 0.29$).

## 5.4 Accuracy Measures

We report accuracy measures based on the metrics introduced by Mackenzie [26] consisting of Target Re-entry (TRE), Target Axis Crossing (TAC), Orthogonal Direction Change (ODC), Movement Variability (MV), Movement Error (ME) and Movement Offset (MO). These measures were taken directly from the *FittsStudy* software [41], except for TRE, as the software reports target entries (TE) instead, where TRE=TE-1. A lower number is better for all metrics except MO, where a closer distance to 0 is better.

| | Unmodeled | | Hyperplanar | | Spherical | |
|---|---|---|---|---|---|---|
| | Mean | Stdev | Mean | Stdev | Mean | Stdev |
| TE | **1.27** | 0.68 | **1.28** | 0.70 | 1.35 | 0.78 |
| TAC | **1.45** | 1.20 | **1.49** | 1.17 | 1.55 | 1.25 |
| MDC | **2.77** | 1.69 | **2.78** | 1.66 | 2.87 | 1.79 |
| ODC | **1.08** | 1.30 | **1.05** | 1.25 | 1.19 | 1.38 |
| MV | 23.50 | 20.73 | **22.94** | 18.85 | 23.83 | 20.06 |
| ME | 26.70 | 20.42 | **25.72** | 18.67 | 26.42 | 19.26 |
| MO | -7.81 | 28.32 | 4.51 | 26.57 | **2.04** | 27.25 |

**Table 5: Mean and standard deviation of accuracy measures metrics taken on day 3 of the experiment.**

### 5.4.1 Target Entries

The *Unmodeled* interaction had the best TE score, followed by the *Hyperplanar* interaction. A repeated measures ANOVA showed a significant difference in the number of Target Entries between interactions ($F(2, 14370) = 27.20$, $p_{GG} < .001$, $\eta_p^2 = 0.004$).

The post-hoc test identified a statistical significance between the *Unmodeled* and *Spherical* interactions ($p < .001$, $d = 0.11$), and between the *Hyperplanar* and *Spherical* interactions ($p < .001$, $d = 0.10$).

### 5.4.2 Task Axis Crosses

The *Unmodeled* interaction had the best TAC score, followed by the *Hyperplanar* interaction. A repeated measures ANOVA showed this to be statistically significant ($F(2, 14370) = 11.054$, $p_{GG} < .001$, $\eta_p^2 = 0.002$). The post-hoc test identified a significant difference between the *Unmodeled* and *Spherical* interactions ($p < .001$, $d = 0.08$). The *Hyperplanar* interaction was also found to be significantly different from the *Spherical* interaction ($p < .05$, $d = 0.04$).

### 5.4.3 Movement Direction Change

The *Unmodeled* interaction had the best MDC score, followed by the *Hyperplanar* interaction. A repeated measures ANOVA showed this to be statistically significant ($F(2, 14370) = 8.262$, $p_{GG} < .001$, $\eta_p^2 = 0.001$). Post-hoc tests showed a significant difference between the *Unmodeled* and *Spherical* interactions ($p < .005$, $d = 0.06$). The post-hoc test also identified a significant difference between the *Hyperplanar* and *Spherical* interactions ($p < .005$, $d = 0.06$).

### 5.4.4 Orthogonal Direction Change

The *Hyperplanar* interaction had the best ODC score, followed by the *Unmodeled* interaction. A repeated measures ANOVA found this to be statistically significant ($F(2, 14370) = 23.786$, $p_{GG} < .001$, $\eta_p^2 = 0.003$). A post-hoc test showed a significant difference between the *Unmodeled* and *Spherical* interactions ($p < .001$, $d = 0.08$), and between the *Hyperplanar* and *Spherical* interactions ($p < .001$, $d = 0.10$).

### 5.4.5 Movement Variability

The *Hyperplanar* interaction had the best MV score, followed by the *Unmodeled* interaction. A repeated measures ANOVA found a significant difference between interactions ($F(2, 14370) = 3.918$, $p_{GG} < .05$, $\eta_p^2 = 0.0005$). A post-hoc tests showed a significant difference between the *Hyperplanar* and *Spherical* interactions ($p$ <.05, $d$ = 0.05).

### 5.4.6 Movement Error

The *Hyperplanar* interaction had the best ME score, followed by the *Spherical* interaction. A repeated measures ANOVA showed this to be statistically significant ($F(2, 14370) = 5.161$, $p_{GG} <$ .01, $\eta_p^2 = 0.0007$). The post-hoc test identified a significant difference between the *Hyperplanar* and *Unmodeled* interactions ($p$ <.005, $d$ = 0.05).

### 5.4.7 Movement Offset

The *Spherical* interaction had the best MO score, followed by the *Hyperplanar* interaction. A repeated measures ANOVA showed this to be statistically significant ($F(2, 14370) = 424.97$, $p_{GG} <$ .001, $\eta_p^2 = 0.06$). The post-hoc test identified a significant difference between the *Spherical* and *Hyperplanar* interactions ($p$ <.001, $d$ =0.09), and between the *Spherical* and *Unmodeled* interactions ($p$ <.001, $d$= 0.36). The post-hoc test also showed that the *Hyperplanar* interaction was significantly different than the *Unmodeled* interaction ($p$ <.001, $d$ =0.45).

## 5.5 Subjective User Feedback

### 5.5.1 Preference

Participants were asked to rank the interactions by preference on a scale of 1-6, with 1 being the best interaction and 6 being the worst. We combined the rounds that used the same interaction. From these rankings we can order the interactions by most preferred to least as such: 1) *Hyperplanar*, 2) *Unmodeled*, 3) *Spherical*, with their respective scores of 2.57, 3.60, 4.33. A Friedman test showed that there was a statistically significant difference in preference rank between the interactions ($\chi^2(2) = 13.505, p = 0.0012$). Post hoc analysis with Wilcoxon signed-rank tests was conducted with a Bonferroni correction applied. The only statistically significance found was that the *Hyperplanar* interaction was significantly preferred over the *Spherical* ($Z = -3.524, p < .001, r = .23$).

### 5.5.2 Usability

|  | Unmodeled | Hyperplanar | Spherical |
|---|---|---|---|
| Operation smoothness | 4.13 | 4.27 | 3.97 |
| Operational effort | 4.20 | 4.30 | 4.03 |
| Accuracy | 3.82 | 4.27 | 3.80 |
| Operation speed | 4.27 | 4.33 | 4.23 |
| General comfort | 4.27 | 4.40 | 4.07 |
| Overall operation | 4.17 | 4.33 | 4.03 |

**Table 6: Mean reported usability & comfort metrics per interaction (1 = Most Negative, 5 = Most Positive).**

Participants were asked to fill out 5-point independent rating Likert scale questions from Annex C. of the ISO 9241-9 which evaluated usability and comfort of the interaction immediately after using the interaction. Table 6 depicts the questions and the mean reported ratings about the usability the interaction. The reported ratings show reasonably high usability in all interactions. Friedman tests showed no statistical significance between interactions.

### 5.5.3 Fatigue

Participants filled out a 5-point independent rating Likert scale questions from ISO 9241-9 Annex C to collect data in regards to fatigue. Table 7 depicts the questions and the mean reported ratings

|  | Unmodeled | Hyperplanar | Spherical |
|---|---|---|---|
| Finger fatigue | 4.53 | 4.50 | 4.50 |
| Wrist fatigue | 4.37 | 4.37 | 4.17 |
| Arm fatigue | 4.33 | 4.33 | 4.33 |
| Shoulder fatigue | 4.57 | 4.53 | 4.40 |
| Neck fatigue | 4.87 | 4.87 | 4.87 |

**Table 7: Mean reported fatigue per interaction (1 = Extreme, 5 = None)**

per interaction. The reported ratings demonstrate a minor presence of fatigue in each interaction. Friedman tests showed no statistical significance between interactions.

### 5.5.4 Borg Scale

|  | Unmodeled | Hyperplanar | Spherical |
|---|---|---|---|
| Arm Effort | 1.20 | 1.37 | 1.27 |
| Shoulder Effort | 0.95 | 1.02 | 1.05 |
| Neck Effort | 0.15 | 0.20 | 0.27 |

**Table 8: Mean reported effort per interaction (0 = Nothing at all, 0.5 = very very weak (just noticable), 1 = very weak, ..., 10 very, very strong)**

Previous work in gestures encouraged the use of the Borg Scale for arm, shoulder, and neck effort [17], and were therefore included in our subjective assessment. We used the Borg scale from ISO 9241-9 Annex C. Table 8 shows the questions and the mean reported ratings for each interaction. The table demonstrates that minimal effort was required when using the interactions. Friedman tests showed no statistical significance between interactions.

## 6. ANALYSIS

The goal of this study was to evaluate the hypotheses using the metrics from the previous section. We report our findings of the hypotheses by splitting hypothesis H2 to better illustrate the results based on each of the interactions.

**H1** Users will learn gestural interaction over time, allowing for an improvement in performance.

We accept **H1** as the performance improvement analysis showed a significant improvement in all models between each day, which is indicative of learning.

**H2a** An interaction with a simple model of the interaction space will perform better than an interaction which does not model the space

We accept **H2a**. This decision was based on a comparison of performance, accuracy and Fitts's law conformance between the *Hyperplanar* and *Unmodeled* interaction.

In terms of performance, The *Hyperplanar* interaction obtained statistically better bivariate throughput than the *Unmodeled* interaction. However, this improvement was minor and not practically significant based on Cohen's interpretation.

With respect to accuracy, the *Hyperplanar* interaction obtained statistically better Movement Offset than the *Unmodeled* interaction, which was found to be a small-medium effect as defined by Cohen. It also had statistically better Movement Error, although the practical significance is minor.

In terms of Fitts' conformance, the *Hyperplanar* interaction demonstrated a strong linear correlation $(R)$ between Movement Time and IDe, had an intercept that was within the ideal range, and a higher goodness of fit $(R^2)$. The *Unmodeled* interaction, on the other hand, demonstrated a weak linear correlation $(R)$, an intercept that was not within the ideal range, and a lower $R^2$. It can also be seen in Table 4 that the *Hyperplanar* interaction demonstrated an improvement over time with regards to Fitts's law, while the *Unmodeled* interaction did not.

Since the *Hyperplanar* interaction was found to be as good, or better, in the individual metrics of performance, accuracy, and predictability as measured by Fitts's conformance, we consider the *Hyperplanar* interaction as a whole to obtain better results than the *Unmodeled* interaction.

**H2b** An interaction which models the interaction space using a sphere will perform better than an interaction which uses a hyperplane.

We fail to reject the null hypothesis in the case of **H2b**. To evaluate this hypothesis we compared the *Hyperplanar* and *Spherical* interactions using each of the collected metrics: performance, accuracy, and Fitts' conformance.

In terms of performance, the *Hyperplanar* interaction obtained statistically better bivariate throughput than the *Spherical* interaction, which was found to be a small-medium effect as defined by Cohen.

In terms of accuracy, *Hyperplanar* interaction obtained statistically better accuracy than the *Spherical* interaction in 5 of the 7 accuracy metrics. None are considered to be practically significant. The *Spherical* interaction obtained significantly better Movement Offset than the *Hyperplanar* interaction, but was not practically significant.

Fitts' regressions demonstrated a strong linear correlation, an intercept within the ideal range, and a relatively high 'goodness of fit' in both the *Hyperplanar*, and *Spherical* interactions. However the *Spherical* interaction was found to have a higher correlation, goodness of fit, and an intercept that was closer to the ideal value when compared to the *Hyperplanar* interaction.

In addition to the aforementioned quantitative metrics, users also showed preference towards the *Hyperplanar* interaction which was shown to be significant. Taking all these into consideration, we cannot conclude that the *Spherical* interaction performs better than the *Hyperplanar*, thus we fail to reject the null hypothesis.

# 7. DISCUSSION AND FUTURE WORKS

Over the course of this work, we found performance improvements between all 3 days of the study which we believe is caused by participants learning the interaction. While this may seem trivially true, current literature has in some cases failed to identify learning in these gestural interfaces [6, 34, 1]. We believe this difference is due to our experimental design, which used a longitudinal study and random-order practice.

We found that fatigue and effort were reported to be minimal from the rested position, as demonstrated in Table 7 and Table 8. This finding further reinforces current literature that has stated that resting the elbow during interaction reduces fatigue [14, 36, 6, 20].

We also found that modeling the interaction space resulted in an interaction which conforms to Fitts's law. Conversely, we found that an interaction which does not model the input space was not well explained by Fitts's law, nor was it within the ideal intercept range in each of the 3 days. This means that the relationship between movement time and IDe is not consistently predictable in the

unmodeled approach, and offers less value to those designing interfaces [37]. The approach used to detect these results was in line with the current standard's encouragement to regress the participant's mean movement time (MT) over their respective effective Index of Difficulty(IDe), as opposed to regressing over mean of means per Index of Difficulty [37].

We found that the interaction which used a simple model was significantly better than the unmodeled interaction in terms of both performance and accuracy, and only the latter was found to be practically significant as interpreted by Cohen. However, we also found that the interaction whose model was more complex in terms of the input space performed significantly worse than the other two models despite its mapping to the biomechanics of the body. This may be caused by the strict assumptions of the model. The two azimuthal $(\theta)$ and elevation $(\phi)$ angles were inferred from the previously measured elbow position and the palm position provided by the Leap Motion. Therefore, this model requires a higher tracking precision in order to perform optimally.

Upon review of the notes taken during the experiment, which included participants' feedback, we identified a few issues with the *Spherical* interaction. A recurring issue was with the static elbow placement. Participants had difficulty finding their calibrated elbow position even when a marker was present. We also found that during the pilot, participants mistakenly knocked the tracker off of its stand during their note-taking between rounds. This did not seem to significantly penalize the more simple models but caused large cursor jitters during the *Spherical* interaction. We attempted to solve this issue by building a new stand using Legos which allowed the tracker to tightly fit into place. While this increased stability, the stand itself was still movable when hit. We posit that a better interaction can be built using a device which directly tracks the arm in terms of relative angles. Another option would be to allow for dynamic elbow tracking in which both the hand and the elbow are dynamically tracked so that the elbow does not need to be in a fixed position. We believe that the better fit offered by the *Spherical* approach could yield positive results if these considerations are addressed.

While we provided overall effect size using $\eta_p^2$, and pairwise effect sizes for performance and accuracy metrics as measured by Cohen's d, interpreting these effect sizes however proved to be difficult. These interpretations are meant to be domain-specific [30], but no such guidelines exist within the domain of pointing device evaluation. We had to therefore fallback on the interpretations provided by Cohen, which are meant to be used as a last resort [22]. By providing the effect size of our study, we aim to provide better context for future research, and to contribute towards establishing guidelines for interpreting effect size within this domain.

# 8. CONCLUSION

In this study we used a longitudinal design to evaluate the two hypotheses. We learned that modeling the interaction space results in an interaction which can be explained by Fitts's law. Conversely, we learned that an unmodeled approach conforms weakly to Fitts's law. We also learned that a simple model of the user's interaction space resulted an interaction that was as fast and more accurate than an interaction which did not model the user's interaction space. Furthermore, we introduced a more complex model of the interaction space which maps the arm movement from a rested position to the 2D screen with no loss of information using the forearm angles as input. This more complex model did not exhibit better performance nor accuracy than the simpler model. We posit that this is due to the interaction having too many constraints and being unsuitable for use with an input device which uses the hand position as input. Finally, we showed that gestural interaction demonstrated performance improvements over multiple sessions, from which we infer learning.

# 9. REFERENCES

[1] Adhikarla, V. K., Sodnik, J., Szolgay, P., and Jakus, G. Exploring direct 3d interaction for full horizontal parallax light field displays using leap motion controller. *Sensors 15*, 4 (2015), 8642–8663.

[2] Bailly, G., Müller, J., Rohs, M., Wigdor, D., and Kratz, S. Shoesense: A new perspective on gestural interaction and wearable applications. In *Proceedings of the SIGCHI Conference on Human Factors in Computing Systems*, CHI '12, ACM (New York, NY, USA, 2012), 1239–1248.

[3] Banerjee, A., Burstyn, J., Girouard, A., and Vertegaal, R. Pointable: an in-air pointing technique to manipulate out-of-reach targets on tabletops. In *Proceedings of the ACM International Conference on Interactive Tabletops and Surfaces*, ACM (2011), 11–20.

[4] Bigdelou, A., Schwarz, L., and Navab, N. An adaptive solution for intra-operative gesture-based human-machine interaction. In *Proceedings of the 2012 ACM International Conference on Intelligent User Interfaces*, IUI '12, ACM (New York, NY, USA, 2012), 75–84.

[5] Bolt, R. A. *"Put-that-there": Voice and gesture at the graphics interface*, vol. 14. ACM, 1980.

[6] Brown, M. A., Stuerzlinger, W., and Filho, E. J. M. The performance of un-instrumented in-air pointing. In *Proceedings of the 2014 Graphics Interface Conference*, GI '14, Canadian Information Processing Society (Toronto, Ont., Canada, Canada, 2014), 59–66.

[7] Carmody, T. Why 'gorilla arm syndrome' rules out multitouch notebook displays. *Wired, Oct 10* (2010).

[8] Cockburn, A., Quinn, P., Gutwin, C., Ramos, G., and Looser, J. Air pointing: Design and evaluation of spatial target acquisition with and without visual feedback. *International Journal of Human-Computer Studies 69*, 6 (2011), 401–414.

[9] Cohen, J. Statistical power analysis for the behavioral sciences.

[10] Cohen, J. A power primer. *Psychological bulletin 112*, 1 (1992), 155.

[11] Criminisi, A., Reid, I., and Zisserman, A. A plane measuring device. *Image and Vision Computing 17*, 8 (1999), 625–634.

[12] Ens, B., Hincapié-Ramos, J. D., and Irani, P. Ethereal planes: A design framework for 2d information space in 3d mixed reality environments. In *Proceedings of the 2nd ACM Symposium on Spatial User Interaction*, SUI '14, ACM (New York, NY, USA, 2014), 2–12.

[13] Fitts, P. M. The information capacity of the human motor system in controlling the amplitude of movement. *Journal of experimental psychology 47*, 6 (1954), 381.

[14] Freeman, D., Vennelakanti, R., and Madhvanath, S. Freehand pose-based gestural interaction: Studies and implications for interface design. In *Intelligent Human Computer Interaction (IHCI), 2012 4th International Conference on*, IEEE (2012), 1–6.

[15] Guinness, D., Poor, G. M., and Jude, A. Gestures with speech for hand-impaired persons. In *Proceedings of the 16th International ACM SIGACCESS Conference on Computers & Accessibility*, ASSETS '14, ACM (New York, NY, USA, 2014), 259–260.

[16] Guna, J., Jakus, G., Pogačnik, M., Tomažič, S., and Sodnik, J. An analysis of the precision and reliability of the leap motion sensor and its suitability for static and dynamic tracking. *Sensors 14*, 2 (2014), 3702–3720.

[17] Hincapié-Ramos, J. D., Guo, X., Moghadasian, P., and Irani, P. Consumed endurance: A metric to quantify arm fatigue of mid-air interactions. In *Proceedings of the SIGCHI Conference on Human Factors in Computing Systems*, CHI '14, ACM (New York, NY, USA, 2014), 1063–1072.

[18] Jota, R., Nacenta, M. A., Jorge, J. A., Carpendale, S., and Greenberg, S. A comparison of ray pointing techniques for very large displays. In *Proceedings of Graphics Interface 2010*, GI '10, Canadian Information Processing Society (Toronto, Ont., Canada, Canada, 2010), 269–276.

[19] Jude, A., Poor, G. M., and Guinness, D. An evaluation of touchless hand gestural interaction for pointing tasks with preferred and non-preferred hands. In *Proceedings of the 8th Nordic Conference on Human-Computer Interaction: Fun, Fast, Foundational*, ACM (2014), 668–676.

[20] Jude, A., Poor, G. M., and Guinness, D. Personal space: User defined gesture space for gui interaction. In *CHI '14 Extended Abstracts on Human Factors in Computing Systems*, CHI EA '14, ACM (New York, NY, USA, 2014), 1615–1620.

[21] Kaptein, M., and Robertson, J. Rethinking statistical analysis methods for chi. In *Proceedings of the SIGCHI Conference on Human Factors in Computing Systems*, CHI '12, ACM (New York, NY, USA, 2012), 1105–1114.

[22] Lakens, D. Calculating and reporting effect sizes to facilitate cumulative science: a practical primer for t-tests and anovas. *Frontiers in psychology 4* (2013).

[23] Lee, T. D., and Genovese, E. D. Distribution of practice in motor skill acquisition: Learning and performance effects reconsidered. *Research Quarterly for Exercise and Sport 59*, 4 (1988), 277–287.

[24] Lin, C.-H. J., Sullivan, K. J., Wu, A. D., Kantak, S., and Winstein, C. J. Effect of task practice order on motor skill learning in adults with parkinson disease: a pilot study. *Physical therapy 87*, 9 (2007), 1120–1131.

[25] MacKenzie, I. S., and Jusoh, S. An evaluation of two input devices for remote pointing. In *Engineering for human-computer interaction*. Springer, 2001, 235–250.

[26] MacKenzie, I. S., Kauppinen, T., and Silfverberg, M. Accuracy measures for evaluating computer pointing devices. In *Proceedings of the SIGCHI conference on Human factors in computing systems*, ACM (2001), 9–16.

[27] MacKenzie, I. S., and Teather, R. J. Fittstilt: The application of fitts' law to tilt-based interaction. In *Proceedings of the 7th Nordic Conference on Human-Computer Interaction: Making Sense Through Design*, ACM (2012), 568–577.

[28] McLester, J., and Pierre, P. *Applied Biomechanics: Concepts and Connections*. Cengage Learning, 2007.

[29] Mentis, H. M., O'Hara, K., Sellen, A., and Trivedi, R. Interaction proxemics and image use in neurosurgery. In *Proceedings of the SIGCHI Conference on human factors in computing systems*, ACM (2012), 927–936.

[30] Morris, P. E., and Fritz, C. O. Effect sizes in memory research. *Memory 21*, 7 (2013), 832–842.

[31] Nagy, J. G., Plemmons, R. J., and Torgersen, T. C. Iterative image restoration using approximate inverse preconditioning. *Image Processing, IEEE Transactions on 5*, 7 (1996), 1151–1162.

[32] Pino, A., Tzemis, E., Ioannou, N., and Kouroupetroglou, G. Using kinect for 2d and 3d pointing tasks: performance evaluation. In *Human-Computer Interaction. Interaction Modalities and Techniques.* Springer, 2013, 358–367.

[33] Richardson, J. T. Eta squared and partial eta squared as measures of effect size in educational research. *Educational Research Review 6*, 2 (2011), 135–147.

[34] Sambrooks, L., and Wilkinson, B. Comparison of gestural, touch, and mouse interaction with fitts' law. In *Proceedings of the 25th Australian Computer-Human Interaction Conference: Augmentation, Application, Innovation, Collaboration*, ACM (2013), 119–122.

[35] Schmidt, R. A., and Lee, T. *Motor Control and Learning, 5E.* Human kinetics, 1988.

[36] Segen, J., and Kumar, S. Look ma, no mouse! *Commun. ACM 43*, 7 (July 2000), 102–109.

[37] Soukoreff, R. W., and MacKenzie, I. S. Towards a standard for pointing device evaluation, perspectives on 27 years of fitts' law research in hci. *International Journal of Human-Computer Studies 61*, 6 (2004), 751–789.

[38] Teixeira, V. *Improving elderly access to audiovisual and social media, using a multimodal human-computer interface.* PhD thesis, Faculdade de Engenharia, Universidade do Porto, 2011.

[39] Triesch, J., and Von Der Malsburg, C. Robotic gesture recognition by cue combination. In *Informatik'98.* Springer, 1998, 223–232.

[40] Wachs, J. P., Kölsch, M., Stern, H., and Edan, Y. Vision-based hand-gesture applications. *Communications of the ACM 54*, 2 (2011), 60–71.

[41] Wobbrock, J. O., Shinohara, K., and Jansen, A. The effects of task dimensionality, endpoint deviation, throughput calculation, and experiment design on pointing measures and models. In *Proceedings of the SIGCHI Conference on Human Factors in Computing Systems*, CHI '11, ACM (New York, NY, USA, 2011), 1639–1648.

[42] Yoo, J., Lee, S., and Ahn, C. Air hook: Data preloading user interface. In *ICT Convergence (ICTC), 2012 International Conference on*, IEEE (2012), 163–167.

# Evaluation of Docking Task Performance Using Mid-air Interaction Techniques

**Vanessa Vuibert**
Centre for Intelligent Machines
McGill University
Montréal QC, H3A 0E9
vvuibert@cim.mcgill.ca

**Wolfgang Stuerzlinger**
School of Interactive Arts +
Technology
Simon Fraser University
Surrey, BC V3T 0A3
w.s@sfu.ca

**Jeremy R. Cooperstock**
Centre for Intelligent Machines
McGill University
Montréal QC, H3A 0E9
jer@cim.mcgill.ca

## ABSTRACT

Mid-air interaction has the potential to manipulate objects in 3D with more natural input mappings. We compared the performance attainable using various mid-air interaction methods with a mechanically constrained input device in a 6 degrees-of-freedom (DoF) docking task in both accuracy and completion time. We found that tangible mid-air input devices supported faster docking performance, while exhibiting accuracy close to that of constrained devices. Interaction with bare hands in mid-air achieved similar time performance and accuracy compared to the constrained device.

## Keywords

3D interaction, 3D docking task, unconstrained mid-air

## 1. INTRODUCTION

Computer-vision-based tracking systems, exemplified by products such as the Kinect One and the Leap Motion, are now easily accessible on the mass-market. Simultaneously stereoscopic displays for gaming and entertainment have also become increasingly popular. These trends support and encourage the possibility of unconstrained mid-air interaction with a virtual 3D world, in a manner that approximates how we interact with the physical world. This vision is also promoted by augmented reality products, such as the Atheers One[1] and Meta [2], which render stereoscopic 3D content and track the users' hand gestures with built-in depth-sensing cameras. But can we, in fact, manipulate virtual 3D content quickly and accurately without the benefit of special-purpose constrained desktop devices?

This question motivated the studies described here. Our intent was to determine how mid-air interaction compares to existing alternatives for a non-trivial task in virtual environments. Specifically, we wanted to evaluate the possibility that efficient and accurate manipulation of 3D content may be supported without the need

---

[1] www.atheerlabs.com
[2] www.spaceglasses.com

for a constrained desktop input device. If so, we would also like to determine whether a hand-held input device is even necessary, or if tracking of the user's hands can potentially suffice.

We chose to study 3D docking as our main task, which requires both orientation and positioning of an object with respect to a target. Our contribution is an exploration of docking performance using various mid-air interaction techniques, and the comparison of this performance to that attained with a desktop device that is considered to be ideally suited for 6 DoF manipulations. The focus of our study was not the docking strategy itself, but rather the performance attainable with various input devices.

Several earlier studies investigated docking tasks using traditional wireframe graphics. However, for our experiment, we chose a richer graphical environment, offering improved depth cues with lighting and shadow effects, as this permits users to reuse existing skills. We also propose a mapping that allows users greater flexibility in the manner in which they manipulate the virtual object. Moreover, we discuss the need to evaluate not only the docking time, but also the accuracy of the final position and orientation of the object.

## 2. RELATED WORK

### 2.1 Evaluation of Input Conditions

There has been significant prior research investigating 3D manipulation using desktop devices, in particular, investigating 3D position and/or orientation tasks. These include the virtual trackball [26], Rockin'Mouse [1], GlobeFish and GlobeMouse [7], multi-touch surfaces used in conjunction with indirect [6] and direct interaction techniques, e.g., DS3 and StickyTools [6, 24, 10, 18], and mid-air interaction techniques such as Go-Go [23], as summarized in Table 1. Very few experiments compared constrained desktop-based devices to unsupported devices that can be manipulated freely in mid-air. A notable exception is early research by Zhai and Milgram [33], which demonstrated that for a docking task, isomorphic manipulation through a 6 DoF unsupported device was faster but less accurate than non-isomorphic manipulation with a 6 DoF elastic-rate-controlled device. However, it was unclear whether the time-accuracy tradeoff was more a result of the differences between isomorphic and rate-controlled input, or supported vs. mid-air interaction.

Placement (3 DoF), orientation (3 DoF) and docking (6 DoF) are fundamental tasks for manipulation of 3D content. However, comparisons of performance between input devices on such tasks are often frustrated by the lack of a standard experimental design. Bérard et al. [2] compared various devices for a 3D placement

| Study | Task | Fastest Technique | Other Compared Techniques |
|---|---|---|---|
| Zhai et al. [33] | docking | mid-air | constrained device |
| Froehlich et al. [7] | docking | GlobeFish & GlobeMouse | mouse |
| Berard et al. [?] | placement | mouse | DepthSlider, SpaceNavigator, mid-air |
| Wang et al. [30] | placement | Phantom | mouse |
| Kratz et al. [14] | orientation | mid-air | multi-touch screen |
| Glesser et al. [8] | docking | Phantom, dual multi-touch surfaces | trackpad, mouse |

**Table 1: Past Research on 3D manipulation tasks.**

task and found that the mouse, used in conjunction with orthographically projected views, was the fastest. However, computer-generated scenes often lack some of the depth cues that we rely on in the physical world to discriminate depth. This factor may account for at least some of the difference in human performance observed for tasks in the virtual compared to the physical world. With the addition of an improved visualization technique to compensate for limited depth cues, Wang et al. demonstrated that the Phantom could achieve higher performance on the same task [30], consistent with results from a more recent study [8].

Most placement, orientation and docking experiments only measure the time it takes participants to dock the cursor [7, 14, 8], but accuracy is often equally important. A docking task involves gross motion and then fine-tuning once near the target. Zhai et al. [33] measured how much the cursor's actual path differed from the shortest path to the target, both in terms of position and orientation. While there is interesting information in such trajectories, we are more interested in the accuracy of the final position and orientation, i.e., the docking result, as the evaluation criterion.

## 2.2 Visualization

Grossman et al. used motion capture cameras to track hand gestures as the fingers interact on the transparent spherical enclosure of a 3D volumetric display [9]. Although such volumetric displays offer the benefit of a true 3D display, consumer-level stereoscopic 3D, as used in many virtual and augmented reality displays, is a considerably more affordable and easily obtainable technology.

Stereoscopic 3D rendering and shadow-casting were found to improve accuracy in positioning tasks and permitted subjects to perform 3D placement tasks faster [13]. However, they did not improve rotation tasks [3]. In a stereoscopic rendering condition, direct mid-air interactions outperformed multi-touch screen techniques when the target was further away from the screen [4]. This may be due, in part, to the fact that while focusing on the finger that touches the multi-touch screen, the stereo image rendered above the screen appears blurred. Although stereoscopic rendering is often associated with simulator sickness, this is not a problem for docking tasks because the scene is static and the user focuses on a single object [25].

## 2.3 Gestures

The choice of interaction gestures is a critical factor in usability and performance. Previous studies [16, 27] used a handle bar metaphor to perform mid-air translations and rotations, where the virtual object being manipulated is imagined to be between the fists of the user. The main limitation of this technique is that the handle bar pose becomes fatiguing when users need to keep their arms extended to manipulate the handle bar for longer periods of time. A study by Hincapie et al. recommended to keep motions between the hip and the shoulder, and to minimize arm extension [11].

Tracking the translation and rotation of one hand is less fatiguing than using the handle bar technique. Levesque et al. proposed using the left hand for selection and the right hand for translation and rotation operations [15]. Cutler et al. proposed a more natural approach by using a pinch gesture to grab the virtual object and performing the 6 DoF operations with the same hand [5], similar to the 6 DoF Hand technique described by Mendes et al. [19]. Although not specified in their published descriptions, we suspect that these techniques require the users to always start their operations with their hand oriented so that it is pointing at the display. For example, if users were to grab the virtual object from the right side with their right hand and twist their wrist around its Z axis (local frame) (Figure 1), the object would rotate around the Z world axis instead of the X axis.

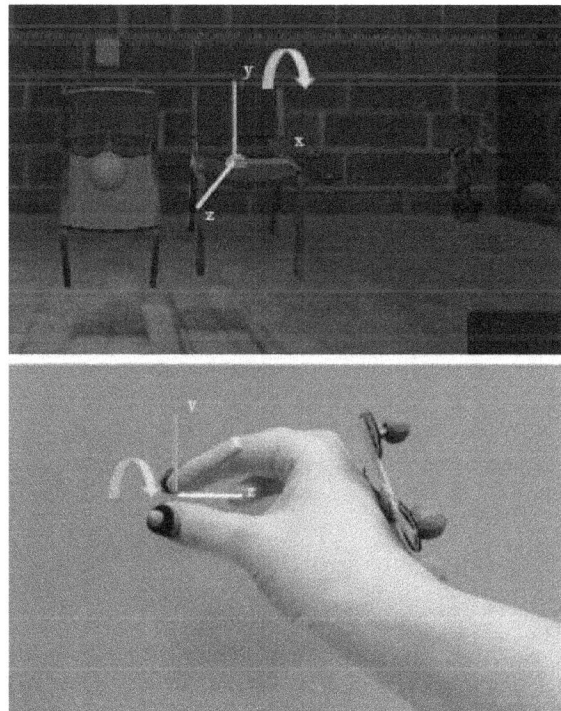

**Figure 1: Rotating the dark blue chair around its X axis with the hand.**

## 3. METHODOLOGY

A docking task was used to compare performance of three mid-air interaction options, using either a physical replica of the virtual object, a wand-like device or the user's hands. As baseline we chose a mechanically constrained input device, the Phantom Omni,

45

which can be used to provide 6 DoF input. This device demonstrated its superiority in terms of time performance in relation to other desktop devices in a recent docking study [8]. For our experiment, participants were asked to dock a moving "cursor" chair using a combination of translation and orientation operations, with a similar lighter colored target that remains fixed in the middle of the screen throughout each trial (Figure 2).

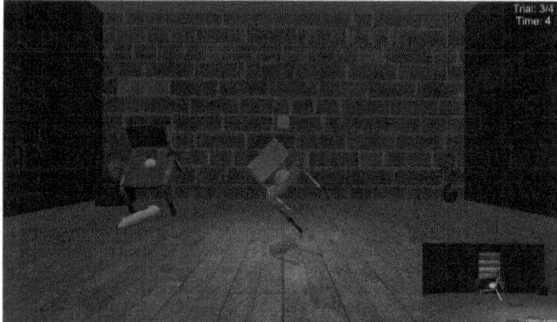

**Figure 2: The virtual representation of the AirPen is visible in the image as an ellipsoid. The second camera on the bottom right shows a view from the right side.**

## 3.1 Experimental Task

Previous docking studies used a set of predetermined target positions and orientations to avoid visual ambiguities [33, 8]. Since we offer a richer virtual environment for the docking task and thus are less affected by the visual ambiguity issue, the moving chair is placed randomly at the start of each trial, within a predetermined distance range from the target, which is assigned a uniformly distributed random orientation. A trial is completed once the participant succeeds in aligning the moving chair to the target position and orientation within a tolerance level, and confirms, either by a confirmation gesture or button-press [30, 8, 3].

While in other studies the timer started after a loud beep [33] or a key press [7], we initiate timing of the first trial when the participant begins manipulating the input device. For subsequent trials, the timer is started as soon as the new target is displayed. Each trial needs to be completed within a given time limit or it is automatically skipped. In this case, a new trial is added to the sequence, ensuring that all participants complete an equal number of trials. The number of completed trials for the current device, as well as the time elapsed since the trial began, is displayed in the top-right corner of the screen. (Figure 2).

## 3.2 Visual Environment

The scene is rendered in stereo and viewed through NVidia 3D Vision RF shutter glasses, thereby providing the participants with stereoscopic depth cues. We used the default stereo settings of the NVidia drivers, because these were picked to be appropriate for a large variety of viewers at desktop viewing distances. We did not attempt to perform any individual calibration of stereo viewing parameters for each participant. Our objective was simply to attain a quality of depth perception commensurate with what one achieves with "out-of-the-box" commodity 3D hardware.

Although stereoscopic rendering is often associated with simulator sickness, this is not a problem for docking tasks because the scene is static and the user focuses on a single object [25]. To assist in visualization of the target orientation, a second camera window, shown at the bottom right of the screen, offers a view of the target from the right side (Figure 2).

Despite the use of a stereoscopic display, Wang et al. [30] raised the concern that depth discrimination may be affected by impoverished depth cues, thus increasing task complexity. To minimize the potential impact of this factor, we designed a more graphically rich virtual environment, in which depth cues are also conveyed by the textures of the floor and walls. Lighting effects and shadows cast by the chairs further improve 3D perception and aid positioning [13]. However, we did not evaluate the improvement in task performance resulting from these factors. Instead, the objective of our experiment was to evaluate human performance with different input devices on the docking task. Theoretically, users can perform such tasks even without the benefit of stereo rendering, as there are enough depth cues available in our virtual environment.

## 3.3 Accuracy Feedback and Error Measures

We use orientation and position errors to measure accuracy. The orientation error is the angle between the quaternions of the chairs and the position error is the Euclidean distance between them. Once the orientation and position errors of the moving chair are within a threshold, a confirmation message appears in the top left panel. If the participant confirms the position and orientation while the chair is docked within the tolerance level, a confirmation sound is played and the trial completes. The tolerance level for orientation and position was determined in a pilot study, described in the following section.

Similar to previous experimental docking studies [3, 7, 8, 33], we provide color feedback as a means of informing participants that they have docked the chair within the required tolerance and can complete the trial. However, we have two additional objectives. First, we wish to determine the limits of accuracy that participants can achieve with the interaction methods under evaluation. Second, we wish to explore the use of auditory feedback to avoid the problem of split visual attention between the docking task itself and visually verifying accuracy feedback.

To encourage participants to achieve the highest accuracy possible, we provide continuous visual and audio feedback regarding their progress in the docking task. Once the position is within tolerance, drums are heard as audio feedback, and the color of the cube shown in Figure 2 changes from yellow to green. The cube remains fixed in position above the target at all times. Similarly, once the orientation is within tolerance, a bass track is heard as audio feedback, and the color of the spheres also changes from yellow to green. Both the volume of the audio tracks and brightness of the visual cues increase as position and orientation improve further.

## 3.4 Apparatus

The experiment was conducted on a computer equipped with a Nvidia Quadro FX 3800 GPU that drove a 1920x1080 120 Hz 53 cm wide display, viewed by participants through NVidia 3D Vision RF shutter glasses. The software environment for the experiment was developed using the Unity3D game engine. Participants manipulated the cursor in mid-air using an "AirPen", a "MiniChair", or the participants' own hand and fingers, as described below. A fourth input device, the Phantom Omni, was employed as control condition. All four input techniques can be seen in Figure 3. For all mid-air conditions, retro-reflective markers were attached to the input device and hand, and tracked by an Optitrack Flex:V100 motion capture system.

Since latency is known to have a stronger effect than spatial jitter on docking task performance [28], another set of measurements was performed to determine whether end-to-end latency might be a factor in our experiment. For these measurements, the scene consisted of a gray circle, which the experimenter translated back and

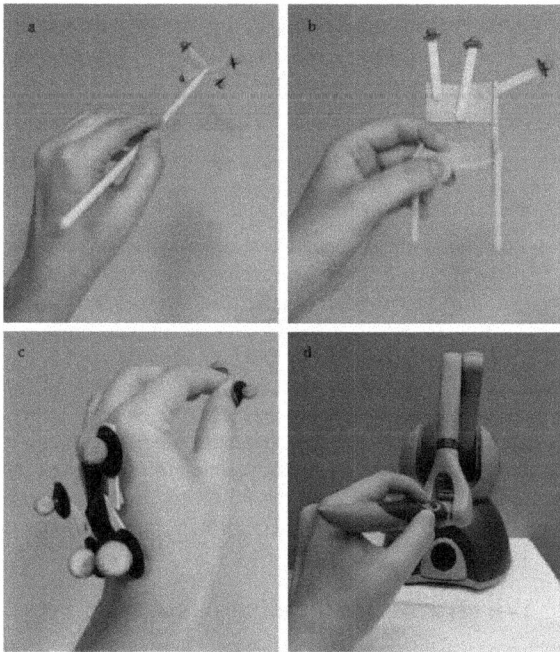

**Figure 3: The input conditions used in the experiment were: (a) AirPen (b) MiniChair (c) Fingers and (d) Phantom Omni.**

forth using the Phantom and the AirPen. The circle was overlaid on a 2D black-and-white checkerboard pattern, chosen to facilitate detection of movement by a high-speed black-and-white video camera, which captured the scene at 250 Hz. This procedure was repeated five times for each device and the recorded frames were reviewed to find the offset between movement of the physical device and the corresponding movement of the virtual device on screen. The results indicated a mean latency for the Phantom of 76.8 ms versus 72.0 ms for our Optitrack motion capture system.

We then sought to also confirm that the comparison of device performance was not affected by the sampling rate of the motion capture hardware or the Phantom. Towards this, we recorded the position and orientation reported through logging for each device over a 1 s interval, during which the experimenter used the device to translate and rotate the virtual chair. This procedure was repeated five times for each device. From inspection of the data, the sampling rate of the Phantom was determined to be approximately 73 Hz, versus 61 Hz for the devices tracked by the motion capture cameras.

In other words, both sampling rates were above 60 Hz, and the absolute difference between their mean latencies was approximately 5 ms. From these measurements, which are consistent with previous work [22], we are confident that neither sampling rate nor latency was substantially different between the Phantom and the other input conditions.

For all devices, translations and rotations are coupled, allowing both operations to be carried out simultaneously. This choice was preferred by all participants in a pilot, contradicting the findings of Martinet et al. [18]. To reduce shoulder fatigue, the width of the tracking volume was designed to reside between the hip and the shoulder of the participants. The need for arm extension and un-ergonomically large hand rotations was minimized through a clutch mechanism [11]. The participants sat approximately 75 cm from the screen and were allowed to rest their elbows on their lap or the armrests of the chair. All interaction involved indirect ma-

nipulation, which was found to be considerably faster than direct manipulation [20].

## 3.5  Input Mapping

To improve the input mapping, and in contrast with the previous work discussed in the Related Works section, we did not limit the locations at which the virtual object could be manipulated. Figure 4b shows how one can rotate the dark blue virtual chair around the Z axis of the AirPen (along the stick) in order to match the orientation of the target. The same mapping was used for all of the devices in our experiment, except for the rotation operation of the MiniChair, on which we elaborate in the following subsection.

The translation of each input device was applied to the virtual chair. Similarly, the virtual chair was rotated based on the change in Euler angles of the orientation of the input device. The virtual device had the same orientation as the real device except for its rotation around the Z axis (local frame), which was always set to $0°$, consistent with the assumptions of our pilot participants. The "up" vector of the virtual device (the Y direction) was transformed from local space to world space. The rotation operation of the virtual chair was performed around the previously obtained axis passing through its center. The same was done with the X and Z axes.

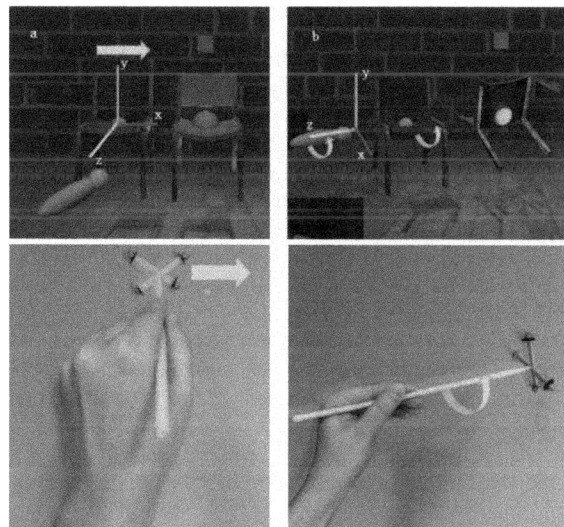

**Figure 4: Mapping of the devices. The light blue target chair is under the floating cube. (a) Translating the dark blue virtual chair by dragging the AirPen to the right. (b) Rotating the dark blue virtual chair around the Z axis of the AirPen.**

## 3.6  Input Conditions

### 3.6.1  AirPen

The AirPen (Figure 3a) was designed to be functionally similar to an unconstrained version of the Phantom stylus. It serves as an example of a familiar object that could plausibly be tracked as an input device by a virtual or augmented reality system, since the Leap Motion is already capable of tracking a stylus. The AirPen consists of a chopstick, to which a set of short sticks affixed with retro-reflective markers was attached perpendicularly to both track the third degree of rotation and to avoid occlusions.

While the AirPen is held in the dominant hand, the non-dominant hand is used for clutching and confirmation gestures. We use a fast tap of the index finger and the thumb of the non-dominant hand as confirmation gesture and a (longer) pinch for clutching. While

47

the user is holding the clutch gesture, movements of the AirPen are applied to the chair cursor, as in previous studies [17, 21, 31]. The confirmation gesture indicates completion of a trial. The pinch gesture is detected by observing the proximity of two spherical retro-reflective motion-capture markers, placed on the index finger and thumb using putty. The threshold distance for the "clutch" was established through calibration on a per-participant basis. A fast "tap" gesture, involving contact between the thumb and index finger of less than 0.3 s, is used to confirm the final docking position and orientation. The experimenter empirically determined the time threshold for the fast tap.

### 3.6.2 MiniChair

Inspired by Hinckley's passive real-world interface props [12], the MiniChair (Figure 3b) is a 3D printed chair, to which we attached sticks with retro-reflective markers. To avoid marker occlusions when the chair is upside down, we constrained the angle between the "up" vector of the target chair and the "down" vector of the virtual world to be greater than $80^o$, a value found empirically to be sufficient. For consistency across conditions, this constraint was applied to all devices. Because of the one-to-one mapping between the orientation of the physical MiniChair and its virtual representation, clutching was unnecessary and inappropriate for performing rotations. In theory, this represents a docking time advantage for the MiniChair for rotation operations. As with the AirPen, clutching by pinching with the non-dominant hand affects translations of the virtual chair. A fast tap was again used for confirmation.

### 3.6.3 Fingers

The easiest input device for users to access is, of course, their own hands (Figure 3c). This is especially true in the mobile context, for which other input devices would need to be carried or worn. As with the stylus, tracking of hands and fingers is available through existing RGB and depth cameras, although doing so robustly often remains a challenge. To avoid this potential confound, retro-reflective motion capture markers, configured as a trackable object, are taped to the back of the dominant hand for our experiment, while single markers are placed on the index finger and thumb. The virtual chair is then manipulated only while the subject is pinching. Since no object needs to be grasped in this condition, a fast tap of the thumb and index finger of the dominant hand is used to confirm docking.

### 3.6.4 Phantom

The Phantom Omni (Figure 3d) is a mechanically tracked, constrained device designed for 6 DoF operations that has demonstrated its superior performance in previous studies [8, 30]. We used the light colored button on the Phantom for clutching and the dark button for confirmation.

## 4. EXPERIMENTS

Before turning to the main study itself, we first describe several preliminary experiments we conducted to establish docking thresholds and the trial time limit, as well as to validate the benefits of using an everyday, textured object as the docking cursor and target.

## 4.1 Tolerance Level and Time Limit

Prior to running the main experiment, we needed to determine an appropriate tolerance level for both position and orientation errors. This was established through a pilot with four unpaid university students, without giving the participants feedback regarding their accuracy.

The pilot began with practice trials, where each device was tested on a series of five targets. Presentation order of the four input devices tested was determined by a four-level Latin square. The first target was presented in a standard orientation, Figure 4a, and the following three targets were rotated $45^o$ around the Y, X and Z axes respectively. The final target was assigned a random orientation, subject to the constraints explained above in the "MiniChair" section.

After completing the practice trials, each participant performed eight trials with each of the four interactions for a total of 32 trials per participant. We arranged the mean orientation and position error by input condition, and chose the biggest errors. The largest errors in both position (1.5 cm) and orientation ($15^o$) were observed in the Fingers condition; these values were then used as the respective tolerances for the position and orientation errors for all conditions in the following experiments. Similarly, analysis of the logged docking times during the practice trials led us to select a time limit of 40 s for trials in the following experiments. This value was sufficient for completion of all trials apart from one outlier (40.1 s).

## 4.2 Wireframe Tetrahedron vs. Chair Pilot

Some docking tasks in previous work used wireframe tetrahedra as target and cursor [3, 33, 8, 7], with a uniform texture or a checkerboard pattern over the background [30, 2] similar to the environment in Figure 5. However, anecdotal reports suggest that the use of a everyday, more familiar, and less symmetrical object, such as a chair, could reduce the perceptual complexity of the docking task. Since the goal of a docking task experiment is to evaluate input methods and not the spatial intelligence of the participants, we conducted a pilot test with three unpaid participants to compare their performance using tetrahedra (Figure 5) and chairs (Figure 2). For the former condition, each edge of the tetrahedron was assigned a different color to avoid ambiguity in perception of orientation, and a checkerboard texture was used as a background.

We chose the AirPen device for this test, since the participants in our pilot studies preferred it. The pilot test consisted of 2 blocks × 6 trials × 2 docking environments for a total of 24 trials per participant. Before starting the trials, the participants completed four practice runs in each docking environment. The participants were instructed to be as accurate as possible within the time limit. The diameters of the bounding spheres of the virtual chair and tetrahedron were 9 cm and 10 cm, respectively.

**Figure 5: A screenshot from our pilot experiment of a typical docking task experiment using wireframe tetrahedra.**

The results in Table 2 show similar accuracy in both environments. However, participants docked the chair noticeably faster than the tetrahedron, and reported greater difficulty docking the tetrahedron, consistent with our hypothesis.

| Environment | Orientation error (degree) | Position error (cm) | Docking time (s) |
|---|---|---|---|
| Tetrahedron | 9.29 | 0.71 | 15.19 |
| Chair | 9.30 | 0.66 | 11.30 |

Table 2: Average accuracy error and docking time for trials using tetrahedra and chairs.

## 4.3 Main Study

The main experiment consisted of 2 blocks × 6 trials × 4 input conditions for a total of 48 trials per participant. The order of the four input conditions tested was determined by Latin squares. A total of 12 participants took part in the experiment, ages ranging from 19 to 27 (median 22), drawn from a population of students. Half of the participants performed 3D virtual tasks at least two to five times per week and the other half less often. Participants began by completing a pre-test questionnaire, reading a document with instructions, and watching a short video explaining the visual and sound feedback provided in the docking task. They then carried out four practice trials before proceeding to the full experiment for each interaction. Following the experiment, participants completed a post-test questionnaire, and were compensated $10 for their time. We used the tolerance threshold found in our pilot study (position: 1.5 cm, orientation: $15°$) and limited the task time to 40 s. The participants were instructed to be as accurate as possible within the time limit.

### 4.3.1 Results

As the data was not normally distributed, we used ART [32] to conduct a non-parametric ANOVA for the docking time, position and orientation errors. All 19 skipped trials were discarded, and we analyzed only the $48 \times 12$ successful trials. The ANOVA test indicated that the interaction method used had a significant effect on the docking time ($F(3, 33) = 6.95, p < 0.05, GES = 0.09$), position error ($F(3, 33) = 4.21, p < 0.05, GES = 0.07$), and orientation error ($F(3, 33) = 3.36, p < 0.05, GES = 0.04$). Pairwise comparison using paired t-tests with a Bonferroni correction was then used to analyze individual effects within these measures.

For docking time, there was a significant difference between all the interaction methods except for the MiniChair-AirPen and Phantom-Fingers pairs. Figure 6 shows that all the tangible mid-air interactions were faster than with the Phantom, a constrained device. The slowest mid-air method, the fingers, was 0.29 s faster (1.37%), on average, than the Phantom. The fastest device, the MiniChair, was 4.79 s faster (23.09%) than the Phantom. Although the MiniChair had the smallest mean docking time, the difference between it and the next fastest device, the AirPen, was not significant.

The Phantom was the most accurate device, allowing participants to achieve the smallest position error among all input conditions tested (Figure 7). The difference was significant, according to the paired t-tests, although the value of this difference was small: the Phantom was 0.14 cm (26.50%) more accurate than the least accurate interaction for placement, the AirPen. Similarly, the orientation error achieved by participants with the Phantom was the smallest, as shown in Figure 8, which was again significantly differ-

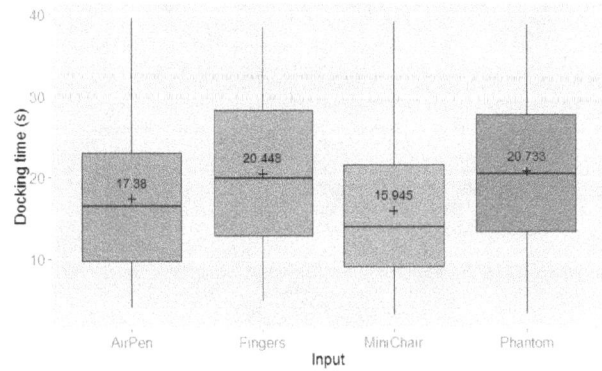

Figure 6: Boxplot of the docking task completion time for each interaction, where (+) is the mean docking time.

ent from all the mid-air interactions according to the t-tests. Even though the Phantom was 20.84% more accurate for rotation operations than the worst mid-air interaction, the fingers, the absolute difference in degrees was minor, at only $1.53°$. Thus, the Phantom was the most accurate device for both position and orientation, but not by a large margin. There was no significant difference in terms of either accuracy measures between the mid-air interaction conditions. A representative illustration of the average accuracy error of Fingers (position: 0.53 cm, orientation: $7.36°$), overall the least accurate interaction condition, is shown in Figure 9.

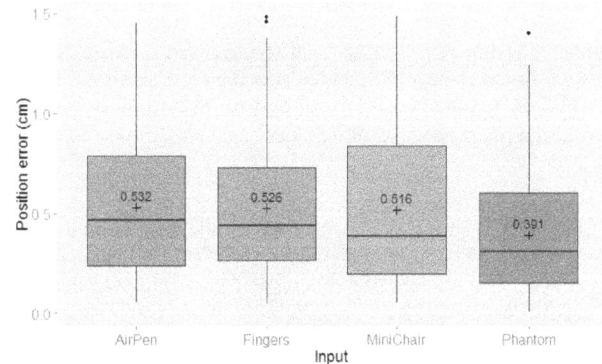

Figure 7: Boxplot of the position error for each interaction, where (+) is the mean position error.

On average, participants, applied transformations to the virtual chair (clutched) during 76% of the total time for each trial. An ANOVA test indicated that input condition had a significant effect on the clutching time ($F(3, 33) = 4.36, p < 0.05, GES = 0.07$). T-tests with a Bonferroni correction identify significance between all pairs of input conditions except for the fingers-AirPen and fingers-Phantom pairs. The average clutching time for the AirPen, fingers, MiniChair and Phantom were 13.62, 15.20, 12.24 and 15.61 seconds, respectively.

We also found that on average the chair cursor was rotated around its three axes almost equally, but participants preferred rotating the input device around its Z axis while applying rotations to the chair cursor. An ANOVA test indicated that the interaction between the input condition and the rotation axis had a significant effect on the number of rotations performed around each axis ($F(6, 66) = 6.75$,

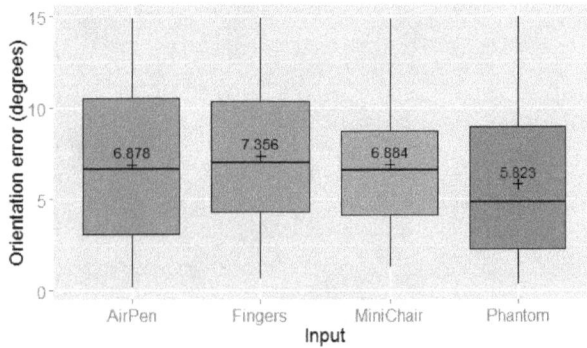

**Figure 8: Boxplot of the orientation error for each interaction, where (+) is the mean orientation error.**

**Figure 9: Visual representation of the average accuracy error for the Fingers interaction, which was the least accurate, overall. The dark blue chair cursor had an orientation error of 7.36° and a position error of 0.53 cm.**

$p < 0.05$, $GES = 0.02$). After separating the data by input condition, the ANOVA tests found that the rotation axes had a significant effect on the number of rotations performed around each axis for the AirPen ($F(2, 22) = 36.56$, $p < 0.05$, $GES = 0.19$), MiniChair ($F(2, 22) = 7.00$, $p < 0.05$, $GES = 0.04$), Fingers ($F(2, 22) = 4.19$, $p < 0.05$, $GES = 0.02$) and Phantom ($F(2, 22) = 31.10$, $p < 0.05$, $GES = 0.16$). T-tests with a Bonferroni correction identify significance between the Z axis and the X and Y axes for all input conditions. Rotations were performed around the Z axis 42.8% of the time for the AirPen, 45.5% for the Phantom, and 37.5% for the Fingers and 38.1% for the MiniChair. The AirPen (X:29.8%, Y:27.3%) and the MiniChair (X:29.1%, Y:32.8%) also had significance between their X and Y axes.

The post-test questionnaire asked participants to rate how favorably they found each interaction, with '5' considered to be strongly favored and '1' strongly unfavorable. Participants also rated the level of fatigue they experienced in their wrist and shoulder for each interaction and were asked their opinion about the auditory and color feedback. Results of this questionnaire indicate that subjects preferred the AirPen and Fingers, while interaction with the MiniChair was the least favored (Figure 10). The level of fatigue reported by the participants was similar across devices. The participants gave the auditory feedback an average rating of 4.42 and the color feedback an average rating of 3.42 out of 5.

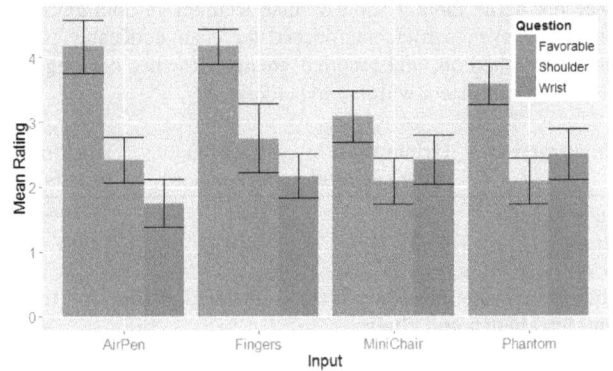

**Figure 10: Participants' response to the post-test questionnaire grouped by favorable interaction, shoulder fatigue and wrist fatigue.**

## 5. DISCUSSION

Overall, we found that the Phantom, a mechanically tracked and constrained device, was the most accurate device for position and orientation, whereas the tangible mid-air interactions (AirPen and MiniChair) were the fastest. This is consistent with previous research [33]. Interestingly, the Phantom interaction exhibited the highest completion time, and the highest clutching time, on average. These observations may be due to the physical limitations of the Phantom's joints, which constrain the possible movements of the stylus, thereby making it more complicated to perform the required manipulations. However, we also found that the tested mid-air conditions achieved an average accuracy that is close to that of the constrained device, which was the most accurate. Our results also highlight that time, orientation error, and position error are all important factors in evaluating docking tasks, since these measures offer insights into suitable applications for the device.

The results of our pilot study indicate that participants were able to dock an everyday virtual object, such as a chair, faster than the traditional wireframe tetrahedron, which has been used in the past for docking tasks. One possible explanation is that a more familiar and less symmetrical object is easier to perceive. As confirmed by the post-test questionnaire data for our main experiment, audio feedback offers the benefit that each musical instrument can provide information regarding a different variable. Even though visual feedback was provided by the color of two dedicated objects (square and sphere), participants preferred the audio feedback. This may have been due to the audio feedback not requiring split attention, or because it was more salient than the visual feedback.

We observed that some participants were more accurate than others, although at the cost of longer trial completion times. This speed-accuracy trade-off is known from Fitts' law research in human-computer interaction and has been observed in 3D selection tasks [29]. Bérard et al. [2] also found a trade-off between time and accuracy, further motivating the imposition of a time limit on trials. Such a limit should be determined through a pilot test, during which one can simultaneously determine an appropriate tolerance level. If the time limit is too high, some participants will become tired trying to achieve the maximum possible accuracy. If it is too low, some participants will not be able to complete the trials successfully.

Since the participants reported similar fatigue for the desktop device and the mid-air interactions, our experiment does not seem to suffer from the "gorilla arm problem". The likely reason is that users kept their movements between the hip and shoulders, as suggested by Hincapie et al. [11], and manipulated the chair during 76% of the trial time, limiting arm extension with the clutching mechanism. For maximum flexibility, we deliberately enabled a larger working volume for the unconstrained interactions than that provided in the Phantom condition. We observed that many participants would initially perform large gestures to avoid clutching, but soon switched to small gestures after realizing that these are less fatiguing, much like what one can observe with typical mouse usage. After the practice trials, most participants used approximately the same volume for all interactions.

Our analysis did not indicate any user preference for rotating the virtual chair around its X, Y or Z axis. This might suggest that participants deliberately select different orientations of the input device around the volume in order to manipulate the virtual object more comfortably, a behavior enabled by our mapping. The target was always assigned a random orientation and the rotations applied to the chair cursor from its reference frame also seemed random. Yet, the log data indicates that participants applied the transformations with their input device in a non-uniform manner, preferring rotations of the AirPen and Phantom device around its Z axis, which they did for 42.8% and 45.5% of all rotations respectively. We believe this to be due to the fact that it is easier to roll the stylus around its longitudinal axis between the fingers, relative to other rotations, which involve moving the wrist.

The MiniChair was the fastest option, likely because it was a replica of the virtual target and did not require clutching for rotation operations. However, participants rated the MiniChair as the least favorable condition, which we speculate was due to its more complex shape, which made it difficult to manipulate. In fact, some participants used both hands to rotate the MiniChair, possibly due in part to their small hand size. While it is not practical to have a replica of every virtual object we want to manipulate, such replicas may still be convenient for some applications, such as action figures in an augmented reality game.

Based on our results, we believe that the AirPen can serve as a multi-purpose device due to its ergonomic shape, speed and the high acceptance from the participants. The Flystick [20] behaves in a similar manner, but is held with a power grip, which precludes rolling around its Z axis, a feature of the stylus preferred by our participants. The user's fingers are a convenient input condition, since there is no need for an extra device. However, this requires accurate and reliable finger tracking in the presence of potentially large hand rotations. While it would have been possible to use the same gestures for clutching across all conditions, the AirPen and MiniChair needed the second hand for clutching, while the Phantom and the fingers conditions were manipulated with the dominant hand. We acknowledge that this might have increased fatigue for the bi-manual conditions, but the participants reported similar levels of fatigue across all conditions.

As described earlier, we determined the maximum position and orientation errors acceptable for the docking task through a pilot experiment. Traditionally, the experimenter chooses such values empirically. Yet, in pilot tests we observed that if the threshold is too high, participants repeatedly make small adjustments until they receive feedback of being within the required tolerance. In that case, the results may be more a reflection of luck than the performance achievable with any given input device. Given these factors, we attempted to set a tolerance threshold that is sufficiently difficult to make the task challenging, but not so difficult that success becomes tedious and overly fatiguing.

## 6. CONCLUSION

We conducted a study to compare the completion time and accuracy achievable on a docking task, performed with a 6 DoF mechanically constrained desktop device, to three alternatives employing mid-air interactions. We found that the constrained desktop device achieved greater accuracy than mid-air unconstrained interactions, as expected. Interestingly, however, the performance difference was very small, and possibly overshadowed by the faster speed of the tangible mid-air interaction methods. Even though the fingers did not outperform the Phantom in accuracy or speed, the difference between these two conditions was small. Thus, fingers may serve as a reasonably accurate and efficient input method, especially for mobile environments. We also found that participants prefer performing rotations around the Z axis of a stylus, and preferred multi-modal audio feedback to visual feedback for accuracy.

Given these results, we believe that rich mid-air interaction with virtual 3D content is not only plausible, but also reasonably fast. Future work should address the challenge of accurately tracking input devices with RGB and depth cameras.

## 7. ACKNOWLEDGEMENTS

We thank Jeff Blum for valuable discussions, Shrey Gupta for help with statistics and Ziad Ewais for the 3D printed chair.

## 8. REFERENCES

[1] Balakrishnan, R., Baudel, T., Kurtenbach, G., and Fitzmaurice, G. The rockin'mouse: integral 3d manipulation on a plane. In *Proceedings of the ACM SIGCHI Conference on Human factors in computing systems*, ACM (1997), 311–318.

[2] Bérard, F., Ip, J., Benovoy, M., El-Shimy, D., Blum, J. R., and Cooperstock, J. R. *Did Minority ReportÂİ get it wrong? Superiority of the mouse over 3D input devices in a 3D placement task*. Human-Computer Interaction-INTERACT 2009. Springer, 2009, 400–414.

[3] Boritz, J., and Booth, K. S. A study of interactive 6 dof docking in a computerised virtual environment. In *Virtual Reality Annual International Symposium, 1998. Proceedings., IEEE 1998*, IEEE (1998), 139–146.

[4] Bruder, G., Steinicke, F., and Sturzlinger, W. To touch or not to touch?: comparing 2d touch and 3d mid-air interaction on stereoscopic tabletop surfaces. In *Proceedings of the 1st symposium on Spatial user interaction*, ACM (2013), 9–16.

[5] Cutler, L. D., Fröhlich, B., and Hanrahan, P. Two-handed direct manipulation on the responsive workbench. In *Proceedings of the 1997 symposium on Interactive 3D graphics*, ACM (1997), 107–114.

[6] de la Rivière, J.-B., Kervégant, C., Orvain, E., and Dittlo, N. Cubtile: a multi-touch cubic interface. In *Proceedings of the 2008 ACM symposium on Virtual reality software and technology*, ACM (2008), 69–72.

[7] Froehlich, B., Hochstrate, J., Skuk, V., and Huckauf, A. The globefish and the globemouse: two new six degree of freedom input devices for graphics applications. In *Proceedings of the SIGCHI conference on Human Factors in computing systems*, ACM (2006), 191–199.

[8] Glesser, D., Bérard, F., and Cooperstock, J. R. Overcoming limitations of the trackpad for 3d docking operations. In *CHI'13 Extended Abstracts on Human Factors in Computing Systems*, ACM (2013), 1239–1244.

[9] Grossman, T., Wigdor, D., and Balakrishnan, R. Multi-finger gestural interaction with 3d volumetric displays. In

*Proceedings of the 17th annual ACM symposium on User interface software and technology*, ACM (2004), 61–70.

[10] Hancock, M., Ten Cate, T., and Carpendale, S. Sticky tools: full 6dof force-based interaction for multi-touch tables. In *Proceedings of the ACM International Conference on Interactive Tabletops and Surfaces*, ACM (2009), 133–140.

[11] Hincapié-Ramos, J. D., Guo, X., Moghadasian, P., and Irani, P. Consumed endurance: A metric to quantify arm fatigue of mid-air interactions. In *Proceedings of the 32nd annual ACM conference on Human factors in computing systems*, ACM (2014), 1063–1072.

[12] Hinckley, K., Pausch, R., Goble, J. C., and Kassell, N. F. Passive real-world interface props for neurosurgical visualization. In *Proceedings of the SIGCHI conference on Human factors in computing systems*, ACM (1994), 452–458.

[13] Hubona, G. S., Shirah, G. W., and Jennings, D. K. The effects of cast shadows and stereopsis on performing computer-generated spatial tasks. *Systems, Man and Cybernetics, Part A: Systems and Humans, IEEE Transactions on 34*, 4 (2004), 483–493.

[14] Kratz, S., Rohs, M., Guse, D., Muller, J., Bailly, G., and Nischt, M. Palmspace: continuous around-device gestures vs. multitouch for 3d rotation tasks on mobile devices. In *Proceedings of the International Working Conference on Advanced Visual Interfaces*, ACM (2012), 181–188.

[15] Lévesque, J.-C., Laurendeau, D., and Mokhtari, M. An asymmetric bimanual gestural interface for immersive virtual environments. In *Virtual Augmented and Mixed Reality. Designing and Developing Augmented and Virtual Environments*. Springer, 2013, 192–201.

[16] Mapes, D. P., and Moshell, J. M. A two-handed interface for object manipulation in virtual environments. *Presence: Teleoperators and Virtual Environments 4*, 4 (1995), 403–416.

[17] Markussen, A., Jakobsen, M. R., and Hornbaek, K. Vulture: a mid-air word-gesture keyboard. In *Proceedings of the 32nd annual ACM conference on Human factors in computing systems*, ACM (2014), 1073–1082.

[18] Martinet, A., Casiez, G., and Grisoni, L. The effect of dof separation in 3d manipulation tasks with multi-touch displays. In *Proceedings of the 17th ACM Symposium on Virtual Reality Software and Technology*, ACM (2010), 111–118.

[19] Mendes, D., Fonseca, F., Araujo, B., Ferreira, A., and Jorge, J. Mid-air interactions above stereoscopic interactive tables. In *3D User Interfaces (3DUI), 2014 IEEE Symposium on*, IEEE (2014), 3–10.

[20] Moehring, M., and Froehlich, B. Effective manipulation of virtual objects within arm's reach. In *Virtual Reality Conference (VR), 2011 IEEE*, IEEE (2011), 131–138.

[21] Muller, J., Geier, M., Dicke, C., and Spors, S. The boomroom: mid-air direct interaction with virtual sound sources. In *Proceedings of the 32nd annual ACM conference on Human factors in computing systems*, ACM (2014), 247–256.

[22] Pavlovych, A., and Stuerzlinger, W. The tradeoff between spatial jitter and latency in pointing tasks. In *Proceedings of the 1st ACM SIGCHI symposium on Engineering interactive computing systems*, ACM (2009), 187–196.

[23] Poupyrev, I., Billinghurst, M., Weghorst, S., and Ichikawa, T. The go-go interaction technique: non-linear mapping for direct manipulation in vr. In *Proceedings of the 9th annual ACM symposium on User interface software and technology*, ACM (1996), 79–80.

[24] Reisman, J. L., Davidson, P. L., and Han, J. Y. A screen-space formulation for 2d and 3d direct manipulation. In *Proceedings of the 22nd annual ACM symposium on User interface software and technology*, ACM (2009), 69–78.

[25] Schild, J., Jr, J. J. L., and Masuch, M. Altering gameplay behavior using stereoscopic 3d vision-based video game design. In *Proceedings of the 32nd annual ACM conference on Human factors in computing systems*, ACM (2014), 207–216.

[26] Shoemake, K. Arcball: a user interface for specifying three-dimensional orientation using a mouse. In *Graphics Interface*, vol. 92 (1992), 151–156.

[27] Song, P., Goh, W. B., Hutama, W., Fu, C.-W., and Liu, X. A handle bar metaphor for virtual object manipulation with mid-air interaction. In *Proceedings of the SIGCHI Conference on Human Factors in Computing Systems*, ACM (2012), 1297–1306.

[28] Teather, R. J., Pavlovych, A., Stuerzlinger, W., and MacKenzie, I. S. Effects of tracking technology, latency, and spatial jitter on object movement. In *3D User Interfaces, 2009. 3DUI 2009. IEEE Symposium on*, IEEE (2009), 43–50.

[29] Teather, R. J., and Stuerzlinger, W. Pointing at 3d targets in a stereo head-tracked virtual environment. In *3D User Interfaces (3DUI), 2011 IEEE Symposium on*, IEEE (2011), 87–94.

[30] Wang, G., McGuffin, M. J., BÃČÂl'rard, F., and Cooperstock, J. R. Pop-up depth views for improving 3d target acquisition. In *Proceedings of Graphics Interface 2011*, Canadian Human-Computer Communications Society (2011), 41–48.

[31] Wang, R., Paris, S., and Popović, J. 6d hands: markerless hand-tracking for computer aided design. In *Proceedings of the 24th annual ACM symposium on User interface software and technology*, ACM (2011), 549–558.

[32] Wobbrock, J. O. Practical statistics for human-computer interaction. In *Annual Workshop of the HCI Consortium*, HCIC (2011).

[33] Zhai, S., and Milgram, P. Quantifying coordination in multiple dof movement and its application to evaluating 6 dof input devices. In *Proceedings of the SIGCHI conference on Human factors in computing systems*, ACM Press/Addison-Wesley Publishing Co. (1998), 320–327.

# A Study on Proximity-based Hand Input for One-handed Mobile Interaction

Florian Müller[1], Mohammadreza Khalilbeigi[1], Niloofar Dezfuli[1],
Alireza Sahami Shirazi[2]*, Sebastian Günther[1], Max Mühlhäuser[1]
[1] Technische Universität Darmstadt, Darmstadt, Germany
[2]Yahoo Labs, 701 First Avenue, Sunnyvale, CA 94089, United States
{florian.mueller, khalilbeigi, niloo, guenther, max}@tk.informatik.tu-darmstadt.de,
alireza@yahoo-inc.com

## ABSTRACT

On-body user interfaces utilize the human's skin for both sensing input and displaying graphical output. In this paper, we present how the degree of freedom offered by the elbow joint, i.e., flexion and extension, can be leveraged to extend the input space of projective user interfaces. The user can move his hand towards or away from himself to browse through a multi-layer information space. We conducted a controlled experiment to investigate how accurately and efficiently users can interact in the space. The results revealed that the accuracy and efficiency of proximity-based interactions mainly depend on the traveling distance to the target layer while neither the hand side nor the direction of interaction have a significant influence. Based on our findings, we propose guidelines for designing on-body user interfaces.

**Categories and Subject Descriptors:** H.5.m. Information Interfaces and Presentation(e.g. HCI): Miscellaneous

**General Terms:** Human Factors, Experimentation

**Keywords:** Human Factors; Design; Measurement.

## 1. INTRODUCTION

Technological advances in (depth) sensors and mobile projectors resulted in the emergence of a new class of interfaces that extend interaction to the surface of our body. These so-called on-body interfaces [6, 7] allow ubiquitous and mobile interaction with digital contents by sensing input and projecting graphical output on the skin. The hand and forearm receive particular attention because they are often unclothed and socially acceptable to touch [12]. These advantages resulted in a large body of research for body-based projective [7, 14, 8, 13], augmented [5] or imaginary [3, 4] interfaces.

In most of these systems, the user's non-dominant hand acts as a two-dimensional interactive surface on which the

*The majority of the work has been conducted while he was a researcher at the University of Stuttgart.

*SUI'15,* August 8–9, 2015, Los Angeles, CA, USA.
© 2015 ACM. ISBN 978-1-4503-3703-8/15/08 ...$15.00.
DOI: http://dx.doi.org/10.1145/2788940.2788955.

**Figure 1: A map application as an example of one-handed (a) proximity-based interaction with a linear layered information space. The user can browse map layers by moving his hand through the space (b).**

opposing hand interacts with the content through (multi)-touch gestures. While useful and practical, the interaction space is bound to the two-dimensional surface of the hand. Moreover, this style of interaction requires both hands and therefore hardly supports situations, where users are encumbered. Similar to [2], we believe that the large number of degrees of freedom offered by our hands and arms can support one-handed interaction styles based on proximity. We can rotate and move our hands away or towards our body or we can hold them at a specified position.

We extend the input space of prior on-body user interfaces by focusing on the degree of freedom offered by the elbow joint, i.e., flexion by moving the hand toward and extension by moving the hand away from the body. We propose to use this proximity dimension as an additional input modality for one-handed mobile interaction. The interaction space alongside the user's line of sight can be divided into multiple parallel-planes. Similar to [11], each plane corresponds to a layer with visual content. The user can move his hands to browse through successive layers (cf. Figure 1). Beyond palm-projected interfaces, our approach can also be used as an additional input dimension for devices such as wearables or head-mounted displays with small input spaces for touch interaction. For such devices, our approach allows to expand the interaction space and provide direct manipulation.

In this paper, we investigate the human capabilities for a proximity-based hand input modality in multi-layer information spaces. We contribute the results of a controlled experiment addressing two main questions:

1. How accurate and efficient users can interact with the layered information space in a search task scenario?
2. How to design the interaction space in terms of layer thickness, number of layers, and convenient boundaries of the physical interaction volume?

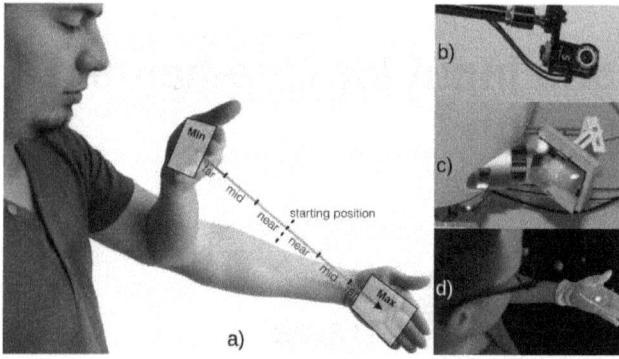

Figure 2: Traveling distance zones (a) and setup of the study (b-d).

Figure 3: Visual feedback in the study: After reaching the starting position (a), the system showed the direction of interaction (b). The participants task was to browse through a stack of white colored numbers (c) to find the one red colored number (d).

In the remainder of this paper, we present the methodology of the experiment followed by detailed report on our results. Finally, we present the implications and limitations.

## 2. CONTROLLED EXPERIMENT

The focus of the study was to investigate how efficiently and accurately users can interact in a multi-layer information space in a searching task. Further, we evaluated the influence of the direction of interaction and the side of the hand.

We recruited 14 participants (P1-P14: 4 female, 1 left-handed), aged between 24 and 29 years ($\mu = 26$, $\sigma = 1.6$), using the University's mailing address. The average height was 177cm ($\sigma = 9.5cm$), the average arm length (measured from armpit to carpus) of 59cm ($\sigma = 3.6cm$). We choose a within-subject design. No compensation was provided.

### 2.1 Design and Task

Similar to [10], we designed a basic multi-layer information space alongside the participants line of sight consisting of randomized integer numbers (each layer displayed one number). We varied the **number of layers** in the available interaction space (which directly correlates with the layers' thickness) as the independent variable with the values of 12, 24, 36, 48, 60 and 72. In addition, we varied the **direction of interaction** between flexion and extension as a second as well as the **side of the hand** (palm or backside) as a third condition. We considered those conditions to assess their influence on the participants performance in terms of accuracy and efficiency.

The participants' first task was to search for the one red colored number in the stack of white colored numbers (cf. Figure 3). Once found, participants confirmed the discovery by pressing a button with their non-interacting hand. Directly after, as the second task, participants had to hold the hand steady at the respective position for 3 seconds to measure the accuracy while trying to hold on a layer.

We defined the maximum boundary of the interaction space with the participant's individual arm-length and the minimum boundary as the near point of the human's eye (not closer than 12.5cm to the user's face). Furthermore, we defined the starting point of all trials as half of the distance between the minimum and the maximum interaction distance, resulting in an elbow joint deflection of around 100 degree. Informal pre-tests showed this to be a natural and relaxed holding position for the hand. To systematically an-

alyze influences of the traveling distance of the users hand, we divided the total available interaction space in each direction into three equal-sized zones: near, medium, and far as shown in Figure 2 a).

### 2.2 Study Setup and Apparatus

We used an optical tracking system (OptiTrack, cf. Figure 2 b) to precisely measure the linear distance between the participant's hand and his eyes alongside the participant's line of sight. To achieve this, we used two trackable apparatuses: a glasses frame and a glove, each augmented with a number of small retro-reflective markers (cf. Figure 2 d), which participants wore during the study. We further used the real time tracking information to fit the projected feedback to the participant's hand. (cf. Figure 3). For each trial, we measured:

1. the **task completion time (TCT)** as the timespan between starting the trial and confirming the discovery of the target.
2. the **overshooting error** as the maximum deviation in distance (in mm) between the center of the target layer and the participant's hand before confirming the discovery.
3. the **holding error** as the maximum distance (in mm) from the starting point of the holding task.

### 2.3 Procedure

We used a repeated measure design with 6 levels for numbers of layers, 2 different hand sides, and 2 directions of inter-action with 6 repetitions (two from each zone) resulting in $6 \times 2 \times 2 \times 6 = 144$ trials. The order of the conditions was counterbalanced using a Balanced Latin Square design for the number of layers and the direction of interaction. We excluded the side of the hand condition from the Latin Square design because remounting the trackable marker resulted in also recalibrating the system. However, half of the participants performed all palm-side trials first, while the other half started with the backside trials.

We introduced the participants to the concept and study setup. We mounted the two trackable apparatuses and calibrated the system to adapt it to the respective arm size. Before starting each trial, the system guided the user to the starting position through visual feedback displayed on the users hand. Once in the starting position, the system displayed the direction of the interaction. Each trial started by pressing the button. Once the target was found, the participant confirmed the discovery through another click. After that, the system informed participants to hold their current position for three seconds. Participants did not receive any

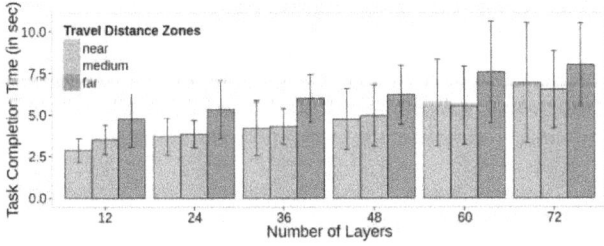

**Figure 4: Mean TCT and SD for different numbers of layers.**

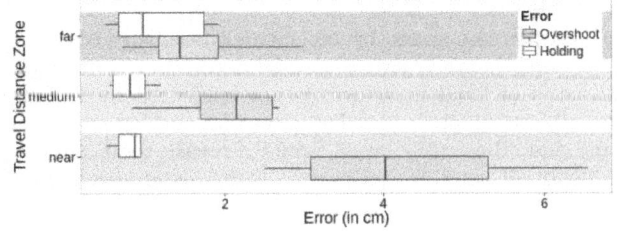

**Figure 5: Error measurements for the three traveling distance zones.**

feedback during the holding task and were not informed on the current layer thickness.

After each condition, participants took a 30 seconds break. We concluded the experiment with a semi-structured interview focusing on their overall opinion about the concept, preferred interaction boundaries (minimum/maximum distance), and differences between the tested conditions. The experiment took 60 minutes per participant.

## 3. RESULTS

We analyzed the data using repeated measures ANOVA. In cases where Mauchly's test indicated a violation of the assumption of sphericity, we corrected the tests using the Greenhouse-Geisser method and report the $\epsilon$. When significant effects were revealed, we applied Bonferroni corrected pairwise t-tests for the post-hoc analysis. For correlation tests, we used Pearson's method.

### 3.1 Task Completion Time

The analysis unveiled that the traveling distance of the hand had a significant effect on the TCT ($F_{2,62} = 23.27; p < 0.001$). Post-hoc tests confirmed that the TCT for near ($\mu=4.7s$, $\sigma=3.6s$) and medium zone ($\mu=4.8s$, $\sigma=2.7s$) targets were significantly smaller (p<0.001) than for those in the far zone ($\mu=6.4s, \sigma=3.4s$). Post-hoc test did not show a significant different TCT between medium and near zone targets.

The number of layers had a significant effect on the TCT ($\epsilon=0.49; F_{2.45,31.36}=45.68$; p<0:001). Post-hoc tests revealed a significantly (p< 0.01) larger TCT for higher numbers of layers. The mean TCT increased from 3.7 sec ($\sigma=1.8s$) for 12 layers to 7.2 sec ($\sigma=4.7s$) for 72 layers. While the mean TCT was faster for extension ($\mu=5.5s$, $\sigma=3.5s$) than flexion ($\mu=5.1s, \sigma=3.1s$), we could not find any significant effects ($F_{1,13}=2.8$, $p = 0.12$). Also, no significant effect of the hand orientation on TCT was found ($F_{1,13}=0.15$, $p = 0.70$, Palm: $\mu=5.2s$, $\sigma=3.2s$, Back: $\mu=5.3s$, $\sigma=3.4s$). We could not find interaction effects between the conditions. Figure 4 shows the TCT for the explored numbers of layers and target layers.

### 3.2 Overshooting Error

The traveling distance also had a significant effect on the overshooting error ($\epsilon = 0.63; F_{1.26,16.38} = 39.44; p < 0.001$). Post-hoc tests showed significant differences between all zones (all p<0.05). We observed that participants initially started with fast movements and slowed down towards their physical boundaries in the far zones, resulting in higher overshooting errors in the near ($\mu=4.4cm$, $\sigma=1.7cm$) and medium ($\mu=2.1cm$, $\sigma=1.0cm$) zones compared to the far

($\mu=1.6cm$, $\sigma=0.7cm$) zone. Figure 5 shows the overshooting error.

The analysis showed neither any significant influence of the direction of interaction on the overshooting error ($F_{1,13} = 0.0008, p = 0.97$; flexion: $\mu = 2.5cm, \sigma = 3.0cm$; extension: $\mu = 2.6cm, \sigma = 3.2cm$) nor the hand orientation ($F_{1,13} = 0.11, p = 0.75$; palm: $\mu = 2.6cm, \sigma = 3.1cm$; back: $\mu = 2.6cm, \sigma = 3.0cm$). Furthermore, we could not find any significant influence ($F_{5,64}=0.64$, p=0.66) of the number of layers (Min: $\mu=2.2cm$, $\sigma=3.1cm$ for 12 layers, Max: $\mu=2.8cm$, $\sigma=3.4cm$ for 36 layers). Also, we could not find any significant correlation between the participant's arm-length and their accuracy ($r(166)=$ âĹŠ0.8376, p=0.40) in our results.

### 3.3 Holding Error

We observed significant effects of the distance between the starting point and the holding point on the holding error ($\epsilon=0.56$, $F_{1.12,14.56}=5.53$, p<0.05). Post-hoc tests showed a significant effect (all p<0.05) between targets in the far ($\mu=1.6cm$, $\sigma=1.8cm$) and the medium ($\mu=1.0cm$, $\sigma=0.9cm$) zone as well as between the far and near ($\mu=1.1cm, \sigma=1.1cm$) zone. The difference between near and medium zones were however not significant ($p > 0.74$). Figure 5 shows the holding error for the travel distance zones.

We could not find either any significant influences of the direction of interaction ($F_{1,13} = 1.65, p = 0.22$; flexion: $\mu = 0.7cm, \sigma = 0.8cm$; extension: $\mu = 0.8cm, \sigma = 0.8cm$) or the hand orientation ($F_{1,13} = 1.37, p = 0.26$; palm: $\mu = 0.8cm, \sigma = 0.8cm$; back: $\mu = 0.7cm, \sigma = 0.7cm$) on the holding error. Furthermore, we could observe a significant ($\epsilon=0.29$, $F_{1.45,18.85}=7.21$, p<0.001) influence on the number of layers. Post-hoc tests confirmed a significant (p < 0.01) bigger holding error for 12 layers ($\mu=1.2cm$, $\sigma=0.9cm$) compared to all higher numbers of layers. The mean hold error further decreased for increasing numbers of layers (min: $\mu=0.6cm$, $\sigma=0.4cm$ for 72 layers) but was not significant.

### 3.4 Qualitative Results

In general, all participants appreciated the idea of being able to interact with multi-layer information spaces through movements of their hand. There was a strong consensus among participants (11 out of 14) that this input modality is suitable for immediate and short-term interactions, such as serendipitous discovery of contents, fast peeking into information or executing a shortcut. From the participants' comments, we derived that convenient boundaries for interaction are approximately the near and middle zones in each direction. Far zones turned out to cause more fatigue on arm and upper arm muscles.

## 4. IMPLICATIONS

**Partition the space by layer thickness** Our results indicate that the accuracy - measured as an error of absolute distance - of hand movement is not influenced by various sizes of participants' arms. For users with smaller arms, too many and, thus, thin layers would decrease the accuracy. On the other hand, for taller users with greater arm length, insufficient numbers of layers would result in greater traveling distances and, therefore, decreased efficiency. Hence, we propose to design the interaction space based on the layer's thickness. This way, the design results in different numbers of layers for different arm sizes, allowing the user to interact within the borders of their physical abilities.

**Use an uneven layer thickness** The traveling distance proved to be the most important factor. We observed that the typical overshooting error decreases towards outer regions. Therefore, we propose to use descending layer thicknesses towards outer regions. This allows for smaller layers in outer regions without increasing the interaction time that is introduced due to overshooting the target. Based on our quantitative results, a layer thickness of 7.8 cm for near, 4.2 cm for medium and 3.0 cm for far targets (the respective mean overshoot plus the double standard deviation) would result in >95% accuracy for all traveling distances.

**Design with convenient boundaries in mind** The qualitative feedback from participants showed that interactions in the far zones are less convenient compared to the closer regions. Therefore, we propose to focus on the near and medium zones for frequent and common interactions. As showed in [1], the slightly uncomfortable hand position in the far zones can be leveraged for important and not reversible actions.

## 5. APPLICABILITY

We believe that our results help to answer fundamental questions related to the design of proximity-based interaction in front of the user. We imagine a real world system implemented as a bracelet using an attached pico-projector along with an infrared proximity array as presented in [9].

Beyond palm-projected interfaces, proximity interaction can also be used in other domains such as head-mounted displays. For stereoscopic **AR glasses**, our approach can leverage the space in front of the user to present a layered information space (virtually projected on the user's palm). Additionally, touch input on the palm can provide direct manipulation possibilities on each layer. **Head-Up Displays** such as Google Glass present floating interfaces in the view of the user. Proximity interaction can act as a selector for different layers of the UI. The respective layout can be imaginary mapped to the palm's surface. Through the sense of proprioception, users can touch interface elements without visual attention to the hand. Similar to [5], the hand's 3D features can be extracted from a RGB-D attached to the head-mounted display.

## 6. CONCLUSION

We presented findings derived from a controlled experiment in which we focused on human capabilities for proximity-based hand input. The results confirmed the viability and feasibility of this input modality. The traveling distance to the target layer proved to be the main influence for the accuracy and the efficiency.

## 7. ACKNOWLEDGMENTS

This work was supported by Institute for Information & communications Technology Promotion(IITP) grant funded by the Korea government(MSIP) (No.B0101-15-1292, Development of Smart Space to promote the Immersive Screen Media Service).

## 8. REFERENCES

[1] S. Benford, C. Greenhalgh, G. Giannachi, B. Walker, J. Marshall, and T. Rodden. Uncomfortable interactions. In *Proc. CHI '12*, page 2005. ACM Press, 2012.

[2] X. A. Chen, J. Schwarz, C. Harrison, J. Mankoff, and S. Hudson. Around-body interaction. In *Proc. MobileHCI '14*, pages 287–290, New York, New York, USA, Sept. 2014. ACM Press.

[3] N. Dezfuli, M. Khalilbeigi, J. Huber, F. Müller, and M. Mühlhäuser. PalmRC: imaginary palm-based remote control for eyes-free television interaction. In *Proc. EuroiTV '12*, pages 27–34. ACM Press, 2012.

[4] S. G. Gustafson, B. Rabe, and P. M. Baudisch. Understanding palm-based imaginary interfaces. In *Pro. CHI '13*, page 889. ACM Press, 2013.

[5] T. Ha, S. Feiner, and W. Woo. WeARHand: Head-worn, RGB-D camera-based, bare-hand user interface with visually enhanced depth perception. In *Proc ISMAR '14)*, pages 219–228. IEEE, Sept. 2014.

[6] C. Harrison and H. Faste. Implications of location and touch for on-body projected interfaces. In *Proc. DIS '14*, pages 543–552. ACM Press, 2014.

[7] C. Harrison, S. Ramamurthy, and S. E. Hudson. On-body interaction. In *Proc. TEI '12*, page 69. ACM Press, 2012.

[8] P. Mistry and P. Maes. SixthSense âĂŞ A Wearable Gestural Interface. In *Sketches. SIGGRAPH ASIA '09*, page 11. ACM Press, 2009.

[9] D. Ryu, D. Um, P. Tanofsky, D. H. Koh, Y. S. Ryu, and S. Kang. T-less: A novel touchless human-machine interface based on infrared proximity sensing. In *Proc. IROS '10*, pages 5220–5225. IEEE, Oct. 2010.

[10] M. Spindler, M. Martsch, and R. Dachselt. Going beyond the surface: studying multi-layer interaction above the tabletop. In *Proc. CHI '12*, pages 1277–1286. ACM Press, 2012.

[11] S. Subramanian, D. Aliakseyeu, and A. Lucero. Multi-layer interaction for digital tables. In *Proc UIST '06*, page 269, New York, New York, USA, Oct. 2006. ACM Press.

[12] J. Wagner, M. Nancel, S. G. Gustafson, S. Huot, and W. E. Mackay. A Body-centric Design Space for Multi-surface Interaction. In *Proc. CHI '13*, page 1299. ACM Press, 2013.

[13] A. D. Wilson and H. Benko. Combining multiple depth cameras and projectors for interactions on, above and between surfaces. In *Proc. UIST '10*, page 273. ACM Press, 2010.

[14] C. Winkler, J. Seifert, D. Dobbelstein, and E. Rukzio. Pervasive information through constant personal projection. In *Proc. CHI '14*, pages 4117–4126. ACM Press, 2014.

# Duet: Improvising Spatial Dialogues with an Artificially Intelligent Agent

**Stephanie Andrews**
Deakin University
221 Burwood Highway
Burwood, VIC 3125 Australia
+61 3 9244 6342
anst@deakin.edu.au

**Jordan Beth Vincent**
Deakin University
221 Burwood Highway
Burwood, VIC 3125 Australia
+61 3 9251 7614
jordan.vincent@deakin.edu.au

**John McCormick**
Deakin University
221 Burwood Highway
Burwood, VIC 3125 Australia
+61 3 9251 7426
john.mccormick@deakin.edu.au

## ABSTRACT

This paper presents an experimental framework for a virtual reality artwork, *Duet*, that employs a combination of live, full body motion capture and Oculus Rift HMD to construct an experience through which a human User can spatially interact with an artificially intelligent Agent. The project explores conceptual notions of embodied knowledge transfer, shared poetics of movement and distortions of the body schema. Within this context, both the User and the Agent become performers, constructing an intimate and spontaneously generated proximal space. The project generates a visualization of the relationship between the User and the Agent without the context of a fixed VR landscape or architecture. The Agent's ability to retain and accumulate movement knowledge in a way that mimics human learning transforms an interactive experience into a collaborative one. The virtual representation of both performers is distorted and amplified in a dynamic manner, enhancing the potential for creative dialogue between the Agent and the User.

## Categories and Subject Descriptors

J.5 [**Computer Applications**]: Arts and Humanities – *performing arts, fine arts*

## General Terms

Experimentation, Human Factors, Design

## Keywords

Aesthetic Interaction; Agents and Intelligent Systems; Virtual Reality; Embodiment; Performance;

## 1. INTRODUCTION

*Duet* is an artistic experiment and prototype that offers a framework for questioning the nature of embodied perception and agency within a virtual reality (VR) environment. This research platform builds on experimental arts practices and methodologies.

*SUI '15,* August 08 - 09, 2015, Los Angeles, CA, USA
Copyright is held by the owner/author(s). Publication rights licensed to ACM.
978-1-4503-3703-8/15/08…$15.00
DOI: http://dx.doi.org/10.1145/2788940.2788952

Unlike a task-oriented collaborative user interface where directed action is of the upmost importance, *Duet's* design is specifically crafted to leave room for questioning and meditation on ideas of body, motion, cognition, and relationships between entities.

*Duet* explores the potential of a User to 'perform' with an artificially intelligent Agent and to shape the visualization of space in response both to the User's own avatar, and the avatar of the Agent (which is also present in the simulation). This kind of interactive artwork is designed to be witnessed from within the VR environment, as opposed to the User 'performing' movement for the benefit of an external audience. The Agent, which is a neural network that takes the form of an avatar in the VR environment, is able to respond to the movement of the User using acquired movement patterns, articulating an embodied metaphorical conversation between avatars.

One goal of this project is to encourage the transformation of the personal perspective of the human from that of a viewer to that of a collaborating performer. This requires a shift in the relationship between the User and the system, as well as a questioning of the boundaries of agency and definitions of identity within that shared system. In *Duet*, this is explored via two primary means: 1) the complexity of interaction with the intelligent Agent and 2) the interplay between the visual representations of the avatars.

The relationship between the Agent and the User is not merely interactive but is linked through the sharing of embodied knowledge and data that happens during the 'performance' as well as afterwards, as the Agent integrates the performative material it has observed into its neural network. Each new User becomes a source of knowledge to cannibalize, creating new and unforeseen artistic outcomes. Because the Agent is accumulating knowledge from multiple human performance partners over a long period of time, the Agent serves multiple purposes including: 1) the creation of an aesthetically pleasing performance as part of a movement dialogue with the User and 2) the garnering of new data from its human partner to augment its growing catalogue of movement knowledge with the aim of providing new and interesting points of inspiration to each successive User. For the User, recognition of the learning capacity of the Agent informs their live movement choices, but also raises questions about the potential and the limitations of enacting a concurrent presence in both physical and VR avatar bodies.

*Duet*, as a conceptual framework, presents a platform for artistic spatial user exploration, in which the interface itself and the interaction it fosters become the primary source for the artwork. There is no traditional overlay or emplacement of a graphical user interface in this scenario; rather, the responsive environment is fundamentally linked to the performance content in real-time. The tracked body in motion becomes the vector for direct interaction, and the layered distinctions between what is and what is not an interface disappear. This work acknowledges and integrates human embodiment, and retains the grounding of a body in multiple worlds, simultaneously.

*Duet* differs from most VR environments in that there are no directly imposed constructs (i.e. objects, clearly delineated environments or architecture, or defined volumes) or required actions (i.e. tasks, goals, games, or fixed triggering points). The very space itself is constructed by the User's movement, which offers the potential for an artwork that is generated from the way people naturally want to explore a new environment. The framework offered by *Duet* allows for the investigation of the nature of agency, as well as the connected and interactive movement choices that inform the overall experience. This approach focuses on interactions and reactions, offering an opportunity to visualize embodied knowledge in a VR scenario. This interplay between the Agent and the User touches on the use of space, our recognition of the relationships of bodies in VR, and understandings of our physical presence as individuals.

# 2. SETUP
## 2.1 Technical Configuration
*Duet* consists of a combined VR and motion capture system, where the visual display is an Oculus Rift DK1 and the motion capture device is a second generation Kinect [Fig.1]. The User's whole body gestures are captured via the Kinect and analyzed by the Agent's algorithms. In order to lessen latency and prevent jitter, the head tracking is enabled within the Oculus device, providing the reference point within the virtual environment for the position and orientation of the Users' camera viewport onto the scene. The computer graphics simulation is rendered in real-time running in the Unity game engine and sent to the Oculus Rift over DVI cable.

## 2.2 Physical Environment
The work is displayed in a modified installation gallery context, where the computing equipment is set up and an experienced attendant is present to guide the user orientation.

**Figure 1. Illustration of User experiencing *Duet* prototype**

## 2.3 Virtual Reality Experience
*Duet* uses a Natural User Interface, or NUI as defined by Blake [1], as a method of placing the User into the space of interactivity, not requiring any type of training with a device or orientation to other GUI representation that would distract from the direct connection and interaction with the Agent. Roupe et al [2] demonstrated that participants find this type of full body interactivity non-demanding and easy to use. This affords a level of directness and comfort in the User, who quickly understands that their movements are reflected in that of the avatar body they inhabit. This is then paired with a level of complexity in the rendering of the avatars, as well as the responsiveness of the Agent to the User. Both the User and the Agent have avatars in the VR space. The motion data points are based on the Kinect skeleton system. They are rendered with an aesthetic approach of preserving a traceable sense of the underlying skeleton structure, but with a degree of abstraction in the visual representation.

## 2.4 The User
When the User first puts on the Oculus Rift, they perceive a black, void-like environment that is initially occupied by only their own body avatar for reference. The human User has an avatar body that is realistic in terms of its basic skeletal, bipedal, humanoid, structural form, though not in its visual rendering. The User avatar corresponds to the positioning of the physical body, but is represented as a non-photo-realistic volume-based rendering of particles, solid enough to give the illusion of a continuous form. The experience of the User does not involve direct tactile or haptic feedback, but rather relies on avatar spatial colocation and high fidelity movement tracking to give the User a feeling of ownership over their avatar. The User is not instructed to perform any given task or action, but rather invited to engage in a fluid and expressive manner with the Agent in the VR space.

## 2.5 The Agent
The Agent is also present in *Duet's* VR space, and has an ethereal body of light streams and particles, similar in rendering to that of the User. In fact, the Agent avatar can even partially inhabit the same spaces as the body of the User.

The Agent is a learning, artificial neural network that uses movement data from humans to inform its own movement behaviors. It has been trained to understand a basic vocabulary of body gestures likely to occur in this setup. It will acquire and analyze new data between sessions, and continue to adapt accordingly, integrating new knowledge into its systems. The Agent can be symbolically interpreted as a kind of hybrid entity, having absorbed and processed the movements of previous performance partners, guided by a set of algorithmic instructions and the received data transmissions from the motion capture system.

The Agent employs a type of Artificial Neural Network (ANN) called a Self-Organizing Map (SOM), also referred to as a Kohonen Feature Map after Teuvo Kohonen who first described them. [3, 4] The SOM is trained for 1000 iterations using motion capture data comprising joint rotations and position of the body using a 24-camera Motion Analysis optical system. This creates a catalogue of clean data of full body postures over which a Synaptic Self-Organising Map (SOSM) is overlaid. As the User engages with the installation, their Kinect skeleton data is passed to the SOSM and the vectors contained in the best matching neuron are used to animate the Agent's avatar. As the postures in the SOSM contain relatively clean postures learnt from the motion capture data, Agent's responses tend to have recognizable and intact body form even when the Kinect skeleton is jittery due to tracking or orientation issues. The synaptic layer of the SOSM is able to create traces from one neuron to the next, effectively linking postures and enabling a facsimile of the movement generated in real time by the User. These links between neurons are accumulated, and are then available for use by the Agent in subsequent User engagements.

## 2.6 Temporal Structure

*Duet* proceeds in a loose narrative arc of four phases, designed to draw out the sensation in the User of being a kind of virtual 'parent.' As the experience evolves, dynamic movements result in the definition of the volume of the VR space, as well as contributing to the development of the corporeality of the agent. As the User moves, the User's avatar sheds particles, which are absorbed by the Agent. This sharing of particles is a metaphor for the feeding of movement data to the Agent.

**Phase 1: Orientation**. This phase introduces the User to their bodily representation within the VR simulation, giving the User time to 'recognize' their own avatar as a volume of coherent particles.

**Phase 2: Emergence.** As the User moves, particles are shed and are absorbed into the body of the Agent, who slowly gains a humanoid form in the space. The agent 'feeds' from the 'life force' of its performative partner (i.e. by gathering particles), the User, and begins to engage in the movement duet.

**Phase 3: Interplay**. The movement relationship between User and Agent becomes increasingly abstracted, with the Agent responding both to real-time motion data input, as well as an accumulated memory catalogue of movement data acquired from previous encounters. The response of the Agent is not perceptibly imitative in a strictly mimicking sense.

**Phase 4: Dissolution**. The avatar particles of User and Agent begin to wink out and disperse, finally leaving the volume that was previously occupied by the visual traces of spatial conversation with only a void, emphasizing the momentary nature of interaction and communication.

## 3. RELATED WORK

*Placeholder* by Benda Laurel, Rachel Strickland, et al is one of the earliest examples of a VR artwork that explored the role of the body and self-identity by giving the user an animal avatar with which to directly inhabit. [5] Until recently, however, most immersive HMD VR-based interactive artworks have not directly addressed the permutations of the User's body representation as a vector for exploration. This is due in large part to technological advances in tracking and the markedly increased access to real-time HMD display hardware.

McCormick et al have previously investigated collaborations between humans and AI agents, in which an expert dancer performed with a projected image (3D stereoscopic) of an artificially intelligent entity. [6, 7] In their series of live performances, the AI entity was trained to respond to the whole body gestures of the expert dancer, using motion capture as the means to absorb movement data, which was then performed live within the stage environment.

Unlike McCormick et al's works that took place in a dance theatre context, *Duet* employs an immersive VR environment, through which the User is also the sole audience member. *Duet* cuts out the 'middle man' (the expert dancer) and instead takes the originating source of its knowledge from movement inspiration

that can come from any User, trained as a dancer or not. It also conflates the role of the audience member with that of the human performer.

## 4. CONCEPTUAL GROUNDING

Burgess [8] has theorized that two systems are utilized to visually decode spatial relationships in human perception: 1) egocentric distance as defined by measuring from the viewer to objects within the space, and 2) allocentric distance where the viewer uses object-to-object context to build a spatial representation. [8] Given the theory that concepts of body schema and peripersonal space are actually emergent properties of a network of cognitive centers related to specific areas of the body [9], *Duet* explores the connections between these centers by intentionally shifting visualizations of bodily relationships. As shown in the work of Mohler [10], more accurate estimations of egocentric distance are made by users who are able to see an articulated and tracked representation of themselves in the VR environment. In *Duet*, a heightened sensation of space as a dialogue between themselves and the Agent is intentional, and the User is not provided with a reference point of a defined architecture or world-like environment. This consciously limits the User's capacity to map spatial relationships via allocentric means.

Morie asserts that the immersed VR user still possesses knowledge of simultaneous embodiment, being aware at some level of both the rendered simulation they currently appear to control and their own physical body still operating in the default reality. [5] This sense of having a 'bifurcated self' exists in parallel with the user's feeling of presence in the simulation. In *Duet*, the introduction of an Agent that draws directly on the User for movement data creates a kind of 'trifurcated self,' through which the presence of the User is extended across three entities at once: the User's physical body, the User's VR avatar, and the Agent. The addition of the third body presence into this scenario, the Agent, may function for the User at different levels of clarity and symbolic interpretation dependent on the mindset of the User, how long they have been interacting with the Agent, the ease with which the movements of the Agent body can be read, and other contextual factors.

In terms of the sense of presence experienced by the User, the typologies defined by Lee in 2004 [11] are useful to explicate *Duet's* artistic intentions. This project investigates the User's unfolding realization that they are interacting with what Lee describes as an 'Artificial Social Agent,' or an entity that reveals itself as present during the Emergence and Interplay sequences in *Duet* [11]. Additionally, *Duet* explores the liminal zone between the Para-authentic Self (a genuine representation of the self in the environment) and the Artificial Self (an entirely constructed representation of the self in the environment), given that the avatar body of the User is initially represented as having a high fidelity of movement and tracking and spatial co-location with the physical body [11]. This psychological attachment the User will experience to the User's avatar will be challenged as the work continues and the form of the User's avatar becomes increasingly fluid and abstract. Related to the sense of ownership over a virtual body, it has been demonstrated that the representation of the avatar self in immersive VR can have a significant cognitive and emotional impact if that body is altered [12] [13], distorted [14], or displaced [15].

This paper argues that part of the experience of *Duet* is the active exploration by the User of the nature of the artificial Agent, and their status as an object that may or may not have social importance and identity. Ianchini et al have shown that both peripersonal reaching space (as defined in neuro-cognitive research) and interpersonal spaces (as discussed in social psychology) are related to embodied perception and social modulation [16]. These factors include perceptions of danger, gender, and social importance or agency imbued to the object.

## 5. ARTISTIC EXPLORATION

*Duet* is motivated by a desire to concentrate the attention of the User on the spatial interactions and fluid interchange of embodied cognition and perception experienced with the Agent. A sense of what a discrete body can be in that space is challenged by the fluid interchange both of physical form and proximity, but also in the interchange of embodied knowledge. The Agent's neural network is formed from the moving bodies of the people it has danced with, and is therefore a sort of scavenger that draws from a catalogue of learned motions that it has accumulated from the humans who have attempted embodied communication with it.

*Duet* intentionally leaves interpretation open to the imagination of the User, thereby encouraging engagement and sense of play, wonder, and exploration. By removing certain contextual cues, this work provokes the User to focus on immediacy and improvisation. This allows for an individual exploration into the poetics of movement and movement visualizations.

Future developments include the addition of haptic feedback to allow physical responses to be made by the Agent and the environment, directed at the User. Wearable haptics will be investigated to provide a sense of touch to further enhance the available range of communication within the VR environment. Other future iterations might include the incorporation of multiple Kinects to provide more robust User tracking and stability.

## 6. CONCLUSIONS

Through its conceptual framework this project explores new metaphors for user interaction. It approaches this investigation using the creative synthesis of technical advances in engineering combined with knowledge of recent research in physical cognition, perception, and interaction paradigms in virtual scenarios. With its grounding in artistic practice, this project offers an investigation that seeks to engage with the cognitive and emotional systems of the User, asking the human participant to experientially explore ideas of spatial interaction, the nature of embodiment, and interpretations of artificial intelligence.

## 7. ACKNOWLEDGMENTS

Our thanks to Kim Vincs, Steph Hutchinson, and our colleagues at the Deakin Motion.Lab and the Center for Intelligent Systems Research at Deakin Universty.

## 8. REFERENCES

[1] Blake, J. Natural User Interfaces. In *.NET –WPF 4, surface 2, and Kinect.* Manning Publications.

[2] Roupé, M., Bosch-Sijtsema, P. and Johansson, M. Interactive navigation interface for Virtual Reality using the human body. *Computers, Environment and Urban Systems*, 43(1/1/January 2014 2014), 42-50.

[3] Kohonen, T. *Self-organization and associative memory*. Springer-Verlag, Berlin ; New York :, 1989.

[4] Kohonen, T. *Self-organizing maps*. Springer, Berlin ; New York :, 1997.

[5] Morie, J. F. Performing in (virtual) spaces: Embodiment and being in virtual environments. *International Journal of Performance Arts & Digital Media*, 3, (2/3 2007), 123-138

[6] McCormick, J., Vincs, K., Nahavandi, S. and Creighton, D. Learning to dance with a human. In *Proceedings of* (Sydney, Australia, 2013). ISEA International, Australian Network for Art & Technology, University of Sydney, Sydney, 2013.

[7] McCormick, J., Vincs, K., Nahavandi, S., Creighton, D. and Hutchison, S. Teaching a Digital Performing Agent: Artificial Neural Network and Hidden Markov Model for recognising and performing dance movement. In *Proceedings of the 2014 International Workshop on Movement and Computing* (Paris, France, 2014), ACM, Paris, 2014.

[8] Burgess, N. Spatial memory: how egocentric and allocentric combine, *Trends In Cognitive Sciences*, 12 2006), 551-558.

[9] Holmes, N. P., Spence, C., Giard, M.-H. and Wallace, M. The body schema and multisensory representation(s) of peripersonal space. *Cognitive Processing*, 5, 2 2004), 94-105.

[10] Mohler, B. J. b. m. t. m. d., Creem-Regehr, S. H., Thompson, W. B. and Bülthoff, H. H. The Effect of Viewing a Self-Avatar on Distance Judgments in an HMD-Based Virtual Environment. *Presence: Teleoperators & Virtual Environments*, 19, 3 (06// 2010), 230-242.

[11] Lee, K. M. Presence, Explicated. *Communication Theory (10503293)*, 14, 1 2004), 27-50.

[12] Kilteni, K., Bergstrom, I. and Slater, M. Drumming in Immersive Virtual Reality: The Body Shapes the Way We Play. *IEEE Transactions on Visualization & Computer Graphics*, 19, 4 (04// 2013), 597.

[13] Banakou, B. Groten, R, and Slater, M. Illusory ownership of a virtual child body causes overestimation of object sizes and implicit attitude changes. In *The Proceedings of the National Academy of Sciences*, 110, 31 (07/30/2013), 12846-51.

[14] Kilteni, K.N., Sanchez-Vives J. M., Slater, M. V. Extending body space in immersive virtual reality: A very long arm illusion. *PLoS ONE, 7, 7 (2012)*

[15] Lenggenhager, B.,Tadi, T., Metzinger, T., and Blanke, O. Video Ergo Sum: Manipulating Bodily Self-Consciousness. *Science*, 317, (24/07/2007) 1096-1099.

[16] Iachini, T., Coello, Y., Frassinetti, F. and Ruggiero, G. Body Space in Social Interactions: A Comparison of Reaching and Comfort Distance in Immersive Virtual Reality. *PLoS ONE*, 9, 11 2014), 1-7.

# Attracting User's Attention in Spherical Image by Angular Shift of Virtual Camera Direction

Ryohei Tanaka, Takuji Narumi, Tomohiro Tanikawa, and Michitaka Hirose

Graduate School of Information Science and Technology, The University of Tokyo,

Hongo 7-3-1, Bunkyo-ku, Tokyo 113-8656, Japan,

{r_tanaka, narumi, tani, hirose}@cyber.t.u-tokyo.ac.jp

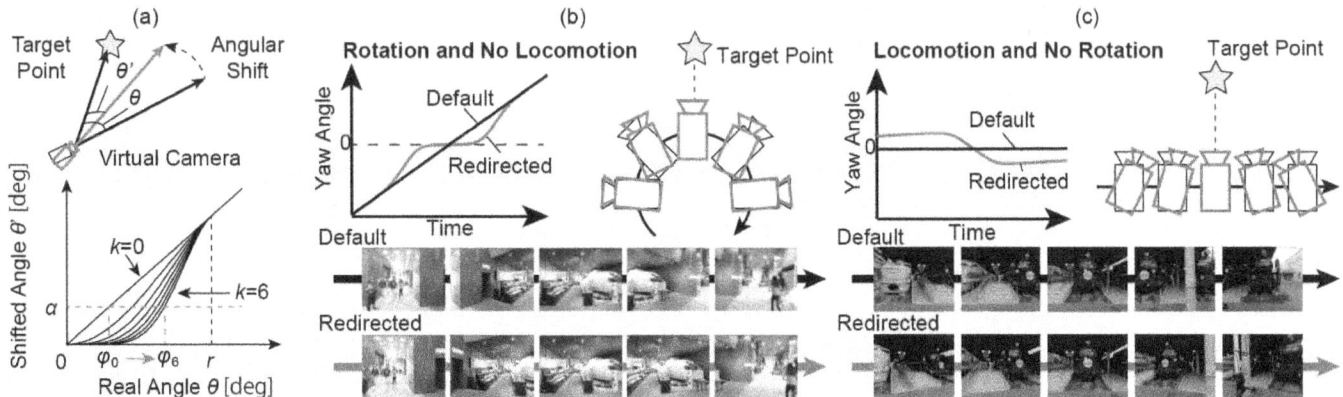

Figure 1. (a) Upper: Concept image of angular shift. Bottom: Relation between real angle and shifted angle. The larger k becomes, the steeper the curve becomes. (b) Redirected camera behavior when the virtual camera rotates in a spherical image. (c) Redirected camera behavior when the virtual camera position moves in the series of spherical images with the rotation fixed

## ABSTRACT

A spherical image can contain the whole information of the landscape, allowing users to look at the point they want to. However, most of the information in a spherical image is often unimportant to the photographer, and only several points in the image are important. If users can view the spherical image completely freely, they may be unable to determine what the photographer thinks is important, and may stop viewing it before they notice the important points in the image. Therefore, a methodology to induce users to look at a selected point in the spherical image while leaving the interactiveness that allows them to look around with their intention is needed. In this paper, we propose a method to induce users to look at a selected point in the spherical image by using an angular shift in the direction of the virtual camera. We introduce a method of a tablet application called "Window to the Past," which was set up as a real exhibition. After analyzing a massive amount of user data obtained from the application, we found that our method worked well for spherical image viewing. The total amount of time during which users looked at selected points was significantly lengthened without feeling interrupted. The result also suggests that the induction method is also effective to make users aware of virtual buttons on the image.

## Categories and Subject Descriptors: H.5.1 [Information Interfaces and Presentation]: Multimedia Information

Systems—artificial, augmented, and virtual realities; H.5.2 [Information Interfaces and Presentation]: User Interfaces—evaluation/methodology, style guides, theory and methods

## Keywords

Spatial User Interface; Spherical Image; Digital Museum.

## 1. INTRODUCTION

A spherical image, which is synthesized from images taken from one spot and from all perspectives, is being used more often because it can contain a larger amount of the information surrounding us than a normal image. Moreover, compared with the virtual spaces constructed by computer graphics, the virtual spaces constructed by spherical images are more realistic, immersive, and easy to construct [1][5]. Applications that use spherical images, such as Google Street View [4], have also become more popular. In those applications, users can interactively view where they want to look in the spherical image.

When a spherical image is taken to show a certain point such as an exhibit in a museum, one of the most important pieces of information is the region of the point. The remaining data in the image, such as corridors, lights, and pillars, are less important to the photographer. A concern is that users will stop viewing the image before they notice the important points. However, the less important regions should not be completely omitted because in the case of museums these regions are designed according to the entire space including lighting, room arrangements, and spatial postures. Therefore, a methodology to induce users to look at a selected point in a spherical image, while retaining the interactiveness that allows them to look around that image, is needed.

In this paper, we propose a method to induce users to look at a selected point in a spherical image by shifting the direction of their virtual camera (**Figure 1(a) Upper**). Since this method adds no information on the screen, occlusions do not occur and there is no need to modify the original images. With regard to museum archives and reliving, we seek to induce users to look at several exhibits. Therefore, we conducted a large-scale experiment to evaluate how our method works when it is used by a great number of people.

## 2. RELATED WORK

### 2.1 Visual Guidance

In a nonspherical image, some methods to enhance the attention of the selected region without occluding that region have been proposed. Parkhurst et al. showed using neuroscience that both luminance contrast and texture contrast contribute to the generation of visual salience and play a role in determining the allocation of overt visual attention [2]. Kim et al. induced the viewer's attention to a selected region of an image by changing the luminance around the region [3]. However, these two methods are not appropriate because the original color of the image is modified, which may interfere with the user correctly understanding the scene. Bailey et al. attracted viewer's attention by modulating a selected region of image when the region is in the viewer's peripheral vision so that the selected region is showed as the original when the region is in the viewer's foveal vision [7]. However, these methods are useless for a spherical image if the selected region does not appear in the visual field of the virtual camera.

### 2.2 Redirected Walking

Razzaque et al. adjusted subjects' virtual camera direction to direct them to a selected point in real world [8]. In their method, extra rotation proportional to the users' angular velocity is added to users' virtual camera direction. In other research, Steinicke et al. set rotation gain defined as the ratio of the virtual yaw angle to the real yaw angle and found that users couldn't tell the distortion if rotation gain is set in the proper range [9].

Our redirection method is close to those researches in the point of virtual camera adjustment. However, since our purpose is not inducing users to face a certain direction in real world but inducing users to look at a certain region in virtual world, we apply the different algorithms from the redirected walking.

## 3. REDIRECTION METHODOLOGY

### 3.1 Algorithms

Spherical image viewer applications have several user interfaces that rotate the virtual camera including the joystick, mouse drag, and buttons on the screen. In this research, the direction of the virtual camera direction is linked with the tablet device. Therefore, when the user moves the device in a specific direction, the virtual camera moves in the same direction. Interactive interfaces that involve physical motion have been reported as providing a deeper understanding of the geometric space and content [6]. The tablet device posture in the real world is obtained from the gyro and acceleration sensor in the device.

To induce the user to look at a selected point in the spherical image, the camera direction is shifted according to the following equations:

$$\begin{cases} \theta' = \theta \sin^k \frac{\pi\theta}{2r} & (if\ \theta < r) \\ \theta' = \theta & (if\ \theta \geq r) \end{cases} \quad (1)$$

In equation (1), $\theta$ represents the angle between the directional vector of the target point and that of virtual camera and $\theta'$ repre-

sents the shifted angle. $r$ is a value that determines the angular range where the angular shift occurs, $k$ is a constant value that determines the strength of the angular shift. In this paper, $k$ is defined as redirection power.

**Figure 1(a) Bottom** shows the relationship between $\theta$ and $\theta'$ when k = 1, 2, …, 6 and constant r = 100°. Once the shifted angle $\theta'$ is calculated, the camera direction is shifted to the direction whose angle to the target direction is the shifted angle, and on the plane defined by the original camera directional vector and the target directional vector. As you can see in **Figure 1(a)**, the difference between the real angle and the shifted angle in the virtual world becomes larger as k increases. **Figure 1(b)** shows an example of camera behavior when the user's camera rotates along the yaw angle in a spherical image.

### 3.2 Theory and Hypothesis

To judge whether the user is looking at the target point, we set a threshold angle $\alpha$. When the angle between the target direction and virtual camera direction is smaller than $\alpha$, then we determine that the user is looking at the target point. We measure how long users look at target points under different terms ($k = 0, 1, …, 6$) and compare the results. Since the threshold angle in the virtual world is fixed, the threshold angle in the real world shifts according to equation (1). In **Figure 1(a)**, the threshold angle of the real angle is $\varphi_0$ when $k = 0$, while the threshold shifts to $\varphi_6$ when $k = 6$. Now $\varphi_i$ is defined as the threshold of the real angle when the shifted angle is $\alpha$ when $k = i$. Since the camera is rotated three-dimensionally, yaw, pitch, and roll angles should be taken into consideration. However, since almost all of the users' rotations to look around the museum are considered to be along the yaw angle, we assume that the angular shift occurs only along the yaw angle for the sake of simplicity. In addition, assuming that the users look around the image without bias, the increased ratio of the amount of time users look at the target point when $k = 0$ to the time when $k = i$ equals the increased ratio of $\varphi_0$ to $\varphi_i$. In the experiment we conducted, $\alpha$ is set at 29.2°, which is two thirds of the screen size with a field of view set at 80°. **Table 1** shows $\varphi_k$ and $\varphi_k/\varphi_0$.

**Table 1. Theoretical value of $\varphi_k$ and $\varphi_k/\varphi_0$**

| $k$ | 0.0 | 1.0 | 2.0 | 3.0 | 4.0 | 5.0 | 6.0 |
|---|---|---|---|---|---|---|---|
| $\varphi_k$ [°] | 29.2 | 45.0 | 53.2 | 58.4 | 62.1 | 65.0 | 67.2 |
| $\varphi_k/\varphi_0$ | 1.00 | 1.54 | 1.82 | 2.00 | 2.13 | 2.22 | 2.30 |

## 4. SPHERICAL IMAGE VIEWER

For a spherical image viewer, we developed an application named "Window to the Past," which depicts a virtual museum space reconstructed with a large sequence of spherical images. The application uses images of the Modern Transportation Museum in Osaka in an area of 10,000 m². The exhibit closed in April 2014. We archived the museum as 7,000 spherical images and developed a walk-through system by properly arranging the images. The distance between two adjacent archive points of the images is approximately 0.15 m, and the maximum walk speed is set at 2.0 m/s. Thus, approximately 12 spherical images are seamlessly shown in 1 s.

In this system, the virtual camera is rotated according to the tablet's posture, as suggested in **Section 3.1**. The locomotion of the viewpoint is operated by a virtual pad on the screen. Users slide the pad in the direction they want to walk.

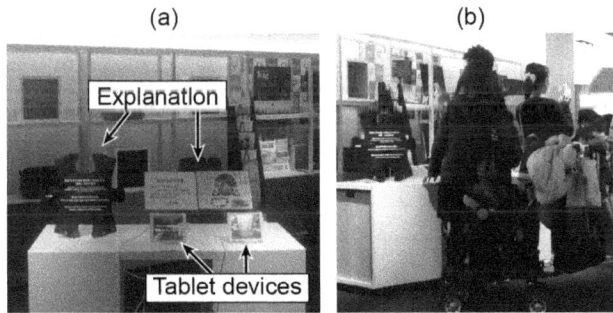

Figure 2. (a) Overview of the exhibit. (b) Scene of the experiment

In this research, we selected 25 exhibits as the targets that should attract attention. We selected these 25 targets because they are introduced in the museum website, and the curators consider these targets more important than other exhibits in the museum.

We set interactive buttons for each target exhibits. The button is displayed on the screen as if it is floating on the target exhibits. If users click them, a detailed explanation of the target exhibits appears, which deepens the users' understanding of the exhibits.

By allowing seamless locomotion through the sequences of the images, another interesting behavior resulting from the angular shift occurs. When a user walks near the target position in the virtual world with a fixed real angle, the virtual camera angle shifts to the target point, or the motion rotates around the point where the camera is directed (**Figure 1(c)**).

## 5. EXPERIMENT IN REAL EXHIBITION

To evaluate our method, we conducted a large-scale experiment in a real exhibition at KNOWLEDGE CAPITAL The Lab. **Figure 2** shows an overview of this exhibit and the scene of the experiment. Two iPad Airs act as the tablet devices, and a simple explanation of the Modern Transportation Museum and how to use the application are placed as shown in the figure. The subjects are people who came to the exhibition and experienced the "Window to the Past" during the 38 days of the experiment. The age groups of the visitors vary from children to seniors. They did not know about the purpose of this experiment and regarded it as a normal exhibit, so they used the application to their hearts' content.

To measure the differences in the redirection power, the application's parameter of redirection power is changed from 0 to 6 every five or six days. During their experience, the real tablet posture, the virtual camera posture, their location in virtual world and the types of clicked interactive buttons were logged. Since the buttons are showed under every redirection power condition, virtual buttons on the targets never affect on the results.

After their experience, subjects are asked to answer a questionnaire. It says, "Could you answer a questionnaire? Your answer are used to improve the system and for the sake of our research." Subjects can choose whether answer or not. In the questionnaire, subjects answer questions such as, "Did you look around along the way?" by a continuous value between 0 and 1, where 0 means "Not at all" and 1 means "Very strongly."

These experiences are passed the ethical check conducted by the research ethics committee of The University of Tokyo.

## 6. RESULT AND DISCUSSION

The total number of the subjects was 4235. **Table 2** shows the number of subjects and the number of answers to the questionnaire under each redirection power. In this table, *k*, *Sub Num*, and

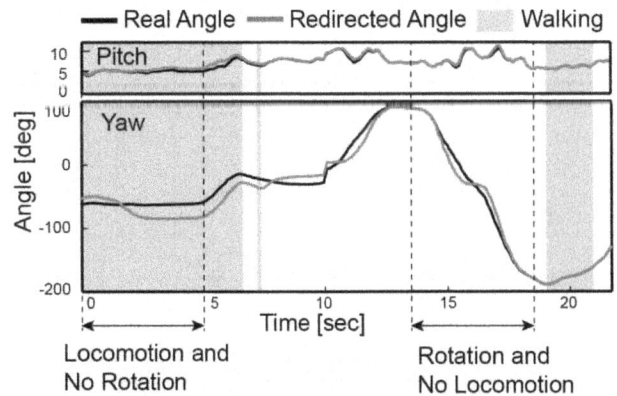

Figure 3. Example of subject's experience data and the behavior patterns

Table 2. Number of the subjects and number of the answers of the questionnaire

| k | 0 | 1 | 2 | 3 | 4 | 5 | 6 |
|---|---|---|---|---|---|---|---|
| Sub Num | 645 | 749 | 321 | 377 | 761 | 456 | 926 |
| Ans Num | 30 | 40 | 24 | 30 | 36 | 21 | 50 |

*Ans Num* represent redirection power, the number of the subjects, and the number of answers to the questionnaire, respectively.

**Figure 3** shows an example of the subject's rotation data experienced when the redirection power is 2. The black and red lines represent the real angle of the tablet device and the virtual camera angle, respectively. The gray area indicates the period when the subject is walking in the virtual world. Between 13 and 19 s, as shown in **Figure 1(b)**, the subject rotated the device constantly along the yaw angle without locomotion, and the virtual camera was redirected to -40°. Between 0 and 5 s, as shown in **Figure 1(c)**, the subject walked through the successive spherical images without rotating, and the virtual camera was redirected to the target exhibition.

Regarding differences in redirection power, it is shown that the larger the redirection power, the longer the viewing time. **Figure 4** shows a box plot of time during which subjects looked at the target point. This plot does not show outliers. The red line represents the median of the data. By using the Mann-Whitney U test, the time of redirection power 0 is significantly lower than that of all other redirection power settings ($p < 10^{-5} \ll 0.01$).

The black points in the **Figure 4** represent theoretical increases compared with the time of a redirection power of 0, which is calculated in **Table 1**. To validate the assumption that the angle shift occurs only along the yaw angle, we compare the sum of the differences between the real yaw angle and the shifted yaw angle and that of the pitch angle. The value represents how much the redirection effects on user's rotation along the yaw or pitch angle. Analyzing all rotation data with the angular shift, the rate of the summed differences in pitch to that of the yaw is calculated to be 10.2%. Judging from the result, the assumption is considered to be valid. The ratio of the experimentally gained median time to the theoretically calculated time is 0.93, 1.09, 1.06, 1.11, 1.12 or 1.10 when the redirection power is 1, 2, 3, 4, 5 or 6 respectively. Remarkably, the time during which subjects looked at the targets is more increased than theoretical value when the redirection power is 2, 3, 4, 5 or 6. This slight increase may result from the fact that with the angular shift, the subjects have more chances to be aware of the targets. Once the subjects become aware of the

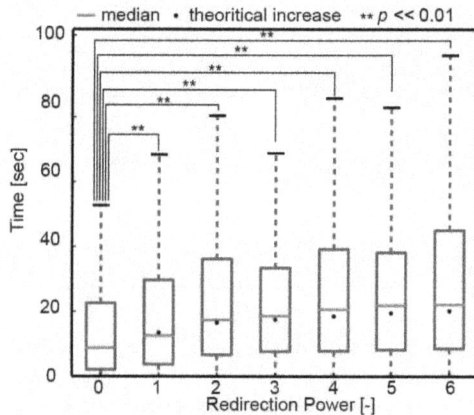

Figure 4. Box plot of the amount of the time during which subjects looked at the targets

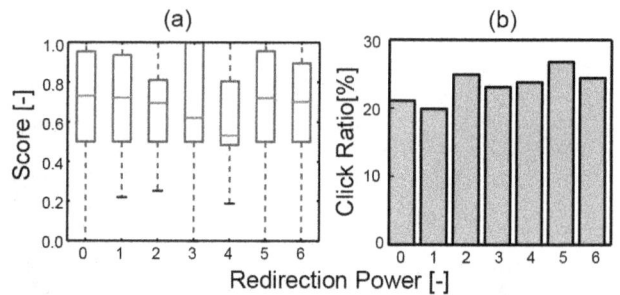

Figure 5. (a) Results of questionnaire asking, "Did you look around along the way?" (b) Rate of the number of subjects who clicked the interactive button at least once to the number of all subjects.

target because of the angular shift, they may become interested in it and feel like looking at it for a longer time.

However, we are concerned that the angular shift causes cybersickness or interrupts arbitrary exploration. In terms of cybersickness, we carefully observed if subjects got sick during the experiment and finally, no subjects got sick. **Figure 5(a)** shows the results for the question, "Did you look around along the way?" Interestingly, significant differences did not exist among any pairs of the redirection powers. This result indicates that even when there is a strong angular shift, users feel no interruptions and can look around the virtual world with the same feeling of freedom. These results, including cybersickness, may change with a more immersive interface such as a head-mounted display or a less immersive interface such as a mouse drag or touch swipe.

An additional positive effect is recorded in the data. **Figure 5(b)** shows the rate of the number of the subjects who clicked the interactive buttons at least once to that of all subjects. From the experimental data, the click rate is only 21.1% without any angular shift. When the redirection power is 2, 3, 4, 5, or 6, the rate increases to more than 23%. This may occur because the time the button is displayed becomes longer according to the time in which the subject looks at the target point. In other words, this method may be effective to make users aware of an interactive object in a virtual space.

## 7. CONCLUSION AND FUTURE WORK

In this paper, we proposed a method to induce users to look at a selected point in virtual space during uninterrupted viewing by shifting the virtual angular direction. From the results of the experiment conducted in a real exhibition, the amount of time during which subjects looked at the targets became significantly longer compared to the time without an angular shift ($p \ll 0.01$). Remarkably, since the time was longer than theoretically estimated value in some redirection power, it is considered that more users get interested in the exhibits by the redirection. Furthermore, the results of the questionnaire suggested that this redirection method does not interrupt the subject's viewing and is effective in making subjects aware of an interactive object in virtual space.

For future work, our method must be useful for watching a live broadcasting with spherical movies. For AR applications, it is possible to redirect user's camera to AR marker objects by using wide-angle cameras instead of spherical cameras in the same way as the digital image stabilization.

## 8. ACKNOWAGEMENT

This work was partially supported by the MEXT, Grant-in-Aid for Scientific Research (A), 25249957. The authors would like to thank West Japan Railway Company and KNOWLEDGE CAPITAL association.

## 9. REFERENCES

[1] Chen, Shenchang Eric. 1995. Quicktime VR: An image-based approach to virtual environment navigation. *Proceedings of the 22nd annual conference on Computer graphics and interactive techniques. ACM,* 1995.

[2] Parkhurst, Derrick J., and Ernst Niebur. 2004. Texture contrast attracts overt visual attention in natural scenes. *European Journal of Neuroscience 19.3 (2004): 783-789.*

[3] Kim Youngmin, and Amitabh Varshney. 2006. Saliency-guided enhancement for volume visualization. *Visualization and Computer Graphics, IEEE Transactions on 12.5 (2006): 925-932.*

[4] Goolge Street View. https://www.google.com/maps/views/u/0/streetview?gl=jp

[5] Takaaki Endo, et al. 1998. Image-Based Walk-Through System for Large-Scale Scenes, *Proceedings of 4th International Conference on Virtual Systems and Multimedia (VSMM'98), Vol.1, pp.269-274, Gifu (Japan).*

[6] Jun Imura, et al. 2014. Reliving Past Scene Experience System by Inducing a Video-camera Operator's Motion with Overlaying a Video-sequence onto Real Environment, *ITE Transactions on Media Technology and Applications (MTA), Vol.2, No.3, pp.225-235.*

[7] Bailey, R., et al. 2009. Subtle gaze direction. *ACM Trans. Graph.* 28, 4, Article 100 (August 2009), 14 pages.

[8] Razzaque, S. et al. 2001, September. Redirected walking. *In Proceedings of EUROGRAPHICS (Vol. 9, pp. 105-106).*

[9] Steinicke, F., et al. 2010. Estimation of detection thresholds for redirected walking techniques. *Visualization and Computer Graphics, IEEE Transactions on, 16(1), 17-27.*

[10] Nescher, T., et al. 2014, March. Planning redirection techniques for optimal free walking experience using model predictive control. *In 3D User Interfaces (3DUI), 2014 IEEE Symposium on (pp. 111-118). IEEE.*

# Spatial Constancy of Surface-Embedded Layouts across Multiple Environments

Barrett Ens[1], Eyal Ofek[2], Neil Bruce[1], Pourang Irani[1]

[1]University of Manitoba
Winnipeg, Canada
{bens, bruce, irani}@cs.manitoba.ca

[2]Microsoft Research
Redmond, WA
eyalofek@microsoft.com

Figure 1. Transitions of application window layouts to world-fixed coordinates are derived from a common body-centric layout (a). This approach maintains relative spatial consistency while integrating application layouts into diverse surroundings (b, c). © B. Ens

## ABSTRACT

We introduce a layout manager that exploits the robust sensing capabilities of next-generation head-worn displays by embedding virtual application windows in the user's surroundings. With the aim of allowing users to find applications quickly, our approach leverages spatial memory of a known body-centric configuration. The layout manager balances multiple constraints to keep layouts consistent across environments while observing geometric and visual features specific to each locale. We compare various constraint weighting schemas and discuss outcomes of this approach applied to models of two test environments.

**Author Keywords**
Head-worn displays; HWD; HMD; window manager; view management; spatial constancy; visual saliency.

**ACM Classification Keywords**
H.5.3 [Information interfaces and presentation]: User interfaces

## INTRODUCTION

A new generation of head-worn displays (HWDs) is rapidly advancing, and lightweight form factors such as Microsoft Hololens are capable of reliably detecting the wearer's surroundings in real time. This spatial information can be leveraged to integrate personal information displays into the

*SUI '15*, August 08 - 09, 2015, Los Angeles, CA, USA
© 2015 ACM. ISBN 978-1-4503-3703-8/15/08…$15.00
DOI: http://dx.doi.org/10.1145/2788940.2788954

environment to support analytic tasks that rely on multiple sources of information [3, 6, 7]. However, the ideal placement remains an open research question; although much work has explored configurations in display space, little attention has been given to content layout on the surface structure of a sensed 3D model of the environment.

This paper explores the transition of window layouts from body-centric to world-based reference frames [6]. For example, imagine a mobile HWD content manager that arranges your favourite apps in a body-centric 'bubble'. When you arrive at your home or office, you can 'pin' this window layout onto the surrounding surfaces (Figure 1). Some key requirements we apply to such transitions are 1) to integrate content with existing surface structure, 2) to maintain the spatial relationship of windows so the user can locate apps quickly, and 3) to prevent app windows from occluding important objects in the environment.

We propose using the device wearer's egocentric coordinate system as a reference frame for world-fixed spatial layouts. This approach serves the dual purpose of leveraging reliance on body-centric spatial memory and maintaining consistency between different environments. However, layouts must also respect geometric differences between different spaces, for instance to avoid overlapping surface boundaries or occluding scene objects. We developed a layout manager that balances multiple constraints, including spatial constancy, visual salience, surface fit, window overlap and relative order.

## RELATED WORK

A line of work following Bell et al. [2] on view management for augmented reality uses constraint-based algorithms for managing virtual content, typically to keep object labels from overlapping and close to their point of origin. Constraints are often combined using force-based algorithms [10], however a greedy approach has been noted to increase dynamic layout stability [9]. We instead apply a random walk approach [8, 14] that observes global layout constraints. Although some recent work has used vanishing line detection to align virtual content with real-world surfaces [13], view management generally occurs in 2D display space or on a set of view-aligned planes [21]. In contrast, we are interested in 3D˙ spatial layouts and draw from early work by Feiner et al. [7] and Billinghurst et al. [3] that imagined multiple windows arranged in body-centric configurations or anchored to world objects.

We follow a use case similar to the Office of the Future [16], in which applications are embedded on walls and other surfaces in the environment. Thus our work overlaps with research on projection-based systems that can detect and adapt to the surrounding 3D structure [5, 15, 17]. One closely-related work [22] describes a multi-projector window-manager that maximizes available projection space, but does not address background saliency. Following the vision of such works on a HWD platform presents specific challenges, in particular the limited field of view (FoV) of current displays [6]. To help mitigate this issue, we aim to leverage spatial memory [1, 17] by applying a constraint of spatial constancy [18, 20], which has received little attention in the context of spatial user interfaces.

# A LAYOUT MANAGER FOR SPATIAL CONSTANCY

We created a layout manager for see-through, stereoscopic HWDs that embeds virtual 2D application windows in a 3D environment. Using a sensor-generated model, layouts are created at run time based on the current pose (i.e. position and orientation) of the user. Each generated layout balances several constraints (described below) to arrive at a given layout. The main goals of the layout manager are threefold:

1) *Conform to surface structure* – Virtual app windows are superimposed on real-world surfaces, observing attributes such as surface boundaries and occluding objects.

2) *Maintain layout consistency* – We apply a spatial constancy constraint to maintain window positions relative to the user. Additional constraints try to maintain relative order and prevent overlap [2, 9, 21].

3) *Preserve background information* – Window positions are adjusted to prevent interference with important scene content. While there are many possible attributes to observe (e.g. colour, texture, contrast, object edges [9]), we focus on visual salience [9], which models human visual importance.

## Implementation

We implemented our layout manager using Unity3D on a desktop computer with an NVIDIA Quadro 600 GPU. We created two mock environments for development and testing, resembling a typical office and living room (Figure 2a, b). Layouts are viewed through an Epson BT-100 stereoscopic HWD with 23° diagonal FoV, tethered by composite video

input. By tracking the HWD with a Vicon system, virtual content appears through the HWD to be accurately superimposed on the physical environments.

## Algorithm

Our layout manager follows a Monte Carlo approach [11] shown to be effective for creating constraint-bases layouts in 3D space [8, 14]. Input consists of data extracted form a mesh model and a single photo of each environment. The mesh models (Figure 2g, h) are created with Kinect Fusion [12] and the photos (Figure 2a, b) are taken with a typical SLR camera with a wide-angle lens (110°). We begin by searching the vertices of the mesh models for regions of uniform surface normal, from which we extract a set of surface polygons (Figure 2c,d) using a greedy search with Hough transforms [19]. Meanwhile, we compute a saliency map of both scenes using the AIM saliency algorithm of Bruce and Tsotsos [4] (Figure 2e, f). We chose this saliency method from many available options because of the high contrast and preserved boundary regions in the saliency map. Finally, we calibrate the model with image space (Figure 2g, h) to allow saliency queries of 3D model points.

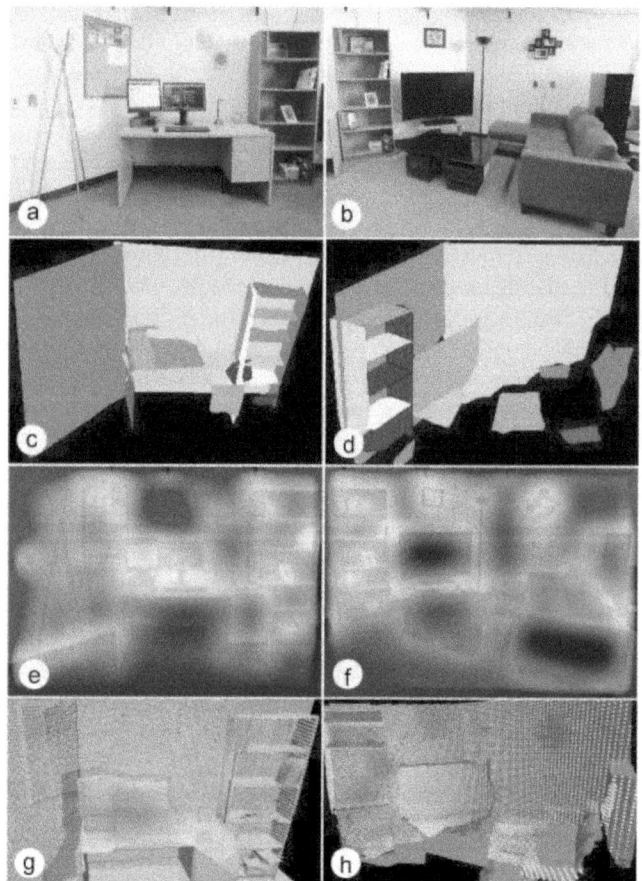

Figure 2. Office (a) and living room test environments (b). Surface polygons (c, d) generated from the mesh models (g, h). Saliency maps using AIM [4] (light regions are high salience, contrast increased for demonstration; e, f). Saliency maps projected on mesh models (red nodes are high salience; g, h).

The layout solution space is a set of all possible assignments of a set of application windows $W$ to unique points in a discretized set $P_E$. We define a 'goodness' function **$Goodness(L) := \sum_i \alpha_i \cdot r_i(L_i)$** where $\alpha_i$ is an optional weight, $r_i: (Oi \subseteq O) \to \mathbb{R}$ is a constraint operating on the parameters $O$, $L$ is a proposed layout solution, and $L_i$ is a layout subset containing windows with constraints $O_i$.

The algorithm iteratively evaluates the goodness function on layouts of randomly positioned windows. Layouts are confined to a region 90° wide × 45° high, centered on the forward view, discretized into points at increments of 5°. Windows are resized to maintain apparent angular width. We update the solution if improvement is found or with probability $p < 0.005$. This factor allows the algorithm to escape local maxima to find better solutions. We run 2000 iterations of this algorithm to generate an initial solution, then an additional 500 iterations for a 'fine-tuning' phase, where the pool of positions for each window is restricted to within 0.2m of the previous iteration. The primary phase finds a 'good' layout from the whole available space and the fine-tuning phase optimizes that layout within the local maxima. Mean run-time of the procedure is 3.26 s.

Our current implementation uses the following constraints:

*Adherence* enforces spatial constancy by minimizing the angular distance of a window's location from its default body-centric position (Figure 3a). The score is calculated as $1 - d^2$, where $d$ *is* the absolute angular displacement normalized by a maximum angle of 30°.

*Nonocclusion* uses visual saliency to minimize the occlusion of important scene objects. The score $1 - s^4$, where $s$ is the salience of the occupied region normalized by the scene's maximal salience value. High scores are given to windows in regions with low salience.

We apply several local window constraints: *View Direction* (to align windows closely to the user's forward view), *Surface Fit* (whether a window lies fully in a polygon), and *Line-of-Sight* (window corners are unoccluded). Additional global layout constraints are *Relative Order* of windows (whether windows maintain their spatial relations e.g. left-of), and *Overlap* (whether windows overlap others).

## DISCUSSION
In preliminary trials we found the nondeterministic algorithm to be relatively consistent. However the number of iterations

can be increased to improve consistency between trials or decreased to reduce run time. One advantage of our approach is that a finer discretization of space will have negligible effect on run time, whereas greedy search [9] complexity would increase with $P_E$.

Figure 3 shows outputs of our layout algorithm with the constraint weighting schemas defined in Table 1, which vary the balance of *Adherence* and *Nonocclusion*. The Balanced schema (Figure 3b) is ideally tuned to balance these contrasting factors in our test environments. Through trial and error, we found that the *Nonocclusion* constraint requires a higher weight than *Adherence* to prevent windows from often overlapping high salience regions, such as the area surrounding the desktop monitors in the office setting (Figure 2g). The Constancy schema (Figure 3c) has a *Nonocclusion* weight of zero. This theoretically causes each window to be projected onto the nearest surface in line with its default position (similar to Figure 1a), however the other constraints cause some deviation. Conversely, the Saliency schema (Figure 3d) has an *Adherence* weight of zero. This causes windows to congregate in low salience basins of the environment's saliency map, regardless of their distance from the default location. We provide the *View-direction* constraint in place of *Adherence* to help prevent windows from moving to extreme distances from the user's forward view.

## LIMITATIONS AND FUTURE WORK
In this work we use a body-centric reference frame for allowing windows to be found quickly given a limited FoV. However, there are other possible interpretations of spatial constancy, for instance placement of objects relative to semantically meaningful objects. We also note that applying a body-centric layout on a world-fixed frame assumes a 'primary' user pose within the room. There are many cases where this holds true, for instance in a typical office or in one's favourite cozy chair. Many interesting research questions are presented with more complex situations. For instance, how should a layout behave if a user frequently rotates between two different orientations? In future, we plan

| Layout | Adherence | Nonocclusion | View-direction |
|---|---|---|---|
| **Balanced** | 1 | 2 | 0 |
| **Constancy** | 1 | 0 | 0 |
| **Saliency** | 0 | 2 | 1 |

**Table 1. Three possible constraint weighting schemas promoting different mixtures of spatial constancy and visual saliency. All other weights are set to their default value of 1.**

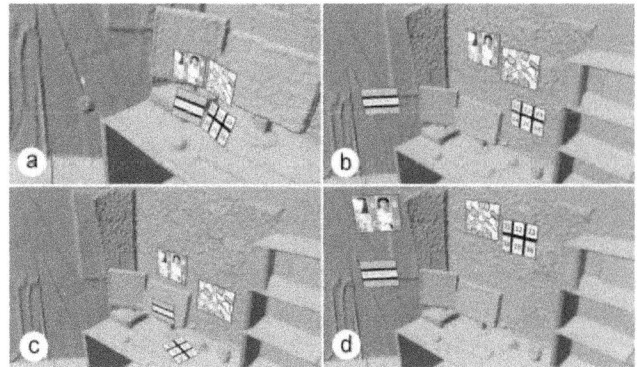

**Figure 3. a) Default window locations set in 'floating' array 50 cm from viewing position (green sphere). Results of weighting schemas b) Balanced, c) Constancy, and d) Saliency.**

to explore the benefits and trade-offs of body-centric vs world-based approaches to spatial constancy and combine these in a single layout manager.

Dynamic environments pose additional questions, for instance whether users would prefer windows to dynamically change position when someone enters the room, or to be temporarily occluded. Planned improvements include real-time extraction of the environment model and layout optimization, for instance by eliminating the mesh model or cropping to reduce raycasting operations used to detect occluded surface regions. This will allow us to explore additional design challenges, such as predicting and reacting to stimuli from people or other moving objects in the environment.

## CONCLUSION

We introduce a HWD layout manager that integrates applications into the built environment. Our implementation focuses on providing spatial constancy for consistency between environments while observing local features such as surface structure and visual saliency. We apply these and some additional constraints on window layouts in two test environments with varying visual information density.

## ACKNOWLEDGMENTS

We thank NSERC for funding this project.

## REFERENCES

[1] Agarawala, A. and Balakrishnan, R. Keepin' it real: Pushing the desktop metaphor with physics, piles and the pen. Proc. *CHI '06*, ACM (2006), 1283-1292.

[2] Bell, B., Feiner, S. and Höllerer, T. View management for virtual and augmented reality. Proc. *UIST '01*, ACM (2001), 101-110.

[3] Billinghurst, M., Bowskill, J., Jessop, M. and Morphett, J. A wearable spatial conferencing space. Proc. *ISWC '98*, IEEE (1998), 76-83.

[4] Bruce, N. and Tsotsos, J. Saliency based on information maximization. Proc. *NIPS '05* (2005), 155, 162.

[5] Cao, X. and Balakrishnan, R. Interacting with dynamically defined information spaces using a handheld projector and a pen. Proc. *UIST '06*, ACM (2006), 225-234.

[6] Ens, B., Finnegan, R. and Irani, P. The Personal Cockpit: A spatial interface for effective task switching on head-worn displays. Proc. *CHI '14*, ACM (2014), 3171-3180.

[7] Feiner, S. MacIntyre, B., Haupt, M. and Solomon, E. Windows on the world: 2D windows for 3D augmented reality. Proc. *UIST '93*, ACM (1993), 145-155.

[8] Gal, R., Shapira, L. Ofek, E., and Kohli, P., FLARE: Fast Layout for Augmented Reality Applications, Proc. *ISMAR '14*, ACM (2014), 207-212.

[9] Grasset, R., Langlotz, T., Kalkofen, D., Tatzgern, M. and Schmalstieg, D. 2012. Image-driven view management for augmented reality browsers. Proc. *ISMAR '12*, IEEE (2012), 177-186.

[10] Hartmann, K., Ali, K. and Strothotte, T. Floating labels: Applying dynamic potential fields for label layout. In *Smart Graphics*, Butz, A., Krüger, A. and Oliver, P. (eds.). Springer, 101-113.

[11] Hastings, W. K., Monte Carlo sampling methods using markov chains and their applications. *Biometrika* 57, 1 (1970), 97-109.

[12] Izadi, S., Kim, D., Hilliges, O., Molyneaux, D., Newcombe, R., Kohli, P., Shotton, J., Hodges, S., Freeman, D., Davison, A., and Fitzgibbon, A. KinectFusion: Real-time 3D reconstruction and interaction using a moving depth camera. Proc. *UIST '11*, ACM (2011), 559-568.

[13] Lee, W., Park, Y., Lepetit, V. and Woo, W. Video-based in situ tagging on mobile phones. *TCSVT 21*, 10, IEEE (2011), 1487-1496.

[14] Merrell, P., Schkufza, E.,Li, Z., Agrawala, M., and Koltun, V. Interactive furniture layout using interior design guidelines. *TOG 30*, 4, ACM (2011).

[15] Raskar, R., van Baar, J., Beardsley, P., Willwacher, T., Rao, S. and Forlines, C. iLamps: Geometrically aware and self-configuring projectors. Proc. *SIGGRAPH '03*, ACM (2003), 809-818.

[16] Raskar, R., Welch, G., Cutts, M., Lake, A., Stesin, L. and Fuchs, H. The office of the future: A unified approach to image-based modelling and spatially immersive displays. Proc. *SIGGRAPH '98*, ACM (1998), 179-188.

[17] Rekimoto, J. and Saitoh, M. Augmented surfaces: A spatially continuous work space for hybrid computing environments. Proc. *CHI '99*, ACM (1999), 378-385.

[18] Scarr, J., Cockburn, A., Gutwin, C. and Bunt, A. Improving command selection with CommandMaps. Proc. *CHI '12*, ACM (2012), 257-266.

[19] Silberman, N., Shapira, L., Gal, R. and Kohli, P. A contour completion model for augmenting surface reconstructions. Proc. *ECCV '14*, ACM (2014), 488-503.

[20] Tak, S., Cockburn, A., Humm, K., Ahlström, D., Gutwin, G. and Scarr, J. Improving window switching interfaces. Proc. *INTERACT '09*, Springer (2009), 187-200.

[21] Tatzgern, M., Kalkofen, D., Grasset, R. and Schmalstieg, D. Hedgehog labeling: View management techniques for external labels in 3D space. Proc. *VR '14*, IEEE, 27-32.

[22] Waldner, M., Grasset, R., Steinberger, M. and Schmalstieg, D. Display adaptive window management for irregular surfaces. Proc. *ITS '11*, ACM (2011), 222-231.

# Design and Evaluation of an "Around the SmartPhone" Technique for 3D Manipulations on Distant Display

Louis-Pierre Bergé, Emmanuel Dubois, Mathieu Raynal
IRIT – University of Toulouse
118 Route de Narbonne, 31062 Toulouse
{Louis-Pierre.Berge, Mathieu. Raynal, Emmanuel.Dubois}@irit.fr

## ABSTRACT
In this paper, we present the "Around the SmartPhone" interaction technique for manipulating 3D elements displayed on a distant screen. The design of the technique is based on the selection of the most appropriate value for characteristics useful to discriminate existing tactile and tangible techniques for 3D manipulations. We perform two user studies to compare this around-device technique for translating and rotating 3D objects, with two existing tangible and tactile solutions, in terms of performance and user's preference. The literature establishes that the tactile technique evaluated is the best tactile technique among the existing tactile techniques for 3D manipulation. Despite this result, our user study reveals that the two others perform significantly better. In addition, when feedback visibility is preserved, the around-device technique offers similar performance results than the tangible one. Finally, the around-device technique is significantly preferred over the two others in every condition.

## Categories and Subject Descriptors
H.5.2. [**Information interfaces and presentation**]: User Interfaces.

## General Terms
Design, Experimentation.

## Keywords
3D interaction; manipulation task; around-device interaction.

## 1. INTRODUCTION
Using 3D content in interactive environment is becoming more and more frequent. 3D interactive virtual environments (3DVE) tend to get out of the sole hands of 3D experts using dedicated devices [11]. Indeed 3DVE can now be found in many private activities such as on web sites to assist house furniture selection [23], in daily mobile contexts [25] and to play public 3D games [41]; in professional contexts to visualize scientific 3D data [38], to explore 3D data during meetings [16] or to create and edit 3D model [2]; and even in museums [29].

Using a smartphone for supporting the interaction with 3DVE in such everyday life situations presents many potential benefits: providing a multi-sensor remote interaction control thus avoiding occlusion; exploiting a personal and familiar device; displaying additional feedback on the smartphone screen. The use of

*SUI 2015*, August 8-9, 2015, Los Angeles, California, USA.
Copyright 2015 © ACM 978-1-4503-3703-8/15/08…$15.00.
DOI: http://dx.doi.org/10.1145/2788940.2788941

smartphone to interact with 3D content on distant display has already been considered for example to manipulate a slice plane [38], to navigate, select or manipulate a 3D object [5, 21, 23]. Combinations of finger movements [39], device orientations [23] and gesture around the device [21] represent many alternatives for implementing smartphone-based techniques for 3D interaction.

Among these works, less attention has been paid to the combined use of around-device techniques, based on a smartphone, with a 3D scene displayed on a distant screen. And yet, "around the smartphone" interaction techniques have already been successfully explored in other settings [17, 20]. The goal of our work is thus to design, implement and evaluate a new interaction technique involving gestures around a smartphone to manipulate a 3D object displayed on a distant screen.

We first review existing smartphone-based interaction techniques with 3D environments displayed on the smartphone and on distant screens. Secondly, we describe a tangible and a tactile smartphone-based interaction technique to manipulate 3D objects: each one is representative of one of these two classes of existing interaction techniques based on a smartphone in such 3D task. We then describe four characteristics related to the specificities of the context and through which exiting tactile and tangible techniques can be analyzed and discriminated. Based on these characteristics, we design a new technique, "Around the SmartPhone" (ASP), which involves hand gestures around the smartphone to manipulate 3D elements displayed on a distant screen. A first user study with training session and a complementary user study ensuring a more realistic use of the smartphone, compare the three techniques in terms of performance, usability and user's preference. Results reveal that our around-device technique (ASP) performs far better than the tactile solution (OSP). Moreover, ASP technique offers equivalent performance than the tangible solution (WSP). In addition, ASP is largely identified as the preferred technique among the three considered.

## 2. RELATED WORK
Many interaction techniques exist in virtual reality (VR) to support 3D manipulations (i.e. 3D elements translations and rotations), such as World-in-Miniature, Virtual Hand or Go-Go techniques [6]. More advanced forms of interaction include tangible interfaces such as the Hinckley's puppet [14] and the Cubic Mouse [10]. In this section, we specifically focus on other advanced interaction techniques in which smartphones have been involved to manipulate 3D objects.

Given the growing computing capabilities of smartphones, 3D content can easily be displayed and interacted with, on a smartphone. A first trend for supporting 3D manipulations consists in using the direct touch modality, i.e. the tactile screen [15]. Based on an adaptation of multi-touch and direct interaction on tabletop, different techniques have been proposed such as the Z-technique [27], useful to translate an object and the Arc-Ball [32] technique useful to rotate an object. Both have been implemented on smartphone [39] and compared to the Dual-Finger technique to manipulate 3D objects. Indirect manipulations through the use of widgets for controlling 3D manipulation have also been developed [8] or adapted from existing widget [21]. One important result related to touch based interaction with 3D is that the separation of Degrees Of Freedom (DOF) increases the performance of 3D manipulations [26]: three touch techniques perform better than one or two single touch techniques [13].

Alternatively, smartphones also integrate multiple sensors that have been used to design new forms of interaction: these forms of interaction can be considered as tangible interfaces. Orientation of the device combined with the use of the touch-screen can be used to manipulate a 3D object [9, 24].

A third set of researches aims to cope with the size of the screen and has therefore investigated around-device interaction technique as a novel approach to interact with 3D content. PalmSpace is a mid-air gesture technique for rotating 3D objects displayed on the smartphone screen [21]. In T(ether) [22], multi-user 3D modeling and animation are supported through gestures above, behind and on a tablet surface. Mid-air gestures have also been explored to support the navigation and the selection of 3D objects [5]. Even more prospectively the combination of mid-air interaction and rendering around a smartphone has been explored to create a true-3D interactive projection [36].

In the works previously mentioned, the 3DVE is displayed on the smartphone screen. But using a smartphone for interacting with 3D content has also been considered in combination with a distant screen: the smartphone becomes a remote controller of the 3D content. In such settings the smartphone has been used to support single touch interaction while exploring and manipulating distantly displayed cultural heritage 3D models [29]. Other works made use of the smartphone to allow the combination of tactile interaction and smartphone movements for controlling a 3D object with a virtual hand [19, 23] on the remote screen. Tangible use of a smartphone for rotating 3D distant element has also been investigated [18]. Different approaches considered the smartphone as a tool palette to explore and annotate 3D medical data [38], or as a carrier artefact to select and share object between several displays, tabletops or other smartphones during meetings [16].

To summarize, we observe that tactile, tangible and around-device solutions have been proposed in the literature to support user's interaction with 3DVE. However, only tactile and tangible solutions have been proposed to support user's interaction based on a smartphone with a 3DVE displayed on a distant screen. And yet, around-device solutions have been identified as promising for tasks in which multiple degrees of freedom must be controlled simultaneously [21].

Our goal is thus to build upon this opportunity and fill the gap left in the existing works by designing and developing an around-device interaction technique, based on a smartphone, for manipulating 3DVE displayed on a distant screen. Among the well-known 3D tasks [6], we focus in this paper on the manipulation task only because this task is more complex as it definitely requires the 6DOF to be controlled.

# 3. CHARACTERISTICS DISCRIMINATING TACTILE AND TANGIBLE INTERACTION TECHNIQUES

We first present the implementation of two interaction techniques, representative of the tactile and tangible sets of existing smartphone-based techniques for manipulating 3DVE on a distant screen. "With the SmartPhone" (WSP) is a tangible interaction

with the mobile device itself, and is similar to tangible interface [10, 14]; "On the SmartPhone" (OSP) is a tactile technique which requires finger gestures to be performed on the smartphone just as in DualFinger [39]. They both constitute a reference among existing interaction techniques for 3D manipulation: WSP corresponds to a very common tangible situation, well known and also validated for its usability [14, 37]; OSP being an implementation of the Dual-Finger technique based on its authors original code, it has been established that OSP, like the original, offers better performance than other tactile applications [39].

To analyze and compare these two sets of interaction techniques we identified four discriminating characteristics. They correspond to design questions that should be raised to design interaction techniques for manipulating 3D on a distant screen: input frame of reference; DOF combination abilities; feedback visibility; and available space in input. We describe the role and possible values of each characteristic, and illustrate them on WSP (tangible) and OSP (tactile).

## 3.1 A Tangible (WSP) and Tactile (OSP) Implementations of Existing 3D Manipulation Techniques

The tangible technique is the "**With the SmartPhone**" (WSP) technique. The behavior of this technique (Figure 1) is very similar to the one described in [14] to manipulate a cutting plane in 3D medical data. Translation offsets of the smartphone are measured in a coordinate system defined by the distant display and directly mapped to the manipulated elements of the 3D scene. Similarly, any rotations of the smartphone are directly mapped to rotations applied to the selected 3D object. For example rotating the smartphone in a plane parallel to the ground, triggers rotations of the 3D object around its vertical axis (Y axis). Such tangible approaches have been very frequently adopted in virtual reality settings with various physical props. Here the prop is the smartphone that embeds a display and other sensors. In addition, tangible interfaces have been proven to be easy to apprehend by newcomers and occasional users [37].

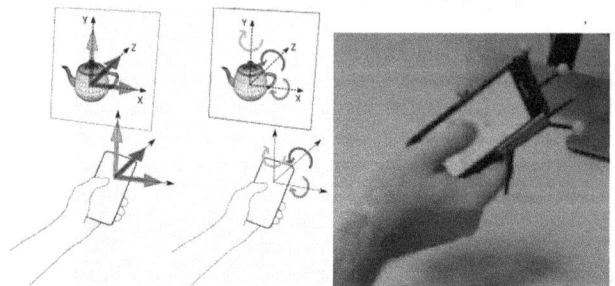

**Figure 1. WSP behavior (translation, rotation) and in use. Colored arrows: input and 3D object movements. Black arrows: input (thin) and 3D (dashed) frame of reference.**

The tactile technique is the "**On the SmartPhone**" (OSP) technique (Figure 2): it is an implementation of the Dual-Finger technique [39]. To perform a translation, if the two fingers are moved jointly up and down on the screen, the 3D manipulated object moves along the Y axis of the 3D scene. If the two fingers are moved apart, the plane defined by the smartphone display is mapped to the (X, Z) plane of the 3D scene, i.e. the ground of the virtual environment. To perform a rotation task, we quote [39]: "*When the user moves both fingers parallel to X axis in the same direction, the object is correspondingly rotated around the Y axis. The same applies to moving the fingers parallel to Y axis in the same direction to rotate the object around X axis. Rotation* *around Z axis is performed by a twisting action by moving the fingers parallel to X axis or Y axis, in the opposite direction*". It was established that Dual-Finger has better performance [39] in comparison to other well-known tactile interaction technique, e.g. the Z-technique [27] and the Arc-Ball [32] technique.

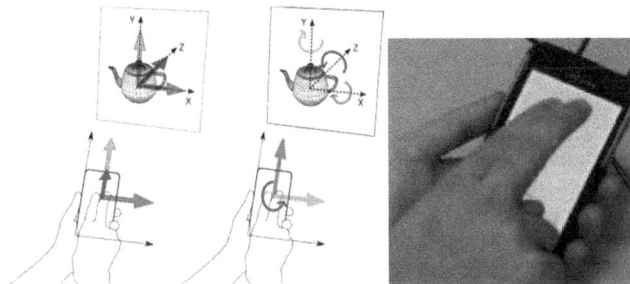

**Figure 2. OSP behavior (translation, rotation) and in use. Arrows: same conventions than Figure 1.**

## 3.2 Four discriminating characteristics

We here describe and illustrate four discriminating characteristics to analyze and compare WSP and OSP that according to the literature may play a role in the usability of the techniques.

A well-known design question in 3D is related to the coordinate system according to which transformations will be applied to elements of the 3D scene. The 3D scene frame of reference represents the frame of reference adopted to apply rotations and translations to rendered elements of a 3D environment [42]. The *egocentric frame of reference* corresponds to a viewer's perspective: it is centered at the user's head. The *room-centered frame of reference* (usually called the world reference) or extrinsic frame refers to unchanging environmental settings: it is based on an absolute reference, fixed in the environment. The *object frame of reference*, or intrinsic frame, refers to the top, bottom, left, right of an object: it is attached to the 3D object manipulated.

Regarding WSP and OSP, the 3D scene frame of reference adopted is the world reference, i.e. the most usual one used in virtual reality settings. Therefore, it is not one of the discriminating characteristics but it is tightly linked to the first one: the input frame of reference.

The **input frame of reference** denotes the frame of reference in which user's inputs are performed to manipulate elements of a 3D scene. Poupyrev notions of *exocentric* and *egocentric* metaphors [34] for manipulation techniques slightly express this consideration. Through the combination of the *Display centricity* and the *Control-Display congruence* axis [31], Milgram better emphasizes the need for considering not only the 3D scene frame of reference but also the frame of reference in which user's controls are initiated. Ware [42] provided an even clearer definition by introducing the *haptic* frame of reference in which the input device used by the user is manipulated. He also shows the importance of adopting a coherent combination of a 3D scene frame of reference and haptic frame of reference.

Regarding WSP, moving the smartphone parallel to the distant display and to its right moves the manipulated 3D objects to the right of the 3D scene. Same behavior applies along the other axis and for the rotations. The input frame of reference is then aligned with the 3D scene frame of reference, i.e. the world reference. Regarding OSP, sliding the finger to the right of the smartphone display moves the manipulated 3D object to the right of the 3D scene. The input frame of reference is therefore attached to the smartphone display. As this display defines only 2DOF, a metaphoric mapping defines a reference for the third rotation

(rotations of two fingers) and an arbitrary mapping defines a reference for the third translation (joint fingers instead of fingers apart).

**DOF combination ability** has an impact on 3D digital tasks. As synthesized in [28] using real object to manipulate 3D elements is quicker than using traditional mouse and keyboard, but simultaneous use of all the DOF does not always lead to the best performance in virtual reality settings. It was also established that separating translation and rotation significantly and positively affects performance [26].

Regarding WSP and OSP, rotations and translations are totally separated: it is impossible to perform them simultaneously in the present setting. WSP allows the three axes to be controlled simultaneously during translations or rotations. With OSP, translation along the Y axis (joint fingers) can only be used separately and rotation can be performed along one axis only at a time.

**Feedback visibility** is one huge benefit of involving a smartphone in such settings instead of physical props as in [14]. The smartphone screen can provide the user with different forms of feedback: a 3D detail of the distant scene as in [5], a textual feedback about the accurate position and orientation of the 3D object, annotations or real pictures of different parts of the 3D scene, etc. In those cases it is important to maintain eye-access to the smartphone screen since it may affect the user's task.

Regarding WSP, the feedback visibility is not always maintained: if the smartphone is translated too far away from the user and under certain combinations of rotations of the devices handed by the user, the display is no longer readable or even visible. Regarding OSP, the traditional finger occlusion issue is raised. Feedback visibility is only partially maintained.

**Available space in input** varies among smartphones and tablets sizes, but comes with a higher weight and delicateness, not compatible with public spaces and mobile devices. Alternatively exploiting the space all-around the devices extends the available space in input and for example efficiently supports input vocabulary on smartphone [20]. Available input space can thus significantly affect the usability.

Regarding WSP, the available space is almost unlimited. It is just constrained by wrist movement (rotation) and by the size of the user's arm (translation). Regarding OSP, the space is limited to the size of the smartphone screen.

## 4. DESIGNING THE "AROUND THE SMARTPHONE" TECHNIQUE

In this section, we present the design of the "Around the SmartPhone" (ASP) technique, an around-device technique based on a smartphone and dedicated to the manipulation of a 3D scene rendered on a distant display.

## 4.1 ASP in Brief

ASP is a smartphone based technique used to manipulate 3D elements displayed on a distant screen. With ASP the user steadily handles the smartphone in the non-dominant hand and performs hand gestures, with the dominant hand, around the smartphone. Translating (resp. rotating) the dominant-hand around the smartphone controls the translation (resp. orientation) of the 3D manipulated object.

Unlike PalmSpace [21] user's hand gestures around the smartphone are not limited to the control of rotations. In addition, our ASP technique is not dedicated to situation in which 3D scene is displayed on the smartphone and mid-air gesture can be continuously produced all around the device.

Another technique similar to ASP was proposed in [5] for a selection task performed in a 3D scene. ASP however is not limited to translations of a single plane and allows different forms of feedback to be displayed on the smartphone screen without restricting it to a detailed portion of the 3D scene. Mid-Air Hand [5] and ASP also differ in terms of control (respectively absolute and relative).

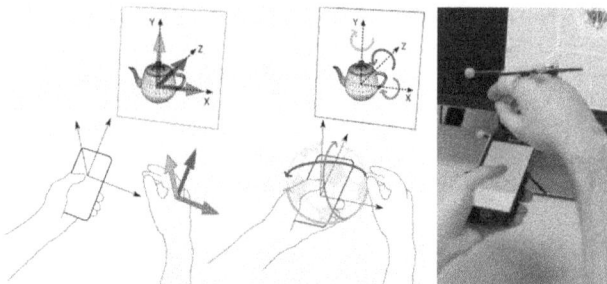

**Figure 3. ASP behavior (translation, rotation) and in use. Arrows: same conventions than Figure 1.**

In comparison to the tactile and tangible techniques introduced above, our ASP technique and the WSP technique are based on the use of mid-air gestures while the OSP technique is a traditional on-screen interaction technique. However, WSP technique involves writ movements while ASP technique involves hand and arm movements around the smartphone thus offering larger mid-air gesture amplitude.

To further refine the design of ASP, we now refer to the four discriminating characteristics introduced and illustrated on WSP and OSP, and instantiate them in a suitable manner to fit the around-device setting (cf. Table 1).

## 4.2 Optimizing the four discriminating characteristics

**Input frame of reference**: ASP being used in front of a distant screen, the user may be not perfectly facing the screen. Therefore adopting the world reference as input frame might be disturbing: if the user looks at the screen with an angle of 45 degrees, hand motions would still have to be performed perpendicularly or parallel to the distant screen!

The goal of ASP is to offer a solution supporting the lack of alignment between the devices used to render the 3D scene and produce the input controls, i.e. to support the use of two different frames of reference for the 3D scene (world reference) and the input (smartphone reference). Therefore, the input frame of reference of ASP must be attached to the smartphone as in OSP. However unlike OSP, it is a true 3DOF input frame of reference not limited to the smartphone-display axes: the third axis is perpendicular to the smartphone screen. It adds a benefit: the user can adjust the position and orientation of the non-dominant hand handling the smartphone in order to allow more comfortable movements of the dominant hand around the smartphone.

As a result, for the translation task (Figure 3), translation offsets of the dominant hand are thus computed with regards to the smartphone orientation and applied to the 3D object.

For the rotation task (Figure 3), the smartphone (resp. its center) materializes the axes (resp. the origin) of the input frame of reference around which hand rotation offsets are measured and then applied to the 3D object.

**DOF combination abilities**: as previously mentioned, separating translations and rotations leads to better performance. Furthermore even if both translation and rotation can be performed jointly users usually perform them independently [30]. We therefore chose for the ASP technique to keep the translation and rotation separated as in WSP and OSP techniques. In addition, we choose to support the combination of the three axes when performing translation (resp. rotations): this is similar to the WSP technique and better takes advantage of the spatial interaction capabilities offered by the around-device setting.

**Feedback visibility**: since ASP relies on gestures performed around the smartphone, the feedback visibility will by construction be maximized. In very limited situations, the dominant arm or hand may occlude the screen from the user's-eye. However head inclinations will overcome these limitations. Among the three considered techniques, ASP supports the largest feedback visibility.

**Available space in input**: when designing ASP, it appeared that the available space in input is slightly different from the available space in WSP: arm size is again constraining the translations movement, but for the rotation, the technique is constrained by the user's motor ability to move the dominant hand and arm around the smartphone.

**Table 1. Discriminating characteristics applied to ASP, WSP and OSP (gray = value is different from ASP)**

|  | ASP | WSP | OSP |
|---|---|---|---|
| Input frame of ref. | smartphone (case - 3D) | world reference | smartphone (display – 2D) |
| DOF combination | T: 3 ; R: 3 | T: 3 ; R: 3 | T: 2 or 1 ; R: 1 |
| Feedback visibility | always | limited by device orientation | limited by finger occlusion |
| Available input space | T: arm size R: arm constraint | T: arm size R: wrist constraint | T: display size R: display size |

## 5. FINALIZING THE IMPLEMENTATION OF ASP, WSP AND OSP

Additional design issues, common to any interaction technique, have been considered to finalize the implementation of the three techniques. They are not specific to a smartphone based interaction technique to manipulate 3DVE displayed on a distant screen but they guided the final implementation of the techniques.

**3D tasks, mode switching**. In the three techniques, manipulation includes 3D translations and 3D rotations which can only be performed separately (cf. section on DOF combination abilities). A mode switching mechanism is thus integrated: the user must press a button, displayed on the smartphone, during the action (translation or rotation).

**Control mode.** Interaction with (WSP), on (OSP), or around (ASP) the smartphone does not provide any force feedback. These techniques can therefore be considered as isotonic and position control of the cursor is preferable [43].

**C/D gain.** Control-Display gain is a recurrent design consideration in HCI community [7]. Two major approaches exist: the ratio can be constant or computed on the basis of a mathematical function applied to movement characteristics. Typically this consideration raises a trade-off between speed and accuracy. The three techniques considered in this paper adopt a constant C/D gain. Regarding WSP, tangible UI physical manipulations are directly applied to the digital world and cannot be accelerated. Regarding ASP, using a constant C/D gain simplifies the use of the technique and limits the learning difficulties. A one to one C/D gain for ASP and WSP is thus used. Now regarding OSP, adopting a constant C/D gain is conform to the initial implementation of the technique [39]: to fit with the 3D environment used in our user study, the adopted C/D gain resulted from a preliminary study allowing the users to adjust the C/D gain to allow a comfortable use of the technique.

**Gesture mapping and clutching mechanism.** Kratz [21] defined four different mappings of hand gestures onto the orientation of a virtual object, that are also applicable to the translation task: absolute control, scaled absolute control, relative control and rate control. The three techniques considered adopt a relative control. This is again in line with the implementation of OSP provided by the authors. Regarding WSP and ASP a relative control induces the presence of clutching and provides more fluidity in the manipulation: whatever the initial position and orientations of the manipulated object, it can be further translated or rotated without having to reposition the dominant hand in the previously reached configuration.

**Figure 4. Visual aids in the 3D scene for the translation (left) and rotation task (center and right).**

**Visual aids.** Many works explored visual aids for guiding and helping the user during the interaction process [6]. The three interaction techniques includes visual aids to ease the perception of the 3D scene frame of reference: the axes of the 3D scene frame of reference are represented on the 3D manipulated object, thus reproducing the feedback provided in modeler software like Maya when manipulating an object. Additional aids are also provided to guide the use of the techniques, i.e. to help performing the appropriate user's input movements. For the OSP technique, fingers contact are displayed on the smartphone to visualize if they are considered joint or apart as originally designed in the Dual-Finger technique [39]. When performing rotations with ASP, a representation of the user's hand position around the smartphone is displayed as a black sphere around the manipulated object in the 3D scene. This is intended to help the user in virtually grabbing one specific vertex of the 3D manipulated object (Figure 4-center). In addition, a wireframe sphere is displayed around the 3D manipulated object: (Figure 4-center). The goal is double: to encourage the user in performing hand movements close to the smartphone and therefore better feel that the smartphone is the center of the rotations; to give the impression that when the hand is moving around the smartphone, it is also stroking the digital wireframe sphere and thus rotating the 3D object included in the sphere.

**Hardware and software tracking solutions.** To support the user experiment, we built a proof-of-concept prototype for WSP and ASP based on the use of an extra tool to localize the smartphone and the user's hand in 6D, as described in section 6.3. The discussion (section 9) mentions alternate embedded solutions. For the WSP technique, the position and the orientation of the smartphone are captured by the tracking system. We used quaternion representation of the orientation of the smartphone in

order to implement a relative control of the rotation movement. For the translation of the ASP technique, the position of the user dominant-hand ($H_{SP}$) is measured with regards to the smartphone position and orientation. Regarding the rotation performed with ASP, converting the position of $H_{SP}$ into an orientation is a technical issue specific to this technique. Our solution relies on the use of axis-angle representation and Rodrigues formula. At each frame, we compute the 3D rotation matrix required to transform the previous $H_{SP}$ into the current $H_{SP}$.

## 6. USER STUDY
The study includes two distinct sessions: the first (resp. second) session consisted in applying 3D translations (resp. rotations) to a 3D object. For these two sessions, the goal of this study is to evaluate and compare the performance, usability and user preference of the three techniques introduced in the previous section. We hypothesize that the around-device technique (ASP) will be more efficient than OSP and WSP because hand gestures are easier to perform, control and understand. ASP will also be preferred over the two others because it is more comfortable to use given the possibility to freely adjust the position and orientations of the smartphone.

### 6.1 Task and Mapping
For the two sessions, participants were instructed to perform the task as quickly and accurately as possible. For the three interactions techniques, participants start and validate each trial by pressing the same button displayed on the smartphone screen.

During the 3D translation task, we asked participants to reach a 3D spherical target in a 3D environment by translating a small 3D spherical cursor (Figure 4-left). The spherical target is always displayed in the center of a 3D cube delimiting the 3D environment. A representation of the axes is attached to the spherical cursor. In addition, stars representing the center of the spherical cursor are projected on two planes of the 3D scene contour. These visual aids are displayed in blue. The same visual aids related to the target sphere are displayed in red. These visual aids provide the user with a support to accurately move and position the object.

The initial position of the spherical cursor is situated in one of the 8 different directions (combining equal x, y and z translations) at two different distances (12.99 and 8.66 units) from the spherical target. The spherical cursor has a fixed radius of 0.5 units. We implemented two different spherical target radiuses (0.5 and 1.7 units) to produce 4 Index of Difficulties (2.6, 3.11, 4.19 and 4.75 bits). The participant can validate the 3D translation task when the cursor collides with the spherical target.

During the 3D rotation task, we asked participants to rotate a tetrahedral cursor until it fits the orientation of the tetrahedral target (Figure 4-center). The two tetrahedral centers are always located in the center of the 3D environment. Spheres of different colors are attached to the vertices of the tetrahedral form. The tetrahedral target is always displayed in green with a fixed orientation. In contrast, the tetrahedral cursor is displayed in brown. These visual aids provide the participant with indications to correctly interpret the current and targeted orientations of the 3D objects.

The initial orientation of the tetrahedral cursor is a combination of rotation axes (XY, XZ, YX, and XYZ) with one of the two angle values (50° and 100°), giving a total of 8 different starting orientations. The participant can validate the 3D orientation task when all the colored spheres of the tetrahedral cursor collide with the corresponding colored spheres of the tetrahedral target.

## 6.2 Design and Procedure

The 3D translation session follows a 3x4 within-participants design with Interaction Technique (ASP, WSP and OSP) and Index of Difficulty (2.6, 3.11, 4.19 and 4.75 bits) as factors. Three blocks were run for each technique, the Interaction Technique factor being counterbalanced by the use of a 3x3 Latin Square. Each block of trials required 32 translations of the target: 8 different directions for each Index of Difficulty. Inside each block the 32 trials were randomly ordered. Each participant performed 3 techniques x 3 blocks x 4 ID x 8 directions = 288 trials.

The 3D rotation session follows a 3x4x2 within-participants design with Interaction Technique (ASP, WSP and OSP), Axes of Rotation (XY, XZ, YX, and XYZ) and Angle (50° and 100°) as factors. As the 3D translation session, three blocks were run for each technique, the Interaction Technique factor being counterbalanced by the use of a 3x3 Latin Square. Each block of trials required 16 rotation of the target: 4 axes of rotation x 2 angle x 2 iterations. Inside each block the 16 trials were randomly ordered. Each participant performed 3 techniques x 3 blocks x 4 axes of rotation x 2 angle x 2 repetitions = 144 trials.

All the participants first perform the 3D translation session followed by a break and the 3D rotation session. They finish with a questionnaire session. Before using a technique for the first time participants perform a training session that consists in 32 translations of the target for 3D translation session and 16 rotations of the target for 3D rotation session. On average, all the experiment lasted 124 minutes.

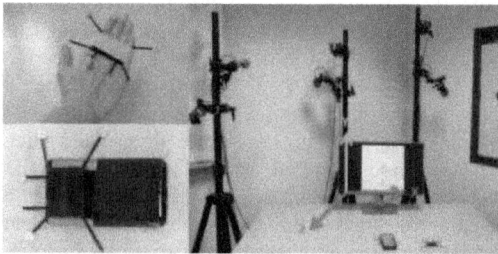

Figure 5. Experimental setting.

## 6.3 Participants, Apparatus, Collected Data

We recruited 12 participants (4 female) aged 28 years on average (SD=6.9). None had previously played 3D games on smartphone. Nine had used gestural interaction (Wiimote or Kinect).

Our setting is composed of a distant display, a smartphone and motion capture for tracking the smartphone and the user's hand (Figure 5). The distant display used is a 24" monitor with a resolution of 1920x1080px. To implement all 3D content, we used the Irrlicht C++ open source engine based on OpenGL. The resolution of the 3D content is a square of 1000px and the 3D environment run at 300fps. For the smartphone, we used a Samsung Galaxy S2 smartphone (6.6x12.5x0.8cm, 116 gr., 4.3" screen) running Android 4.1.2. The motion capture is based on infrared optical markers tracked by 8 OptiTrack cameras (1mm precision, 100fps). One marker is attached to the back of the smartphone using Velcro touch fastener. The second marker is fixed to the hand participant with a self-adhering bandage.

We logged all tracking data and measured completion time from stimulus onset. We asked participants to rank the three techniques according to their preference after the 3D translation session, after the 3D rotation session and once again after having achieved rotations and translations. We also measured the usability of each technique via the System Usability Scale questionnaire (SUS) [4]

and their attractiveness via the AttrakDiff questionnaire [3] AttrakDiff informs on the attractiveness of a technique according to three distinct dimensions: the pragmatic quality (PQ) indicates whether the user can achieve his goals; the hedonic quality (HQ) indicates to what extent the technique enhances the possibilities of the user; the attractiveness (ATT) expresses how the user values each technique based on its quality and engagement.

## 7. RESULTS

### 7.1 3D Translation

**Task completion time** data do not follow a normal distribution (Shapiro-Wilk test, $p<0.001$). We did not find any data transformation that would allow us to use parametric tests. Our statistical analysis is thus based on non-parametric tests.

Figure 6-a summarizes the task completion times for each technique: "Around the SmartPhone" (ASP), "On the Smart-Phone" (OSP) and "With the SmartPhone" (WSP). A Friedman test reveals a significant effect of the Interaction Technique factor on task completion times ($\chi^2(2)=18.17$, $p<0.001$). A post-hoc test using Wilcoxon with Bonferroni correction establishes a significant difference between ASP (2.54s) and OSP (6.87s) ($p<0.001$) and between WSP (2.43s) and OSP ($p<0.001$). No significant difference exists between ASP and WSP.

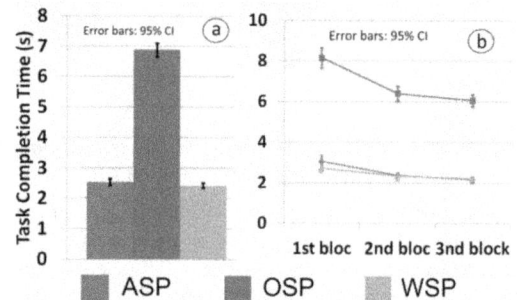

Figure 6. Task completion time (a) and learning effect (b) for 3D translation.

Friedman tests reveal a significant effect of the **block order** on task completion time for WSP and OSP techniques (WSP: $\chi^2(2)=7.82$, $p=0.02$; OSP: $\chi^2(2)=12.18$, $p=0.002$). A post-hoc test using Wilcoxon with Bonferroni correction shows a significant difference between the first and the last block for WSP and OSP techniques (Figure 6-c). Completion time is reduced of 18.5% (0.5s) for WSP ($p<0.001$) and 34.6% (2s) for OSP ($p<0.001$). These results confirm the difficulty to learn gestures required with the OSP technique. Concerning the WSP technique, the learning effect may be explained by the need to find an appropriate way of handling the smartphone during the first trials. Regarding the ASP technique, although the reduction of the completion time is close to the one observed with OSP technique (ASP: 28.6%, 0.9s), the difference is not significant ($p=0.08$).

After performing the translations only, 8 participants rated WSP technique as the **preferred technique** and 4 the ASP technique. In contrast, all the participants ranked OSP technique in last position. For the statistical analysis, we gave a score of 1 to the most preferred technique and a score of 3 to the least preferred technique. A Friedman test reveals a significant effect of the interaction technique on the score representing the user preference ($\chi^2(2)=18.67$, $p<0.001$). A post-hoc test using Wilcoxon with Bonferroni correction shows a significant difference between ASP (1.67) and OSP (3.0, $p=0.005$) and between WSP (1.33) and OSP ($p=0.005$): ASP and WSP techniques are preferred to the OSP technique when performing translations.

## 7.2 3D Rotation

**Task completion time** data does not follow a normal distribution (Shapiro-Wilk test: p<0.001). Our statistical analysis is thus based on non-parametric tests.

Figure 7-a summarizes the task completion time for each technique. A Friedman test reveals a significant effect of the Interaction Technique on task completion time ($\chi^2(2)$=10.67, p=0.005). A post-hoc test using Wilcoxon with Bonferroni correction establishes significant differences (p<0.001) between each technique: OSP (8.43s), ASP (6.81s), WSP (5.40s). The discussion section further refines these results.

These results remain similar and significant when considering the different values of the Angle factor independently. However, we did not observe any significant effect of the Axes of Rotation factor on task completion times for each Interaction Technique (ASP: $\chi^2(3)$=1.9, p=0.593; WSP: $\chi^2(3)$=5.5, p=0.138; OSP: $\chi^2(3)$=6.3, p=0.098).

Friedman tests reveal a significant effect of the **block order** on task completion time for WSP technique only ($\chi^2(2)$=12.17, p=0.002). A post-hoc test using Wilcoxon with Bonferroni correction shows a significant difference between the first and the last block for this technique (Figure 7-b): completion time is reduced of 28.8% (1.4s) for WSP (p=0.006). As in the translation session, this learning effect may be explained by the need to find an appropriate way for handling the device in the first trials. Although the task completion time reduction with ASP (28.6%, 1.7s) is comparable to the one measured for the WSP technique, the learning effect is not statistically significant for this technique. Interestingly, the reduction of completion time with OSP between the first and third block is limited to 13.3% (1s). This improvement is below the one observed with the other technique: it is probably due to the fact that the gestures required in OSP for triggering the rotations are similar to those required to perform the translations and the rotation session always came after the translation session. Participants were thus used to the technique.

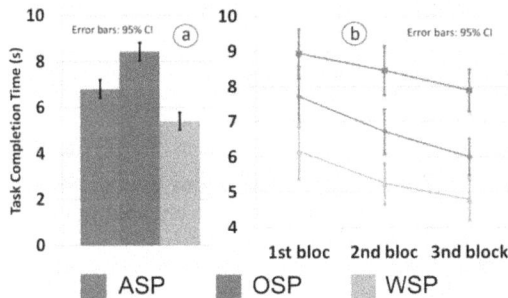

**Figure 7. Task completion time (a) and learning effect (b) for the 3D rotation.**

Following the rotation session, 7 participants rated ASP technique as the **preferred technique** and 5 the WSP technique. In contrast, 9 participants ranked OSP technique in the last position. For the statistical analysis, the same scoring was applied than in the translation session. A Friedman test reveals a significant effect of the interaction technique on this score representing the user preference ($\chi^2(2)$=10.17, p=0.006). A post-hoc test using Wilcoxon with Bonferroni correction reveals a significant difference between ASP (1.58) and OSP (2.75, p=0.033) and between WSP (1.67) and OSP (p=0.017). ASP and WSP technique are preferred to OSP when performing rotations.

## 7.3 Overall Task Results

Given that combining 3D translations and 3D rotations affects performances [26], these two tasks were separated in our user study. However, as tools supporting both of them, we asked the participants to evaluate the three techniques in terms of usability, attractiveness and user preference.

A **SUS score** was computed for each technique [4]: given this score the usability of the WSP technique is rated "excellent" (89.17, SD=9.73), the ASP technique is "good" (76.67, SD=16.11) and the OSP technique is "ok" (51.04, SD=17.04). A Friedman test reveals a significant effect of the interaction techniques on the SUS score ($\chi^2(2)$=14.6, p<0.001). A post-hoc test using Wilcoxon with Bonferroni correction shows a significant difference between ASP and OSP scores (p=0.009) and between WSP and OSP scores (p<0.001).

To measure the **attractiveness** of the three techniques we relied on the Attrakdiff method [3]. We summarize in Figure 8, the results of the Pragmatic Quality (PQ) and Hedonic Quality (HQ) dimensions. According to the Attrakdiff report, ASP technique is rated as "rather desired". With regards to PQ and HQ dimensions, the Attrakdiff report concludes there is room of improvement in terms of usability but the technique is very hedonic: the user identifies with the technique, which motivates and stimulates him. WSP technique is rated "practice oriented": the technique assists the user optimally but there is room of user's stimulation improvement. Finally the OSP technique is rated "neutral": there is room for improvement in terms of usability and user's stimulation.

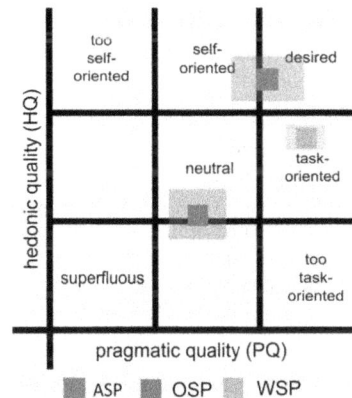

**Figure 8. Portfolio generated using the AttrakDiff method.**

In addition the overall user's impression (Attractiveness ATT) of ASP (ATT=2) and WSP (ATT=1.5) techniques is considered very attractive. For the OSP technique the overall impression is moderately attractive (ATT=-0.8).

When considering the overall 3D manipulation task, 7 participants rated ASP technique as the **preferred technique** and 5 the WSP technique. In contrast, 10 participants ranked OSP technique in the last position. When applying the scoring process previously described, difference between these three results appear to be statistically significant. They are also coherent with those obtained in the translation and rotation sessions.

Globally, users expressed that the ASP technique is funny, accurate and original. But they noticed that it requires a little time of adaptation and it is a two-handed interaction technique. The WSP technique is considered easy to understand and intuitive but tiring due to the weight of the smartphone. In addition they mentioned that it needs many twisting of the wrist. Finally, participants stated that the OSP technique is convenient to use.

But they underlined the lack of accuracy and difficulty for combining the use of two fingers, especially during 3D translations.

# 8. COMPLEMENTARY USER STUDY: ENHANCING FEEDBACK VISIBILITY

The main difference between the two best performing techniques (ASP and WSP) is that ASP allows a permanent access to the feedback provided on the smartphone screen, while many manipulations of WSP results in turning the smartphone screen away from the user's eye. If annotations or pictures for example were displayed on the smartphone screen, WSP would have to be modified to allow a permanent access to this visual feedback. More clutching would thus be required than in the current version of WSP, thus affecting its performance.

To evaluate the impact of such constraints on the performance measured in the first study, we performed a complementary study focusing on the rotations task only. For this user's study we introduced two revised versions of WSP that constrained the user to apply small rotations only to the smartphone: it ensures that eye-access to the smartphone screen is always possible.

The goal of this complementary study is to compare the two newly introduced techniques called WSP_45 and WSP_70, with which rotation angles applied to the smartphone were respectively measured up to 45° and 70°, to WSP_WC in which rotation angles applied to the smartphone were measured without constraint as in the WSP technique used in the first user study.

## 8.1 Experimental settings

**Tasks and mapping.** Only the 3D rotation task session performed in the first experiment was proposed to the user in this second user's study (see section 6.1).

**Design and procedure.** The rotation task to achieve was the same as in the first study. The study followed a 3 (IT) x 4 (rotation axis: XY, XZ, YX, XYZ) x 2 (angles: small, large) within-participants design as the first study, except that interaction techniques considered here are WSP_45, WSP_70 and WSP_WC. Techniques were counterbalanced over the 6 participants. For each technique, participants performed one block as defined in the first study. A training session included one block with WSP_WC first and one with WSP_45.

**Participants, Apparatus, Collected Data.** We randomly recruited 6 participants among the 12 involved in the first study. The same apparatus than in the first experiment is used (see section 6.3). We logged all tracking data and measured completion time from stimulus onset.

## 8.2 Results

A Friedman test reveals a significant effect of the technique on task completion times ($\chi^2(2)=6.33$, p=0.042). A post-hoc test using Wilcoxon with Bonferroni correction establishes a significant difference between WSP_45 (4.53s) and WSP_WC (3.16s) (p=0.001) and between WSP_45 (4.53s) and WSP_70 (3.40s, p=0.043). No significant difference exists between WSP_70 and WSP_WC. As hypothesized, limiting the rotations angles increases clutching and reduces the performance.

Focusing on the 6 participants involved in the complementary study only, no significant difference exists in terms of completion time between WSP (first study, 3.19s) and WSP_WC (3.16s, Wilcoxon test: p=1.00). This allows us to compare the results of this study with other results of the first study.

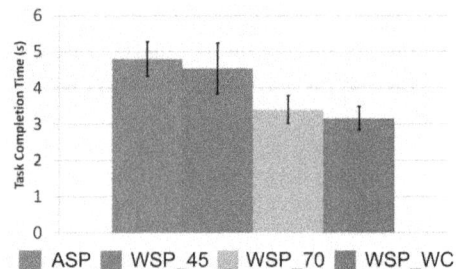

**Figure 9. Task completion time for the 3D rotation with ASP and the three different WSP techniques.**

When comparing the new WSP versions to ASP (Figure 9), a Friedman test reveals a significant effect of the interaction technique (ASP, WSP_WC, WSP_70, WSP_45) on task completion time ($\chi^2(3)=12.6$, p-value=0.006). In addition to the results of the first study, a post-hoc test using Wilcoxon with Bonferroni correction still establishes a significant difference between WSP_70 (3.40s) and ASP technique (4.80s, p<0.01): but combined rotations of 70° around 2 or 3 axes may result in situations where the smartphone screen is no longer readable.

Very interestingly, no significant difference exists between WSP_45 and ASP (p=0.47): they both perform similarly for applying rotations with a distant 3D display and are both compliant with a permanent eye access to the smartphone screen.

# 9. DISCUSSION

Our study reveals that the OSP technique, i.e. one of the best tactile interaction techniques available in the literature, is worse than ASP and WSP, since the first trial, in terms of **user's performance** when achieving a 3D manipulation task on a distant screen displaying the 3D scene. Performances of the tactile (OSP), tangible (WSP) and around-device (ASP) techniques are equally sensible to the difficulty of the task (angle, number of rotation axis, target size and distance). Unlike our initial assumption, in our studies users do not perform better with ASP than WSP: no significant difference has been observed for 3D translation and 3D rotations when the smartphone-screen must remain visible to the users. Without this constraint, the tangible technique (WSP) performs significantly better the 3D rotations only, but obviously does not any more support the possibility to visualize additional feedback on the smartphone since the screen may be hidden.

In terms of **usability, attractiveness and user preference**, OSP is far below ASP and WSP. Focusing on ASP and WSP, their usability score is similar and high (SUS > 75). ASP is preferred over WSP and was evaluated more attractive and desired than WSP. All these results are statistically significant. Different reasons can explain these results. Indeed, with the WSP technique the phone is moved in the air during the tasks: its weight may be a first cause for reducing the attractiveness of this technique. Furthermore, rotating the wrist is cumbersome: participants may be afraid of dropping the smartphone. As opposed to WSP, ASP is based on the motion of an empty hand around the device: it is safer, lighter and easier, thus preferred.

We now analyze the results related to the characteristics that have driven the design of ASP (cf. Table 1). In terms of **input frame of reference**, using the coordinate system of the displayed environment (i.e. world reference) as the reference for user input is the most common approach in VR. Furthermore, mismatches between the input and 3D scene frames of reference affect the performance [42] partly because people typically lack experience with rotation about an axis that has an arbitrary spatial relationship to the object [33]. Although the input frames of reference of WSP and ASP are respectively world reference and the smartphone, we did not observe in these studies significant difference between the users' performance with WSP and ASP. We believe that the design of ASP provides an original and appropriate solution to cope with such frame of reference mismatch issues because the smartphone can be seen as a physical landmark. This landmark contributes to overcome the arbitrary relationship between the two frames of reference because it reifies the coordinate system in which gestures has to be performed to move an object in 6DOF. This hypothesis is in line with previous work related to bimanual interaction [12]. Future works are required to precisely establish under which conditions an around-device technique provides a better support for interacting with a distantly rendered 3D scene, and especially for situations involving predefined and high mismatches of frames of reference, similar to those involved in Ware's experiment [42].

**DOF combination** and **input space** were more limited in OSP than in ASP and WSP. We believe that this is partly responsible for the low OSP performance results. The **visibility of the feedback** provided by the smartphone was not concretely evaluated in our study, since no dynamic information relevant to the task was provided to users. However, the complementary user study clearly established the effect of this characteristic on the performances.

Finally, one limitation of our study is the detection mechanisms of the hand and smartphone motions in the WSP and ASP techniques: the technology used in this study is external to the smartphone and will very unlikely be available in many places. But, this solution was used to ensure robust and accurate measures to support the evaluation of the technique. Thinking in terms of a proof-of-Concept version of the technique might however rely on many existing solutions: proximity sensors on some Samsung devices already allow page browsing based on hand-motions detection; camera resolution are always increasing on current smartphone; small depth camera sensor [21] also constitute an alternative.

Social acceptability issue is a second limitation of around-device techniques. Would a user accept to move his/her hand around the smartphone to interact with a distant display in an office or public context? Recent works started to explore this acceptability question [35] and we will explore it through in-situ evaluation.

## 10. CONCLUSION AND FUTURE WORK

In this paper, we presented the first around-device interaction technique ("Around the SmartPhone" - ASP), based on a smartphone and used to manipulate 3D elements displayed on a distant screen. The design was guided by reasoning on four characteristics discriminating existing smartphone-based tactile and tangible interaction techniques with 3DVE.

To evaluate this new interaction technique, we performed two controlled user studies to compare ASP to a tangible ("With the SmartPhone" - WSP) and a tactile ("On the SmartPhone" - OSP) smartphone-based techniques taken from the literature. These evaluations reveal that WSP and ASP perform better than OSP in 3D translation and rotation. WSP and ASP perform similarly in 3D translation. They also perform similarly in 3D rotation when eye-access to the smartphone-screen is maintained all along the task. Otherwise, WSP is significantly faster that ASP but does no longer support an access to additional feedback provided on the smartphone screen.

From a qualitative point of view, ASP is the most attractive and preferred technique. It also minimizes the risk of dropping the smartphone and physically materializes the input frame of reference.

This work confirms that an "around the smartphone" interaction technique to control distant 3D is a very good alternative to tactile and tangible solutions: this is in line with results observed when interacting with 3D scenes directly displayed on the smartphone. We also revealed the need to further explore the impact of the smartphone, considered as a physical handled landmark, on the user's ability to cope with mismatch between input and 3D scene frames of reference. In the future, we plan to integrate ASP and WSP techniques in a concrete public scenario in order to observe limitations inherent to an in-situ context and to explore further optimizations of ASP and WSP, such as in [1, 40], in order to reduce the need for clutching.

## 11. ACKNOWLEDGMENTS
We would like to thank Gary Perelman for his help during the implementation of the 3D environment of this work and all the participants who generously shared their time for the study. We are also grateful to the anonymous reviewers for their valuable comments and suggestions to improve the quality of the paper.

## 12. REFERENCES
[1] Appert, C. and Fekete, J. 2006. OrthoZoom scroller: 1D multi-scale navigation. In Proc. of *CHI' 06*, ACM, 21–30.

[2] De Araùjo, B.R., Casiez, G. and Jorge, J.A. 2012. Mockup builder: direct 3D modeling on and above the surface in a continuous interaction space. In Proc. of *GI '12*, 173–180.

[3] AttrakDiff: 2014. http://attrakdiff.de/index-en.html. Accessed: 2015-04-07.

[4] Bangor, A., Kortum, P.T. and Miller, J.T. 2008. An empirical evaluation of the System Usability Scale. *International Journal of Human-Computer Interaction*. 24, 6, 574–594.

[5] Bergé, L.-P., Serrano, M., Perelman, G. and Dubois, E. 2014. Exploring smartphone-based interaction with overview+detail interfaces on 3D public displays. In Proc. of *MobileHCI '14*, ACM, 125–134.

[6] Bowman, D.A., Kruijff, E., LaViola, J.J. and Poupyrev, I. 2004. *3D User Interfaces: Theory and Practice*.

[7] Casiez, G., Vogel, D., Balakrishnan, R. and Cockburn, A. 2008. The Impact of Control-Display Gain on User Performance in Pointing Tasks. *Human-Computer Interaction*. 23, 3, 215–250.

[8] Cohé, A., Dècle, F. and Hachet, M. 2011. tBox: a 3d transformation widget designed for touch-screens. In Proc. of *CHI '11*, ACM, 3005–3008.

[9] Daiber, F., Li, L. and Krüger, A. 2012. Designing gestures for mobile 3D gaming. In Proc. of *MUM '12*, 3–8.

[10] Frohlich, B., Plate, J., Wind, J., Wesche, G. and Gobel, M. 2000. Cubic-Mouse-based interaction in virtual environments. *Computer Graphics and Applications*. 20, 4, 12–15.

[11] Gomes De Sá, A. and Zachmann, G. 1999. Virtual reality as a tool for verification of assembly and maintenance processes. *Computers & Graphics*. 23, 3 (1999), 389–403.

[12] Guiard, Y. 1987. Asymmetric division of labor in human skilled bimanual action: the kinematic chain as a model. *Journal of motor behavior*. 19, 4 (1987), 486–517.

[13] Hancock, M., Carpendale, S. and Cockburn, A. 2007. Shallow-Depth 3D Interaction: Design and Evaluation of One-, Two- and Three-Touch Techniques. In Proc. of *CHI '07*, ACM, 1147–1156.

[14] Hinckley, K., Pausch, R., Goble, J.C. and Kassell, N.F. 1994. Passive real-world interface props for neurosurgical visualization. In Proc. of *CHI '94*, ACM, 452–458.

[15] Jankowski, J. and Hachet, M. 2014. Advances in Interaction with 3D Environments. *Computer Graphics Forum*.152–190.

[16] Jeon, S., Hwang, J., Kim, G.J. and Billinghurst, M. 2009. Interaction with large ubiquitous displays using camera-equipped mobile phones. *Personal and Ubiquitous Computing*. 14, 2, 83–94.

[17] Jones, B., Sodhi, R., Forsyth, D., Bailey, B. and Maciocci, G. 2012. Around device interaction for multiscale navigation. In Proc. of *MobileHCI '12*, 83-92.

[18] Katzakis, N. and Hori, M. 2010. Mobile devices as multi-DOF controllers. Proc. of *3DUI '10*, IEEE, 139–140.

[19] Katzakis, N., Teather, R.J., Kiyokawa, K. and Takemura, H. 2015. INSPECT: Extending Plane-Casting for 6-DOF Control. Proc. of 3DUI '15, IEEE, 165–166.

[20] Ketabdar, H., Roshandel, M. and Yüksel, K.A. 2010. MagiWrite: Towards Touchless Digit Entry Using 3D Space Around Mobile Devices. Proc. of *MobileHCI '10*, 443–446

[21] Kratz, S., Rohs, M., Guse, D., Müller, J., Bailly, G. and Nischt, M. 2012. PalmSpace: continuous around-device gestures vs. multitouch for 3D rotation tasks on mobile devices. In Proc. of *AVI '12*, ACM, 181–188.

[22] Lakatos, D., Blackshaw, M., Olwal, A., Barryte, Z., Perlin, K. and Ishii, H. 2014. T(ether): spatially-aware handhelds, gestures and proprioception for multi-user 3D modeling and animation. In Proc. of *SUI '14*, ACM, 90–93.

[23] Lee, D., Hwang, J.-I., Kim, G.J. and Ahn, S.C. 2011. 3D interaction using mobile device on 3D environments with large screen. In Proc. of *MobileHCI '11*, ACM, 575–580.

[24] Liang, H.-N., Williams, C., Semegen, M., Stuerzlinger, W. and Irani, P. 2012. User-defined surface+motion gestures for 3d manipulation of objects at a distance through a mobile device. In Proc. of *APCHI '12*, ACM, 299–308.

[25] Magliocchetti, D., Conti, G. and De Amicis, R. 2012. I-MOVE: towards the use of a mobile 3D GeoBrowser framework for urban mobility decision making. *IJIDeM Journal*. 6, 4, 205–214.

[26] Martinet, A., Casiez, G. and Grisoni, L. 2012. Integrality and separability of multitouch interaction techniques in 3D manipulation tasks. *IEEE transactions on visualization and computer graphics*. 18, 3, 369–80.

[27] Martinet, A., Casiez, G. and Grisoni, L. 2010. The design and evaluation of 3D positioning techniques for multi-touch displays. In Proc. of *3DUI' 10*, IEEE, 115–118.

[28] Martinet, A., Casiez, G. and Grisoni, L. 2010. The effect of DOF separation in 3D manipulation tasks with multi-touch displays. In Proc. of *VRST '10*, ACM, 111-118.

[29] Marton, F., et al. 2014. IsoCam: Interactive Visual Exploration of Massive Cultural Heritage Models on Large Projection Setups. *Journal on Computing and Cultural Heritage*. 7, 2, 1–24.

[30] Masliah, M.R. and Milgram, P. 2000. Measuring the allocation of control in a 6 degree-of-freedom docking experiment. In Proc. of *CHI '00*, ACM, 25–32.

[31] Milgram, P. and Colquhoun, H. 1999. A Taxonomy of Real and Virtual World Display Integration. *Mixed Reality: Merging Real and Virtual Worlds*. 1 (1999), 1–26.

[32] OpenGL Programming/Modern OpenGL Tutorial Arcball *http://en.wikibooks.org/wiki/OpenGL_Programming/Modern_OpenGL_Tutorial_Arcball*. Accessed: 2015-04-07.

[33] Parsons, L.M. 1995. Inability to reason about an object's orientation using an axis and angle of rotation. *Journal of Experimental Psychology: Human Perception and Performance*. 21, 6, 1259–1277.

[34] Poupyrev, I., Weghorst, S., Billinghurst, M. and Ichikawa, T. 1998. Egocentric Object Manipulation in Virtual Environments: Empirical Evaluation of Interaction Techniques. *Computer Graphics Forum*. 17, (1998), 41–52.

[35] Serrano, M., Ens, B.M. and Irani, P.P. 2014. Exploring the use of hand-to-face input for interacting with head-worn displays. In Proc. of *CHI '14*, ACM, 3181–3190.

[36] Serrano, M., Hildebrandt, D., Subramanian, S. and Irani, P. 2014. Identifying suitable projection parameters and display configurations for mobile true-3D displays. In Proc. of *MobileHCI '14*, ACM, 135–143.

[37] Shaer, O. and Hornecker, E. 2009. Tangible User Interfaces: past, present, and future directions. *Foundations and Trends® in Human–Computer Interaction*. 3, 1-2, 1–137.

[38] Song, P., Goh, W.B., Fu, C.-W., Meng, Q. and Heng, P.-A. 2011.WYSIWYF:exploring and annotating volume data with a tangible handheld device. In Proc. of *CHI '11*,1333–1342.

[39] Telkenaroglu, C. and Capin, T. 2012. Dual-Finger 3D Interaction Techniques for mobile devices. *Personal and Ubiquitous Computing*. 17, 7, 1551–1572.

[40] Tsandilas, T., Dubois, E. and Raynal, M. 2013. Modeless pointing with low-precision wrist movements. In Proc. of *INTERACT 2013*, 494–511.

[41] Vajk, T., Coulton, P., Bamford, W. and Edwards, R. 2008. Using a Mobile Phone as a "Wii-like" Controller for Playing Games on a Large Public Display. *International Journal of Computer Games Technology*. 2008, 1–6.

[42] Ware, C. and Arsenault, R. 2004. Frames of reference in virtual object rotation. In Proc. of *APGV '04*, 135–141.

[43] Zhai, S. 1995. *Human Performance in Six Degree of Freedom Input Control*. University of Toronto.

# Combining Direct and Indirect Touch Input for Interactive Desktop Workspaces using Gaze Input

Simon Voelker[1], Andrii Matviienko[1], Johannes Schöning[2], Jan Borchers[1]

[1] RWTH Aachen University
Aachen, Germany
{voelker, matviienko, borchers}@cs.rwth-aachen.de

[2] Expertise Centre for Digital Media
Hasselt University – tUL – iMinds, Diepenbeek, Belgium
johannes.schoening@uhasselt.be

## ABSTRACT

Interactive workspaces combine horizontal and vertical touch surfaces into a single digital workspace. During an exploration of these systems, it was shown that direct interaction on the vertical surface is cumbersome and more inaccurate than on the horizontal one. To overcome these problems, indirect touch systems turn the horizontal touch surface into an input devices that allows manipulation of objects on the vertical display. If the horizontal touch surface also acts as a display, however, it becomes necessary to distinguish which screen is currently in use by providing a switching mode. We investigate the use of gaze tracking to perform these mode switches. In three user studies we compare absolute and relative gaze augmented selection techniques with the traditional direct-touch approach. Our results show that our relative gaze augmented selection technique outperforms the other techniques for simple tapping tasks alternating between horizontal and vertical surfaces, and for dragging on the vertical surface. However, when tasks involve dragging across surfaces, the findings are more complex. We provide a detailed description of the proposed interaction techniques, a statistical analysis of these interaction techniques, and how they can be applied to systems that involve a combination of multiple horizontal and vertical touch surfaces.

## Keywords

Interactive Surfaces and Tabletops; Workspaces; Touch; Indirect Touch; Gaze-based Interaction; Tabletop interaction

## Categories and Subject Descriptors

H.5.2 [**Information Interfaces and Presentation**]: User Interfaces Input Devices and Strategies

## 1. INTRODUCTION & MOTIVATION

Direct interaction with vertical displays is as old as the history of graphical user interfaces. In 1963, Sutherland's Sketchpad [21] already used a light pen to draw on the system's vertical screen. However, this style of interaction is inherently difficult for the human physique, since holding one's arm in mid-air while interacting

**Figure 1: With help of the users gaze one can interact on the horizontal surface using direct touch and on the vertical surface via indirect touch.**

with a vertical display leads to fatigue, a phenomenon known as the *Gorilla Arm effect* [18, 27]. Desktop user interfaces quickly moved input to the horizontal surface in front of the screen, leading to indirect graphical input devices. This allows users to rest their arms on the surface while interacting. Mouse and trackpad are relative, graphic tablets are absolute indirect input devices.

Projects such as Tognazzini's Starfire [22] envisioned future desktop workplaces by including both vertical and horizontal touch surfaces. In the last few years we have seen a rise of interactive surfaces and tabletops [14]. Multi-touch tabletop research projects such as Curve [28], BendDesk [27], and Magic desk [2] have made such setups increasingly feasible, but they also showed that direct interaction with a vertical surface is difficult and less accurate than interacting with the horizontal surface [27]. The first commercial products now exist that make use of a vertical and horizontal touch surface such as Sprout (sprout.hp.com).

Indirect multi-touch allows users to interact with the vertical surface in a comfortable way [13, 26]. Most recently with the new version of iOS 9 for iPad, Apples touch-sensitive QuickType keyboard now also features a indirect touch mode, which transform the keyboard into a trackpad whenever one set down two fingers on the keyboard portion of the screen. Indirect touch also allows the users of interactive workspace, to comfortably interact with the vertical surface using multi-touch input on the horizontal surface. Instead of touching the vertical surface directly, the touch points are transferred using an absolute mapping from the horizontal to the vertical display.

However a drawback of indirect touch is that the horizontal surface is only used as an input area. Should the horizontal input surface also become a output surface, a mode switching problem arises: users need somehow to specify if a touch was meant for a direct control of the horizontal display they physically touched, or if it should provide an indirect control over the vertical display in front of them. We present two different gaze-based mode switching techniques and compare them to the direct touch system with horizontal and vertical touch screens. The key idea of our approaches is to use the user's gaze at the moment of the initial touch to select the right surface. In the technique called Indirect Touch Surface Selection (ITSS), the gaze is used to select a screen to which the touch is mapped absolutely. In the other technique called Indirect Touch Object Selection (ITOS), the gaze is used to map the touch directly onto an object displayed on the vertical surface.

In our experiments, we investigate a system which combines one horizontal touch surface that is also an output surface (multi-touch desk), and one vertical input/output touch surface (vertical screen) in front of the user. Our interaction techniques can be a first step to make future interactive workspaces, as for example envisioned by Tognazzini et al. [22], more user friendly. The techniques could overcome important limitations of current interactive workspaces, which hinder users to use them on a day to day basis.

To summarise, our paper addresses the following three important aspects to improve future interactive workspaces:

1. We present two gaze-based interaction techniques that allow users to switch between direct touch interaction on a horizontal and indirect touch on a vertical surface.

2. We provide an empirical evaluation of the users' performance with these techniques compared to the direct touch system with both horizontal and vertical surfaces.

3. We outline how these results could be used to study multi-screen environments.

## 2. RELATED WORK

In the following subsections we discuss the related work in the fields of direct and indirect touch input and gaze supported touch interaction.

## 2.1 Direct and Indirect Touch Input

Weiss et al. [27] and Wimmer et al. [28] show how direct touch can enrich interactions for interactive workspaces, although it is cumbersome and tiring when interacting with the vertical screen. It is also shown that operating on the horizontal surface is faster and less exhausting than on the vertical [26]. To improve the users performance on vertical touch surfaces, Schmidt et al. [13] propose an approach that allow users to comfortably interact with a vertical screen of the interactive workspace utilizing indirect multi-touch. In such a setup, the neck pain and strain can be reduced as users do not have to bend over the horizontal surface. The problem of the proposed system is that users are not able to directly click or select a target object. A hover state is needed to indicate where the touch point is mapped onto the vertical surface. Schmidt et al. address this problem by projecting the shadow of the arm hovering above the horizontal input surface onto the vertical display. This require the users to constantly hover their arms above the horizontal surface, which is, according to his users, again cumbersome and uncomfortable. The problem of the missing hover state was later

picked-up by Voelker et al. [26] by extending Buxton's [4] common two state interaction model of touch interfaces with a *tracking* state that allow users to touch the surface without directly manipulating the object below the touch point. This allow users to rest their arms on the horizontal display without unintentionally manipulating an object displayed on the vertical surface. Gilliot et al. [7] analyzed in impact of size and aspect ratio differences between the input and the output surfaces on indirect pointing tasks. Their studies showed that especially a different aspect ratio between input and output surface has a strong negative effect on the users performance. In contrast to the related work, we show how to switch between the two modes (direct and indirect touch)and we overcome the problem of indirect touch systems where the horizontal touch surface is degraded to merely an input surface.

## 2.2 Touch and Gaze Input

Results by Stellmach et al. [20] indicate that gaze input may be used as a natural input channel as long as certain design considerations are taken into account. Other researchers conclude that due to the inaccuracy, the *double role of eye gaze*, and the *Midas Touch* problem [19], it is ineffective to use eye gaze to directly manipulate digital content or control cursors. The study by Turner et al. [23] show that manual input conditions outperform gaze in transferring objects from a personal device to a public display and vise versa. Also, it is shown that a dwell time method is slower in comparison to techniques that allow users to confirm their actions using touch [24]. Eye focus selection as an independent channel of input is used in several research projects due to its high speed, familiarity and naturalness [17, 18, 25]. The eyes typically acquire a target well before manual pointing is initiated, following the principle "what you look at is what you get" [29]. Users tend to look at a target before issuing a command, starting an interaction, and look at the screen of interest, which makes gaze tracking a good interaction technique for window targeting [15, 25]. Using gaze as an additional input modality was also studied with a variety of user modalities other than touch. A study by Ashdown et al. [1] shows that combining head tracking with mouse input for a multi-monitor system is preferred by the users due to reduced mouse movement. Head motion is more stable, less accurately indicates the user's focus of attention, because eyes can move independently of the head.

The MAGIC (Manual And Gaze Input Cascade) technique proposed by Zhai et al. [30] is a combination of mouse and gaze input for fast target selection. Fono and Vertegaal [6] present an attentive windowing technique that uses eye tracking for focus selection, evaluated four focus selection techniques, and conclude that eye-controlled zooming windows with key activation provides efficient and effective alternative to current focus windows selection techniques. Eye tracking with key activation is, on average, about as twice as fast as mouse or hotkeys. Fono and Vertegaal results also show that despite the difference in speed between automatic activation and key activation for eye input, the eye input with key activation is a more effective method overall for focus window selection (about 72% faster than manual conditions), and was also preferred by most of the participants. Nancel et al. [11] investigated high precision pointing techniques for remotely acquiring targets and concluded that using head orientation for coarse control of the cursor and touch for precise selection was the most favorable and successful technique.

There are several approaches to combine gaze with manual interaction. Turner et al. [23, 24] combine gaze with mobile input modalities in order to transfer data between public and close proximity

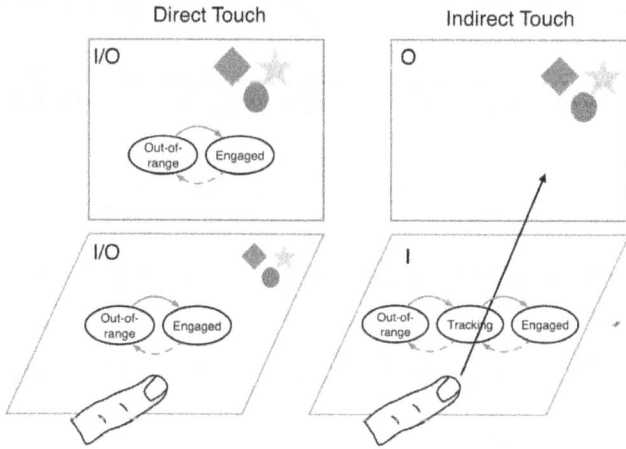

**Figure 2: Direct and indirect touch interaction models for interactive workspaces**

personal displays. The techniques for interaction in such environments are already outlined [15, 24]. Turner et al.'s study shows that manual input conditions outperform gaze positioning, which gives an advantage to the usage of manual input and leaves gaze a supporting role as a switching technique between the screens of interest. As recently shown by Pfeuffer et al. [12], the user's gaze can be used to perform this mode switch. They use gaze in combination with a single tabletop to place the user's touch points at the point of the display where the user is looking at by following the principle "gaze selects & touch manipulates". Their qualitative user study confirms the benefits of combining gaze and touch such as reachability, no occlusion, speed, less fatigue and less physical movement, and they provide a design space analysis of the properties of combining gaze and touch versus direct touch, and present several applications that explore how gaze-touch can be used alongside direct touch.

In contrast to Pfeuffer et al. and other related work, we make use of the user's gaze in interactive workspaces and extend the existing interaction models by two new variants. To our knowledge gaze supported touch input for interactive workspaces has not been investigated or researched before. Both modalities (touch and gaze) have been researched before separately or in combination, but in different contexts and especially not in the context of interactive workbenches as described in this paper. We also provide quantifiable results with a series of controlled experiments. Although gaze in combination with touch has been researched in recent years, we think that our results are important to get a better understanding for how gaze and touch can complement each other in other contexts, such as an interactive workbench that we investigate in detail in this paper.

## 3. INTERACTION TECHNIQUES

Currently, the default way to interact with interactive desktop workspaces is to use Buxton's [4] two-state touch model for both surfaces, as shown in Figure 2 (left). This allows the users to interact with both surfaces in the same way (namely direct touch) without having to change between different interaction techniques. Furthermore, it allows the users to interact with both surfaces using both hands and multiple finger at the same time. In our evaluation we use direct touch (DT) as a baseline condition to compare against the two new techniques we introduce in the paper. For DT a strong

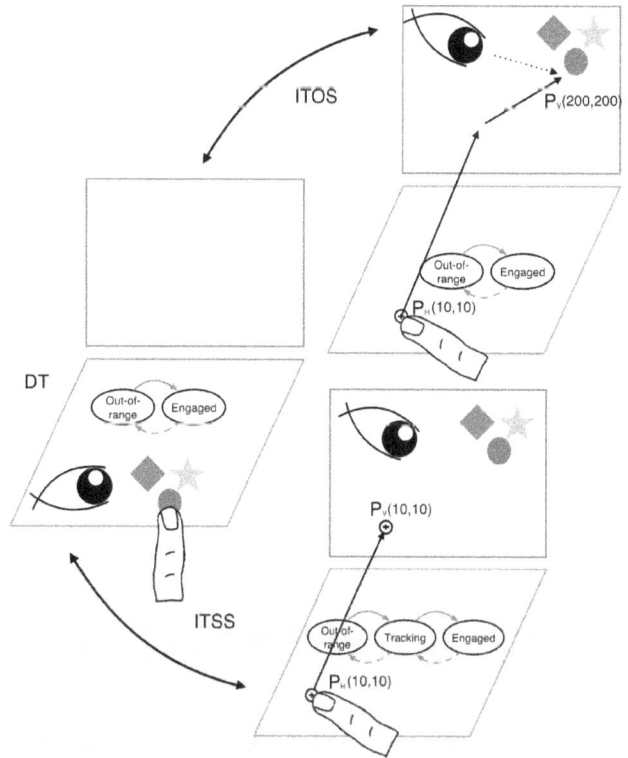

**Figure 3: DT– traditional direct touch interaction. While using ITSS, user's touch from the horizontal screen is absolutely mapped to the vertical screen, if the user is looking at it. While using ITOS, user's touch is directly mapped to the object on the vertical screen that is in the user's focus.**

predictor for the time to point to a certain target is Fitts' law [5]. Recently, it has been adapted and extended to predict the pointing performance on modern touch screens [3]. As both of our new interaction techniques use a combination of touch and gaze, Fitts' law cannot be directly applied. Fitts' law was designed to predict the time needed for rapid aimed pointing tasks only. Therefore it cannot be used to predict the output of our studies. Nevertheless, similar to what is predicted by Fitts' law for simple target acquisitions, we also observed that both new interaction techniques (ITTS and ITOS) follow a similar, but more complex, model, that could be formalised in future research. As mentioned earlier, interacting with the vertical surface using DT can be cumbersome [27] and users prefer to provide input mainly on the horizontal surface. To overcome this problem, users can make use of indirect touch (IT) as illustrated in Figure 2 (right). The touch input on the horizontal surface is mapped to the vertical surface and allows users to remain in a comfortable seating positing, while interacting with the vertical surface. Again the users can use both hands and multiple fingers at the same time. One could assume the following situation: If users selects a target with our gaze supported technique, there could be a case where they simply need to confirm their gaze supported selection without even moving their hand. In this case, the link between the time needed to select a target and the distance to this target in the real world is broken. In addition, we also evaluate our interaction techniques with different dragging operations. The main difference to direct touch is that the users is not directly touching the objects anymore. The user rather has to estimate the area of the horizontal surface which maps to the object they want to touch.

This and the fact that in the common touch interaction model each touch directly manipulates the object that was hit by the touch lead to the problem that the user could unintentionally manipulate other objects while trying to hit one specific target using indirect touch. Therefore, a *tracking* [26] state is needed that allows users to aim for an object without manipulating the other objects (Fig. 2 right).

Furthermore, in an IT system the horizontal surface is only used as an input and not as an output device. In this paper, we present two novel interaction techniques, which combine both direct touch on the horizontal surface and indirect touch on a vertical surface. Since both interaction techniques could use the horizontal surface for input, the system needs to decide if the touch point created by the user should be used to directly interact with the horizontal surface (DT) or used to indirectly interact with a vertical surface (IT). We make use of the user's gaze to do this, as gaze input can be easily used as an additional input channel [20]. Furthermore, it was also shown by several research project that especially the combination of touch and gaze input works very well [12, 18, 19]. The problem of using the user's gaze is inconsistency of the eye due to its constant movement [10] and the fact that it can be easily distracted by unexpected events. For those reasons, our interaction techniques are using the user's gaze only for the *non-critical tasks* such as selecting the surface, area, or object which the user is currently looking at and to translate the initial position of the touch point. Every other operation, such as translating or manipulating the object, is done by the user's touch to prevent errors and reduce the impact of the gaze on the usability of the system.

In the following, we present two novel interaction concepts that use a gaze supported switching mechanism. Both are also illustrated in the attached video.

## 3.1 Indirect Touch Surface Selection (ITSS)

The first interaction technique, named ITSS, combines absolute DT and absolute IT: If the gaze is directed towards the horizontal touch surface, the system maps the touch point to the horizontal screen, allowing the user to interact with the object using the two-state DT interaction model (Fig. 3 left). If the user is looking at the vertical surface, the touch is translated using an absolute mapping to this particular vertical surface. For example, if both surfaces have the same size and resolution, when a user touches at point $P_H(10, 10)$ on the horizontal screen, the touch point is mapped to point $P_V(10, 10)$ on the currently looked at surface. Now, instead of using the two state interaction model, the three state indirect touch model [26] is used. Each new touch point that is mapped to a vertical surface is in a *tracking* state, which allows the user to move the finger over the surfaces without manipulating any object. To change the touch to the *engaged* state, which allows object manipulation, the user has to execute a *lift-and-tap* gesture as suggested by Voelker et al. [26]. This process is illustrated in Figure 3. In order to provide feedback, a cursor represents the touch point, displayed on the surface to which it is mapped. In both cases, if the touch is mapped to the horizontal or to a vertical surface, the touch stays on the surface until the user releases the finger from the input surface.. However, this is not the focus of this paper.

For the ITSS interaction technique we used an absolute mapping to prevent confusion when multiple cursors are present on the screen. Especially usage scenarios which involve multi-touch and bi-manual multi-touch input, cognitive load from mapping multiple touches and multiple cursors would be overwhelming.

## 3.2 Indirect Touch Object Selection (ITOS)

The first step of the ITOS interaction technique is the same as ITSS. Again, if the gaze is directed towards the horizontal touch surface, the system maps the touch point to the horizontal screen, allowing the user to interact with the object using the two-state DT interaction model.

For the second step, we initially planed to use the user's gaze not only to select the surface as in ITSS, but instead transfer the initial touch point to the position of the surface where the user is currently looking at. However, to the constant movement of the eyes, it ís complicated to determine the exact position where the user is looking at as shown by Stellmach et al. [18].

Therefore, we choose to use a similar snapping mechanism for the ITOS technique as proposed by Pfeuffer et al. [12]. If the user is looking at the vertical surface or outside the horizontal screen, the touch is now translated to the object, on which the users gaze is concentrated. In this case, the user's gaze selects an object by highlighting it and a touch confirms this selection. To determine which object the user is currently looking at, we use an approach similar to the Bubble Cursor technique introduced by Grossman and Balakrishnan [8]. If a user touches the surface while he is looking at the vertical screen, the system calculates the area at which the user look at in the last 50 ms. If this area contains only one object this object is selected. If multiple objects are located in this area, the system calculates the center of the area and then selects the object which is closest to this center. For example, if a user touches point $P_H(10, 10)$ on the horizontal screen, and looks at the object on the vertical screen that is located at $P_V(200, 200)$, the touch point $P_H(10, 10)$ is mapped to point $P_V(200, 200)$. In contrast to the ITSS technique, using ITOS requires no *tracking* state, since the system highlights an object to which a touch is mapped before the user touches the screen. This allows the user to be sure to interact with one specific object without manipulating other objects.

## 4. USER STUDIES

We designed three different experiments to compare users interacting with different interaction techniques. We compared ITSS and ITOS against a DT baseline condition for a *tapping*, *dragging* (dragging an object on the vertical or the horizontal surface) and *cross dragging* (dragging an object from the vertical to the horizontal surface and vice versa) task. Even so it is known that interacting with a vertical display using DT leads to fatigue, as described in the introduction, we believe that users of future interactive workspaces will prefer direction manipulation [16] using touch instead of still relying on mouse and keyboard input typically used for GUIs, because the use of mouse and keyboard would require switches between different input concepts.

In this paper, we focus only on single-touch tasks to first understand how users perform using our two proposed interaction technique in basic tasks. In the future we plan to also evaluate more complex tasks that involve multiple fingers and both hands. Our experiments aims to answer the following questions:

1. Which technique is preferred in the indirect touch setup?

2. Which technique allows users to complete tasks faster and more accurate?

All three experiments were within subject experiments and we used the same setup and general procedure.

## 4.1 Participants

We recruited 14 participants (five female and nine male) aged between 23 and 36 (mean age 27.0). Twelve of the participants were right handed and two were left handed. All three experiments were conducted with the dominant hand of the user. On average, it took the participants about 1.2 h to complete all three experiments.

## 4.2 Apparatus

Participants sat at a desk with two touch displays, as shown in Figure 1. As a horizontal, screen we used a capacitive touch-sensing 27" Acer Touch display embedded in a custom made table at a height of 72 cm following ISO9241-5. For the vertical screen, we used a 27" Perceptive Pixel display, which was placed 55 cm from the edge of the table. Both displays had the same resolution of 2560 x 1440 pixels and the size of 597 x 336 mm. Both displays were connected to a Mac Pro running the software for the experiments. The effective touch frame rate for both displays was set to 60 Hz.

To determine the gaze of the users, we used the *Dikablis Glasses* by Ergoneers[1]. The *Dikablis Glasses* are a head-mounted eye tracking system that is able to detect the position of the user's gaze in a visual marker coordinate system. Two markers were placed around the vertical display, as shown in Figure 1. By doing so, we can convert the gaze coordinates into the the pixel coordinate system of the vertical screen with an accuracy of about 1.5 cm (63 px). The effective frame rate of the eye tracker was also set to 60 Hz. The eye tracker was calibrated with a standard routine that comes with the eye tracker for each user before conducting the user study. This calibration process took about 30 seconds.

## 4.3 General Procedure

The participants conducted each experiment with all three interactions techniques (DT, ITSS and ITOS). Each participant conducted the experiments in a random order. No learning effects were observed by the experimenter or appeared in the data. Before the experiments, the users could run a ten minute test trials to familiarize themselves with the new interaction techniques and the different techniques. It was emphasized to solve a task as fast and as accurately as possible.

## 4.4 Experiment 1: Tapping

In the first experiment, we investigated the effect of the three different interaction techniques on the users' performance by running the tapping task on both the horizontal and vertical surface.

### 4.4.1 Task

Participants were asked to touch blue circles, which were displayed alternating on the horizontal and vertical surface. As soon as the user touched the circle he had to hold his finger for 0.5 seconds on the circle before the circle disappeared and a new target circle on the other surface appeared. The task time was measured from the moment the target circle was visible till the moment it was successfully touched by the user. In order to complete one trial, users had to repeat this task for 50 targets, 25 on the vertical and 25 on the horizontal surface. The exact position of these targets was predefined and was the same for all the users. During a trial the circle size was fixed. The users had to conduct one trial for three different circle radii—63 px (1.5 cm), 126 px (3 cm), 252 px (6 cm). The 1.5 cm circle represents the smallest touchable button on a mobile device such as the Apple iPhone, the 3 cm circle

[1]http://www.ergoneers.com/

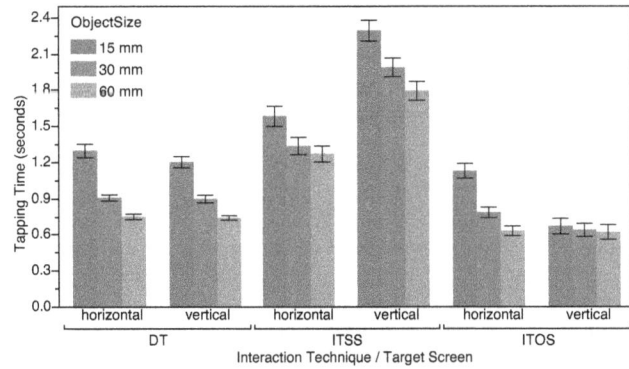

**Figure 4: Users tapping times using all three interaction techniques in the Tapping experiment. Whiskers denote 95% confidence interval.**

a control element, and the 6 cm circle a picture or a document. The experimental design was a 3 (interaction technique) × 3 (target size) × 2 (target surface) mixed design with repeated measurements, which summarizes to a total of 450 tapping tasks per user. Since the required arm movement in the ITSS condition is expected to be smaller compared to ITTS and DT, we hypothesized the following outcome:

**H1:** Touching a target displayed on the vertical surface using indirect touch object selection is faster than using indirect touch surface selection and direct touch.

### 4.4.2 Results

The measured values were logarithmically transformed, according to the logarithmic distribution of the data. The data was analyzed for all dependent variables *interaction technique*, *target size* and *target surface* using a repeated measures ANOVA. We saw a significant main effect for the factor *interaction technique* in the ANOVA results ($F(2, 221) = 438.8255; p = 0.0001$). The post-hoc Tukey HSD test comparison showed that overall tapping durations using ITOS (mean 0.61 sec) were 32% shorter than while using DT (mean 0.9 sec) and 60% shorter than ITSS (mean 1.54 sec). The ANOVA showed a significant main effect of the factor *target size* ($F(2, 221) = 78.7119; p = 0.0001$). The post-hoc Tukey HSD comparison showed that the tapping time on the objects with a size of 63 px (1.5 cm) (mean 1.14 sec) was 19% longer than on the objects with a size of 126 px (3 cm) (mean 0.92 sec) and 29% longer than on the objects of size 252 px (6 cm) (mean 0.8 sec) for all three techniques. The main effect of the factor *target surface* was not significant. The ANOVA showed a significant interaction effect between the factors *interaction technique, target size* and *target surface* ($F(4, 221) = 4.301; p = 0.0001$). The post-hoc Tukey HSD comparison revealed among other results the following: Using ITSS on the vertical screen the tapping times for all three target sizes was significantly slow compared to both other interaction techniques. On average the users need 2.15 sec to tap the small circles, 1.87 sec to tap the medium circles, and 1.68 sec to tap the large circles. Compared to both other interaction techniques, the users were faster using ITOS (H1). On average the users need 0.52 sec to tap the small circles, 0.5 sec to tap the medium circles, and 0.49 sec to tap the large circles.

### 4.4.3 Discussion

As expected, the ITOS technique was overall the fastest tapping technique in comparison to DT and ITSS (Fig. 4). This can be explained by observing how users executed these tapping tasks. At the moment the new target was displayed, the users already touched the horizontal surface, since they previously touched a target object on the horizontal surface. So they only had to find and look at the new target to trigger the selection process. As soon as the target was highlighted, they only had to lift and tap anywhere on the horizontal surface again. Both of these actions can be executed very fast, especially finding and looking at a object on a nearly empty display. But also executing a lift and tap gesture on the horizontal surface can be done very fast, the users did not have to hit the same position on the display which they touched before releasing the finger. In comparison to other interaction techniques, ITSS required a longer interaction sequence. In the direct touch condition, the users had to move their entire arm to touch an object on the vertical surface, which required more time, since not only the arm muscles are involved in the movement, but also the shoulder. In the ITSS condition, the users also had to find and look at the new target, but instead of lifting and tapping anywhere on the surface, the users had to execute a more complex sequence of actions. First, the users had to estimate to which of the surfaces their touch is currently mapped. Secondly, the users had to move their arms to the estimated area and touch the horizontal surface with their fingers. Next the users had to identify whether the cursor on the vertical surface was actually on the target. If so, the user had to execute a lift-and-tap gesture, in order to successfully hit the target. If not, the users had to move their fingers until the cursor was on the target and then execute the gesture. In contrast to the lift and tap gesture in the ITOS condition, the users had to make sure that they tapped on the target.

Considering the object size, the objects with a bigger size were selected faster than smaller ones. However, this is not true in the ITOS condition for targets that where displayed on the vertical surface. For these targets, no significant differences were observed. This can also be explained by the fact that finding and looking at an object on an otherwise empty screen is very fast and is in this experiment not influenced by the size of the object. In other use cases, where in a small area of the surface a lot of object are displayed (e.g. menu with multiple buttons), the user would require more time to find the desired object. Also, due to the constant eye movement, the system would have taken longer time to decide at which of the object the user is currently looking.

## 4.5 Experiment 2: Parallel Dragging

After we analyzed how three interaction techniques influenced the users performance on tapping the objects, we wanted to explore how the users' performance is influenced by our interaction techniques while dragging the objects on the horizontal and vertical surfaces. Furthermore, for the direct touch condition, we wanted to check whether the vertical dragging introduces a fatigue effect that influences the users' performance.

### 4.5.1 Task

Users were asked to drag blue circles (160 px) to yellow rings (160 px) within the same display on the horizontal and vertical screens one after another. The initial scene displayed two circle ring pairs with a fixed distance of 1300 px (30 cm). Users were instructed to first start an the horizontal screen. The object is accounted as being at the destination if the position of the circle matches the destination ring within a range of 20 px. When circle and ring match and the user releases the hand, both objects disappear from the scene. This task is then repeated on the vertical surface. The next trial starts from the screen where the previous one

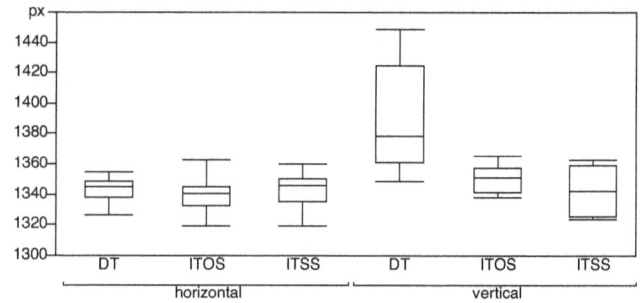

**Figure 5: User's dragging trajectory length using all three interaction techniques subtask in the Dragging experiment. Scale starts at 1300 px which was the minimal distance the user had to drag. Whiskers denote 95% confidence intervals.**

was finished. To complete this task, users had to drag 25 objects into its targets on each screen. As depended variables we measured the dragging times on vertical and horizontal screens. Time was measured from the moment the circle was touched by the user until it was successfully released in its target ring on the same surface. Furthermore, the length of dragging trajectories was recorded.

The experimental design was a 3 (interaction technique) × 2 (surface) mixed design with repeated measurements, which summarizes to a total of 300 dragging tasks per user. Based on previous research [27], that investigated the use of DT for an interactive workspace, and based on the fact that the user cannot rest their arms while interacting directly with the vertical surface, we hypothesized the following outcomes for the second experiment:

**H2:** Direct dragging is faster than indirect.

**H3:** Direct dragging an object on the vertical surface is less accurate than direct dragging on the horizontal and indirect dragging on the vertical surface.

**H4:** The dragging trajectory length increases over time while dragging objects on the vertical surface using DT.

### 4.5.2 Results

Due to the logarithmic distribution of the measured values for both depended variables, dragging time and trajectory length were logarithmically transformed. We analyzed both depended variables using a repeated measures ANOVA. For the *trajectory length*, the ANOVA reported a significant main effect of the factors *interaction technique* ($F(2, 65) = 13.4972; p = 0.0001$) and *surface* ($F(2, 65) = 18.5804; p = 0.0001$). The interaction also showed a significant effect ($F(2, 65) = 12.5804; p = 0.0001$). The post-hoc Tukey HSD showed that the dragging trajectory for the DT (mean 1368 px) was significant longer then the dragging trajectories for ITSS (mean 1347 px) and ITOS (mean 1346 px). It also showed that the trajectory length on the vertical surface (mean 1362 px) was significant longer than the trajectory length on the horizontal surface (mean 1345 px). The post-hoc Tukey HSD for the interaction showed that the trajectory length for the DT condition on the vertical surface (mean 1391 px) was significant longer than the other conditions (mean 1344–1350 px), as shown Figure 5. For the variable *time*, the ANOVA reported a significant main effect of the factors *interaction technique* ($F(2, 65) = 27.6531; p = 0.0001$) and *surface* ($F(2, 65) = 19.2332; p = 0.0001$). The interaction

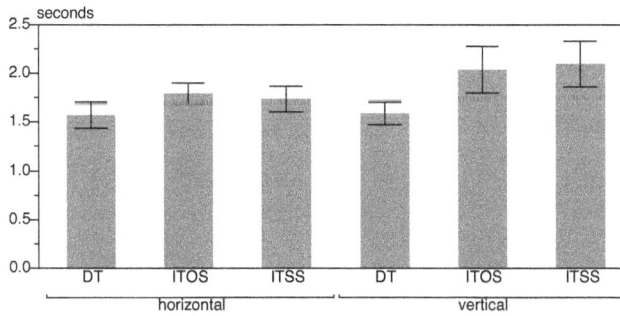

**Figure 6: Users dragging times using all three interaction techniques subtask in the Dragging experiment. Whiskers denote 95% confidence interval.**

| | df | | F | p |
|---|---|---|---|---|
| Overall time | | | | |
| Interaction technique | 2 | 276 | 57.1986 | <.0001 |
| Dragging direction | 2 | 276 | 12.7149 | <.0001 |
| Vertical time | | | | |
| Interaction technique | 2 | 276 | 10.9089 | <.0001 |
| Dragging direction | 2 | 276 | 146.1459 | <.0001 |
| Switching time | | | | |
| Interaction technique | 2 | 276 | 33.1058 | <.0001 |
| Dragging direction | 2 | 276 | 15.3929 | <.0001 |
| Overall trajectory | | | | |
| Interaction technique | 2 | 276 | 65.3526 | <.0001 |
| Dragging angle | 2 | 276 | 29.1385 | <.0001 |
| Vertical trajectory length | | | | |
| Interaction technique | 2 | 276 | 3.4964 | .0316 |
| Dragging angle | 2 | 276 | 9.5764 | <.0001 |
| Dragging direction | 2 | 276 | 26.3364 | <.0001 |
| Horizontal trajectory length | | | | |
| Interaction technique | 2 | 276 | 6.7045 | .0014 |
| Dragging angle | 2 | 276 | 9.5764 | <.0001 |
| Dragging direction | 2 | 276 | 12.0905 | <.0001 |

**Figure 7: Significant main effects and interaction for the dependent variables in the CrossDragging experiment.**

also showed a significant effect ($F(2, 65) = 6.9140; p = 0.0001$). The post-hoc Tukey HSD showed that the dragging time for the DT (mean 1.583 sec) was significant shorter than the dragging trajectories for ITSS (mean 1.901 sec) and ITOS (mean 1.8729 sec). It also showed that the dragging time on the horizontal surface (mean 1.869 sec) was significantly shorter than the dragging time on the vertical surface (mean 1.695 sec). The post-hoc Tukey HSD for the interaction (Fig. 6) showed that the dragging time for the ITOS and the ITSS condition on the vertical surface (mean 1.994 sec; 2.08 sec) was significantly longer than the other conditions (mean 1.571–1.75 sec).

### 4.5.3 Discussion

As shown in Figure 5, the user's dragging trajectory is longer while dragging an object directly on the vertical surface in comparison to dragging it directly on the horizontal or indirectly on the vertical surface. As this could be expected, this can be explained by the understanding of the user's dragging operation execution. Movement of the fingers on the horizontal surface involves mostly the movement of the forearm and the wrist. However, users are able to rest their hands on the table during the horizontal dragging operation. When users are directly touching the vertical surface, the dragging movement mostly involve the upper arm and shoulder joints, which is more inaccurate as shown by Hammerton et al. [9]. Interestingly, as shown in Figure 6, the DT technique was overall the fastest dragging technique on the vertical screen in comparison to the other two. The shorter task-completion time in the DT condition might be caused by a fatigue users experienced after some time of interaction. Therefore, physical exhaustion decreases the time users want to spend holding their hands in the air. Furthermore, this could also indicated that dragging an object using indirect touch is cognitively more challenging than dragging it directly. Both points need to be taken into consideration, when designing interaction workspace for all-day use.

Considering the distance an object traveled on the vertical screen, it was longer for the DT technique than for the other two techniques, which could be explained by the loss of accuracy after a long-term DT interaction on the vertical screen. Physical movement of the hand while using ITSS and ITOS was always performed on the horizontal surface, which was causing less fatigue over time, because users were resting their hands on the surface while interacting. This shows an interesting interplay between the vertical and the horizontal surface. After this dragging experiment, mostly all users (twelfth) stated that especially dragging objects in the DT condition was extremely exhaustive. However, H2 was rejected since our recorded data did not show that this had any effect on the dragging time or trajectory length. But since the experiment took only about 3–5 minutes maybe it was too short to show a fatigue effect using direct touch on the vertical surface.

## 4.6 Experiment 3: Cross Dragging

After analyzing dragging operations that were only involving one of the surfaces, we wanted to explore how the interaction techniques affect the user performance in dragging tasks that involve switching from one to the other surface. Furthermore, we also wanted to explore if the effect that Weiss et al. [27] found in their cross surface dragging experiment can be observed using our interaction techniques. They showed that in diagonal dragging operations that involved a horizontal and a vertical surface the user dragging trajectories are significant longer than in dragging operations that go straight up or downwards.

### 4.6.1 Task

The task setup is similar to the cross dragging experiment conducted by Weiss et al. [27]. Users were asked to drag a blue circle (160 px) placed on the one surface into a white ring (160 px) placed on the other surface. To execute this task, users had to drag the blue circle to the edge of the surface such that it is visible on the other surface. Then they had to switch to the other surface to continue dragging the circle. The initial scene displays a circle ring pair on the fixed distance of 1631 px (37 cm). Trials appeared in seven different movement angles: $45°$, $30°$, $15°$ to the left, $0°$ (which is straight up or downwards) and $15°$, $30°$, $45°$ to the right.

Dragging had to start either on the horizontal (upwards) or vertical (downwards) display. The object is accounted as being at the destination if the position of the circle matches the destination ring within a range of 20 px. When the circle and ring match and the users releases their hand, both objects disappear and a new pair appears. Participants worked through 35 upwards and 35 downwards trials for each of the three interaction techniques, which results in a total of 210 dragging operations per user. The system automatically stores horizontal/vertical distance, and vertical, horizontal, and switch time.

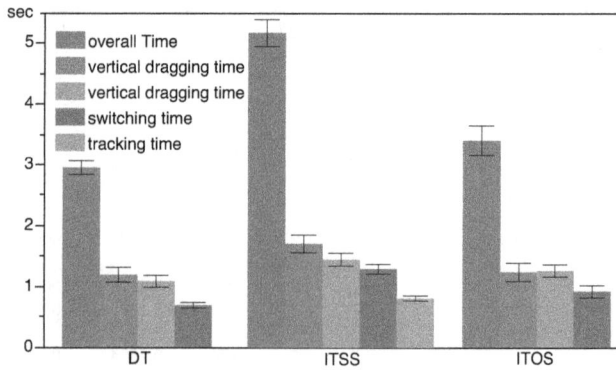

**Figure 8: Users dragging times for the different subtask in the CrossDragging experiment. Whiskers denote 95% confidence interval.**

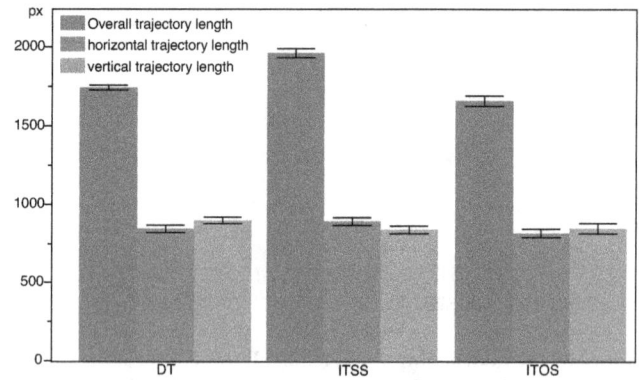

**Figure 9: Users dragging trajectory length in the CrossDragging experiment. Whiskers denote 95% confidence interval.**

The experimental design was a 3 (interaction technique) × 2 (vertical direction) × 7 (dragging angle) mixed design with repeated measurements. With five repetitions per target, each user had to perform 210 cross surface dragging operations. Again, by extrapolating the results of the study conducted by Weiss et al. [27] (H7) and based on the assumption that users can glance at an object faster than touching the object (H5, H6), we hypothesized the following outcomes:

**H5:** Overall, users complete the dragging operations faster using ITOS than using the other interaction techniques.

**H6:** Using ITOS, the time in which the user switches from interacting with one surface to interacting with the other surface is the shortest.

**H7:** The overall dragging trajectory is longer for larger dragging angles.

### 4.6.2 Results

Due to the logarithmic distribution of the measured values for all dependent variables, such as *overall time* (overall task completion time), *vertical time* (time needed to move an object on the vertical screen), *switching time* (time needed to switch from the horizontal to the vertical screen and vice versa), *overall trajectory* (overall physical distance user's finger traveled on both screens), *vertical trajectory length* ( physical distance user's finger traveled on the vertical screen), *horizontal trajectory length* (the physical distance user's finger traveled on the horizontal screen), all of them were logarithmically transformed. A repeated measures ANOVA was conducted to compare the effect of interaction technique, dragging direction, and dragging angle as well as their interactions on the overall, horizontal and vertical dragging trajectory length, time, and switching time. The significant results are shown in Figure 7. For the post-hoc test the Student's t-test was used for the dragging direction variable. For the other variables we used the Tukey HSD test.

The post-hoc test for the *interaction technique* showed that the overall time using ITSS (4.99 sec) was significantly shorter than ITOS (3.183 sec) and DT (2.87 sec). Furthermore, upwards dragging (3.87 sec) was significantly slower than the downwards dragging (3.29 sec). The post-hoc test for the *vertical time* revealed the same results as for the overall time. Using ITSS (1.54 sec) was significantly slower than ITOS (1.06 sec) and DT (0.98 sec). Also,

dragging upwards on the vertical surface (1.78 sec) took significantly longer than dragging downwards (0.77 sec). Similarly, for the horizontal dragging time, the post-hoc test revealed for the *interaction technique* the same results as for the overall time. Using ITSS (1.29 sec) was significantly slower than ITOS (1.08 sec) and DT (0.95 sec). Dragging upwards (0.94 sec) on the horizontal surface was significantly faster than dragging downwards (1.53 sec).

Switching using DT (0.59 sec) was significantly faster than ITOS (0.83 sec), which was significantly faster than ITSS (1.32 sec). Switching form the vertical to the horizontal surface (0.74 sec) was faster than switching from horizontal to the vertical (1.01 sec).

The post-hoc test for the *interaction technique* showed that the *overall length* using ITOS (1568 px) was significantly shorter than for DT (1689 px) and ITSS (1879 px). For the *deltaAngle* factor the post-hoc test showed that *overall length* for 0° angle (1707 px) was significantly shorter than for 15° (1756 px), 30° (1809 px) and 45° (1851 px). The same tendency was shown for the factor *horizontal length*: for 0° angle *horizontal length* (802 px) was significantly shorter than for 15° (831 px), 30° (857 px) and 45° (879 px).

### 4.6.3 Discussion

As expected, the overall time and time on the vertical surface were longer for the ITSS technique than for the other two (Fig. 8). The primary reason is the existence of an additional *tracking* state in the interaction model. Users spend a lot of time on the moving the cursor to the object they want to select, while for DT, they could directly physically reach the target or for ITOS just look at the object of interest, which requires a much smaller amount of time. However, since no difference between the users performance between using ITOS and DT was found, H5 was rejected. A not obvious factor is the physical distance the user's arm had to travel in the air while switching between the vertical and horizontal surface. For DT, this distance is fixed and the smallest, and equals to the distance between the lower edge of the vertical screen and the upper edge of the horizontal. For ITOS, this distance is not fixed and depends on the strategy the user has chosen to use. As far as the user is not restricted by the touch area, after reaching the border between the horizontal and vertical screen, the distance depends on where the user touched the horizontal surface. Therefore, it equals the distance between the lower edge of the vertical screen and the point on the horizontal surface the user touched, which lays between the higher and lower edges of the horizontal screen. In the case of ITSS, traveling distance is always equal to the maximum—

**Figure 10: Concept how our gaze supported interaction techniques can be applied to multi-screen environments.**

the distance between the lower edge of the vertical screen and the lower edge of the horizontal. Moreover, for both the upward and downward moving direction those distances were the same. For this reason, the switch time as shown in Figure 8 is the longest for ITSS and comparably shorter for ITOS and DT. Furthermore, since in this case DT outperformed ITOS in terms of switching time H6 also does not hold.

Considering the overall time duration on the horizontal screen, it was the longest for ITSS in comparison to the other two techniques. The horizontal time for the three techniques for the upward direction is the same; because they repeat the same sequence of actions, the most influential part lays on the downward direction. As mentioned above, for the DT technique the physical movement distance in the air is static for both upwards and downwards directions. However, for the ITOS technique, users could overcome the border between the screens without re-grabbing an object and move it for some time on the horizontal screen without reaching the target. Therefore, the time needed for the movement on the horizontal screen was comparably lower than for ITSS, where users always had to move an arm from the lower edge to the upper edge of the horizontal screen. H7 was confirmed by our results and it seems that the dragging trajectories are longer for more diagonal dragging operations. These results show, that this effect is not only true on curved surfaces [27], but also for systems that combine horizontal and vertical surfaces that are not connected by a curved surface. Interestingly is that this effect is also true if the users are not directly interacting with the vertical surface. If we look at the results for the horizontal and vertical dragging trajectories, this effect is only visible for the horizontal surface. This leads to the assumption that users try to minimize their movement on the vertical surface even when they are not directly interacting with it. In general these results indicate that even if interaction using indirect touch and direct touch are execute on the same surface user tend to prefer direct touch over interact touch in basic operations.

## 5. MULTI-SCREEN WORKSPACES

Both interaction techniques, ITSS and ITOS, can be extended to system setups that include multiple vertical surfaces (Fig. 10). Instead of switching only between horizontal and vertical screens for ITSS, the system allows switching among a number of vertical surfaces and activating the screen that is currently in the user's focus. Using ITOS, it does not matter for the system how many displays

are presented in the setup, since the user selects an object using its gaze. Selection can be done for objects on one horizontal surface or $n$ vertical surfaces as long as the user is able to see an object on one of the surfaces. However, in a setup with multiple vertical screens that are far away from the user using ITSS seems to be a better solution. The reason is the easiness of determining whether a user is looking at a large screen that is far away or identifying one small object on that screen. Moreover, for ITSS low-cost head- or eye-trackers can be used. We also envision head- or eye-tracking technology, that is embedded in the displays, that could replace the head-mounted head- or eye-tracker and could open up further interaction contexts. Using the head position as a focus 'pointer' is more robust and precise, and usage of external eye-gaze trackers is more comfortable, especially for a long time interaction.

## 6. CONCLUSION & FUTURE WORK

In this paper, we propose two novel gaze-based interaction techniques, namely ITSS and ITOS, for easy touch interaction for interactive workspaces. With the help of these gaze supported interaction techniques it is possible to enrich the interaction with interactive workspaces as first envisioned by Tognazzini's Starfire [22] concept. By introducing gaze as a additional modalities we are able to reduce the time that is needed to reach targets on the vertical screen as well as reduce effort that is needed to interact with the system. This enables users to comfortably interact with interactive workspaces for a longer time (e.g. a full working day). Nevertheless further studies are needed to investigate these long-term effects. We evaluated the performance of these interaction techniques compared to DT for different standard tasks, such as tapping and dragging an object within or between the screens. Our results indicate that ITOS outperforms the DT and ITSS in terms of tapping speed. ITOS was about 32% faster than DT. We believe that these techniques can make interactive workspaces more user friendly in the future.

With the help of our studies we analyzed the characteristic of these interaction techniques compared to DT. In the case of the dragging an object on a screen, DT outperformed ITOS and ITSS in speed on the vertical screen, but was least accurate, reporting the longest traveled distances on the vertical screen. Results of cross dragging between the screens indicate that moving an object downwards over all techniques was faster than upwards. The traveled distance of the finger on the screen was increasing with the angle between the object and the target. For this task, and in terms of speed, direct touch outperformed ITSS by 42% and ITOS by 9%. We conclude that ITOS provides an efficient and effective alternative in some situations for manipulation with indirect touch systems. We only explored basic single finger tasks in which only few objects were displayed on the surfaces. In use cases where multiple small objects are displayed in the same area of a vertical surface, using ITOS could become more difficult. In these cases, it is more complicated for the system to decide at which object the user is looking at, which could lead to a wrong object selection.

We believe that our new techniques can be used in different interaction contexts, even so both require the users to wear a eye-tracker. These interaction contexts include future office spaces or traffic control rooms. Gaze-based interaction offers a new direction of using systems that combine one or more horizontal and vertical touch screens and is not only limited to interactive workspaces. In the future, we want to investigate the usage of our proposed interaction techniques for setups with one horizontal, but multiple vertical touch screens. We also believe that advantages in technology will make setups with continuous surfaces possible as originally envisioned by Curve [28] and BendDesk [27]. It would also be interesting to extend or adapt Fitts' law to predict the time needed to select a certain target with ITTS or ITOS. Furthermore, we also want to explore mobile settings, where the horizontal surface is, for example, an iPad, and the users interacts with multiple screens situated in their environment. This will lead to new application designs, where eye gaze can be used complementary to direct touch interaction. Additionally, we intend to specify the limitations of such systems, use cases.

## 7. ACKNOWLEDGEMENTS

This work was partially funded by the German B-IT Foundation. We would like to thank the anonymous reviewers for their valuable comments. We are grateful to Davy Vanacken for proof-reading the paper.

## 8. REFERENCES

[1] Ashdown, M., Oka, K., and Sato, Y. Combining Head Tracking and Mouse Input for a GUI on Multiple Monitors. In *CHI EA*, ACM (New York, USA, 2005), 1188–1191.

[2] Bi, X., Grossman, T., Matejka, J., and Fitzmaurice, G. Magic Desk: Bringing Multitouch Surfaces into Desktop Work. In *Proc. CHI*, ACM (New York, USA, 2011), 2511–2520.

[3] Bi, X., Li, Y., and Zhai, S. FFitts Law: Modeling Finger Touch with Fitts' Law. In *Proc. CHI*, ACM (New York, USA, 2013), 1363–1372.

[4] Buxton, W. A Three-State Model of Graphical Input. In *Proc. INTERACT*, North-Holland Publishing Co. (Amsterdam, The Netherlands, 1990), 449–456.

[5] Fitts, P. M. The Information Capacity of the Human Motor System in Controlling the Amplitude of Movement. *Journal of experimental psychology 47*, 6 (1954), 381.

[6] Fono, D., and Vertegaal, R. EyeWindows: Evaluation of Eye-controlled Zooming Windows for Focus Selection. In *Proc. CHI*, ACM (New York, USA, 2005), 151–160.

[7] Gilliot, J., Casiez, G., and Roussel, N. Impact of Form Factors and Input Conditions on Absolute Indirect-touch Pointing Tasks. In *Proceedings of the SIGCHI Conference on Human Factors in Computing Systems*, ACM (New York, USA, 2014), 723–732.

[8] Grossman, T., and Balakrishnan, R. The Bubble Cursor: Enhancing Target Acquisition by Dynamic Resizing of the Cursor's Activation Area. In *Proc. CHI*, ACM (New York, USA, 2005), 281–290.

[9] Hammerton, M., and Tickner, A. H. An Investigation into the Comparative Suitability of Forearm, Hand and Thumb Controls in Acquisition Tasks. *Ergonomics 9* (1966), 125–130.

[10] Kern, D., Marshall, P., and Schmidt, A. Gazemarks: Gaze-based Visual Placeholders to Ease Attention Switching. In *Proc. CHI*, ACM (New York, USA, 2010), 2093–2102.

[11] Nancel, M., Chapuis, O., Pietriga, E., Yang, X.-D., Irani, P. P., and Beaudouin-Lafon, M. High-precision Pointing on Large Wall Displays Using Small Handheld Devices. In *Proc. CHI '13*, ACM (New York, USA, 2013), 831–840.

[12] Pfeuffer, K., Alexander, J., Chong, M. K., and Gellersen, H. Gaze-touch: Combining Gaze with Multi-touch for Interaction on the Same Surface. In *Proc. UIST*, ACM (New York, USA, 2014), 509–518.

[13] Schmidt, D., Block, F., and Gellersen, H. A Comparison of Direct and Indirect Multi-touch Input for Large Surfaces. In *Proc. INTERACT*, Springer-Verlag (Berlin, Heidelberg, 2009), 582–594.

[14] Schöning, J. Touching the Future: The Rise of Multitouch Interfaces. *PerAda Magazine* (2010), 5531.

[15] Shell, J. S., Vertegaal, R., Cheng, D., Skaburskis, A. W., Sohn, C., Stewart, A. J., Aoudeh, O., and Dickie, C. ECSGlasses and EyePliances: Using Attention to Open Sociable Windows of Interaction. In *Proc. ETRA*, ACM (New York, USA, 2004), 93–100.

[16] Shneiderman, B. Direct Manipulation for Comprehensible, Predictable and Controllable User Interfaces. In *Proceedings of the 2Nd International Conference on Intelligent User Interfaces*, IUI '97, ACM (New York, USA, 1997), 33–39.

[17] Smith, J. D., and Graham, T. C. N. Use of Eye Movements for Video Game Control. In *Proc. ACE*, ACM (New York, USA, 2006), Article 20.

[18] Stellmach, S., and Dachselt, R. Look & touch: Gaze-supported target acquisition. In *Proc. CHI*, ACM (New York, USA, 2012), 2981–2990.

[19] Stellmach, S., and Dachselt, R. Still Looking: Investigating Seamless Gaze-supported Selection, Positioning, and Manipulation of Distant Targets. In *Proc. CHI*, ACM (New York, USA, 2013), 285–294.

[20] Stellmach, S., Stober, S., Nürnberger, A., and Dachselt, R. Designing Gaze-supported Multimodal Interactions for the Exploration of Large Image Collections. In *Proc. NGCA*, ACM (New York, USA, 2011), 1:1–1:8.

[21] Sutherland, I. E. Sketch Pad a Man-machine Graphical Communication System. In *Proc. DAC*, ACM (New York, USA, 1964), 6.329–6.346.

[22] Tognazzini, B. The "Starfire" Video Prototype Project: A Case History. In *Proc. CHI*, ACM (New York, USA, 1994), 99–105.

[23] Turner, J. Cross-device Eye-based Interaction. In *Proc. UIST Adjunct*, ACM (New York, USA, 2013), 37–40.

[24] Turner, J., Bulling, A., and Gellersen, H. Combining Gaze with Manual Interaction to Extend Physical Reach. In *Proc. PETMEI*, ACM (New York, USA, 2011), 33–36.

[25] Vertegaal, R., Mamuji, A., Sohn, C., and Cheng, D. Media Eyepliances: Using Eye Tracking for Remote Control Focus Selection of Appliances. In *CHI EA*, ACM (New York, USA, 2005), 1861–1864.

[26] Voelker, S., Wacharamanotham, C., and Borchers, J. An Evaluation of State Switching Methods for Indirect Touch Systems. In *Proc. CHI*, ACM (New York, USA, 2013), 745–754.

[27] Weiss, M., Voelker, S., Sutter, C., and Borchers, J. BendDesk: Dragging Across the Curve. In *Proc. ITS*, ACM (New York, USA, 2010), 1–10.

[28] Wimmer, R., Hennecke, F., Schulz, F., Boring, S., Butz, A., and Hussmann, H. Curve: Revisiting the Digital Desk. In *Proc. NordiCHI*, ACM (New York, USA, 2010), 561–570.

[29] Zhai, S. What's in the Eyes for Attentive Input. *Commun. ACM 46*, 3 (Mar. 2003), 34–39.

[30] Zhai, S., Morimoto, C., and Ihde, S. Manual and Gaze Input Cascaded (MAGIC) Pointing. In *Proc. CHI*, ACM (New York, USA, 1999), 246–253.

# GyroWand: IMU-based Raycasting for Augmented Reality Head-Mounted Displays

Juan David Hincapié-Ramos[1], Kasım Özacar[2], Pourang P. Irani[1], Yoshifumi Kitamura[2]

[1] University of Manitoba
Winnipeg, Manitoba, Canada
{jdhr, irani}@cs.umanitoba.ca

Research Institute of Electrical Communication,
Tohoku University, Sendai, Miyagi, Japan
{kozacar, kitamura}@riec.tohoku.ac.jp

## ABSTRACT

We present GyroWand, a raycasting technique for 3D interactions in self-contained augmented reality (AR) head-mounted displays. Unlike traditional raycasting which requires absolute spatial and rotational tracking of a user's hand or controller to direct the ray, GyroWand relies on the relative rotation values captured by an inertial measurement unit (IMU) on a handheld controller. These values cannot be directly mapped to the ray direction due to the phenomenon of sensor drift and the mismatch between the orientations of the physical controller and the virtual content. To address these challenges GyroWand 1) interprets the relative rotational values using a state machine which includes an anchor, an active, an out-of-sight and a disambiguation state; 2) handles drift by resetting the default rotation when the user moves between the anchor and active states; 3) does not initiate raycasting from the user's hand, but rather from other spatial coordinates (e.g. chin, shoulder, or chest); and 4) provides three new disambiguation mechanisms: Lock&Twist, Lock&Drag, and AutoTwist.

In a series of controlled user studies we evaluated the performance and convenience of different GyroWand design parameters. Results show that a ray originating from the user's chin facilitates selection. Results also show that Lock&Twist is faster and more accurate than other disambiguation mechanisms. We conclude with a summary of the lessons learned for the adoption of raycasting in mobile augmented reality head-mounted displays.

## Categories and Subject Descriptors
• Human-Computer Interaction ~ Interaction Techniques
• Computer Graphics ~ Mixed/augmented Reality.

## Keywords
GyroWand, raycasting, IMU, head-mounted displays

## 1. INTRODUCTION

Optical head-mounted displays (HMDs) enable augmented reality (AR) applications by blending virtual objects with the real world. Devices like EPSON's Moverio [7], Sony's SmartEyeglasses [26], and META's SpaceGlassess [14] are commercially-available HMDs that support these novel AR experiences in a mobile form-factor and at a fraction of the cost of earlier solutions. At the core of this new generation of devices are low-cost tracking technolo-

*SUI '15*, August 08 - 09, 2015, Los Angeles, CA, USA
© 2015 ACM. ISBN 978-1-4503-3703-8/15/08 $15.00
DOI: http://dx.doi.org/10.1145/2788940.2788947

gies that allow HMDs to interpret users' motion in the real world in relation to the virtual content for the purpose of navigation and interaction. Whereas previous AR devices required external and expensive equipment to track the users' motion, newer devices use techniques such as marker-based tracking [19], SLAM [30], and IMU-based dead-reckoning [18][32]. These tracking technologies enable AR applications to take place outside the research lab, in mobile settings without the need of fixed tracking infrastructure, and at an affordable price.

However, the advantages of pervasive tracking come at the cost of limiting interaction possibilities. Off-the-shelf devices often still depend on peripherals such as keyboard and mouse for user input (yet again reducing mobility) or hand-held touchpad controllers: input mechanisms that were created for other settings and conditions of use. Hand-gestures and other natural user interfaces (NUI) offer a compelling alternatives to peripherals, yet are limited to interacting with content relatively close to the user (direct manipulation) and are prone to tracking errors and arm fatigue [10].

Raycasting, an interaction technique widely explored in traditional virtual reality (VR), is another alternative available for AR [1]. Extensive research has explored the benefits of raycasting over other interaction techniques and there exist multiple design options to improve its performance [3]. Raycasting generally requires absolute tracking of the user's hand or of a hand-held controller (known as a wand), but the limited tracking capabilities of novel AR devices make it difficult to track this controller. Even when the HMD is equipped with cameras to track the environment or hand gestures, a hand-held controller is still normally outside the field-of-view (FoV) of the camera, for comfortable use. Our goal is to explore how to bring raycasting to AR HMDs, even when the controller lies outside the HMD camera's FoV.

Our approach to this research is to devise a way to reduce the tracking requirement from both the wand's exact position and

Figure 1. GyroWand enables raycasting in HMDs. In this example, the ray origin is the user's chin. The ray direction is controlled using the IMU on the hand-held controller.

rotation to simply its rotation. The wrist is highly dexterous [24], and with sensors readily available with HMDs ([7][26]), we consider how best to design a raycasting interface. In principle, the IMU rotation cannot be used directly to determine the direction of the ray due to intrinsic problems such as magnetic interference and sensor drift. Moreover, the user's movement in space creates a situation in which the display contents and ray direction are often not aligned with the HMD's FoV.

To address these challenges, and the central contribution of this paper, we introduce a raycasting technique called GyroWand (see Figure 1). GyroWand enables raycasting in AR HMDs using IMU rotational data from a handheld controller. GyroWand introduces four fundamental design differences from traditional raycasting:

- GyroWand interprets IMU rotational data using a state machine which includes an *anchor* state, an *active* state, an *out-of-sight* state, and a *disambiguation* state (see Section 4);
- GyroWand compensates for drift/interference by taking the orientation of the hand-held controller as the initial rotation (zero) when moving from the *anchor* to the *active* state.
- GyroWand does not initiate raycasting from the user's hand, but rather from any spatial coordinate (e.g. chin, shoulder);
- GyroWand provides three novel disambiguation methods: Lock&Drag, Lock&Twist and AutoTwist.

Our second contribution is an experimental exploration of how best to design GyroWand for 3D content selection. We present results of two controlled user studies revealing the most suitable design parameters: the origin of the virtual ray and the disambiguation mechanism. Our final contribution is a discussion of the lessons learned for the adoption of raycasting in AR HMDs.

## 2. RAYCASTING IN 3D INTERFACES

Raycasting has a long tradition in 3D user interfaces for virtual reality applications [1][3][22]. In raycasting, a virtual ray is casted from a point of origin along a given direction in the virtual environment. When a trigger event is issued by, for example, pressing a button on a hand-held controller, the system selects one of the virtual objects crossed by the ray – typically the object closest to the ray. Benefits of raycasting include having a precise pointer, jitter control and being a natural metaphor for distant pointing. However, raycasting also presents limitations such as poor control for object manipulation (translation, rotation) and the need to disambiguate among possible targets in depth when working in dense 3D environments. Despite these limitations, experimental results show that raycasting outperforms other 3D interaction techniques in selection tasks [3].

Raycasting implementations vary in various aspects including how the ray is controlled, the ray shape, and the method to disambiguate among possible targets. Controlling the ray requires a point of origin and a direction. These two values can be provided by tracking the position and orientation of a controller or wand [9][17][22], the bare user hands [4][14], the head [28], or a mix of hands and head [23]. For example, in Occlusion Selection the ray starts from the head and goes through the user's hand before hitting the target [23]. Another proposal is to use both hands to control the ray which adds the capacity to bend the ray by rotating the dominant hand [22]. Nonetheless, the most common approach relies on tracking a hand-held controller which can also help trigger selection events.

Another important variation is the shape of the ray: it can be an actual line in 3D space [1], or it can have an aperture angle providing a cone [8]. Using a cone improves the selection of

smaller targets and compensates for hand trembling and jitter, while increasing the need to disambiguate between possible targets.

Finally, another variation between raycasting implementations is the disambiguation mechanism, to distinguish which object on the ray's depth is of interest. When no disambiguation mechanism is offered, the system selects the object on the ray's path which is closest to the ray origin. This approach can be frustrating when the desired object is not the first one the ray crosses. Argelaguet and Andujar [1] classify disambiguation mechanisms in three types: manual, heuristic and behavioral. Manual disambiguation allows the user to perform a secondary selection between the initial set of highlighted objects, laying out the objects differently, such as with a linear or a flower menu [9], or by allowing the user to press a button on the controller to iterate among the selectable objects [27]. Another alternative is to use a 3D cursor along the ray: the object closest to the cursor is selected [9]. Heuristic disambiguation uses a predefined algorithm to "guess" the target the user wants to select. A common approach is to select the object closest to the ray or to the central axis of the cone. A more elaborate approach uses probabilistic models to determine the selection target. Finally, behavioral disambiguation takes into account the user's actions in a given time window to rank objects before the selection event is triggered [5][27][21]. Ranks can take into account distance-to-cone axis, the time the object has been inside the cone, the number of visible pixels, etc.

In this paper we explore similar aspects of control, shape and disambiguation for AR HMDs. Particularly, we use IMU-data to control the ray when the location and orientation of the controller are unknown. We also propose a cone of adjustable aperture as the ray shape. Finally, we investigate different disambiguation mechanisms that rely solely on rotational data.

Control, shape and disambiguation are three important aspects of a raycasting solution, although not the only ones. A more detailed account of the design and evaluation of selection techniques for 3D environments, and the design space of raycasting techniques in particular, can be found in [1].

## 3. THE NEED FOR IMU-DATA

Optical head-mounted displays for augmented reality require three key components: a computing unit, an optical element capable of showing digital content alongside the real-world, and a set of image and movement sensors. Such sensors have been the focus of considerable research aimed at providing spatial tracking without relying on external infrastructure. Research efforts include computer vision (CV) techniques like camera-based feature extraction and matching now available in commercial SDKs such as Metaio [15] or Vuforia for Smart EyeWear [31]; simultaneous location and mapping (SLAM) using depth sensors [25] and traditional low-end RGB cameras [30]; and dead-reckoning based on improved IMU data processing algorithms [32].

The main purpose of these approaches is the accurate positioning of the HMD in relation to the virtual world. Therefore, they provide limited support for the tracking of objects out of range for the HMD sensors (i.e. camera). Objects need to be within the field of view of the camera. This way, users need to position their hands or objects within the camera FoV by either raising them in front of the HMD or by looking downwards towards the object. Not only are these adjustments physically demanding (raising the hands [10]) and uncomfortable (looking down), but they also interfere with the user's task. Such limited tracking also impacts the way in which raycasting can be realized in AR HMDs, particularly its control mechanisms: only raycasting from the head [28] and from the head through the hand [23] seem to be available.

In our research we aim to leverage sensors not located on the head piece for interacting with content. For example, the EPSON Moverio BT-200 is made of an optical HMD and a hand-held controller [7]. The controller contains the computing unit and a touchpad for interacting with the HMD applications. The controller also provides a 9-axis IMU which can capture the controller orientation. Our approach is to leverage this rotational data for controlling the direction of the ray. For other HMDs without a hand-held controller (such as the announced Microsoft HoloLens [16]), we imagine using external objects to capture rotational data such as Bluetooth connected wands, rings or even smartphones.

## 3.1 Challenges associated with IMU data

Despite the convenience of using an available hand-controller, the rotational data gathered from IMUs has several known problems: noise, sensor drift and magnetic interference, and axis mapping.

Noise relates to the quality of the measurement. A noisy sensor can exaggerate the amount of rotation or report rotational movement where there was none. Noise handling is important because raycasting derives its naturalness from being an isomorphic interaction technique, i.e. there is a one-to-one mapping between movement of the controller and the virtual ray. Traditional noise reduction strategies such as thresholding or a control-display (CD) ratio are inconvenient because they compromise isomorphism. The ultimate solution to the noise problem is higher quality IMU electronics. For raycasting, noise means that the direction of the ray will present jitter or trembling even if there is none.

Sensor drift is a related problem where the sensor might report a slow yet continuous change in rotation where there is none. Newer IMU sensors appear to successfully handle drift: the direction of gravity can be used to cancel out drift in the X and Z axis, while the compass can stabilize drift along the Y axis. Nonetheless, both strategies fail when the amount of movement is beyond or below the sensors' tolerance or when there is magnetic interference that affects the compass. Better tracking algorithms are able to reduce drift [13][32] but not eliminate drift. For raycasting, drift means that the same controller orientation results in different ray directions as drift accumulates.

Finally, the relation between the coordinate systems of the virtual content and that of the controller's IMU changes as the user interacts with the application or moves in the real world. For example, if the HMD application uses view-centric content (content that is always visible regardless of the head orientation) and the user rotates his general orientation 90 degrees on $y$, the resulting virtual ray moves also 90 degrees in relation to the virtual content, that is, out of view for the user. Similar mismatches occur when the user turns around to continue interacting with the virtual counterpart of a physically moving object. In both cases, the user has to accommodate the orientation of the controller in relation to the real world, instead of in relation to the virtual world. In the first example, after rotating the body 90 degrees, the user would have to maintain the controller in the same orientation in the real world as before rotating his body. This mismatch in coordinate systems leads to an unnatural mapping between the movements of the controller and the ray, which is one of the strengths of raycasting.

In summary a raycasting solution using rotational data as provided by an external IMU should address the following requirements:

R1 – Provide mechanisms to compensate for noise-induced jitter.

R2 – Assume an interaction model acknowledging the continuous effect of sensor drift in the direction of the ray.
R3 – Recognize the changing relation between the coordinate systems of the handheld controller and the virtual content.

Also, from the existing raycasting literature we know that a raycasting solutions should:

R4 – Provide an alternative origin for the virtual ray given that the actual controller position cannot be tracked.
R5 – Propose disambiguation techniques that leverage the degrees of freedom available to the controller.

Section 4 presents the design of GyroWand, focusing on R1-3. To address R4 we explored various regions for originating the virtual ray which we present in Section 5. For R5 we created and evaluated three novel disambiguation mechanisms presented in Section 6.

## 4. GyroWand – IMU-BASED RAYCASTING

GyroWand is a raycasting technique for self-contained AR HMDs. By self-contained, we refer to the lack of external tracking of the head piece, hand or objects. GyroWand directs a ray originated at a predefined location in virtual space (see Section 4) using rotational data acquired from an IMU in the user's hand.

## 4.1 Dynamic Apex

To address R1, the effect of noise on jitter and selection accuracy, GyroWand uses a dual approach. First, we filter the data with a moving window from the last five data points. We do so to reduce jitter while maintaining isomorphism between the movements of the controller and the ray. Second, we use a cone shape with a 2 degrees aperture apex (as used in [9]). Moreover, users can decrease the aperture apex to 0 degrees by twisting the controller 45 degrees inwards (pronation). Similarly, users can increase the aperture apex to 6 degrees by twisting the controller 45 degrees outwards (supination). Figure 2 shows the effect of GyroWand's dynamic apex on the apex diameter at 1 meter away from the origin. A dynamic apex leverages best-practices (2 degrees default) while allowing users to control the apex according to the level of noise produced at a given moment. It is important to note that, regardless of the apex value, the system renders the ray as a single line.

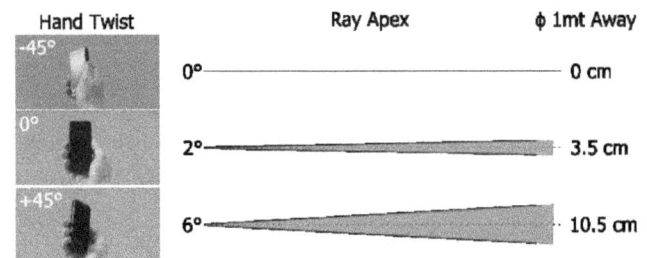

| Hand Twist | Ray Apex | φ 1mt Away |
|---|---|---|
| -45° | 0° | 0 cm |
| 0° | 2° | 3.5 cm |
| +45° | 6° | 10.5 cm |

**Figure 2. Pronation and supination control the apex aperture.**

There are other alternatives to the manual control of the aperture apex. For example, the system could monitor the noise level and automatically adjust the apex to the noise, providing a wider apex when the noise level is high and a narrow one when the noise level is low. Another alternative would increase the apex aperture according to the phase of the selection task. In the ballistic phase, when the user is moving from one target to another with large movements and thus generating more noise, the apex can be wider. In the corrective phase, when the user is refining the selection with small movements and therefore generating less noise, the apex can be narrower.

## 4.2 A State-Machine for Raycasting

GyroWand addresses R2 (drift) and R3 (coordinate mapping) using the state machine presented in Figure 3. GyroWand is always in one of four states: *Anchor*, *Active*, *Out-of-Sight*, or *Disambiguating*. GyroWand transitions between states manually by rotating or touching the controller, or automatically via timeouts. The initial state is *Anchor*, and it is set during the initialization process. In the anchor state GyroWand points its ray to a pre-defined coordinate in space relative to the HMD called the *anchor point*. When users move or rotate their heads in virtual space the anchor point remains at the same position relative to the HMD and therefore the ray, which points to the anchor point, seems static to the user. Rotational data has no effect on the ray direction. The ray is presented in a dark red color, indicating to the user that it is in the anchor state and therefore disabled for interaction.

Tapping on the controller's touchpad activates the GyroWand, transitioning from the *Anchor* state to the *Active* state. During this transition, the GyroWand captures the orientation of the controller and uses it as the initial or baseline rotation; i.e., the rotation at which the active ray points at the anchoring point. All rotational movement of the controller is now applied to the ray direction. The GyroWand notifies all the virtual objects it crosses. A quick tap event (< 150ms) selects the hovered object closest to the ray.

Users can transition back from the active to the anchor state in two ways: a rotation timeout or a TwistUp gesture. The rotation timeout, currently set at 5 seconds, transitions the state back to anchor when the total rotation on all axes is smaller than a given threshold. This timeout serves as an implicit interaction to disable the ray when the user places the controller on a surface (e.g. a table) in order to work with real world objects. The user can also issue a TwistUp gesture (akin to pulling a fishing rod) which is implemented as a rotation on the *x* axis for more than 45 degrees in less than 150 milliseconds.

In the presence of drift (R2) the ray slowly changes direction even as the physical controller is still, leading eventually to the ray leaving the display area. Naturally, a user compensates drift by rotating the controller in the opposite direction. However, when drift is large, users can reset the initial rotation by moving back into the anchor state (TwistUp gestures) and back again into the active state (tapping the touchpad). Similarly, moving between the anchor and active states, thus setting the hand-held controller initial or baseline rotation, helps users to manually deal with conflicting coordinate systems (R3). If the user is moving around while the GyroWand is active, he can reset the baseline rotation by going back into anchor state and back again to active.

The GyroWand's ray can at times be out of the user's sight, that is, outside the small FoV of the HMD. For example, the EPSON Moverio BT-200 has a diagonal FoV of 23 degrees (~11.2 degrees vertical). Accumulated drift or user movement in the real world could end up with an out-of-sight ray. User interactions with the hand-held controller or an accommodation of the hand to reduce fatigue can also lead the controller to an orientation that takes the ray of out sight. A ray out of the user's FoV can be challenging to recover because the user has no indication of how the hand-held controller must be rotated to bring the ray back into view. GyroWand enters into the *Out-of-Sight* state automatically when it judges the ray is out of the HMD's FoV. In the *Out-of-Sight* state touch input is ignored to avoid triggering selection events on virtual objects out of the user's view. The user can bring the GyroWand back into active state rotating the controller until the ray is back into view. The user can also issue a TwistUp gesture to anchor the

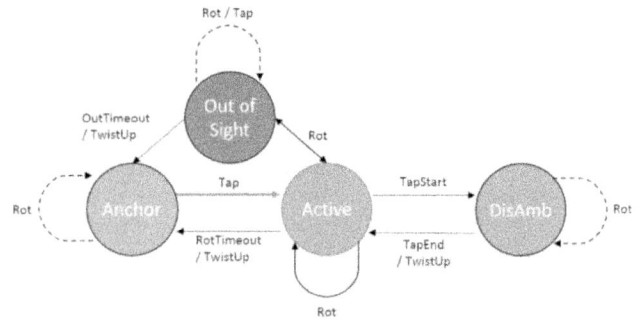

**Figure 3. The state machine for IMU-based raycasting has four states: anchor, active, out-of-sight, and disambiguating. The transition from Anchor to Active sets the current controllers orientation as the baseline for the GyroWand movement.**

ray, and then go back to active state. If the user does not correct the ray direction and no TwistUp gesture is issued within a given timeout (currently 5 seconds), GyroWand transitions into the anchor state automatically. This transition is aimed at reducing the time a user spends "looking" for the ray.

The *Disambiguation* state is where users refine the actual target they want to select in depth. The GyroWand goes into the *Disambiguation* state only when a tap is started from the active state and the ray crosses more than one virtual object. Taps in the anchor and out-of-sight states are ignored. In the *Disambiguation* state the ray is locked on the position and orientation where the tap was initiated. The default selection target changes from the object closest to the ray to the one closest to the origin. The user can then use any disambiguation method to iterate over the highlighted objects and specify a new selection target. Disambiguation ends when the user releases the finger from the touchpad, issuing the selection event on the current selection target and returning to the active state. Section 6 presents three disambiguation mechanisms which the user controls while in the *Disambiguation* state.

## 5. ON-BODY RAYCAST ORIGIN

Given that GyroWand uses only rotational data, it does not know the spatial location of the controller in the real-world. Therefore, we must determine a suitable body location for the origin of the ray. Our initial idea was to use the eyes' center as the origin. However the visual representation of such a ray is confusing at best: the ray is shown too close to the users' eyes resulting in poor 3D visual effect (often visible in one eye only), occupies considerable display real estate, and causes eye strain. Therefore we chose to explore different body locations (see Figure 4) inspired partly by our observations of the way in which people hold and carry the HMD controller, and by our own design assumptions.

The first ray origin is Middle Side (MS) and is located at (15,-40, 20), that is 15 cm to the user's dominant side, 40 cm below the virtual camera and 20 cm in front of the user. We chose this location because it most closely resembles a user's hand position when holding the HMD controller while standing. The second ray origin is the Chest (CT) and is located at (0, -30, 10). The Chest captures the hand position of users who hold the HMD controller in front of their chest, similar to the way smartphones are held when typing. The third ray origin is the Shoulder (SH) and is located at (15, -20, 0). We selected the shoulder to compensate for differences in the physical dimensions, mainly height, between users. The final ray origin is the Chin (CN) and is located at (0, -12, 0). We study the chin because the effect of the distance to target on the ray direction is less severe than that of other locations. For example, when content is very close to the eyes, the controller would have to be held almost vertical when coming from the chest, and almost lateral when coming from the shoulder. These orientations cause a mismatch between the hand movement and the capacity to acquire a target. A ray coming from the chin would almost always move forward and within the HMD FoV. Nonetheless, these differences minimize rapidly as the distance to the target increases.

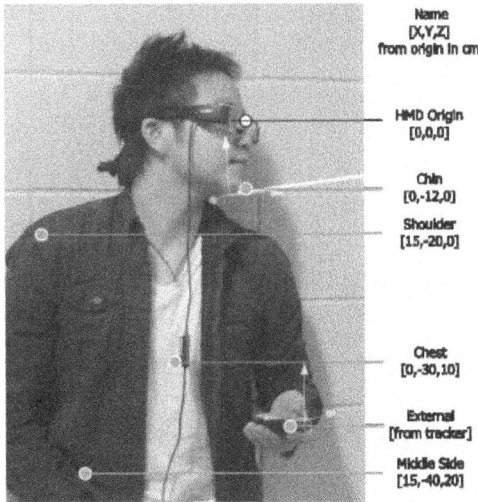

**Figure 4. We explored four possible virtual positions for the GyroWand's ray origin: chin, chest, shoulder, and middle side. External represents the actual controller location measured with an optical tracker and used as baseline.**

## 5.1 Experiment 1: Raycast Origin

In this experiment we investigated user efficiency and physical exertion for the different ray origins in 3D selection tasks in different reference frames. We compared the virtual origins to the origin of traditional raycasting (i.e. the actual controller location).

*Apparatus* – Head registration was provided with an external optical tracking system OptiTrack with 4 cameras covering a cube of dimensions 1 (wide) x 1 (depth) x 2 (height) meters. The middle of the cube is located at 1 meter height from the floor. The system tracked the location and orientation of the smart glasses at 60 FPS and transmitted the data to the smart glasses via UDP over WiFi at a 40 FPS (a 30% reduction due to networking overhead). The participants stood in the center of the tracking cube. For the smart glasses we used the EPSON Moverio BT-200 with a 23 degree diagonal FoV, a 960x540 pixel display resolution, and a focal depth of 5 meters. We created stereoscopic 3D graphics using the side-by-side approach at 50 FPS. Touch input was received through the touchpad of the Moverio BT-200.

*Subjects* – 15 participants (5 female) volunteered, ages 18-33 (mean 26), all right handed. Four participants had previous experience with head-mounted displays, three had experience with virtual reality, and none of them had experience with raycasting.

*Task* – For each session participants had to sequentially select 16 targets in a circular layout on the same plane. The system shows all targets in grey, and the target currently crossed by the ray in light green. The next selection target is shown in red. When the selection target is crossed by the ray its color changes to a brighter red. Selection was triggered upon releasing the finger from the touch pad. Upon selection the system shows the target in magenta, and highlights in red the object in front of the current one as the new target. A line colored red-to-blue also indicates the location of the new target, guiding the participant. This is an important

consideration for situations when the new selection target is located out of the field-of-view (see Figure 1). The session ended when the participant selected all 16 targets. A selection error was marked when selection was triggered on another object or the void.

*Design* – Independent variables were ray origin and reference frame. We used a 5x3 within-subject design to compare user performance. We considered the four ray origins (Chin, Chest, Shoulder and Middle Side) and the real controller location as baseline (tracked with an optical tracker). We located 3D content at the same distance from the HMD (50 centimeters away) but on different reference frames. We are interested in the effects of reference frame rather than distance for two reasons. First, it can be safely assumed that as the distance increases the impact of the origin is negligible because their differences are less than the distance to the target. On the other hand, when objects are close to the user, the origin of the ray can greatly impact the rotational movement needed to reach a target. Second, for content close to the user the reference frame makes a difference as content reacts differently to user movement. We evaluated three reference frames: view, body and world [6]. With the View reference frame content remains fixed in the field-of-view regardless of any head movement. On the Body reference frame content is always at the same location in relation to the body. For example, content positioned on the right of the body will always be visible when the user turns his head to the right, but not when he looks forward. Finally, content on a world reference frame remains fixed in space irrespective of the user location or gaze direction; we located the targets at the center of the tracking cube and 1.5 meters high, participants stood 50 cm away. Targets appeared at approximately the same pixel size in all reference frames.

Random variables were target size and target distance (diameter of the circle). We considered target sizes of 1 and 2 centimeters of diameter. We considered target distances of 7 and 9 centimeters. We chose these seemingly small dimensions because of their large size in the HMD – particularly for the view reference frame in which all targets must fit within the display (see Figure 5).

Participants were asked to hold the Moverio BT-200 controller in their dominant hand. All rotational information was calculated using the internal IMU of the Moverio BT-200 controller. For the real controller location and orientation (controller condition), we

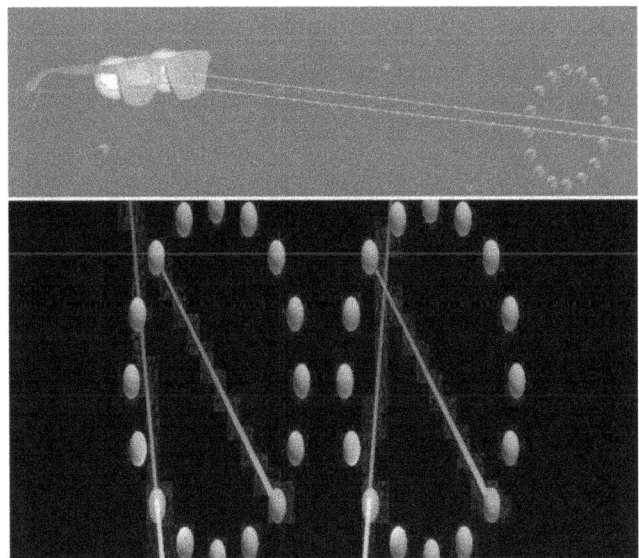

**Figure 5. Targets of 1cm width and 9cm separation.**
**Top: Targets are located 50 cm in front of the HMD.**
**Bottom: Stereoscopic rendering of the user view.**

used optical tracking, so that it could be accurately attached to the user hand. At the start of each condition, the experimenter asked the participant to hold the controller in an initial and comfortable position; this position was set as the rotation baseline (the ray was horizontal and forward from the active source).

The experimenters demonstrated the task and participants were allowed to train for 10 minutes. A minimum of 20 selections with each ray location were required to complete the training session. The trials were counter-balanced using a latin-square design on the 15 conditions. Target size and distance appeared in random order. With a total of 5x3 = 15 conditions per participant and 16x2x2 = 64 selections per condition, we registered 15x64 = 960 selections per participant or 14400 selections in total. All participants completed the experiment in one session lasting approximately 60 minutes.

*Measures* – For each trial we recorded task completion time and selection errors. For each condition we collected Borg RPE ratings of physical effort.

## 5.2 Results
We removed outliers after 3 standard deviations of completion time. Figure 6 presents the results we analyzed using analysis of variance (ANOVA) and post-hoc tests with Bonferroni corrections.

*Completion time* – Results showed a main effect for origin ($F_{4,56}$ = 5.080, p = 0.001, $\eta^2_{partial}$ = 0.266) and reference frame ($F_{2,28}$ = 5.448, p = 0.01, $\eta^2_{partial}$ = 0.280). There were no significant interaction effects for origin × reference frame (p = 0.385). Post-hoc tests showed significant differences between all origins (p < 0.001) except, between Chest and Shoulder (p = 0.250) and between Middle Side and real controller origin (p = 1.0). Chin and Shoulder were the origins with the fastest completion time at 1.737 sec (stdev = 0.663) and 1.798 sec (stdev = 0.698) respectively. Post-hoc tests showed significant differences between all reference frames (p < 0.001), except between Body and View (p = 0.096). Participants were fastest in View (1.826 sec, stdev = 0.708) followed by Body (1.854 sec, stdev = 0.713) and World (1.921 sec, stdev = 0.734).

*Selection errors* – Results showed a main effect for origin ($F_{4,56}$ = 9.293, p = 0.001, $\eta^2_{partial}$ = 0.398) and reference frame ($F_{2,28}$ = 7.307, p = 0.003, $\eta^2_{partial}$ = 0.342). There were no significant interaction effect for origin × reference frame (p =0.057). Post-hoc tests showed significant differences between all origins (p < 0.05), except between Chest and real controller (p = 1.0), between Chest and Shoulder (p = 1.0), between Chin and Shoulder (p = 0.096), and between Shoulder and real controller (p = 0.504). Chin and Shoulder were the origins with the lowest errors rate across all reference frames at 0.17 (stdev =0.455) and 0.21 (stdev =0.517) respectively. Post-hoc tests showed significant differences between all reference frames (p < 0.05). Participants recorded the least number of selection errors in Body (0.21, stdev = 0.499) followed by View (0.23 sec, stdev = 0.53) and World (0.26, stdev = 0.57).

*Borg RPE* - Results did not show a main effect for origin (p = 0.091) or reference frame (p = 0.06).

## 5.3 Discussion
These results show that an origin near to the user's chin seems to be the best choice, regardless of the reference frame. We observed significant differences for the View and Body reference frames, and an equivalence to other origins relatively close to the HMD (Chest and Shoulder) on the World reference frame. This finding supports our assumption that when content is close to the user, the relative distances between the origins are an important factor. The observed advantage of Chin over the other origins was not only in terms of completion time, but we also observed a low error rate; which tells

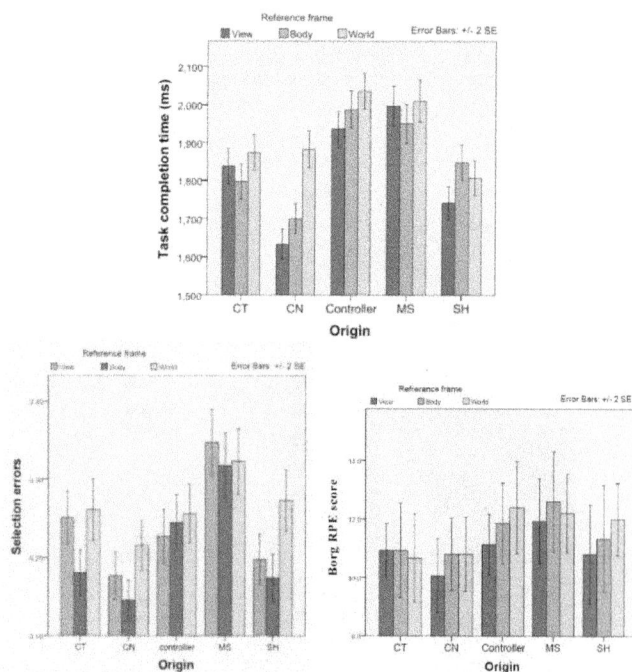

**Figure 6. Quantitative results comparing different ray origins. The baseline condition of the actual controller location, equivalent to traditional raycasting.**

us about the controllability of the GyroWand on a particular origin. Moreover, participants did not report any extra fatigue on the Chin, compared to other origins. From these results we recommend GyroWand to employ a location near the user's Chin as the origin.

An interesting observation is that raycasting from the actual controller location shows some of the worst performance metrics. It shows, together with Middle Side which tries to mimic it, the slowest completion time and higher error rate. This means that users actually struggle with selecting content within arm's reach with a ray coming from their hands, even when they could accommodate the controller in a more convenient position. This is an important result which could have implications on the use of raycasting in other scenarios such as virtual environments.

## 6. IMU-BASED DISAMBIGUATION
Common approaches to disambiguating among potential targets when using raycasting include marking menus and the movement along the axis of the ray [9][11]. While the use of marking menus such as the Flower Ray [9] and similar approaches that spread out conflicting targets is an interesting direction, we are interested in approaches that do not require complementary user-interfaces. Moreover, moving the controller along the axis of the ray is not an option because our design goal is not to depend on external tracking mechanisms, and IMU-based estimations of spatial movement is still unreliable for the consumer-level IMUs included in off-the-shelf devices. Therefore we focus our exploration on techniques that use IMU-based rotational movement and touch input.

## 6.1 Lock and Drag (LD)
Our first technique is Lock and Drag (LD) and is shown in Figure 7. In LD the user directs the ray toward a set of objects including the object to select. Highlighted objects are shown in blue (light and dark), not highlighted objects are shown in gray. Putting the finger on the touchpad transitions GyroWand into the *Disambiguation* state: locking the ray and painting it green. As long as the finger presses the touchpad the ray position and orientation remain

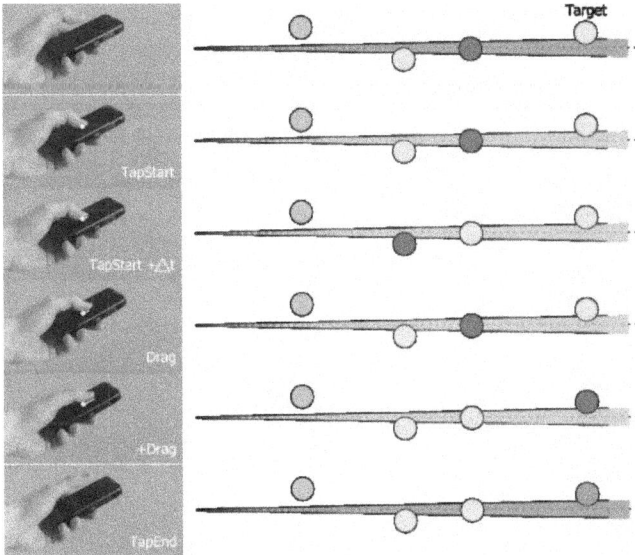

**Figure 7. Lock&Drag. The finger down starts the disambiguation. Dragging the finger up and down refines the selection. Lift the finger to confirm the selection event. Objects not hovered in gray, objects hovered in light blue, selection candidate in dark blue, and selected object in magenta. Active ray is pink, disambiguation ray is green.**

unchanged. Initially, the object closest to the ray is the selection candidate, and colored dark blue. If the user does not remove the finger within a given Δt (<150 ms), the object closest to the ray origin becomes the selection candidate[1]. The user drags the finger in any direction away from the initial point of contact and after a set threshold (50px) the next object away from the origin becomes the selection candidate and turns dark blue, and the previous selection candidate turn light blue. Therefore, to select the first object on the ray path a simple tap + Δt is enough. Drag the finger one time the threshold to select the second object, two times the threshold to select the third, and so on. Dragging the finger back and closer to the point of contact moves the selection candidate back to the previous object. Selection is triggered when the user removes the finger from the touch pad (magenta in Figure 7).

Locking can be a source of errors in itself. For example, the finger movement necessary to activate locking is often accompanied by hand rotation and sometimes full body movement. This small spatial and rotational displacement might cause the ray to lock at a different location and orientation by the time the lock is activated. This phenomenon is known as the Heisenberg effect [4] and has an equivalent manifestation when the user lifts the finger to confirm the selection. Our implementation corrects for Heisenberg effects by correcting the rotation and position of the ray to their respective values 50 milliseconds before locking the ray and triggering the selection event (we arrived to this number iteratively, further research is necessary for a more finely defined value). Nonetheless, even after correcting for Heisenberg effects, users might still activate the ray at the wrong position because of their manipulation of the controller or normal operational or perceptual errors. We minimized the possibility of unintentional locking by limiting the locking operation to situations in which the ray is actually intercepting an object and the intersection point with such object is inside the users' field of view. Users can unlock the ray (out of

_Disambiguation_ and into the _Active_ state) by issuing a TwistUp gesture (rotation on _x_ at 130 degrees/second).

Finally, our research device (Moverio BT-200) provides touchpad data as a mouse cursor, resulting in several challenges to take into account for the LD disambiguation technique. First, the defined threshold for switching the selection candidate is defined in display units (50px) instead of actual physical units of movement and thus subject to the Control-Display ratio provided by the manufacturer. This means that faster finger movements result in larger pixel movements, even if the actual finger displacement was shorter than a larger slower movement – making it harder for novel users to understand the functioning of the technique. We explain this issue to the experiment participants and demonstrated it during training. Another consequence of obtaining the touchpad data as a cursor is that its movement stops upon reaching the edges of the display, which means that if the user had been dragging his finger forward, the user might perceive the disambiguation as not-functioning when the cursor reaches the display edge. Therefore GyroWand provides an arrow on the display suggesting a finger dragging direction always away from the edges.

## 6.2 Lock and Twist (LT)

Our second disambiguation technique is Lock and Twist (LT) and is shown in Figure 8. Similar to [20], LT leverages the extra degree of freedom in wrist movement that is not normally used in our implementation of raycasting operations. Our implementation uses flexion rotation along the _x_ axis, and ulnar and radial deviation for rotation along the _y_ axis. LT leverages pronation and supination (a twist movement of the wrist) as an available degree of freedom. Similar to the previous technique, the user points the ray toward a set of objects including the selection target and moves into the _Disambiguation_ state by placing the finger on the touchpad. Upon starting disambiguation, locking the ray, and waiting for a Δt (<150 ms), the first object to encounter the ray is the selection candidate. The user changes the selection candidate by turning the wrist outwards (supination) by a given threshold. Based on [24] we implemented a linear segmentation of the available rotational space

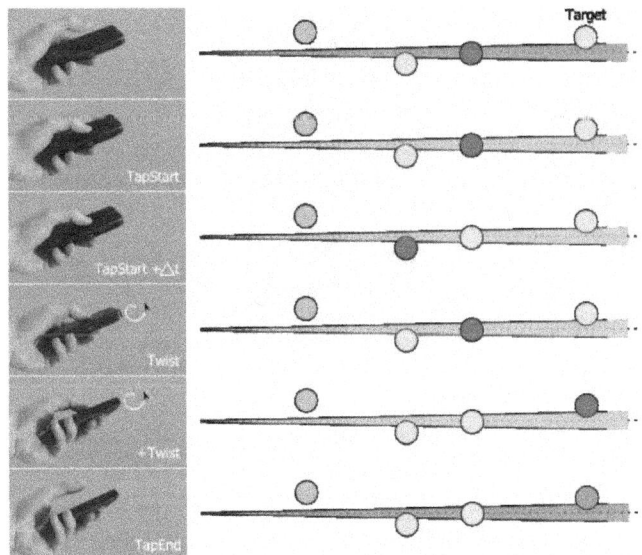

**Figure 8. Lock&Twist. The finger down starts the disambiguation. Supination refines the selection. Lift the finger to confirm the selection event.**

---

[1] GyroWand combines heuristic and manual disambiguation.

at 4 spaces (60 degrees available for supination divided by a 15 degrees threshold). The selection event is triggered when the user lifts the finger from the touchpad. Similar to LD, we handle Heisenberg effect by correcting location and orientation at 50 milliseconds before the locking of the ray and the selection event.

## 6.3 Autolock and Twist (AT)

Our final disambiguation technique is Autolock and Twist (AT), or simply AutoTwist and it is presented in Figure 9. The difference between AT and LT is the way in which the GyroWand enters the *Disambiguation* state. In AT the user points the ray toward the set of objects including the selection target and issues a quick supination movement. After iterative testing we settled for a rotational change in the *z* axis of 7.5 degrees within 150 milliseconds (50 deg/sec). Once the trigger twist is detected, the system corrects the ray's orientation and position to those at the start of the movement. The system also corrects for Heisenberg effect at 100 ms before the final selection event.

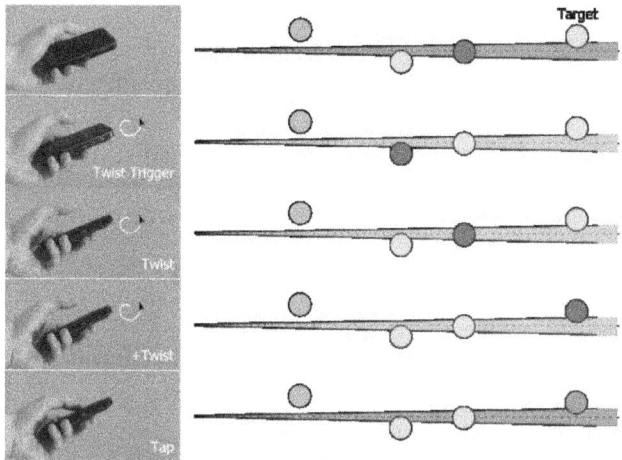

**Figure 9. Autolock &Twist. A quick twist starts the disambiguation. Supination refines the selection. A tap confirms the selection.**

## 6.4 Experiment 2: Disambiguation

In this experiment we investigated the efficiency of the designed raycasting disambiguation techniques in a 3D selection task.

*Apparatus* – Similar to experiment 1, head registration for the Moverio BT-200 was provided by an external optical tracking system. In this case we used a Vicon Tracking system with 8 cameras covering a cube of dimensions 2 (wide) x 2 (depth) x 2 (height) meters. The middle of the cube was at 1 meter height from the floor. The system tracked the location and orientation of the smart glasses at 60 FPS and transmitted the data to the smart glasses via UDP over WiFi at 40 FPS (a 30% reduction due to networking overhead). The participants stood in the center of the tracking cube.

*Subjects* – 12 participants (1 female) volunteered, ages 18-33 (mean 26), all right handed. Four participants had previous experience with head-mounted displays, three had experience with virtual reality, and none had experience with raycasting.

*Task* – For each condition participants had to sequentially select 45 targets located behind 1, 2 or 3 wall obstacles (see Figure 10). In each selection, the participant had to disambiguate selection between the obstacles and the selection target. In the example shown in Figure 10 the target is located behind the third obstacle wall. All crossed objects are shown in light blue, the selection candidate is displayed in dark blue. To select the target (sphere) the

participant has to disambiguate three times, skipping the three obstacle walls, before selecting the target. For all disambiguation techniques and the baseline (PC – point cursor, see below) selection is triggered upon releasing the finger from the touch pad. Upon selection the system highlights the target in magenta, and moves it to a new location in space. A line colored red-to-blue indicates the displacement to the new location, guiding the participant. This is an important consideration for situations when the selection target is relocated out of the current field of view. The task finished when the participant selected 45 targets. All targets were randomly positioned. A selection error was marked when selection was triggered on an object different than the current target.

*Design* – Disambiguation technique was the independent variable. We used a within-subject design to compare user performance with each technique. We considered the three disambiguation techniques (LD, LT, and AT) and Point Cursor (PC) selection as a baseline (similar to the approach used in [9]). The number of obstacles (1, 2 or 3) was a random variable with equal amounts of selections.

We leveraged the results of experiment 1 and used the "chin" as origin. Participants were asked to hold the Moverio BT-200 controller in their dominant hand. All rotational information was calculated using the internal IMU of the Moverio BT-200 controller. For the point cursor we used the optical tracking system to determine the Moverio BT-200 controller location and orientation, so that its source was effectively located at the participant hand (this was done to provide a reliable baseline). The point cursor was located at a fixed length of 50 cm from the controller location and in the ray direction. For all disambiguation techniques except PC participants stood 50 cm in front of the first obstacle wall. For PC participants could walk freely in the space to be close enough to be able to select the target. At the start of each condition, the experimenter asked the participant to hold the controller in an initial and comfortable position; this position was set as the rotation baseline.

The experimenter demonstrated the selection task with each disambiguation technique and participants were allowed to train for 10 minutes. A minimum of 20 selections with each technique were required to complete the training session. The trials were counter-balanced using a latin-square design on the 4 disambiguation mechanism. With a total of 4 conditions per participant and 45 selections per condition, we registered 4x45 = 180 selections per participant or 2160 selections in total. All participants completed the experiment in one session lasting approximately 30 minutes.

*Measures* – For each selection trial we recorded task completion time, disambiguation time (calculated as the time to complete the task minus last time of arrival), and selection errors. For each condition we collected Borg RPE ratings of physical exertion – a subjective scale aimed at helping users report the perceived required effort in performing a task [2].

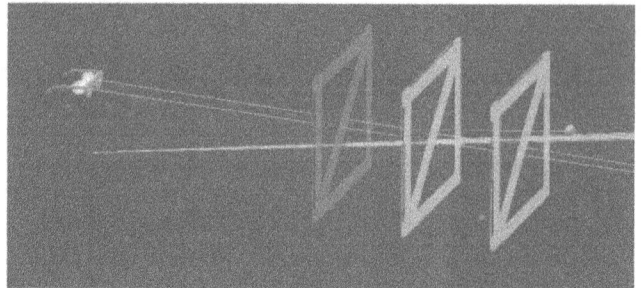

**Figure 10. Three obstacle walls and one target (better seen in color).**

## 6.5 Results

We removed outliers after 3 standard deviations of completion time. Figure 11 presents the results we analyzed using analysis of variance (ANOVA) and post-hoc tests with Bonferroni corrections.

*Completion time* – Results showed a main effect for disambiguation mechanism ($F_{3,33} = 13.431$, $p < 0.001$, $\eta^2_{partial} = 0.550$) and obstacles ($F_{2,22} = 10.449$, $p = 0.001$, $\eta^2_{partial} = 0.487$). Results also showed an interaction effect between disambiguation mechanism × obstacles ($F_{6,66} = 3.225$, $p < 0.01$, $\eta^2_{partial} = 0.225$). Post-hoc tests showed significant differences between all mechanisms ($p < 0.01$). PointCursor was fastest at 4.044 sec (stdev = 1.931), followed by Lock&Twist at 4.851 sec (stdev = 1.963), Lock&Drag at 5.162 sec (stdev = 2.222) and AutoTwist at 5.691 sec (stdev = 2.432). Post-hoc tests showed significant differences between all number of obstacles ($p < 0.001$) except between 1 and 2 obstacles ($p = 0.243$). Participants selected targets with 1 obstacle in 4.864 sec (stdev = 2.127), against 2 in 4.822 sec (stdev = 2.194) and against 3 in 5.267 sec (stdev = 2.3).

*Disambiguation time* – Results showed a main effect for disambiguation mechanisms ($F_{3,33} = 152.827$, $p < 0.001$, $\eta^2_{partial} = 0.933$) and obstacles ($F_{2,22} = 19.599$, $p < 0.001$, $\eta^2_{partial} = 0.640$). Results also showed an interaction effect between disambiguation mechanism × obstacles ($F_{6,66} = 5.760$, $p < 0.001$, $\eta^2_{partial} = 0.343$). Post-hoc tests showed significant differences between all mechanisms ($p < 0.001$). AutoTwist disambiguation was fastest at 2.144 sec (stdev = 0.859), followed by Lock&Twist at 2.516 sec (stdev = 0.796) and Lock&Drag at 2.789 sec (stdev = 1.173). PointCursor did not entail a disambiguation. Post-hoc tests showed significant differences between obstacles ($p < 0.003$). Participants disambiguated 1 obstacle in 1.841 sec (stdev = 1.049), 2 in 2.048 sec (stdev = 1.215) and against 3 in 2.184 sec (stdev = 1.213).

*Selection errors* – Results showed no main effect for disambiguation mechanism ($p = 0.204$) or obstacles ($p = 0.298$). Error rate was similar for all condition at 0.22 (stdev = 0.56).

*Borg RPE* – A Friedman $\chi^2$ test did not show significant differences between disambiguation mechanisms ($p = 0.06$).

## 6.6 Discussion

The experimental results show that Lock&Twist is the mechanism which is in general fastest than the others without any particular extra effect on error rate or perceived physical exertion. This advantage was present even when AutoTwist presented a faster disambiguation time. We believe the overall advantage for Lock&Twist is because of the perceived difficulty participants encountered in the initial ray lock of the AutoTwist technique, even with the -100 ms time we used for handling Heisemberg effects.

Logically, the PointCursor is even faster than Lock&Twist but it cannot be used in AR HMDs because of the need of tracking its spatial location, thus relying on external sensors. Nonetheless it serves as a good baseline (and hence why we included it in the study). With PointCursor, total selection time at around 4 sec, Lock&Twist adds 0.8 sec. This seems like a large amount of time, but considering that the user doesn't have to move in space it appears to be a reasonable trade-off.

Therefore, we recommend using Lock&Twist when the number of targets to disambiguate is small. This is because having to navigate through a large list of objects by twisting the arm does not scale well, leading the users to twist their arms to uncomfortable positions. A possibility to deal with scalability (or even motoric problems) is a disambiguation mechanism combining Lock&Twist and Lock&Drag. Allowing the user to switch to the more time-

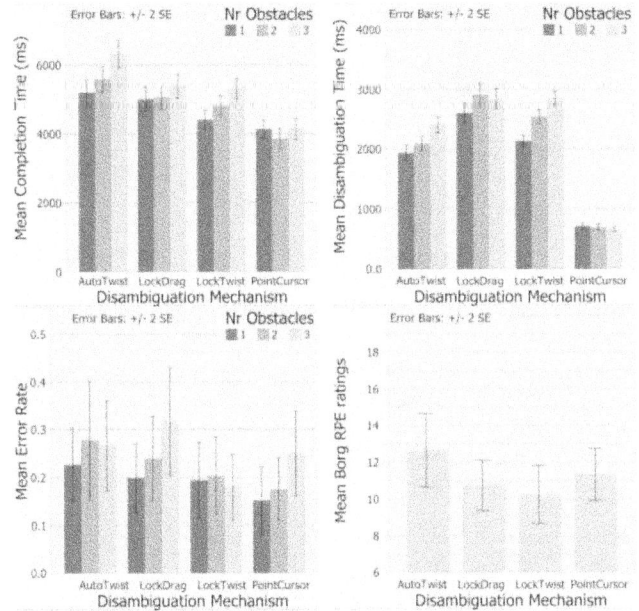

**Figure 11. Quantitative results the disambiguation techniques in selections with 1, 2 and 3 obstacles.**

consuming finger dragging navigation when the twist movement is inconvenient.

## 7. LESSONS LEARNED

Our studies highlight (a) the potential for using raycasting, even when full tracking is not available, as in outdoors environment; (b) the need to carefully select a raycasting origin; and (c) the ability to design suitable target disambiguation approaches even with an IMU sensor. From our results, we learn that:

1) IMU sensing alone, is a suitably good approach for target selection in AR HMD platforms. In the absence of external tracking, as is the case with mobile environments, raycasting is only slightly less efficient than a fully-tracked solution.

2) Raycasting using IMU data can originate at a location away from the controller (as when there is limited full-body tracking). An origin from the user's chin is a good candidate. This is particularly important for close-by targets, as was tested in our study. Our results support Jota et al. [12] which found origins close to the eye to provide "good performance for both targeting and tracing tasks".

3) Using small hand rotations, particularly wrist pronation and supination, are good design options for disambiguating targets laid out in 3D. In combination, a mechanism to switch into a disambiguation mode, such as the Lock&Twist approach we took, provides a suitable balance to mitigate unwanted movement and precise selection.

## 8. IMPLEMENTATION DETAILS

We implemented GyroWand for the EPSON Moverio BT-200 in Unity 4.6 for Android 4.0. Tracking data captured by the optical tracking systems (OptiTrack and Vicon) was received by a Unity application running on a desktop computer. The data was passed to the Moverio BT-200 via UDP packages using Unity's multiplayer gaming capabilities. To create the stereoscopic rendering in Unity we use the Stereoskopix FOV2GO Unity package created by the MxR group at the University of Southern California (USC). Our experiments were carried out in two places. Experiment 1 was performed using an OptiTrack system with 4 cameras. Experiment 2 was carried using a Vicon tracking system with 8 cameras.

To determine rotational movement we evaluated both Android's own orientation vector and Madgwick's x-AHRS [6]. Contrary to [9] the Android implementation appeared more stable and less prone to drift. Nonetheless, the EPSON Moverio BT-200 platform we used seemed to have frequent problems of sensor malfunction which required re-starting the controller for the IMU to provide clean data. We observed this problem on several EPSON Moverio BT-200 units we tested.

## 9. CONCLUSIONS AND FUTURE WORK

We explore the possibility of using accessible inertial measurement unit (IMU) sensing to bring into mobile AR a common interface for interacting with objects in 3D. Since its first proposal, raycasting, a line projecting away from the user's arm and into a scene, as an interface tool has witnessed numerous developments. Many of these rely on external tracking approaches, which are not readily available in mobile contexts for augmented reality applications on head-mounted displays. Instead, most commercially available devices are equipped with controllers that sense the relative 3D hand orientations using gyroscopes. We propose GyroWand, a raycasting interface for 3D object selection. In our design we address a number of challenges, such as identifying the source point of the ray and the ability to disambiguate the selection. GyroWand also uses a state machine to mitigate sensing and drift errors arising from such sensors, as well as involuntary 3D movements. Overall, our results suggest that raycasting can be adopted for AR HMDs.

In future work, we will consider other disambiguating approaches, such as using a quadratic distribution function on the wrist tilt for more accurate disambiguation. We will also consider how such an approach affects interaction while on the move, an area less explored with raycasting solutions that have primarily been tested in indoor environments. We will also investigate how such an approach compares both in performance, as well as comfort, against natural user interfaces, that involve natural arm movements. Finally, we will explore the potential of such an approach, when the controller is miniaturized for ease of use, such as when the IMU is available on a ring-based device.

## 10. ACKNOWLEDGEMENTS

Part of this work was supported by the Cooperative Research Project Program of the Research Institute of Electrical Communication, Tohoku University, and Grants-in-Aid for Scientific Research (KAKENHI) grant number 15H01697.

## 11. REFERENCES

[1] Argelaguet, F. and Andujar, C. 2013. A survey of 3D object selection techniques for virtual environments. Computers & Graphics, 37 (3).

[2] Borg, G. 1998. Borg's Perceived Exertion and Pain Scales. Human Kinetics.

[3] Bowman, D.A., Kruijff, E., LaViola Jr, J.J., and Poupyrev, I. 3D user interfaces: theory and practice. Addison-Wesley. 2004.

[4] Bowman, D.A., Wingrave, C.A., Campbell. J.M, and Ly, V.Q. Using Pinch Gloves™ for both Natural and Abstract Interaction Techniques in Virtual Environments, In Proc. HCI'01.

[5] De Haan, G. Koutek, M., Post, FH. IntenSelect: using dynamic object rating for assisting 3D object selection; 2005.

[6] Ens, B., Hincapié-Ramos, J.D. and Irani, P. 2014. Ethereal planes: a design framework for 2D information space in 3D mixed reality environments. In Proc. SUI '14. ACM.

[7] Epson Moverio, http://www.epson.com/moverio

[8] Forsberg, A., Herndon, K., Zeleznik, R. Aperture based selection for immersive virtual environments. In Proc. UIST '96. ACM.

[9] Grossman, T. and Balakrishnan, R. The design and evaluation of selection techniques for 3D volumetric displays. In Proc. UIST '06. ACM.

[10] Hincapié-Ramos, J.D., Guo, X., Moghadasian, P. and Irani, P. 2014. Consumed endurance: a metric to quantify arm fatigue of mid-air interactions. In Proc. CHI '14. ACM.

[11] Hinckley, K., Pausch, R., Goble, J.C., Kassell, NF. A survey of design issues in spatial input. In Proc. UIST '94.

[12] Jota, R., Nacenta, M.A., Jorge, J.A., Carpendale, S., and Greenberg, A. 2010. A comparison of ray pointing techniques for very large displays. In Proc. GI '10. Canadian Information Processing Society, Toronto, Ont., Canada.

[13] Madgwick, S.O., Harrison, A.J. and Vaidyanathan, R. Estimation of IMU and MARG orientation using a gradient descent algorithm. In Proc. ICORR '11. IEEE.

[14] META SpaceGlassess, https://www.getameta.com/

[15] Metaio SDK, http://www.metaio.com/products/sdk/

[16] Microsoft HoloLens, https://www.microsoft.com/microsoft-hololens/en-us

[17] Mine, M., Frederick Brooks, J., And Sequin,C. 1997. Moving objects in space: exploiting proprioception in virtual environment interaction. In Proc. SIGGRAPH'97.

[18] Mulloni, A. Seichter, H. and Schmalstieg D. Handheld augmented reality indoor navigation with activity-based instructions. In Proc. MobileHCI '11. ACM.

[19] Nakazato, Y., Kanbara, M., Yokoya, N. Wearable augmented reality system using invisible visual markers and an IR camera. In Proc. ISWC'05. IEEE.

[20] Ni, T., McMahan, R. P., and Bowman, D. 2008. Tech-note: rapMenu: remote menu selection using freehand gestural input. In Proc. 3DUI 2008. IEEE.

[21] Olwal, A., Benko, H., Feiner, S. SenseShapes: using statistical geometry for object selection in a multimodal augmented reality system. In: ISMAR '03. IEEE

[22] Olwal, A., Feiner, S. The flexible pointer: an interaction technique for selection in augmented and virtual reality. In Proc. UIST '03. ACM.

[23] Pierce, JS., Forsberg, A., Conway, MJ., Hong, S., Zeleznik, R., Mine MR. Image plane interaction techniques in 3D immersive environments. In Proc. I3D'97.

[24] Rahman, M., Gustafson, S., Irani, P. and Subramanian, S. Tilt techniques: investigating the dexterity of wrist-based input. In Proc. CHI '09. ACM.

[25] RGBDSLAM, https://openslam.org/rgbdslam.html

[26] Sony SmartEyeglass, https://developer.sony.com/devices/mobile-accessories/smarteyeglass/

[27] Steed, A. Selection/towards a general model for selection in virtual environments. In Proc. 3DUI'06. IEEE.

[28] Tanriverdi, V., Jacob, RJK, Interacting with eye movements in virtual environments. In Proc. CHI '00, ACM.

[29] Tsandilas, T., Dubois, E. and Raynal, M. 2010. Free-space pointing with constrained hand movements. In Proc. CHI EA '10. ACM.

[30] Ventura, J., Arth, C., Reitmayr, G., Schmalstieg, D., Global Localization from Monocular SLAM on a Mobile Phone, Visualization and Computer Graphics, In Proc. TVCG'14. IEEE.

[31] Vuforia for Smart EyeWear, https://www.qualcomm.com/products/vuforia

[32] Zhou, P., Li, M. and Shen, G. Use it free: instantly knowing your phone attitude. In Proc. MobiCom '14. ACM.

# Comparing Direct Off-Screen Pointing, Peephole, and Flick&Pinch Interaction for Map Navigation

Khalad Hasan[1], David Ahlström[2], Pourang P. Irani[1]

[1]University of Manitoba,
Winnipeg, Manitoba, Canada
{khalad, irani}@cs.umanitoba.ca

[2]Alpen-Adria-Universität Klagenfurt
Klagenfurt, Austria
david.ahlstroem@aau.at

## ABSTRACT

Navigating large workspaces with mobile devices often require users to access information that spatially lies beyond its' viewport. To browse information on such workspaces, two prominent spatially-aware navigation techniques, peephole, and direct off-screen pointing, have been proposed as alternatives to the standard on-screen flick and pinch gestures. Previous studies have shown that both techniques can outperform on-screen gestures in various user tasks, but no prior study has compared the three techniques in a map-based analytic task. In this paper, we examine these two spatially-aware techniques and compare their efficiency to on-screen gestures in a map navigation and exploration scenario. Our study demonstrates that peephole and direct off-screen pointing allows for 30% faster navigation times between workspace locations and that on-screen flick and pinch is superior for accurate retrieval of workspace content.

## Categories and Subject Descriptors

H.5.2. Information interfaces and presentation (e.g., HCI): User Interfaces – Interaction styles.

## Keywords

Spatial interaction; Direct off-screen pointing; Peephole displays;

## 1. INTRODUCTION

Mobile devices with touchscreens are often used to navigate large information spaces such as maps, text documents, images, and web pages. These information spaces are often considerably larger than what can be viewed at once on the available display. Consequently, the user has to engage in extensive navigation activities, using pinch and flick gestures, to view information that is located in distant parts. Using these gestures to explore large information spaces, however, often involves considerable effort [6] and the user has to deal with screen occlusion and fat-finger situations [16].

As an alternative to on-screen gestures, numerous researchers have investigated peephole displays (e.g., [4, 9, 10, 12, 13, 17]) where the mobile device is aware of its position in relation to the workspace that is 'pinned' to the environment directly surrounding the device. As illustrated in Figure 1a, with a peephole display, the content shown on the screen is updated according to device movements across the underlying workspace: for example, moving

SUI '15, August 08 - 09, 2015, Los Angeles, CA, USA
© 2015 ACM. ISBN 978-1-4503-3703-8/15/08 $15.00
DOI: http://dx.doi.org/10.1145/2788940.2788957

the device 5cm to the left shows content located 5cm to the left in the workspace. Several earlier projects have compared the efficiency of a peephole display to the use of pinch and flick interaction in workspace navigation tasks, but with partly contradicting results. While some studies demonstrate clear advantages for the spatially-aware peephole technique [13, 16], others report similar [9] or inferior [8, 10] navigation performance compared to flick and pinch (Rädle et al. [14] provide a comprehensive overview of peephole vs. flick and pinch studies).

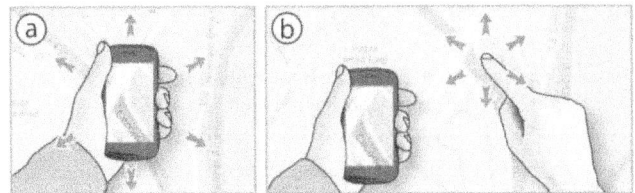

Figure 1. Map navigation with a peephole display (a) and with direct off-screen pointing (b).

Another promising and envisioned approach–motivated by the rapid advancement and miniaturization of optical sensing and tracking technologies–to improve interaction on mobile devices is to make the device spatially-aware of finger gestures in the air around the device. For instance, Jones et al. [8] demonstrate the potential of using in-air gestures instead of on-screen gestures to navigate within large workspaces. Ens et al. [3] explore the concept of directly pointing into a virtual workspace that extends beyond the screen where items that reside outside the screen are selected by moving a finger to their corresponding in-air location. Ens et al. present a performance model which captures this type of 'direct off-screen pointing' and show that user performance is largely dependent on on-screen guidance cues, such as a mini-map or an overview of the workspace. Hasan et al. [6] expand on the idea and study how off-screen space can be divided into discrete 'storage bins' with bin-content being shown on the screen as the tracked off-screen pointing finger moves from bin to bin.

Despite the growing interest in identifying how best to harness spatially-aware techniques, such as peephole displays and in-air finger detection, for improving workspace navigation on mobile devices, we know little of how these two approaches perform in comparison to one another. To this end we contribute an empirical understanding of their strengths and limitations. We explore how direct off-screen pointing can be used for navigating and browsing content in a continuous workspace, such as a map. Figure 1b illustrates: the device tracks the user's finger and updates screen content according to the off-screen finger's current position so that the content 'under' the finger is displayed on the screen. In a user study we compare the performance of off-screen pointing against the standard on-screen flick and pinch interaction and the peephole technique in a map navigation task. Results show that participants were faster navigating the workspace with the spatially-aware techniques, particularly in the presence of an on-screen visual cue.

## 2. EXPERIMENT

**Task**: Our experimental task captured a scenario wherein a user is interested in examining biometric and environmental data collected with a sports bracelet during a morning jog. After the jog, the user can combine the recorded data with geographical information for detailed analysis in an exercise app on a smartphone. Jogging-related information–heart rate, running speed, elevation, air temperature, and humidity–are shown in callout boxes associated with markers positioned on a digital map, as shown in Figure 2a and b. In each experimental trial, the participant was prompted to find and select the marker containing the highest or lowest, value on one of the five variables, such as "Find the location with the greatest elevation" or "Find the location with the highest speed".

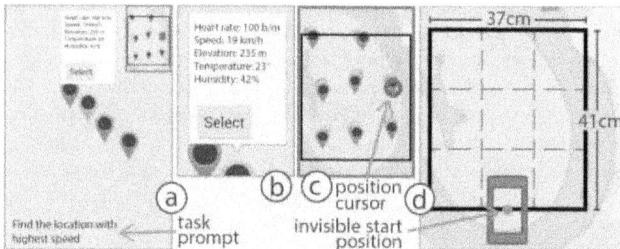

**Figure 2. a) Task screen with an open callout box, the overview, and task prompt. b) Enlarged callout box. c) Enlarged overview. d) Map area with black guiding boundary.**

Figure 2d shows the map we used. A black outline defined the relevant map area to the participants. We divided the relevant area into nine cells (dashed lines in Figure 2d, the lines were invisible during the experiment) and placed a cluster of four markers (Figure 2a) in each cell but the upper-right cell. Each cluster contained one potential orange target marker with a callout box displaying exercise information (Figure 2a and b) and three blue markers with callout boxes showing irrelevant information (as commonly found in map applications). We considered the blue markers as distractors. A trial started with a window containing the task prompt and a 'start' button. Timing started with a tap on the button. This dismissed the window and displayed the area around a fixed start position at the bottom of the lower middle map cell, as visualized in Figure 2d (the task prompt remained visible but at the bottom of the screen). The map was zoomed to Google Maps' zoom level 20. At this zoom level, a paper version of the relevant map area would measure 37×41cm. We used a 1:1 mapping for the motor space and the display space where moving the smartphone (peephole) or finger (off-screen pointing) 1cm would move the map area by 1cm.

We encouraged the participants to search the map for the orange target marker that matched the task prompt as fast as possible. When participants believed they had found the correct target, they could end the trial with a tap on the 'select' button in the marker's callout box (Figure 2a & b). Selecting the correct marker ended trial time and displayed the task window for the next trial. An error dialogue was shown if the wrong marker was committed and the search could continue after dismissing the dialogue.

The marker cluster within a map cell and the orange target marker within a cluster were randomly positioned for each trial. Across a series of five trials, the correct target marker was located once in each of five different and randomly selected map cells. Five different task prompts were randomly selected from a pool of ten task prompts for each series of five trials.

**Apparatus & Map Navigation Techniques**: All participants performed series of trials using direct off-screen pointing (OP), a peephole display (PD), and the standard on-screen pinch and flick gestures (FP) while standing in a quiet room. The study software ran on a Google Nexus 5 smartphone with a 4.95-inch screen (1080×1920 pixels resolution). For the PD and OP techniques we used a Vicon system (with eight T-Series cameras) to emulate a spatially-aware smartphone and to ensure reliable and noise-free data. The system tracked the position of the smartphone when the PD was used, and both the smartphone and the user's right-hand 'in-air' index finger when OP was used. The study software was built on Android 4.4.2 (API 19). Google Maps Android API (v2) was used to implement the map features in the study software.

With FP, participants held the smartphone in their left hand and performed on-screen manipulations with their dominant right hand: flick to pan the map, pinch to zoom, and tap to select map markers, the 'start' button, and the 'select' button in callout boxes.

To avoid ambiguities involved in zooming with spatially-aware displays [8, 12], such as identifying suitable interactions for clutching and zoom adjustment, map navigation with PD and OP was restricted to 2D-panning (zooming was only enabled with the FP). Furthermore, during implementation of the spatially-aware techniques we noticed that accurately homing in on and tapping small map markers was cumbersome as any jitter from device–or the user's in-air pointing finger–causes small erratic displacements of the displayed map area and its markers. As a solution, for OP and PD we opted for a two-step selection approach similar to TapTap [15]. That is, a first tap anywhere on the screen froze the screen content and a second tap, if on a map marker, opened the corresponding callout box. If the second tap occurred elsewhere, the freeze was released and any open callout box was closed. In cases with an open callout box, an additional tap outside the callout box closed the box and released the freeze. Unlike the original TapTap, we did not scale the target sizes.

When using OP, participants held the smartphone in their non-dominant left hand and used their right-hand index finger to point in mid-air around the device to navigate the map. On-screen interactions (taps to freeze the screen, select map markers and buttons) were performed with the left-hand thumb. With PD, for stable and accurate map navigation and little on-screen jitter, participants were encouraged to use their dominant right hand to move the peephole display (smartphone) across the stationary map and to use their right-hand thumb or left hand for on-screen interactions (all participants chose to use only their right hand). With OP and PD, the start position on the map (Figure 2d) was 'anchored' to a point in physical space: with OP to the center of the phone, with PD to a set of tracking markers placed on the floor in front of the participants' assigned standing position.

Several earlier studies have demonstrated strengths and weaknesses of various techniques to visualize the positions of objects that reside outside the currently visible part of the workspace in different user tasks, such as Halos [2], Wedges [5, or overviews [e.g., 7, 11]. Accordingly, we were also interested in investigating how map navigation performance with the two spatial techniques is influenced by such on-screen guidance. Informed by earlier work [3, 7], we opted for an overview visualization of the relevant map area with marker clusters and a blue circular position cursor that indicated what area of the map was currently displayed on the screen. All three techniques were tested with and without an on-screen overview. In trials with the overview, the overview was positioned in the upper right corner of the screen and roughly took 1/15 of the display space, as shown in Figure 2a.

**Measurements**: The study software recorded the number of markers that were opened during a trial, the time spent on manipulating markers (incl. time needed to open callout boxes, reading marker information, and to tap the 'select' button and to close callout boxes), the time taken to navigate between markers, the total trial time (marker+navigation time), and the accumulated distance 'travelled' in a trial (measured in centimeters, distances at different zoom levels with *FP* were normalized to the Google Maps' zoom level 20, as used for *PD* and *OP*). We analyzed the results using 2×3 RM-ANOVAs with *guidance* (*No Overview*, *With Overview*) and *technique* (*OP*, *PD*, *FP*) as independent factors.

**Participants**: Twelve right-handed smartphone owners (8 male) aged 21 to 28 years (mean 25.0, $\sigma$=2.7) participated. All were unfamiliar with spatially-aware interaction techniques. Participants performed two sets of five timed trials with each technique. The first set with assistance from an on-screen overview, the second without an overview. The order of techniques was counter-balanced between participants. Before a participant started with a new set of timed trials with a new technique, we demonstrated the technique and the participant had two untimed practice trials. We collected 12 (participants) × 3 (*techniques*) × 2 (*guidance* conditions) × 5 = 360 timed trials. With short breaks and practice trials, each session lasted around 45 minutes.

## 3. Results

**Errors & outliers**: Participants committed a wrong target marker once or twice before they committed the correct target marker in 30 of the 360 trials (the erroneous trials were roughly evenly distributed between the six *techniques-guidance* combinations and participants). Understandably, erroneous trials had markedly longer trial times (caused by more marker selections and error messages to react to) than trials where only one marker (the correct one) was committed. We removed the erroneous trials and then identified and removed nine outlier trials with a trial time outside of ± 4 S.D. from the mean time for the corresponding *technique-guidance* combination (outliers were roughly evenly distributed between *technique-guidance* conditions).

**Learning**: Figure 3a plots the mean trial time for the first, second, third, fourth, and fifth trial with each *technique-guidance* combination. For all combinations we see a trend toward faster times in later trials. However, one-way ANOVAs (one for each *technique-guidance* combination) did not show any significant differences between early and late trials for any of the six *technique-guidance* combinations. We conclude that there were no significant learning effects and continue with all trials.

**Marker visits & marker time**: An optimal trial would include inspecting the information in all eight target markers and while navigating between these remembering the position of the 'currently best' marker and then, after having inspected all eight target markers, returning back to the correct target marker which includes information matching the task prompt. Accordingly, the optimal trial includes 8+1 or 8 marker visits (8 in cases where the last marker visited contains the correct information). On average, during a trial participants inspected the information in 10.8 callout

boxes. There were no significant differences in the mean number of visited markers between the three techniques (*FP* 10.5, *PD* 11.3, *OP* 10.6 markers) or between the two *guidance* conditions (*No Overview* 11.2, *With Overview* 10.5 markers). Unsurprisingly, as shown in Figure 3b, using the dominant hand for on-screen manipulation (*FP*) was significantly faster ($F_{2,22}$ = 42.0, p < 0.001, $\eta^2$ = 0.79) than using the thumb on the hand holding the device (*PD* and *OP*). Using the thumb took about twice as long as using fingers on the dominant hand (*FP* 13.8s, *PD* 28.0s, *OP* 27.6s). As expected, having access to the on-screen overview did not influence the time needed to manipulate markers.

**Navigation time & path length**: Overall, across *techniques*, participants needed significantly more time (26%) to navigate between markers in trials with no guiding overview than in trials with a guiding overview (46.8s vs. 37.2s, $F_{1,11}$ = 32.4, p < 0.001, $\eta^2$ = 0.75). As shown in Figure 3c, the overview was only effective in combination with *FP* or *OP* (interaction effect: $F_{2,22}$ = 7.6, p < 0.01, $\eta^2$ = 0.41). The overview reduced navigation time by 10.2% when used with *FP* and by 45.0% when used with *OP*.

Overall, across the two *guidance* conditions, navigation time differed depending on *technique* ($F_{2,22}$ = 42.0, p < 0.001, $\eta^2$ = 0.79). Bonferroni adjusted post-hoc comparisons showed that *FP* with 49.5s required significantly longer navigation time than both *PD* with 38.7s and *OP* with 37.5s (27.7% resp. 31.9% slower, p's < 0.016), which did not differ. Clearly, gross hand and arm movements–as used with a *PD* or *OP*–are more suitable for quick navigation than the familiar, but minute, on-screen panning and zooming actions used with *FP*.

Figure 3c reveals why participants were faster navigating the map when assisted by the overview. With the overview participants were able to navigate more directly towards marker clusters, as visible in the significantly different accumulated distance traversed during trials with and without the overview (160.4cm with and 204.8cm without the overview; $F_{1,11}$ = 65.5, p < 0.001, $\eta^2$ = 0.86). In this way, navigation time was reduced when the overview was combined with *FP* or with *OP*. User comments provide a likely explanation for the overview's ineffectiveness when combined with *PD*: several participants reported that it was difficult to follow the small position cursor in the overview and to switch visual focus between the overview and the map while moving the smartphone. Accordingly, many participants ignored the overview.

**Trial time**: Figure 3d summarizes the previous analyses and shows the total trial times (marker time + navigation time) for the six different *technique-guidance* combinations. The bar labels show the percentage of total trial time spent on marker manipulation resp. on navigation between markers. Across the two *guidance* conditions, trial time did not differ between the three techniques: *FP* 63.3s, *OP* 65.1s, *PD* 66.8s. The short *marker time* and relatively long *navigation time* with *FP* sum up to a total trial time comparable to the sum of the long *marker times* and short *navigation times* with *PD* and *OP*.

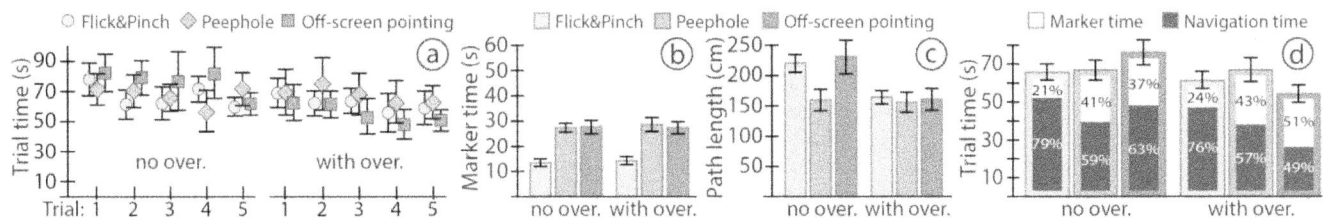

Figure 3. a) Trial time across trial series. b) Marker time. c) Path length. d) Trial time. Error bars show ± 2 S.E.

For all three *techniques*, guidance from the overview significantly reduced trial time ($F_{1,11} = 25.3$, $p < 0.001$, $\eta^2 = 0.70$) by 13.1%, from 69.7s to 60.5s. As visible in Figure 3d, the overview was mainly effective in combination with *OP* (interaction effect: $F_{2,22} = 6.5$, $p < 0.001$, $\eta^2 = 0.37$) where the overview helped participants to reduce their average trial time by nearly a third (29.1%), from 76.1s to 54.0s. *OP* with the overview was the fastest combination at a trial time of 54.0s. *FP* with the overview was the second fastest combination with 61.1s, 13% slower than *OP* with overview.

## 4. DISCUSSION & CONCLUSIONS

Our results clearly highlight the important advantages and critical disadvantages of each of the techniques we evaluated. Results reveal that traditional flick and pinch gestures exhibit superior marker selection capabilities as it employs fingers on the dominant hand to open marker information. On the contrary, the tested spatially-aware techniques are slower for accessing marker information on maps. This is largely because users used the thumb for such interaction with the spatially-aware interactions, which is less efficient than using the index finger. For navigating from one map location to another, peephole and direct off-screen pointing demonstrate improved performance over flick and pinch. The latter requires many minute operations, such as flicking through screens, resulting in less efficient map navigation. Additionally, all the techniques show strong reliance on the overview. Such an on-screen cue helps users to traverse directly towards the targets, particularly in the case of direct off-screen pointing.

Our results also confirm prior results [6, 12, 17]: performance with spatially-aware techniques can be affected by the chosen task. Our task is one that is common for data exploration and analytics [1], which involves inspecting items across the entire workspace and remembering which ones match best a certain search criteria. Similar results have been reported in prior studies involving analytic tasks [6]. Additionally, flick and pinch could be the choice technique in a task that requires frequent touch interactions. Pahud et al. [12] saw similar results wherein participants were as efficient with flick and pinch as with spatial input.

Overall, we provide a first attempt at examining the performance of two spatial navigation techniques, direct off-screen pointing and peephole with standard flick and pinch. Results show that spatially-aware techniques can be a promising alternative for map navigation. With a controlled experiment, we demonstrate the advantages and limitations of each technique for a map navigation and exploration task. This work could be extended in several directions. In the experimental design, we only considered the design factors critical for the proper operation of the spatially-aware techniques we tested. Further experimentation is needed to extract additional design parameters that are suitable to these techniques. For instance, zooming and clutching mechanisms need to be carefully explored for the spatially-aware techniques as such mechanisms are necessary to enable users to navigate larger workspaces than those limited to within arm-reach, as was the case in our study. Our participants had no previous experience with navigating maps using spatially-aware techniques. We believe this can be addressed through extended exposure (i.e., multiple blocks over multiple days) as seen in [12]. Furthermore, we expected that spatially-aware techniques (peephole and direct off-screen pointing) have pronounced navigation movements which support participants in developing an accurate spatial model of the workspace. The standard touch input, which includes minute pan and zoom actions, could make it harder for the user to develop a sense of the spatial relations. However, the on-screen guidance influenced participants' navigation pattern and assisted them to move directly toward the targets, which may diminish the learning effect. It is worthwhile to explore the learning effects when revisiting objects on the map as repeated exposure and navigation could help eliminate the need for on-screen guidance.

## 5. REFERENCES

[1] Amar, R., Eagan, J., and Stasko, J. Low-level components of analytic activity in information visualization. In *Proc. INFOVIS 2005*, 111-117.

[2] Baudisch, P. and Rosenholtz, R. Halo: a technique for visualizing off-screen objects. In *Proc. CHI 2003*, 481-488.

[3] Ens, B., Ahlström, D., Cockburn, A., and Irani, P. Characterizing user performance with assisted direct off-screen pointing. In *Proc. MobileHCI 2011*, 485-494.

[4] Fitzmaurice, W.G. Situated information spaces and spatially aware palmtop computers. *Comm. ACM 36*, 7 (1993), 39-49.

[5] Gustafson, S., Baudisch, P., Gutwin, C., and Irani, P. Wedge: clutter-free visualization of off-screen locations. In *Proc. CHI 2008*, 787-796.

[6] Hasan, K., Ahlström, D., & Irani, P. AD-Binning: leveraging around-device space for storing, browsing and retrieving mobile device content. In *Proc. CHI 2013*, 899-908.

[7] Irani, P., Gutwin, C., Patridge, G., and Nezhadasl, M. Techniques for interacting with off-screen content. In *Proc. INTERACT 2007*, 234-249.

[8] Jones, B., Sodhi, R., Forsyth, D., Bailey, B., and Maciocci, G. Around device interaction for multiscale navigation. In *Proc. MobileHCI 2012*, 83-92.

[9] Kaufmann, B. and Ahlström, D. Studying spatial memory and map navigation performance on projector phones with peephole interaction. In *Proc. CHI 2013*, 3173-3176.

[10] Kerber, F., Krüger, A, and Löchtenfeld, M. Investigating the effectiveness of peephole interaction for smartwatches in a map navigation task. In *Proc. MobileHCI 2014*, 291-294.

[11] Nekrasovski, D., Bodnar, A., McGrenere, J., Guimbretière, F., and Munzner, T. An evaluation of pan & zoom and rubber sheet navigation with and without an overview. In *Proc. CHI 2006*, 11-20.

[12] Pahud, M., Hinckley, K., Iqbal, S., Sellen, A., and Buxton, W. Toward compound navigation tasks on mobiles via spatial manipulation. In *Proc. MobileHCI 2013*, 113-122.

[13] Rädle, R., Jetter, H.-C., Butscher, S., and Reiterer, H. The effect of egocentric body movements on users' navigation performance and spatial memory in zoomable user interfaces. In *Proc. ITS 2013*, 23-32.

[14] Rädle, R., Jetter, H-C., Müller, J. & Reiterer, H. Bigger is not always better: display size, performance, and task load during peephole map navigation. In *Proc. CHI 2014*, 4127-4136.

[15] Roudaut, A., Huot, S., and Lecolinet, E. TapTap and MagStick: improving one-handed target acquisition on small touch-screens. In *Proc. AVI 2008*, 146-153.

[16] Siek, K., Rogers, Y., and Connelly, K. Fat finger worries: how older and younger users physically interact with PDAs. In *Proc. INTERACT 2005*, 267-280.

[17] Spindler, M., Schuessler, M., Martsch, M., and Dachselt, R. Pinch-drag-flick vs. spatial input: rethinking zoom & pan on mobile displays. In *Proc. CHI 2014*, 1113-1122.

# Upper Body Leaning can affect Forward Self-Motion Perception in Virtual Environments

Ernst Kruijff[1*], Bernhard E. Riecke[2*], Christina Trepkowski[1], Alexandra Kitson[2]

[1] Bonn-Rhein-Sieg University of Applied Sciences, Grantham-Allee 20, 53757 Sankt Augustin, Germany

[2] Simon Fraser University, 250 –13450 102 Avenue Surrey, BC, V3T 0A3, Canada

## ABSTRACT

The study of locomotion in virtual environments is a diverse and rewarding research area. Yet, creating effective and intuitive locomotion techniques is challenging, especially when users cannot move around freely. While using handheld input devices for navigation may often be good enough, it does not match our natural experience of self-motion in the real world. Frequently, there are strong arguments for supporting body-centered self-motion cues as they may improve orientation and spatial judgments, and reduce motion sickness. Yet, how these cues can be introduced without having to allow for physical user motion is not well understood. Actuated solutions such as motion platforms can be an option, but they are expensive and difficult to maintain. Alternatively, within this article we focus on the effect of upper-body tilt while users are seated, as previous work has indicated positive effects on self-motion perception. We report on two studies that investigated the effects of static and dynamic upper body leaning on perceived distances traveled and self-motion perception (vection). Static leaning (i.e., keeping a constant forward torso inclination) had a positive effect on self-motion, while dynamic torso leaning showed mixed results. We discuss these results and identify further steps necessary to design improved embodied locomotion control techniques that do not require actuated motion platforms.

## Categories and Subject Descriptors

H.5.1. [**Information Interfaces and Presentation**]: Multimedia Information Systems—Artificial, augmented, and virtual realities; H.5.2. [**Information Interfaces and Presentation**]: Information Interfaces and Presentation: User Interfaces—Ergonomics.

## General Terms

Measurement, Performance, Experimentation, Human Factors

## Keywords

Navigation; virtual environments; 3D user interface; body-centric cues; leaning, self-motion perception; vection; embodied interfaces.

* The first and second author contributed equally to this article.

## 1. INTRODUCTION

Enabling effective yet intuitive spatial orientation and locomotion in 3D environments is a timely and highly relevant research problem. In particular with the rapid advent of head mounted display (HMD) systems such as the Oculus Rift[tm] or Valve VIVE[tm], research on natural locomotion metaphors and techniques is stimulated as users are increasingly interested in highly engaging, immersive interfaces. However, these HMDs come with a series of new challenges and opportunities as they are head-worn and providing a much larger field of view (FOV) than traditional gaming displays. Well-designed locomotion interfaces can improve the experience and performance in virtual environments (VE) [22]. Yet, despite recent advances in virtual reality (VR) technology, supporting effective spatial orientation and providing a compelling sensation of self-motion through the VE remains challenging [27]. While modern VR systems allow for photorealistic graphics, users typically perceive simulated self-motions not as actual and embodied self-motion, but rather as camera motion [26]. Even more so, when HMDs are combined with traditional input methods like gamepad or joystick they can quickly lead to motion sickness and disorientation, reducing overall usability and user experience [32]. As such, there is a clear need for improved techniques to support spatial orientation and self-motion perception for HMD-based systems.

Freely moving around through a physical environment while navigating through virtual content still provides an unsurpassed self-motion experience [32]. Real-world viewpoint changes normally involve upper body and head movements that provide a rich set of cues. However, in many VR applications users cannot move around freely. While some systems are designed for standing [34,35] or leaning while standing [14,20,39], most users of HMD applications, in particular game-driven, are still seated. Despite a few notable developments [1,14,15,25,29], most existing 3D navigation interfaces for seated users do not take advantage of body-centric physical cues, nor is it well understood how these cues work for seated user interfaces [6]. Rather, most interfaces rely on using our hands – mostly deploying mouse, joystick or even gestures – which may reduce usability, especially because we cannot use our hands for other purposes like natural gesturing. This situation introduces an interesting design requirement: how can we design novel navigation techniques that provide suitable self-motion cues while users are seated?

The starting point for the studies reported in this article was the analysis of what cues, besides visual information, we may introduce to users to enhance self-motion perception. Different motion behavior patterns in real life seem to affect our sensation of movement through a real environment at first glance. For example, people tend to lean forward further when running or bicycling faster. In contrast, other motions force users to lean backward – think about accelerating quickly in a fast vehicle, being pressed into a chair. Previous work, as we will show in the next section, informed us that upper body tilt could have a positive effect on self-motion perception [9,13,21]. As a result, we were interested in investigating if and to what degree we could provide useful body-centered cues by simply employing upper body tilt in seated users, where leaning forward and backward is straightforward and requires little personal or technical effort.

Inspired by previous work, we designed two studies in which users wore a HMD while being seated. We looked closely at how upper body tilt can affect self-motion perception, while also briefly exploring differences with leaning in a standing posture. In particular, we studied the effects of **static leaning** (asking participants to keep a tilted posture throughout a trial) versus **dynamic leaning** (changing the upper-body inclination dynamically throughout a trial) because these introduce different kinds of cues to the user, cues that previously have been shown to positively affect self-motion. Through the studies, we aimed at identifying possible effects of different kinds of leaning and potential needs for further studies. In addition, based on study results we targeted the formulation of initial design guidelines for novel and more embodied navigation interfaces. Throughout the paper, we will show that static leaning indeed does have a positive effect on self-motion perception in that it enhanced perceived self-motion velocity. Yet, to our surprise, the dynamic tilting produced mixed results. Informed by previous work, we expected the additional cues of dynamically tilting would strengthen self-motion perception. However, we could not find such a positive effect. In the study reflection, we will unravel the results, identifying how the outcomes of  are useful for interface designers. We believe that specific physical devices may be designed that may adapt to specific velocities that in return can improve the user's experience of speed in a specific environment. We will also show that more research is needed, to understand better the differences between static and dynamic leaning.

## 2. RELATED WORK

Navigation is one of the key tasks performed in both our real world and virtual environments and encompasses both physical and psychological aspects. Physical navigation interfaces have been studied widely and can increase the overall usability and user experience of the system [5,6,23], enhance spatial perception and orientation, which is important for a wide range of tasks [6], and reduce motion sickness [3]. Self-motion, affecting navigation to a large extent, spans various research areas and has been studied extensively too, although there are still large gaps in our understanding. Among others, researchers have looked into the integration of visual and non-visual cues for self-motion perception [11,17] and information storage thereof [2]. Some studies focused specifically on vestibular cues [18], auditory cues [28,36] and tactile/biomechanical cues [30]. Many researchers have also experimented with vestibular stimulation to induce self-motion [16,31]. Our studies were motivated by several previous experiments that investigated how static or dynamic body tilt might affect perceived self-motion. For example, several prior studies indicated that static body tilt could affect various aspects of our visual and non-visual perception. Bringoux et al. showed that blindfolded participants' estimation of earth-referenced horizon (i.e., horizontal with respect to gravity) was systematically affected by their body tilt [9]. Tilting their chair forward yielded lower horizon estimates, and backwards body tilt resulted in elevated estimates. Similar effects of body tilt have been shown when judging the elevation of a visually presented object and one's judged ability to pass under it [8]. Body pitch has

also been shown to affect our perceived self-motion direction [4]. When judging one's perceived direction of self-motion in an expanding optic flow field simulating forward translation with or without some upward/downward component, forward/backwards body tilt (pitch) resulted in systematic downward/upward bias.

With respect to seating postures, an upright posture has been shown to yield stronger illusory self-motion (linear forward vection induced by an optic flow field) than lying postures [13]. However, it is largely unknown if merely statically leaning forward or backwards might be sufficient for affecting our self-motion perception. From an applied standpoint, it is often unfeasible to have users completely lie down, whereas forward/backwards leaning can be easily accomplished in most natural user settings without additional cost or simulation effort.

In a small study with four participants, Nakamura and Shimojo compared linear vection induced in observers sitting either upright or tilted backward 30, 45, or 60° [21]. While horizontal (sideways left-right) vection was not affected by body tilt, vertical (aka elevator) vection was reduced for upright posture and increased to the level of horizontal vection as body tilt increased. However, they did not investigate forward linear vection, and it remains an open question how static body tilt might affect forward linear vection. If there was any effect, this could provide a simple and affordable means of enhancing (or reducing) self-motion perception without the need for expensive equipment. Our study was designed to address this gap.

Dynamically tilting users or the whole motion simulator during simulated accelerations is standard practice in moving-base motion simulators such as high-end driving or flight simulators, and has been shown to improve the realism of linear self-motion as well as the percentage of users experiencing embodied illusions of self-motion (linear vection) [12]. However, dynamically tilting users comes with considerable cost and technical complexity. Moreover, the optimum level of dynamic body tilt depends on a number of factors including the type, velocity, and acceleration of the visual stimulus and the amount of physical translation, which can make it challenging to tune a system [12,33].

As a step towards reducing technical complexity and cost, Beckhaus, Riecke, and others proposed to remove all external actuation and instead let users actuate actively providing their own motion cueing while seated [1,19,25,29]. By using a modified manual wheelchair [29] or a leaning gaming chair [25], they demonstrated that user-powered full-body translational or translational and tilting motion cueing could enhance both forward linear and curvilinear vection [29]. However, to the best of our knowledge there is no prior research investigating if upper body leaning by itself could also affect perceived self-motion. If so, this could be of considerable interest for designing more affordable, usable, and effective self-motion simulation and navigation paradigms for VR and gaming that do not require costly actuated methods.

With respect to spatial navigation interfaces, some connection exists to walking-in-place interfaces [34,35], as well as natural motion interfaces such as supported through treadmills [10]. Yet, these studies focus on standing poses, whereas our study looks at seated users. Moreover, these studies were not focused on navigation. Finally, our study relates directly to various physical leaning-based interfaces for navigation in virtual environments, including the usage of the Wii balance board [15,37,38]and other types of leaning interfaces [14,20,39]. The results of our study can inform the design of such interfaces, as we will discuss later in this article.

# 3. Research questions

In an attempt to address some of the above-mentioned gaps and challenges, we wanted to investigate if self-motion perception and realism could be enhanced by simpler means than a moving-base simulator or other means to move the whole user. We also asked whether forward or backward leaning of the upper body might by itself enhance our sensation of forward motion, and how the velocity of the simulated self-motion might mediate this. Furthermore, as supported through self-motion literature [18], we were interested in the effect vestibular cues (in particular acceleration cues) would have when a body is moved dynamically. That is, what are the differences between keeping a fixed leaned posture and dynamically leaning (moving the upper body forward or backward) on self-motion perception? Furthermore, how can the results inform the design of novel navigation interfaces? And, what further steps may be needed to refine design requirements and improve interfaces?

To this end, we designed two studies in which we investigated whether static (Study 1) or dynamic (Study 2) tilting of just one's upper body might provide at least some of the benefits of full-scale dynamic motion cueing.

**Figure 1: Experiment setup showing a participant in the upright (0°) condition wearing the HMD and backpack (left). Visual stimuli of the optic flow environment (right).**

# 4. STUDY 1 – STATIC LEANING

## 4.1 Methods

### 4.1.1 Stimuli and apparatus

In both studies, visual stimuli were presented through a head-mounted display (HMD), the Oculus RIFT[tm] DK2. This low-cost HMD provides stereo graphics at a resolution of 960×1080 pixel per eye and a binocular FOV of about 100 degrees. The experiments were programmed in Unity3D[tm] and rendered at 60Hz. The head tracking embedded in the RIFT was enabled, and participants were instructed to to keep the cross-hair (and thus their head) leveled during all leaning conditions (see Figure 1, right). Participants were asked to use a joystick to control forward linear self-motion through a simulated 3D optic flow field. The virtual environment consisted of a particle field of white blobs on a black background, designed to provide strong optic flow when moving through it but no absolute size cues, distance cues, landmarks, or a horizon that could have biased results. No auditory or other cues were provided in the VE. Participants were asked to use a Sony Dualshock® 3 gamepad to control movement through the environment and travel the instructed distance while motion was constrained to forward-only. To measure participants' torso leaning angle (posture), they wore a lightweight backpack frame on which a high-resolution

inclination sensor was mounted (PhidgetSpatial 1042), as illustrated in Figure 1. Before the experiment, the fit of the backpack was adjusted such that the inclination sensor readings for sitting upright were similar between all users. Participants were seated on an office chair with armrests to enable the user to keep a constant angle of leaning forward. For the backward leaning condition, participants could lean comfortably against the backrest. In the second study, we also added extra padding in the lower back to enable steeper leaning angles. The participants' leaning angle was displayed on a control monitor, was closely monitored by the experimenter, and corrected during the experiment when necessary. All experiments were logged automatically; variables included the condition, the travelled distance and time, velocity parameters, and the answers to ratings. All experiments were videotaped for further analysis.

### 4.1.2 Experimental design and procedure

The first study was designed as a two-stage study. Experiment 1 was conducted as a within-subject study, employing a 3×3×3 factorial design. Each participant completed 54 trials in randomized order, consisting of a factorial combination of 3 leaning angles {forward 10°, upright (0°), backward 10°}, 3 instructed distances {10, 15 and 20 meters}, 3 speed mappings {half, normal and double speed} and 2 repetitions per condition. Note that due to the lack of absolute size cues there is no obvious mapping of virtual environments units to meters. From the data we can calculate a mean perceived speed of about 3.5m/s for the normal speed mapping, though. In order to discourage participants from simply counting seconds as a means to estimate traveled distance, we modified the maximum movement velocity per trial by using the three speed mappings between the joystick deflection and the resulting simulated velocity. After signing informed consent and receiving written and oral instructions, participants were seated and donned the backpack and HMD. Before the experiment started, participants were asked about demographics and computer gaming experience, and rated their level of mental and bodily fitness (on a 1-11 Likert scale) to measure possible motion sickness effects after the experiments. Before each trial, participants were instructed about the desired posture and to-be-traveled distance via a pop-up in the immersive environment. The leaning (posture) was static in this experiment and participants were asked to adopt the respective posture before starting a trial and keep it throughout the trial. Participants used the joystick to move the desired distance through the environment. After each trial, participants rated perceived vection intensity and vection realism on a scale of 1 (low) to 11 (high) using a simple rating mechanism in the Unity application. We use introspective vection measures as customary the vection research, as the experience of self-motion is by definition introspective, and there are no reliable alternative physiological or behavioral indicators of vection. As participants were engaged in controlling the velocity with their joystick during a trial to produce instructed distances, we refrained from asking them to also report vection onset latencies, as this would have resulted in a dual-task paradigm with potential unknown consequences. Participants could keep the HMD on throughout the experiment. The second experiment was of a more explorative nature and designed to get further insights into what kinds of body movements participants would naturally choose, and guide the design of study 2 (experiment 3 and 4). To this end, participants completed three trials where they were asked to try out and experiment what kind of dynamic, static leaning or whole-body movements might be most conducive in enhancing their self-motion sensation. While standing or sitting as they preferred, they were asked to freely adjust their body posture and motion to produce the most compelling self-motion while at the same time using the joystick to move freely through the environment (forward only). Each participant completed three trials using the same half, normal and double speed mappings. After the experiments participants answered 13 questions about user comfort and ergonomics, and described further possibilities for improving natural motion cues in an open-ended questionnaire. The answers were expected to help us in designing study 2 as well as devise design guidelines for leaning interfaces.

### 4.1.3 Participants and demographics

Explorative data analysis identified that one participant produced notable outliers, for which reason their data were excluded. Data from 15 participants (5 females / 10 males, aged from 19 to 55; mean age: 25.67) were analyzed, producing a total of 810 trials. 80% (12/15) of the participants stated they played games daily or weekly, 20% (3/15) played monthly or more rarely. The preferred medium for playing was online (9/15, 60%) followed by playing offline on their computer (2/15, 13.3%), game consoles (13.3%), handheld devices (6.7%) and cell phones (6.7%). The majority of participants had no prior experience with HMDs like the Oculus RIFT (8/15, 53.3%) or used it just once (5/15, 33.3%). Only two participants had used HMDs several times in the past (13.3%).

## 4.2 Results and discussion

### 4.2.1 Experiment 1 – Static leaning

Because the optic flow-based virtual environment was devoid of absolute size cues, participants' velocity perception and distances traveled varied considerably between participants. Thus, we converted distances traveled in from VE units to normalized distances in meters by dividing the traveled distance per trial and participant by the mean distance per participant, and multiplying it by the mean instructed distance of 15m. This way, mean normalized distances per participant are by definition 15m. This reduced between-subject variability, and allowed us to focus more on the effect of self-motion cues. Data were analyzed using repeated-measures 3×3×3×2 ANOVAs for the independent variables learning angle, instructed distance, velocity mapping, and repetition for the dependent measures relative distance traveled, vection intensity, and vection realism. Significant main effects and interactions are presented below and summarized in Figure 2. Bonferroni correction was applied as needed.

### 4.2.1.1 Effect of leaning

Our main focus of the study, the effect of **leaning** on self-motion perception, showed a significant main effect on normalized distance traveled ($F(2, 28) = 3.33$, $p = .05$, $\eta_p^2 = .192$). As can be seen in Figure 2 (right) and confirmed by planned contrasts, participants travelled significantly less far when leaning forward ($M = 14.34$, $SD = 5.40$) compared to upright ($M = 15.31$, $SD = 6.34$), $p = .039$, or backward postures ($M = 15.35$, $SD = 6.63$), $p = .023$. This suggests that merely leaning forward can significantly increase our perceived speed of forward self-motion, without any need for external actuation or motion cueing. Unexpectedly, however, leaning did not show any significant main effects on vection intensity ($F(2, 28) = 1.26$, $p = .300$, $\eta_p^2 = .83$) or vection realism ($F(2, 28) = .577$, $p = .568$, $\eta_p^2 = .040$).

### 4.2.1.2 Interaction effects

We found a significant three-way interaction between **leaning, velocity mapping, and repetition** ($F(4, 56) = 2.596$, $p = .046$, $\eta_p^2 = .156$). As can be seen in Figure 3, the second iteration shows a clearer fall-off of relative distance traveled for increasing speeds and forward leaning, whereas first repetition does not show such a consistent tendency. This suggests that potential effects of

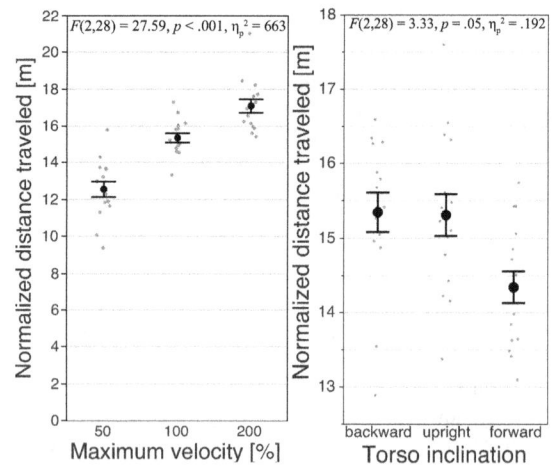

**Figure 2: Mean normalized distances traveled for different speed mappings (left) and torso inclinations (right). Whiskers depict standard errors, gray dots depict mean individual participants' data. Top insets show ANOVA main effects.**

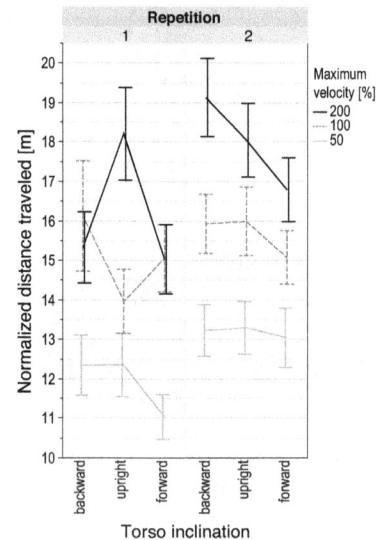

**Figure 3: Three-way interaction between leaning, speed and repetition.**

movement velocity and leaning become more consistent with increasing practice on the task.

### 4.2.1.3 Effect of speed mapping

Traveled distances also showed a significant main effect of the **speed mappings**, $F(2, 28) = 27.587$, $p < .001$, $\eta_p^2 = .663$, with higher speed mappings resulting in further traveled distances (cf. Figure 2). Planned contrasts showed that distances traveled were significantly higher for the 200% speed mapping ($M = 17.09$, $SD = 4.74$) than for the 100% mapping ($M = 15.36$, $SD = 6.18$), which in turn was higher than for the 50% condition ($M = 12.55$, $SD = 4.74$). That is, participants could not fully compensate for the different maximum travel speeds, and might to some degree have used timing to estimate distance traveled. Note, however, that merely using travel time to estimate distances would have resulted in distanced traveled of 7.5m, 15m, and 30m for the speed mappings of 50%, 100%, and 200%, respectively, indicating that participants predominately could to a large degree compensate for the different motion speeds.

### 4.2.1.4 Effect of instructed distance

**Instructed distances** showed significant main effects on the dependent measures normalized distance traveled ($F_{(2,28)}$ = 134.09 $p < .001$, $\eta_p^2 = .905$), vection intensity ($F_{(2,28)}$= 5.86, $p = .007$, $\eta_p^2 = .295$) and vection realism ($F_{(2,28)}$= 4.50, $p = .020$, $\eta_p^2 = .243$). As illustrated in Figure 4 (left), the normalized distance traveled was very close to the predicted distances as indicated by the dashed gray line, for 10m instructed distances (M = 10.98, SD = 3.61), 15m (M = 14.97, SD = 5.44), and 20m (M = 19.04, SD = 6.22). That is, participants were overall quite sensitive to the to-be-instructed distance and could reproduce different distances based on the various motion cues received, and showed very little regression toward mean responses. The effect size of $\eta_p^2 = .905$ indicates that 90.5% of the variability in the distances traveled could be accounted for by the instructed distance.

As vection generally has an onset latency of several seconds and gradually builds up, one would expect the largest to-be-produced distance to yield the highest vection ratings. However, this was not the case: Post-hoc comparisons showed that vection intensities were significantly higher for the 15m condition (M = 58.3%, SD = 16.4%) than for both the 20m (M = 56.2%, SD = 17.2%), $p = .022$ and 10m condition (M = 55.8%, SD = 26.9%), $p = .017$. Similarly, vection realism ratings were higher for the 15m condition (M = 54.9%, SD = 18.9%) than for 10m (M = 51.7%, SD = 18.7%), $p = .020$ condition, but not significantly higher than for the 20m condition (M = 53.3%, SD = 19.3%), $p = .167$. Some users noted they had difficulties in reliably judging vection. For this reason, we included a vection familiarization procedure in study 2. Further studies would be needed to confirm this unexpected finding and potential underlying reasons. Given that vection ratings only differed by about 3% between these conditions, this finding might not be as important as the other observed effects.

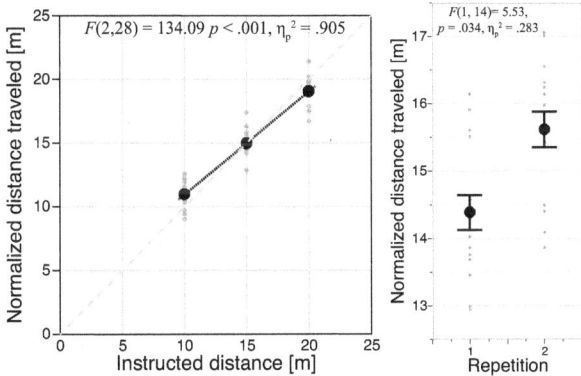

**Figure 4: Mean normalized distances traveled for the different instructed distances (left) and repetitions (right).**

### 4.2.1.5 Effect of repetition of conditions

As depicted in Figure 4 (right), participants travelled significantly further for the second repetition as compared to the first repetition ($F_{(1, 14)}$= 5.53, $p = .034$, $\eta_p^2 = .283$). While further studies are needed to better understand this effect, it might be related to participants getting slightly desensitized to the motion simulation over time, in the sense that longer exposure leads to reducing self-motion velocity estimates.

### 4.2.2 Experiment 2 – Free exploration

In the second experiment, participants tried out and experimented with what kind of dynamic or static leaning and whole-body movements might be most conducive in enhancing their self-motion sensation for the different velocity mappings (half, normal, double speed), and stated which one felt most intense

with regard to the feeling of self-motion. Users were allowed to take any position and perform any kind of motion. When asked to state their preferred posture (see Figure 5), participants' response patterns were fairly similar for the half-speed and normal-speed conditions, where the upright posture was the most common preference (5/15 participants). For the double-speed condition, however, participants tended to prefer forward leaning (6/15) and slight forward leaning (5/15), as well as backward leaning (3/15), whereas only one participant preferred upright posture. Together with verbal reports from the post-experimental debriefing, this suggests that leaning might be a sensible method especially for faster simulated self-motions in VR. For example, one participant stated "leaning forward makes it a bit more realistic when the motion speed is set to high". Three more explicitly noted that leaning forward was the best fit for the fast movement velocity, and that this lead to the strongest sensation of self-motion.

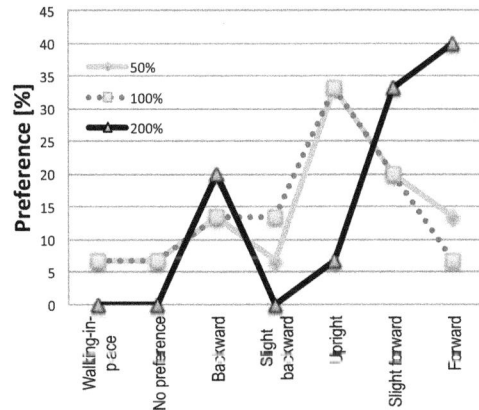

**Figure 5: Leaning and motion preferences depending on velocity mapping.**

Finally, one participant preferred walking-in-place for the slow and medium velocity, but not the fast velocity, whereas another participant stated that body position did not influence their perception of self-motion for the slow and medium velocity mappings. Note that all but two participants clearly preferred seating to standing postures for the slow and medium velocities, and none preferred standing postures for the fast velocity.

In sum, with increasing speed the rather heterogeneous valuation in the half and normal speed mode became more consistent as participants tended to prefer a forward or at least a slightly forward leaning position in the double speed mode.

The participants' choices are in line with what we found in the statistical analysis in phase 1, with direct statement of the positive effect of forward leaning on self-motion perception especially for the faster motions. At this point, it is unclear if the choice for leaning is due to the fact most users tend to sit while working and playing games. Most users did not have experience with the Oculus RIFT or similar head-mounted display devices. Even though participants were invited to stand up and experiment walking around, it may be that they were not accustomed to moving and walking around with the HMD (and constrained by the cables) to mimic natural motion.

### 4.2.3 Pre/post questionnaires

Questionnaire data are summarized in Table 1. Overall, participants stated they felt comfortable and relaxed, meaning the leaning or other experimental procedures did not seem to discomfort them. Also, no motion sickness was reported. Participants noted low excitement, which is not surprising due to the abstract nature of the experiment. Participants were somewhat aware of the real environment while, similarly, the user's attention was somewhat caught by the virtual reality, showing medium immersion. Additionally, the graphics were rated as sufficient to perform the experiment task, while they could concentrate well on the task and had no problems with using the interface. Subjectively, participants noted the body position (posture) had some influence on the perception of self-motion.

| | mean | SD |
|---|---|---|
| General comfort | 8.07 | 2.22 |
| Posture comfort | 7.27 | 2.02 |
| Motion sickness | 1.87 | 1.69 |
| Dizziness | 2.40 | 2.67 |
| Muscle relaxation | 7.20 | 3.14 |
| Excitement | 3.33 | 1.40 |
| Awareness real environment | 5.40 | 2.20 |
| Immersion | 5.33 | 2.80 |
| Graphics task suitability | 6.53 | 2.50 |
| Concentrate on task | 8.20 | 2.20 |
| Problems with interface | 2.07 | 2.02 |
| Fresh and relaxed – before exp. | 5.67 | 1.05 |
| Fresh and relaxed – after exp. | 7.87 | 2.00 |
| Effect of posture on self-motion | 6.60 | 2.92 |

**Table 1 – Pre and post questionnaire ratings on an 11-point Likert scale from 1 = strongly disagree to 11 = strongly agree.**

Yet, while opinions varied quite widely, this also shows there is room for improvement. The variation in opinion on the effect of leaning on self-motion was also reflected in the open questions at the end of the questionnaire. Some participants reported that leaning forward felt best for movement, especially for moving fast. Some participants specifically reported that the faster you moved forward the more you should lean forward to maximize the feeling of self-motion. In the open questions, there were also some contradicting expressions of the effect of forward versus backward leaning to match faster speeds, an effect which we also saw in the leaning and motion preferences reported in Figure 5. Interestingly, only a few participants experimented with dynamic leaning motions, likely because they had extensive exposure to static leaning before. Those who did experiment with dynamic leaning, however, stated that this helped to render the self-motion experience more intense and realistic. This was one motivation for use of investigating user-controlled dynamic leaning motions in the second study. Further motivation comes from the promising results of dynamic leaning in prior studies (see Section 2). Unfortunately, these studies did not directly assess vection or velocity/distance perception, so it remains an open research question to determine what kind of leaning or other self-motions might be most suitable to enhance the user's sensation of self-motion in immersive media. To this end, we designed the second study to investigate how dynamic leaning motions might affect self-motion perception and produced distances, using an experimental paradigm similar to study 1.

# 5. STUDY 2 – DYNAMIC LEANING
## 5.1 Methods
### 5.1.1 Procedure and design

The second study was also designed as a two-stage study, deploying similar procedures as study 1. Once again, in phase 1 each participant completed 54 trials, consisting of a factorial combination of 3 leaning angles {forward 10°, upright (0°), backward 10°}, 3 instructed distances {10, 15 and 20 meters}, 3

speed mappings {half, normal and double speed} and 2 repetitions per condition. Below we only describe those aspects of the methods and procedures that differ from study 1. Motivated by the effect of repetition on performance in study 1, the randomization of conditions was now performed within each of the repetitions. Users first went through all conditions in randomized order in repetition one before repeating all conditions again. Furthermore, instead of adopting and keeping a static posture before the each trial started as instructed in experiment 1, users were now asked to only start leaning forward as they tilted their joystick forward and started the simulated self-motion through the VR. As such, each trial included an initial dynamic stage (dynamically tilting the body forward or backward as instructed) followed by a fairly static stage (keeping the posture during the constant-velocity simulated motion). Because some participants in experiment 1 mentioned that judging vection was difficult without a clear reference of what, e.g., 50% or 100% vection intensity refers to, we added a familiarization phase before the experiment designed to give them a strong sensation of vection that could later act as a reference point of what strong vection should feel like [24]. To this end, participants were asked to move backwards through the environment at double speed for about 15 seconds.

While the maximum leaning angle in phase 1 was only 10° and chosen to match the static leaning angles in experiment 1, it is possible that this leaning might not be extensive enough to show any clear effects. To investigate how not only the direction but also the amount of leaning might affect self-motion perception, phase 2 employed three different maximum leaning angles. That is, each participant performed 7 trials in randomized order, with maximum leaning angles of 0° as well as 5°, 15° and 30° both forward and backward. As participants needed feedback to be able to match these different leaning angles, the experimenter gave them verbal feedback once they reached the desired leaning angle for each trial. For each trial, participants were requested to travel 10 meters with normal speed and no repetitions per condition. In both experiments, participants were asked to report on their background, as well as fill out a questionnaire with 21 questions about general comfort and ergonomic issues.

### 5.1.2 Demographics and user background

16 users participated in experiment 3 and 4 (4 female/12 male, aged 20-30 years, mean: 24.19 years). Each participant performed 54+7 trials, adding to a total of 976 trials. 25% (4/16) played games daily, 31.3% (5/16) weekly, 25% (4/16) monthly, 12.5% (2/16) every half a year, and 6.7% (1/16) every year. The most favored platforms were online PC games (50%, 8/16), 25% (4/16) played cellphone games, while offline PC and console both received 12.5% (2/16). 68.8% (11/16) of participants never used an Oculus RIFT before, 18.8% (3/16) used it once, and 12.5% (2/16) used it a few times before.

## 5.2 Results and Discussion
### 5.2.1 Experiment 3 – limited dynamic leaning

In line with our first experiment, participants were able to reproduce instructed distances fairly consistently (Figure 6). The instructed distance had a significant main effect on the normalized traveled distance ($F(2, 30) = 156.79$, $p < .001$, $\eta_p^2 = .913$), with $\eta_p^2 = 91.3\%$ of the variability in the distances traveled being accounted for by the instructed distance. In contrast to experiment 1, the normalized traveled distance did not show any significant main effects of repetition, velocity, or leaning. In comparison to the first experiment where vection was not influenced by any of the independent variables, experiment 3 showed several effects, potentially due to the added vection familiarization phase: the maximum velocity had a significant effect on vection intensity ($F_{(1.11, 16.71)} = 12.82$, $p = .002$, $\eta_p^2 = .461$), with higher velocities yielding more intense vection (Figure 7 (left)). This is in agreement with the vection literature, where at least up to a certain "optimal velocity" vection tends to increase with stimulus velocity[7]. Furthermore, there was a two-way interaction between torso inclination and repetition on vection intensity ($F_{(2, 30)} = 4.679$, $p = .017$, $\eta_p^2 = .238$), see Figure 7 (right).While there was a tendency for more intense vection for the second repetitions in the upright posture, the forward and backward leaning conditions showed no such trend.

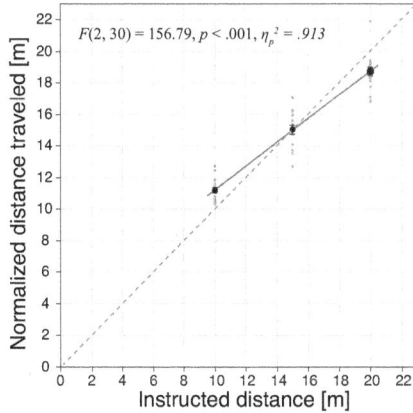

**Figure 6: Traveled normalized distance versus instructed distance**

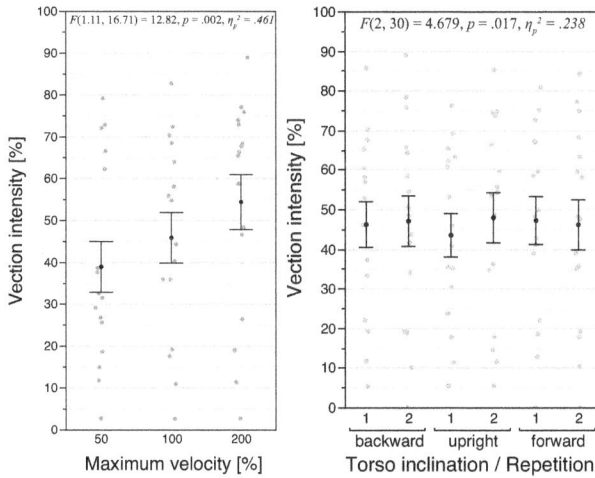

**Figure 7: Effects on vection intensity**

While these findings are interesting and novel, further research is needed to corroborate them and better understand underlying reasons. We also found a two-way interaction between torso inclination and maximum velocity on vection realism ($F_{(1.90, 28.50)} = 3.473$, $p = .047$, $\eta_p^2 = .188$), see Figure 8. While vection in the backward and forward leaning conditions were rated more realistic with larger movement velocity, the upright conditions showed the opposite effect. Similar to the results found in experiment 2, this suggests that leaning is particularly effective in enhancing self-motion perception for faster movement velocities, whereas it provides little benefit for slower movements. Although the ratings of vection intensity and realism indicate some effect of leaning on self-motion perception, in contrast to our first study, leaning did not have any significant effect on the produced distance, $F_{(2, 30)} = .332$, $p = .720$, $\eta_p^2 = .022$. This did surprise us, since we assumed the additional body-centric acceleration and

dynamic motion cues provided by physically leaning forward or backward would have a stronger effect than merely statically leaning. Moreover, tilting users during simulated accelerations and decelerations is commonly used in moving-based motion simulators [12,33] as well as simpler human-powered leaning methods have often been shown to improve self-motion perception [14,15,18,20,37,39]

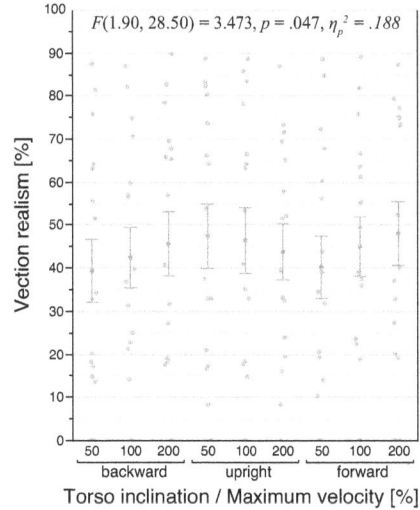

**Figure 8: Effects on vection realism**

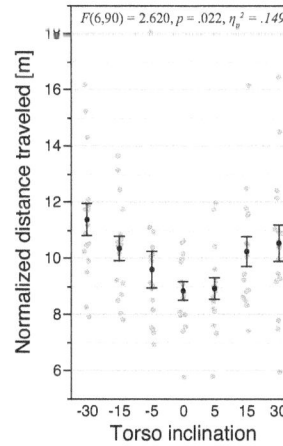

**Figure 9: Effects of leaning on traveled distances**

*5.2.2    Experiment 4 - extended dynamic leaning*

In contrast to experiment 3, analysis of experiment 4 where participants dynamically leaned 0°, 5°, 15° and 30° forwards and backwards showed no significant effects of leaning on vection intensity and realism. Instead, we found a significant effect of torso inclination on normalized traveled distance ($F_{(6, 90)} = 2.620$, $p = .022$, $\eta_p^2 = .149$): As indicated in Figure 9, the further users leaned forwards or backwards, the longer the traveled distance. It is important to note that the direction of the effect was actually the opposite of what would be expected based on the literature and experiment 1, which would have predicted an increased perceived speed and thus a reduction (not increase) in distanced traveled the further the user leaned. We will further discuss this issue in the reflection section 6.

## 5.3    Pre/post questionnaires

The analysis of the pre and post questionnaires (Table 2 and Figure 10) provided some insights in addition to our findings of the distance distribution. As in the first study, a 11-point Likert scale was used. Generally, the comfort in all leaning conditions seemed good – in all postures, users provided medium-high ratings (about 7-8 for all postures) for the comfort and muscle relaxation metrics. Also similar to study 1, the user-excitement was low, while users could nicely concentrate on the task and noted medium immersion. The interaction itself posed no problems, and the graphics were useable for performing the task.

Yet, many users wished for more cues. While we intentionally used a simple and abstract environment in the current studies to reduce potential confounds, it would be interesting to see how users would perform with additional cues such as landmarks and absolute size cues. Motion sickness and dizziness was not an issue, with the exception of one user who had to take a short break. In general, participants were fresh and relaxed before and after the experiment and, hence, we do not expect any negative performance effects of potential posture discomfort or motion sickness. As indicated in Table 2, participants rated that their muscles were more relaxed for the upright as compared to the forward or backward conditions. There was also a non-significant tendency towards higher general comfort and posture-specific comfort ratings for the upright posture compared to forward and backward leaning. At the same time, there was a non-significant trend towards higher self-motion sensations for the forward and backward leaning conditions compared to the upright condition.

| | mean | SD |
|---|---|---|
| Motion sickness | 1.69 | 2.50 |
| Excitement | 2.31 | 1.66 |
| Dizziness | 2.12 | 2.58 |
| Awareness real environment | 4.56 | 2.27 |
| Immersion | 6.25 | 3.36 |
| Graphics task suitability | 6.81 | 3.06 |
| Concentrate on task | 7.88 | 3.10 |
| Interaction problems | 2.69 | 2.27 |
| Fresh and relaxed – before  exp. | 8.81 | 1.72 |
| Fresh and relaxed – after exp. | 7.75 | 2.84 |

**Table 2. Pre/post questionnaire results**

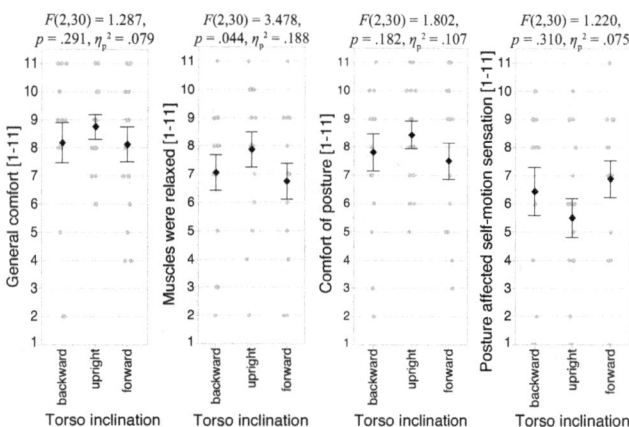

**Figure 10: Effects of leaning on questionnaire ratings.**

This trend was confirmed in the open questions: while 4/16 users noted no effect of posture on self-motion perception, the remaining 12/16 users (75%) reported at least some benefit of leaning on self-motion perception, with 3/16 participants (19%) only stating a minimal benefit. Participants, however, did not agree on whether forward or backward leaning was more

instrumental: while 5/16 (31%) reported a stronger benefit of forward leaning, 3/16 (19%) mentioned a larger benefit for backward leaning. This suggests considerable individual differences in the preferred leaning type, which might be important to consider in the design of leaning-based motion interfaces. For example, it might be sensible to give users an option to choose their preferred leaning direction. Overall, only 4/16 users (25%) commented on the amount of leaning, and those agreed that a medium amount of leaning was most effective (15° here). Still, while these ratings are in line with the subjective ratings of vection realism and intensity, the distance distribution did not reflect these statements directly.

## 6. REFLECTION AND CONCLUSION

Both studies showed that leaning has an effect on self-motion perception. However, a comparison between the two studies reveals there are quite a few differences and surprising results.

### 6.1 Effects on self-motion perception

**Leaning forward can positively affect self-motion perception:** Within our first experiment, we showed that statically leaning forward did significantly affect self-motion perception by reducing distances traveled, likely because of an increase in perceived speed of self-motion. The results are in line with and extending previous body tilt studies we discussed in section 2 [9,13,21]. This suggests that even a simple manipulation such as statically leaning forward while sitting can enhance our self-motion perception in VR, thus providing an extremely simple and affordable approach. However, statically leaning forward reduced traveled distances by only about 6% and, thus, might by itself only have limited applied benefit. In addition, statically leaning forward might not be ergonomically feasible for longer durations.

**Leaning subjectively enhances self-motion perception and is preferred especially for higher speeds:** In experiment 2, participants experimented with different static and dynamic leaning motions and either reported no clear preference or remarked that leaning can enhance their sensation of self-motion and overall realism, especially for faster simulated self-motions. In the debriefing after experiment 4, 75% of participants stated that dynamic leaning enhanced self-motion perception at least somewhat. However, they disagreed as to whether forward leaning (31%) or backward leaning (19%) was more suitable, although they seemed to agree that a moderate amount of leaning (less than the maximum of 30° used in experiment 4) was most instrumental and that the faster motions are best accompanied by more extensive leaning. These findings are overall in alignment with results from experiment 2, where users showed a stronger preference for leaning compared to upright postures for the fastest simulated self-motion.

**Vection unaffected by leaning, at least for current procedure:** It was surprising that vection measures showed no clear main effect of either static leaning (experiment 1) or dynamic leaning (experiment 3 and 4), even though prior work, using somewhat different procedures, did report such benefits [12,21,25]. Post-experimental debriefing suggests that this lack of a vection-facilitating effect, especially in experiment 1, might have been related to participants' difficulty in reliably judging their self-motion sensation without a clear reference stimulus and anchored response scale. For experiment 3, we tried to address this by including a vection familiarization phase, and we observed somewhat higher sensitivity to experimental manipulations and larger variations in vection responses, although a more extensive vection demonstration and practice phase might have yielded clearer effects in all experiments reported here. This highlights the importance of careful experimentation and providing a reference experience to sufficiently ground any introspective scale.

**Exposure/learning effects:** Experiment 1 suggests that longer exposure might lead to lower perceived self-motion velocities. In terms of guidelines for experimentation, this highlights the importance of carefully designing studies in order to take exposure effects into account, for example by counter-balancing different conditions. The 3-way interaction observed in experiment 1 further emphasizes the importance of taking exposure effects into consideration, in that effects of experimental parameters can become more clear and consistent with exposure.

**Dynamic leaning shows unexpected results:** In experiment 3, where participants dynamically leaned up to 10° forward and backward, we observed no significant main effects of leaning on either distance traveled or vection ratings. When the amount of dynamic leaning was varied in experiment 4 (5°, 15° and 30°), we actually observed the opposite of what we would have predicted based on experiment 1 and 2 and the literature [9,13,21]: That is, for steeper leaning inclinations, participants actually traveled further, not less as predicted. While this result was puzzling, the qualitative data from the exit interviews and the video analysis could provide us with some pointers towards a potential explanation. It seemed like users often tended to first concentrate on dynamically leaning forward to reach the desired posture, with steeper postures taking slightly longer to adopt, before concentrating on judging how far to move forward. This leads to the assumption of a two-stage process in the action selection and planning phase in human information processing [40], and matches observations from the video analysis. If participants employed such a 2-stage strategy and did not fully incorporate the distance travelled during the dynamic leaning phase before reaching the maximum leaning extent, this would predict longer distances traveled especially for the most extreme leaning angles, which is exactly what we observed in experiment 4. In contrast, experiment 3 only used leaning angles of 10° and showed no effect of leaning on produced distances. In retrospect, this could be related to the potential effects of leaning being compensated for by the above-mentioned 2-stage approach of first leaning before starting to fully concentrate on the to-be-travelled distance. Further experiments are needed and planned to investigate this.

## 6.2 Conclusions and outlook

Although many questions await further research, designing leaning-based and, thus, more embodied locomotion interfaces seems overall like a promising avenue for further research and might ultimately help to enhance self-motion perception, user experience and engagement, as is also suggested by prior work [1,12,14,20,21,25,29,39]. Generally, we did not see any negative effects of static or dynamic leaning on user comfort, and most ratings were positive. However, it should be noted that participants only had to keep the leaning postures for a short time. Supporting leaning, especially forward leaning, for extended durations will likely require ergonomic supports.

In general, there are a number of potential usability issues that can counteract potential benefits of more embodied locomotion interfaces. For example, in the current study, locomotion through VR was only controlled by a joystick and not directly affected by users' leaning. While this was necessary for experiment 1 and 2, multiple users commented that they would like to directly control the simulated self-motion with their body inclination, using a "human-as-a-joystick" metaphor. This would likely also help to address the two-stage control issue described above. As we discussed in section 2, such leaning-control approaches have been

employed by a number of studies ranging from standing-leaning interfaces to sitting-leaning interfaces using a modified gaming chair or leaning stool interface [1,14,15,19,20,25,37,39].

In conclusion, our study provide first indications that upper body leaning can improve self-motion perception and user experience, which could inspire the design of improved user interfaces that are more embodied yet affordable as the do not require external motor actuation. At the same time, it suggests that decoupling torso leaning from the VE velocity control (by using a joystick in the current study) might be problematic and conceals potential benefits of dynamic torso leaning. On reason might be the lack of direct visual feedback from torso leaning, which might have added cognitive load and resulted in participants in dynamic leaning conditions to first concentrate on the leaning before fully engaging on the distance production task as discussed earlier. Together, this highlights the importance of providing direction action-perception coupling – while separating different parameters can be valuable in fundamental research to disambiguate influences of different factors, immediate and intuitive coupling of user actions to observable effects is essential for designing user interfaces that are both effective and intuitive.

Based on and inspired by our findings and participant feedback, we are currently designing a study using the human-as-a-joystick direct input metaphor using different inclination/speed mappings and incorporating rotations and translations in both forward/backward and left/right direction, as well as comparing upper-body-only motion like in the current experiment to a leaning chair stool paradigm inspired by [1,19,25].

## 7. REFERENCES

[1] Beckhaus, S., Blom, K., and Haringer, M. 2005.Intuitive, Hands-free Travel Interfaces for Virtual Environments. Proceedings of the 3D user interface workshop, IEEE Virtual Reality Conference.

[2] Berthoz, A., Israël, I., Georges-François, P., Grasso, R., and Tsuzuku, T.1995. Spatial memory of body linear displacement: what is being stored? Science , 269, 5220, 95–8.

[3] Bos, J., Bles, W., and Groen, E. 2008. A theory on visually induced motion sickness. Displays 29, 2, 47–57.

[4] Bourrelly, A., Vercher, J.-L., and Bringoux, L. 2010. Pitch body orientation influences the perception of self-motion direction induced by optic flow. Neuroscience letters 482, 3, 193–7.

[5] Bowman, D., Koller, D., and Hodges, L.1998. A Methodology for the Evaluation of Travel Techniques for Immersive Virtual Environments. Virtual Reality: Research, Development, and Applications 3, , 120–131.

[6] Bowman, D., Kruijff, E., LaViola, J., and Poupyrev, I. 2005. 3D user interfaces : theory and practice. Addison-Wesley.

[7] Brandt, T., Dichgans, J., and Koenig, E. 1973. Differential effects of central versus peripheral vision on egocentric and exocentric motion perception. Experimental Brain Research 16, 5.

[8] Bringoux, L., Robic, G., Gauthier, G., and Vercher, J. 2008. Judging beforehand the possibility of passing under obstacles without motion: the influence of egocentric and geocentric frames of reference. Experimental brain research 185, 4, 673–80.

[9] Bringoux, L., Tamura, K., Faldon, M., Gresty, M., and Bronstein, A. 2004. Influence of whole-body pitch tilt and

kinesthetic cues on the perceived gravity-referenced eye level. Experimental brain research 155, 3, 385–92.

[10] Darken, R., Cockayne, W., and Carmein, D. 1997. The Omni-Directional Treadmill: A Locomotion Device for Virtual Worlds. Proceedings of the ACM Symposium on User Interface Software and Technology, 213–221.

[11] DeAngelis, G. and Angelaki, D.2012. Visual–Vestibular Integration for Self-Motion Perception.

[12] Groen, E.L. and Bles, W. 2004. How to use body tilt for the simulation of linear self motion. Journal of vestibular research : equilibrium & orientation 14, 5, 375–85.

[13] Guterman, P., Allison, R., Palmisano, S., and Zacher, J.. 2012. Postural and viewpoint oscillation effects on the perception of self-motion. Journal of Vision 12, 9, 576–576.

[14] Guy, E., Punpongsanon, P., Iwai, D., Sato, K., and Boubekeur, T. 2015. .LazyNav: 3D Ground Navigation with Non-Critical Body Parts. Proceedings of the IEEE Symposium on 3D User Interfaces.

[15] De Haan, G., Griffith, E., and Post, F. 2008. Using the Wii Balance Board as a low-cost VR interaction device. Proceedings of the ACM symposium on Virtual reality software and technology, 289.

[16] Harris, L., Jenkin, M., and Zikovitz, D. 1999. Vestibular Cues and Virtual environments: Choosing the Magnitude of the Vestibular Cue. Proceedings of IEEE Virtual Reality'99, 229–236.

[17] Harris, L., Jenkin, M., and Zikovitz, D. 2000. Visual and Non-Visual Cues in the Perception of Linear Self Motion. Experimental Brain Research 135.

[18] Ivanenko, Y.P., Grasso, R., Israël, I., and Berthoz, A.1997. The contribution of otoliths and semicircular canals to the perception of two-dimensional passive whole-body motion in humans. The Journal of physiology 502,Pt 1, 223–33.

[19] Kitson, A., Riecke, B.E., Hashemian, A., and Neustaedter, C. 2015. NaviChair: an embodied interface to navigate virtual reality. Proceedings of the ACM Symposium on Spatial User Interaction.

[20] Marchal, M., Pettre, J., and Lecuyer, A. 2011. Joyman: A human-scale joystick for navigating in virtual worlds. 2011 IEEE Symposium on 3D User Interfaces, 19–26.

[21] Nakamura, S. and Shimojo, S. 1998. Orientation of selective effects of body tilt on visually induced perception of self-motion. Perceptual and motor skills 87, 2, 667–72.

[22] Peterson, B., Wells, M., Furness, T., and Hunt, E. 1998. The Effects of the Interface on Navigation in Virtual Environments. in Proceedings of Human Factors and Ergonomics Society 1998 Annual Meeting.

[23] Riecke, B., Bodenheimer, B., McNamara, T., Williams, B., Peng, P., and Feuereissen, D. 2010. Do we need to walk for effective virtual reality navigation? physical rotations alone may suffice, 234–247.

[24] Riecke, B., Feuereissen, D., and Rieser, J. 2009. Auditory self-motion simulation is facilitated by haptic and vibrational cues suggesting the possibility of actual motion. ACM Transactions on Applied Perception 6, 3, 1–22.

[25] Riecke, B. and Feuereissen, D.2012. To move or not to move: can active control and user-driven motion cueing

[26] Riecke, B.and Schulte-Pelkum, J. 2013. Perceptual and Cognitive Factors for Self-Motion Simulation in Virtual Environments: How Can Self-Motion Illusions ("Vection") Be Utilized? In F. Steinicke, Y. Visell, J. Campos and A. Lécuyer, eds., Human Walking in Virtual Environments. Springer New York, New York, NY, 27–54.

[27] Riecke, B. and Schulte-Pelkum, J.2014. An integrative approach to presence and self-motion perception research.

[28] Riecke, B.E., Väljamäe, A., and Schulte-Pelkum, J. 2009. Moving sounds enhance the visually-induced self-motion illusion (circular vection) in virtual reality. ACM Transactions on Applied Perception 6, 2, 1–27.

[29] Riecke, B. 2006. Simple user-generated motion cueing can enhance self-motion perception (Vection) in virtual reality. Proceedings of the ACM symposium on Virtual reality software and technology, 104.

[30] Rupert, A. and Kolev, O. 2008. The Use of Tactile Cues to Modify the Perception of Self-Motion.

[31] St George, R.. and Fitzpatrick, R.2011. The sense of self-motion, orientation and balance explored by vestibular stimulation. The Journal of physiology 589, Pt 4, 807–13.

[32] Steinicke, F., Visell, Y., Campos, J., and Lecuyer, A., eds. 2013. Human Walking in Virtual Environments. Springer Verlag.

[33] Stratulat, A.M., Roussarie, V., Vercher, J.-L., and Bourdin, C. 2011. Does tilt/translation ratio affect perception of deceleration in driving simulators? Journal of vestibular research : equilibrium & orientation 21, 3, 127–39.

[34] Templeman, J.N., Denbrook, P.S., and Sibert, L.E.2009. Virtual Locomotion: Walking in Place through Virtual Environments. Presence: Teleoperators and Virtual Environments 8, 6, 598–617.

[35] Usoh, M., Arthur, K., Whitton, M.C., et al.1999. Walking > Walking-in-Place > Flying in Virtual Environments. Proceedings of ACM SIGGRAPH '99, 359–364.

[36] Väljamäe, A., Larsson, P., Västfjäll, D., and Kleiner, M.2006. Vibrotactile Enhancement of Auditory-Induced Self-Motion and Spatial Presence. Journal of the Audio Engineering Society 54, 10, 954–963.

[37] Valkov, D., Steinicke, F., Bruder, G., and Hinrichs, K.2010. Traveling in 3D Virtual Environments with Foot Gestures and a Multi-Touch enabled WIM. Proceedings of Virtual Reality International Conference, 171–180.

[38] Wang, J. and Lindeman, R. 2012.Leaning-based travel interfaces revisited: frontal versus sidewise stances for flying in 3D virtual spaces. Proceedings of the ACM symposium on Virtual reality software and technology, 121.

[39] Wang, J. and Lindeman, R.W.2011. Silver Surfer: A system to compare isometric and elastic board interfaces for locomotion in VR, 121–122.

[40] Wickens, C. and Carswell, C. 1997. Information processing. In G. Salvendy, ed., Handbook of Human Factors and Ergonomics. Wiley & Sons, New York, 130–149.

# Creature Teacher: A Performance-Based Animation System for Creating Cyclic Movements

### Andreas Fender
Department of Computer
Science
Aarhus University, Aarhus,
Denmark
andreasfender@cs.au.dk

### Jörg Müller
Department of Computer
Science
Aarhus University, Aarhus,
Denmark
joerg.mueller@acm.org

### David Lindlbauer
TU Berlin
Berlin, Germany
david.lindlbauer@tu-berlin.de

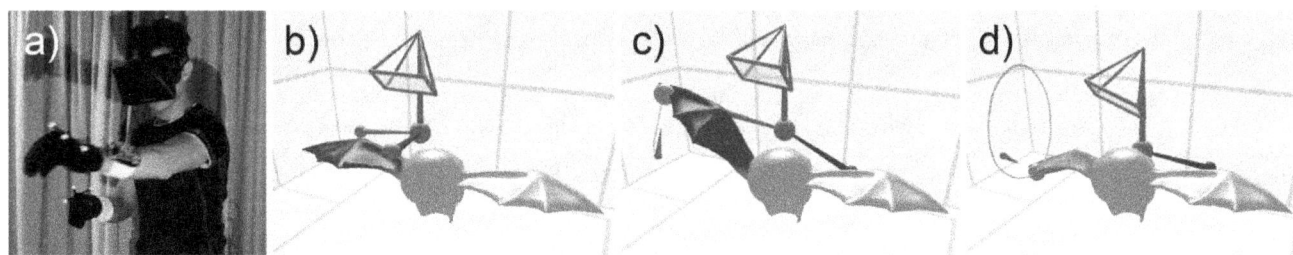

Figure 1: With *Creature Teacher* users can quickly create organic movements by successively selecting and manipulating parts of a virtual creature. (a) The user is wearing an HMD and pinch gloves. (b) Body parts are selected using the left hand. (c) Selected parts are manipulated using the right hand. (d) Periodic movements are detected and played back repeatedly.

## ABSTRACT

We present *Creature Teacher*, a performance-based animation system for creating cyclic movements. Users directly manipulate body parts of a virtual character by using their hands. Creature Teacher's generic approach makes it possible to animate rigged 3D models with nearly arbitrary topology (e.g., non-humanoid) without requiring specialized user-to-character mappings or predefined movements. We use a bimanual interaction paradigm, allowing users to select parts of the model with one hand and manipulate them with the other hand. Cyclic movements of body parts during manipulation are detected and repeatedly played back - also while animating other body parts. Our approach of taking cyclic movements as an input makes mode switching between recording and playback obsolete and allows for fast and seamless creation of animations. We show that novice users with no animation background were able to create expressive cyclic animations for initially static virtual 3D creatures.

## Categories and Subject Descriptors

H.5.m. [**Information Interfaces and Presentation (e.g. HCI)**]: Miscellaneous

## Keywords

Animation; 3D User Interface; Performance-Based; Virtual Reality; 3D Interaction and Graphics

## 1. INTRODUCTION

Animation is a powerful tool used in movies and games to give life to fictional characters and creatures. Those characters can convey emotions, motivations and intentions to viewers just by the way they are moving through space. This can be achieved by *cycle animations* which are repeatedly played back to make a character's locomotion look active. For example, when a game character is moving on the ground, a walking, sneaking or running cycle, depending on the current speed of locomotion, is played back repeatedly. Cycle animations are not only used for locomotion. Movements like breathing, chewing, dancing etc. are examples of cycle animations to be played back even when the virtual character is not changing location.

In general, 3D computer animation is implemented with virtual *articulated figures*, that is, hierarchical *limbs* are defined within the 3D model to deform it locally. With *joints*, we refer to the ends of the limbs or the connections of two limbs. The combination of all limbs yield the *skeleton* of the articulated figure. All limb transformations together yield the *posture*.

Creating convincing and expressive animations is challenging for various reasons. Depending on the number of limbs, a posture can have a large number of degrees of freedom (DOFs). Furthermore, animation introduces a time domain. Much knowledge and experience is required to create animations with state-of-the-art modeling and animation tools like *Blender* and *Autodesk Maya*.

In the recent years, an increasing number of 3D games include content creation by players as a core aspect. Many games enable players to easily personalize the look of their avatar or even to build whole worlds, thus those games are essentially heavily simplified and specialized modeling tools. Current content creation by players, however, is mostly limited to the specification of the appearance of game assets and does not include animation. As noted by Walther et al. [35], games generally do not provide expressive tools for players to create convincing animations. By now, animations of avatars and creatures inhabiting the game worlds are typically predefined or generated. We believe that animation can become a very important and expressive part of content creation by players. In our work, we want to take a step in this direction and allow users to playfully create animation without requiring expert knowledge.

An additional challenge is that due to the fictional nature of games, the virtual game characters can be of arbitrary morphology. Therefore we refer to them as creatures. If a game offers tools for the player to create such creatures, then their morphology might even be unknown at programming time. This makes the creation of specialized animation tools (unlike with specialized creation tools) even more challenging.

We developed Creature Teacher, an immersive virtual reality (VR) system to rapidly and easily create cyclic movement animations for virtual creatures. The main focus is the creation of expressive animations to be played back during locomotion, i.e., to specify how a creature moves through space. The system does not rely on preprocessing steps, specialized mappings or predefined animations. Equipped with a head-mounted display (HMD) and pinch gloves, users directly manipulate a virtual creature to easily create individual and expressive cyclic animations. Previous systems, while allowing for easy creation of smooth movements, often lack flexibility. We contribute by presenting a bimanual selection and manipulation approach to address the problem of providing expressive real-time control over different virtual creatures with arbitrary limb structure. We further present an approach to create cyclic animations by leveraging users' ability to perform repetitive motions and use those as an input method.

## 2. RELATED WORK

The two dominant approaches for computer animation are *keyframing* and *performance animation*, which are discussed in this section. Other techniques like inverse kinematics or behavioural animation exist, aiming to make the animation more realistic and simplify the creation process. However, those techniques are outside the scope of this paper since most of them are orthogonal (or potential additions) to the actual interaction techniques employed in our system.

Table 1 is an overview of previous animation interfaces for articulated figures, which we categorize by four dimensions. The first dimension specifies the input dimension (i.e., *WIMP*, *Sketch*, or *Tangible*), including tracking as input.

For tracking, we distinguish between *Tracking: Mimicking* (acting out movements) and *Tracking: Guiding* (controlling from a third person view). The second dimension specifies the handling of the animation time domain. This includes *keyframing* as well as different types of performance animation systems. *One-take systems* only need one recording take to create the complete animation, thus the animation time passes only once. With *multi-pass systems*, the animation time passes multiple times and users control different DOFs in each take. The other two levels specify if a system is immersive and the level of control. Level of control defines the granularity with which users can edit postures and movements. On one side, users have fine grained control over every single limb (i.e., *low-level*). On the other side, only pre-defined movements are remapped or movements are created automatically (i.e., *high-level*). Note that the table only contains animation systems for articulated figures and hence does not contain interfaces that only support rigid object transformations. Furthermore, the table does not account for pre- and post-processing steps.

### 2.1 Keyframing

With keyframing, only keyframe postures need to be created. The large number of DOFs of an articulated figure can be handled by users accurately one after another without animation time passing. This leads to the advantage that compared to the output, only a limited number of DOFs is necessary as input. Current state-of-the-art software contains sophisticated implementations of the keyframing technique. Those interfaces are very powerful, however, can be difficult to use for novices. In particular, making motions look organic is a very demanding task. Furthermore, keyframing is generally very time consuming, even for professional animators.

Besides established tools such as *Blender* and *Maya*, other user interfaces make use of the keyframing technique. The main focus of those interfaces is making the posing process easy and quick. The *HoloSketch* system is a stereoscopic sketching and animation interface with 3D user input [5]. Users can grasp virtual objects and apply transformations to pose and animate them. In contrast to our work, transformations can only be applied to whole objects rather than postures of articulated figures. With [20], [2] and [4], animations can be created by sketching the keyframe postures of the articulated figure by hand on a piece of paper. Eitsuka et al. [7] created an augmented reality based animation system, with which the user manipulates the key postures of a virtual character with his or her finger. Jacobson et al. [12] presented a modular input device, overcoming the limitations of specialized input devices. Single physical joints can be assembled and manipulated, making the system very flexible.

Even though those tools simplify the creation of postures, performance-animation tools often outperform keyframing approaches in terms of time required to create convincing animations.

### 2.2 Performance animation

In contrast to keyframing, performance animation systems rely on the user's physical timing and coordination skills. One well known technique is *motion capturing*: the performer's motions are mapped onto a virtual character. In most cases, a 1:1 mapping is used to achieve realistic

| | WIMP | Sketch | Tangible | Tracking: Mimicking | Tracking: Guiding |
|---|---|---|---|---|---|
| **Keyframing** | *Blender*<br>*Maya* | *MotionMaster* [20]<br>*Chao* [2]<br>*Davis* [4] | *Jacobson* [12]<br>*Monkey* [8] | | Eitsuka [7]<br>***Osawa* [25]** |
| **One-take** | Laszlo [18] | Motion Doodles [33] | Komura [15]<br>Zhiqiang [21]<br>Numaguchi [23]<br>Kim [14]<br>Krause [17]<br>Mobile Animator [10] | Shin [28]<br>Creature Features [27]<br>Yamane [36]<br>Vögele [34]<br>KinÊtre [3]<br>**ThatcherWorld [30]**<br>Ishigaki [11] | SmurVEbox [1] |
| **Multi-pass** | Yamane [37]<br>Kim [13] | | *Oore* [24]<br>Oshita [26] | Dontcheva [6] | Shiratori [29]<br>Kostandov [16]<br>**CAT [22]**<br>*Creature Teacher* |

**Table 1: Overview of interfaces for animating articulated characters. Bold entries are immersive. Italic entries allow for fine grained limb level control. Conventional interfaces can be found at *WIMP-Keyframing*.**

and natural human-like animations. The main drawback of motion capturing is the restriction to human or humanoid characters. Furthermore, only animations that are physically possible can be created directly. Digital puppetry [32], another performance based approach, aims at overcoming these limitations by not using a 1:1 mapping.

### 2.2.1 Most similar systems

Shiratori et al. [29] created a digital puppetry plugin for *Maya*. Users can move and rotate a tracked device freely to manipulate the associated limbs of any articulated 3D figure. However, 3D input is only used for manipulation. Other tasks, like selection and setting up the mappings, is done through *Maya*. Therefore, users need a certain level of expertise, whereas our system is self-contained and does not need any setup of mappings. Kostandov et al. [16] presented a poster with the idea of an immersive VR character animation system with a direct manipulation interface. Using a 3D input device, users can grasp joints of an articulated figure and record the motions for subsequent playback. The system is suitable for non-humanoid characters, but only feasible for relatively simple limb structures. We build on their approach. However, our system is designed to also animate creatures with more complex limb structures. Martin et al. [22] presented a 3D input animation system called *CAT*, which lets users author animations by grasping and moving the limbs using a handheld controller. However, the system is specialized on quadruped creatures, relying on predefined and automated movements.

### 2.2.2 Performance-based: One-take

*Creature Features* [27] and other systems (e.g., [34]) focus on non-humanoid creature animations. Users are tracked and their movements are mapped onto the creature's movements. The systems rely on a set of predefined animations for each creature to puppeteer in order to blend between them according to the performance. The system of Kim et al. [14] uses a haptic input device and virtual physically simulated marionette strings, to create complex character

animations. With *KinÊtre* [3], the object to animate is deformed according to the user's performance. Yamane et al. [36] use human motion capture data and map the motion to non-humanoid creatures. While one-take animation systems can be advantageous in terms of creation speed, several challenges emerge. For example, movements must be physically possible for the actor to perform, otherwise specialized mappings or predefined animations need to be employed.

### 2.2.3 Performance based: Multi-pass

Kim et al. [13] proposed a performance-based desktop system. Users drag joints of physically simulated 3D-creatures with the mouse. Oore et al. [24] used two bamboo tubes for a bimanual real-time control of the selected limbs. In [6], movements of a handheld device are automatically mapped onto the virtual character's movements. The multi-pass approach tries to balance creation speed and flexibility. A larger number of DOFs can be handled subsequently by creating superimposed animations, often in an additive manner.

## 3. WALKTHROUGH

We now illustrate Creature Teacher in the context of animating a game asset (see Figure 2). Since our system is intended for games in which content creation is important, giving users the ability to express individuality in the animations is a key point. In the example of this walkthrough, a skull with wings shall be animated. More specifically, animation cycles for flying forward, flying backward and flying on the spot need to be created by the player to specify how the skull can move through the game world. The starting point (or input) for Creature Teacher is a rigged 3D model of a creature, containing the mapping from limb transformations to mesh deformations.

Figure 2 depicts the rapid creation of one possible flying-on-the-spot animation. The player can give individual details to the movements. The individualism also comes naturally, since Creature Teacher is performance-based. Therefore, variances in the players' hand movements or even flawed and unwanted movements make the end result unique.

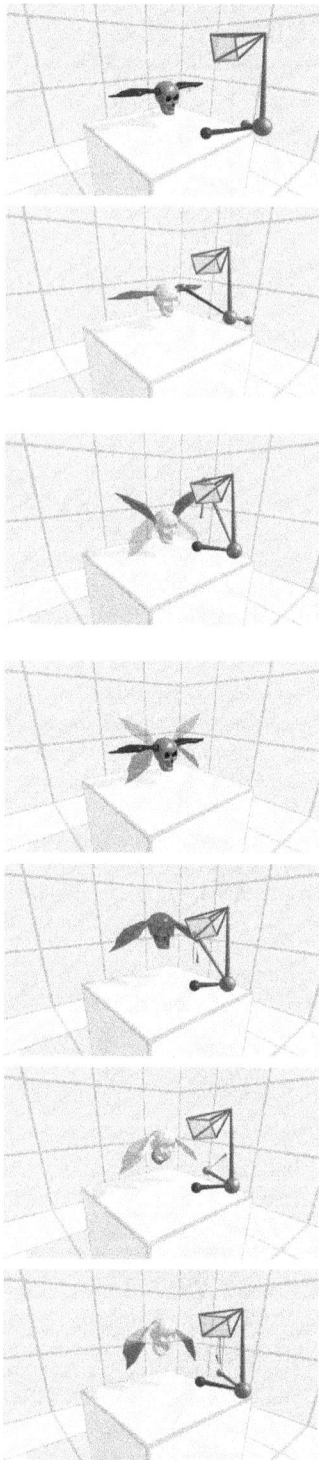

**1.** The user sees the virtual creature.

**2.** At first, the user selects both wings using the left hand (blue arm).

**3.** The wing's posture is manipulated using the right hand (green arm). The hand's motion is mapped onto the orientations of the wings in real-time. By moving the hand up and down, the user creates a wing-flap-motion.

**4.** After repeating the motion a couple of times, the motion is recorded. The skull repeats the motion from then on. Now other parts of the skull can be animated or the wing flap can be refined.

**5.** An up and down motion according to the wing flaps is given to the whole creature. The user has to select the whole creature and to move it up and down in the correct rhythm.

**6.** To add more life, a chewing-like motion is given to the mouth.

**7.** The user gives a delayed flap motion to the pinions to make the animation look more organic.

**Figure 2: Walkthrough for the rapid creation of a flying-on-the-spot animation.**

## 4. CREATURE TEACHER

This section provides details of interaction techniques, the workflow and some implementation details of Creature Teacher.

### 4.1 Overview

Users wear pinch gloves and move their hands in mid-air. The two hands are tracked and represented as two 3D volumetric cursors with different colors. Users see the cursors through an HMD and perceive the position at the actual hand positions. The two hands of the users have different roles, i.e., the non-dominant hand is mainly used for selection and the dominant hand is mainly used for manipulation (cf. [9]). For simplification, the right hand is considered as the dominant hand in this paper (however, Creature Teacher allows for configuring this).

### 4.2 Setup

The main hardware components of the system are two custom made pinch gloves, an *Oculus Rift* (Development Kit 1) and an *OptiTrack* system. Markers are attached to each glove to be tracked by the *OptiTrack* system, which transmits position data to the Creature Teacher software. Further markers are attached to the *Oculus Rift* to get the camera position. For camera orientation, the build-in sensors of the *Oculus Rift* are used. The software is implemented using *Java*, 3D rendering is based on *OpenGL*.

### 4.3 Selection

The selection process starts as soon as the left hand is close to the creature. All previously animated movements of the creature are paused. The creature becomes semi-transparent and its texture is removed. This way, users can concentrate on animating the actual creature while gaining some insights into the underlying structure. We found this to be a good balance between low visual complexity and enough information to create animations. The body part closest to the left hand is highlighted. When pinching, the highlighted part is selected, which is visualized by a change in color of the part. Users can hold the pinch and move the cursor through the creature to select multiple parts in a row. Typically, we observed that users first coarsely reach into the figure to pause the movement, move the hand to the body part to select until the respective body part is highlighted and eventually start pinching. Users can freely select multiple body parts or extend the selection by pinching again with the left hand. Deselection is achieved by starting to pinch within already selected body parts. Users can pinch shortly outside of the range of the creature for complete deselection.

To enable quick selection of large structures as well as accurate selection of small parts, the effective volume of the selection cursor is proportional to the velocity of the hand movement. Slow movements allow for fine grained selection of single parts, since the cursor volume is small. When moving the hand very fast, large parts or even the whole creature can be selected very quickly without having to move through every single body part. This technique is inspired by the *Harpoon Selection* proposed by Leitner et al. [19], but applied to a 3D cursor instead of 2D pen input.

Selected body parts are shaded in blue. We refer to connected selected body parts as *rigid bodies*. The *anchor* of a rigid body is a point at the body part that has non-selected neighboring body parts. The *rigid body vector* is generated as following and depicted in Figure 3. The direction points from the anchor to the joints' center of mass within the rigid body. The magnitude equals the distance of the joint or the joints which are furthest apart from the anchor. Adding the rigid body vector to the anchor yields the *tip*.

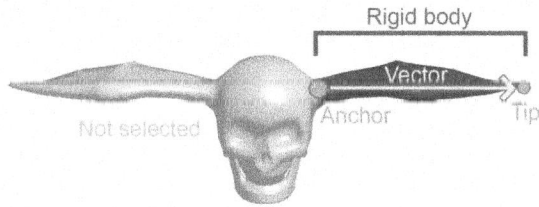

**Figure 3:** Example for a rigid body: The whole wing is selected, indicated by blue shading. The rigid body's anchor is at the transition between the head and the wing. Its tip is at the pinion.

## 4.4 Manipulation

After selection, users can manipulate the created rigid bodies. The manipulation technique is related to the *Handle Bar Metaphor* [31]: Song et al. proposed using a virtual handle which is controlled bimanually to apply transformations on selected objects. Users shift two ends of a virtual handle to rotate, translate and scale it. The resulting transformation of the handle is applied to the selected object. The main motivation of the *Handle Bar Metaphor* is coping with low precision tracking, i.e., with technical inaccuracies. The *OptiTrack* system we use is rather accurate, but nevertheless the orientation control is much more fine grained, when using this technique instead of, e.g., hand rotation. In our system, every rigid body vector can be thought of being such a handle bar, whereas one end is at the rigid body anchor and the other end is controlled by the right hand when pinching. The result transformation is applied to all limbs of the respective rigid body.

To start the manipulation, users pinch with the right hand. Moving the right hand moves the tip of every rigid body, which changes the orientations of the rigid body vectors. All limbs of a rigid body are transformed accordingly. By default, the magnitudes of the rigid body vectors remain constant, therefore, even if users describe a straight line, the tip moves along an arc. Thus, only the orientation is changed. The basic principle is depicted in Figure 4.

If users start the manipulation at a rigid body tip, then the manipulation is collocated. However, from our experiences, it is more important for users to have a good overview of the creature than collocated manipulation. Therefore, users can find the best spot to start the manipulation and not necessarily have to start at the tip. Every rigid body tip is shifted according to the movement of the right hand, i.e., delta movements of the hand are applied to each rigid body tip. This behavior is especially important when multiple body parts are selected (see Figure 4). Furthermore, by not enforcing collocation, user fatigue is potentially reduced, because users can perform manipulations while being in a convenient posture instead of e.g., having to lean to the respective body part during manipulation.

In general, only 2 DOFs of the orientation are manipulated with the right hand, i.e., only yaw and pitch are changed. To enable roll, users have to additionally pinch with their left hand during manipulation. Moving the left hand around the right hand applies a roll transformation to all rigid bodies around their vectors.

If scaling is enabled (toggled through a 3D menu), then not only the orientation, but also the magnitude of the rigid

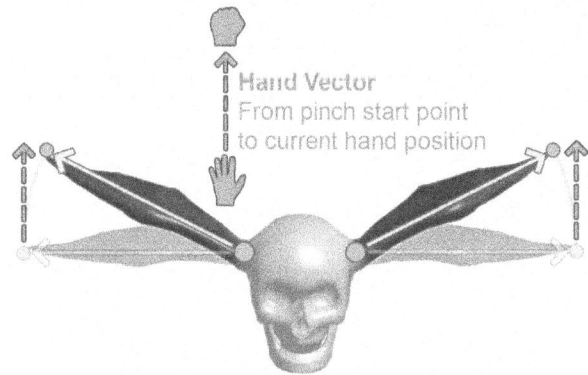

**Figure 4:** Manipulation with two rigid bodies: In this example, the user started to pinch with the right hand at an arbitrary point in the air and moved the hand straight upwards. The rigid body tips are both moved upwards according to the hand vector. The distance of the tip to the anchor, i.e., the magnitude of the rigid body vector, remains constant. Non-selected body parts are not influenced at all.

body vectors can be manipulated. By moving a rigid body tip towards the rotation anchor, the rigid body and its body parts become smaller. By moving it away, it gets bigger. In our current implementation, scaling is uniform.

If a rigid body has no anchor, e.g., when the whole creature is selected, then the movement of the right hand is applied to the translation of the rigid body, instead of the orientation. To rotate such rigid bodies, users need to pinch with the left hand during manipulation and to move the left hand around the right hand (cf. [31]).

Every created animation is additive, i.e., if the body part to manipulate is already animated, then the new motion is added to the prior motion. Therefore, users can first define a coarse motion of a large body part and then add fine grained motions to sub parts or vice versa.

## 4.5 Loops

Movements are recorded only when users perform cyclic movements, thus no record button exists and no explicit mode-switching is required. Users can simply perform cyclic movements until the result looks satisfactory, which allows for fast trial and error.

During manipulation, movements of body parts are saved as soon as users perform a cyclic movement during manipulation. We refer to these cyclic movements as *loops*. As soon as the system detects a loop, the respective body parts are shaded green during manipulation. Users can continue the manipulation to improve the movement. Loops are confirmed by stopping to pinch with the right hand, or cancelled by shortly pinching with the left hand.

Only the most recent cyclic movement is saved. Previous loops are discarded whenever a new cycle is detected. We decided to not average the movement over previous valid cycles, because we believe that the recent loop has the highest likelihood to be the desired one. This way, users can release whenever they are satisfied with the result and the subsequent playback will look exactly like the last motion they have done during manipulation. The cyclic movements of the selected body parts are then played back repeatedly, also while animating other body parts.

### 4.5.1 Loop algorithm

Since robustly finding motion loops is not the focus of this paper, we will only coarsely describe how we detect loops in Creature Teacher. However, Creature Teacher's system architecture allows for the implementation of different algorithms, including more sophisticated methods such as spectral analysis or dynamic time warping. With our current approach, finding loops is reduced to the task of finding the last movement the user did at least twice in a row. This simplifies the problem considerably, since there is no need to detect all cycles and patterns that have been created before. More specifically, if there was a recent repetitive movement, then it is not important if the same movement was done earlier during the manipulation.

When pinching with the right hand, a spatiotemporal curve is created to describe the motion of the right hand. The hand motion is sampled with a constant time interval and saved as an array of 3D points. Releasing and pinching again creates a new curve. No previous curves are taken into account.

Creature Teacher applies a continuous online loop detection during manipulation. For every input point, our algorithm searches for the closest of the previous input points. The closest point must have a distance smaller or equal than 3.5 inches. Furthermore, there must be points within the interval between the point pair with a larger distance. For example, two successive points of the curve have a close distance, but do not count as a pair, since there are no points with a larger distance in between. As soon as a point pair is found, Creature Teacher analyzes the curve between the found and the current point. Curves are marked as loops if two successive curve parts match each other in terms of duration. Additionally, every sampling point of one curve part within a loop must have a matching counterpart (i.e., a point within a distance of 3.5 inches) on the other curve part.

After a loop is detected, the motion of the selected body parts within the found time interval is copied to the resulting animation. Smoothing is performed to make the end point of the loop curve fit with the start point, thus allowing for seamless playback of the loop.

## 4.6 Posing

If users stop pinching before a loop was detected, the selected body parts remain in the manipulated position. Therefore users can seamlessly adjust postures and create cyclic movements without a mode switch. For example, users can first set the creature's posture to then create a cyclic movement based on the posture. Body parts can still be adjusted after they are already animated, that is, a constant orientation can be added to cyclically moving parts.

## 5. DESIGN PROCESS

This section describes the design process of the system including the rationales of design decisions and some dead ends during development.

## 5.1 Immersive virtual reality

Because of the rise of immersive virtual reality and tracking devices in the consumer market especially in gaming, we have chosen to utilize respective 3D interaction concepts to make 3D animation feasible. Using an HMD can be seen as the chosen navigation technique: The immersive setup frees the user from having to explicitly control the virtual camera. No mode switch or extra button is needed and thus users can fully concentrate on the interactions with the creature. The camera is controlled very naturally by moving and rotating the head while having the hands free. To avoid cybersickness, a 1:1 mapping from the physical movements to the virtual movements is used.

Besides the navigation, there are other advantages. For example, users get a better idea of the size and proportions of the virtual creature. The selection is collocated to utilize the proprioception abilities of users.

## 5.2 Visualization

We believe that it is very important that users seamlessly see the effects and results when editing the animation. If users are idle, the cycle animation keeps running and the creature is rendered in its original appearance with its texture and no additional visualizations. Many animation user interfaces render the skeleton within the mesh as an abstraction of the posture and to visualize the topology. In contrast, we do not visualize the skeleton to reduce the visual complexity and the cognitive load. Users are supposed to get a feeling of directly moving body parts instead of manipulating an underlying skeleton. Furthermore, a skeleton would possibly distract from local deformations of the creature's body parts during manipulation. To visualize the topology, body parts near the left hand are highlighted as areas with blue shading during selection. This way, users can explore the topology with the left hand and also predict the selection. The selection is generally related to the *Silkcursor* of Zhai et al. [38], since it makes use of partial occlusions in a similar way. One difference to the *Silkcursor* is the fact that not the cursor, but the creature is semi-transparent. This way, users can see through the creature and reach parts which would normally be occluded.

## 5.3 Bimanual interaction

Instead of using a conventional input like a mouse, we decided for 3D input. The main reason is that users should have the possibility to freely describe 3D trajectories, instead of e.g., only trajectories on a plane. We decided against using specialized input devices to be flexible regarding topology of the creature and motions that can be created.

The main aspects that define the quality of an animation are timing and weight. Novices using a keyframe animation interface in general have trouble in giving the right timing and making the body parts look like they have weight. The resulting animations often appear unnatural or robotic. Using the hands however makes use of organic hand movements and inherent human skills. Users have a sense of timing and rhythm which they can express through the hands. Furthermore, users have a feeling of how objects with different weights move and can approximately simulate the trajectories with their hands.

Users continuously alternate between selection and manipulation, i.e., the left and the right hand are alternating between resting and being active. With this we aim at reducing user fatigue.

## 5.4 Cyclic movements

The initial idea was to intuitively teach movements to the creature. One way of teaching is repetition which led to cyclic motions as input methodology. With cyclic motions as input, users can simply perform motions repeatedly and refine them until the result is satisfactory. Most of previous work need explicit mode-switching for animation recording.

## 5.5 Iterations

Throughout the development, we constantly invited users to test our system. We observed interaction with the system and used a think aloud protocol. We also collected their feedback in open ended interviews.

The first prototype version of the system was a straightforward naive approach: All joints could be pinched individually with the left or with the right hand, that is, there was no prior selection. Therefore, no more than two joints could be controlled directly. When moving joints, the whole model reacted physically very similar to [16]. However, users found it to be very difficult to control, even with very simple skeletons. As the number of joints increased, interaction quickly became unfeasible with this technique. Therefore a technique for improved, simultaneous control over multiple joints was needed. With the selection technique, body parts are selected and when manipulating, the number of joints within the selection can be nearly arbitrary, since they all undergo the same transformations. Summarizing, the selection simplified the interaction significantly and made animating feasible.

Not all users preferred to walk around the figure to see it from different angles. Some even wanted to sit down. Therefore it is also possible to adjust the creature's orientation. Users can either stand and walk around the creature or sit down at a table and still reach all body parts by adjusting the orientation. A table potentially reduces fatigue since the non-active hand can rest on it.

## 6. USER STUDY

In order to explore the usability of Creature Teacher, we conducted a user study with 13 participants. The user study was done at the end of the iterative design process. The goal of the study was to get insights into the usage of the system and to evaluate the interactions and algorithms specific to our system, i.e., selection and manipulation of models and the creation of cyclic movements.

## 6.1 Participants

We recruited 13 participants (5 female), between 23 and 29 years old ($Mdn = 26$) to test our system. All participants were right-handed (based on self-reports) and all of them had very little or no experience with using animation software. All participants had very little or no experience using immersive virtual reality systems and none of them had used Creature Teacher before.

## 6.2 Apparatus

The study was conducted in a quiet experimental room (room size approximately 4 by 3 meters). We used the apparatus as described in the Implementation section.

## 6.3 Procedure

Participants were introduced to the setup, followed by a 5 minute tutorial guided by the experimenter. Within this tu-

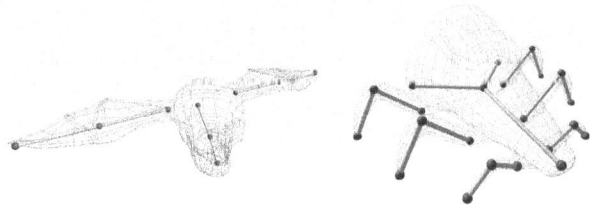

**Figure 5: Users had to animate two models. The first one consists of 6 limbs and the second one consists of 15 limbs.**

**Figure 6: Sample user animations after using the system for the first time.**

torial, participants selected and manipulated a simple pendulum (consisting of one limb) and were guided through the process of creating an oscillating movement of the weight of the pendulum around its pivot.

After the tutorial, participants created animations with two provided 3D models. The first model was a skull with wings (6 limbs, see Figure 5 left) for which participants were asked to create a flying-on-the-spot animation. Secondly, participants animated a walk-cycle with a roach-like creature (15 limbs, see Figure 5 right). No further instructions or templates on how the final animations could look like were given to the participants. Users created both animations multiple times and experimented with the system.

Participants were allowed to ask questions to the experimenter at any time. After completion, we conducted a semi-structured interview with questions on ease of use for each interaction technique (e.g., selection, manipulation, loops), rated on a 5-point Likert scale from 1 (strongly disagree) to 5 (strongly agree). Additionally, we encouraged participants to suggest improvements and missing features of Creature Teacher. Each session took approximately 60 minutes.

## 6.4 Results and Discussion

In general, participants quickly got used to the system and described the animation process as playful and enjoyable. In the following, we will describe feedback on the different interaction techniques included in Creature Teacher as well as results from the questionnaires.

### 6.4.1 Learning

After the guided tutorial, participants became familiar with Creature Teacher within approximately 5 to 10 minutes. The creation of the skull's flying-on-the-spot animation usually took between one and two minutes. This learning curve was expected and we observed this during our iterative design process with several other naive users. Participants became increasingly confident and were able to complete animations without guidance or help of the experimenter. Users were able to rapidly create their desired animation ($Mdn = 4$, "I was satisfied with the result animations."). They were able to fully focus on the outcome of the creation process and not the system itself. Users reported that they were working efficiently ($Mdn = 5$, "I had the feeling that I was working efficiently").

### 6.4.2 Selection and Manipulation

In the beginning, most participants constantly mixed up the handedness of selection and manipulation. This changed after a short time and users felt that they understood the interactions and possibilities ($Mdn = 5$, "I understood how to interact with the system."). Some users first tried to select by pointing towards a body part from the distance, i.e., they expected a raycast selection. However, users quickly got used to the selection technique, which is reflected in the subjective ratings ($Mdn = 4$, "It was easy to select body parts."). Users first started with exploring the models using the left hand to highlight the selectable body parts. During manipulation, users explored the effects of the right hand to the selected body part to then create the actual movement. After some time of exploration, users stated that the movements got more and more purposeful. Again, this is reflected in high ratings of acceptance for the proposed manipulation techniques ($Mdn = 4$, "I was able to purposefully create movements.").

### 6.4.3 Loops

Users reported that the loop detection was working well and they were able to achieve their desired results. Cyclic movements were in most cases detected when they were intended ($Mdn = 4$). However, some users reported that small cyclic movements were not detected at all. We are working on this issue for future versions of Creature Teacher. Additionally, we adjusted the thresholds of our algorithms according to the results and our observations.

Finally, participants reported having no difficulties in repeating similar hand movements in order to create loops ($Mdn = 4$, "I was able to perform repeated hand movements for loop creation.").

### 6.4.4 Problems

Most of the problems were related to technical issues. One major problem was, that due to the tracking inaccuracies, many users always felt an offset between the cursors and the hands in the immersive setup. This made coordination difficult in the beginning and needed some time of adaption. Especially one user, an amateur musical conductor, reported even small differences as interfering with his intents. Furthermore, users felt an offset and a slight delay between the real and virtual head movements.

### 6.4.5 Conclusion

The goal of the user study was to give an initial validation of the system's quality. To us it was especially important to know if novice users are able to quickly create satisfying animations. One main aspect we wanted to gain insights into was if users are able to purposely do cyclic movements to create motions. The overall ratings and user opinions are very promising. This was the very first time these users interacted with the system. Therefore we only provided creatures with a simple limb structure to let users concentrate on the interaction. More complex models were only tested informally during development. Advanced users will be the subjects of our future investigations.

## 7. LIMITATIONS AND FUTURE WORK

The system in its current state concentrates on rotating limbs, since in most cases this is sufficient for posing and animating. Further effort is required for the design and implementation to also fully support individual scaling along each axis and translation of individual limbs. However, depending on the application, it might not be necessary to support transformations other than rotation. Many other animation interfaces for novices are also only supporting changes in orientation.

Creature Teacher uses few input DOFs considering that it is performance-based, i.e., only 12 DOFs consisting of 6 DOFs for the head and 3 DOFs per hand are used. Only position tracking is needed for the hands, since the interaction does not rely on the hand orientations. This makes the system also realizable with simpler 3D input devices than the *OptiTrack* system. The limiting factors are the accuracy and the latency of the input device. However, tracking devices which become available in the consumer market are likely to soon allow for a cheaper solution than the *OptiTrack* system. Furthermore, to also be open to non-immersive setups, other output devices than an HMD could be used without major changes to the basic interaction. Therefore, to reduce the technological overhead, we would like to try out simpler input and output devices. However, one advantage of our current setup is the possibility to naturally walk around the virtual creature.

During the user study, we informally asked some of the participants to also try out Creature Teacher with a regular display positioned in front of them. While a formal comparison of immersive and non-immersive user experience is outside the scope of this work, comments hint the benefits of using an immersive virtual reality system. Most users especially pointed out the collocated selection when using the immersive setup.

With its current implementation, Creature Teacher only contains a very minimalist toolset to move the body parts. However, in general there are no restrictions in including common concepts used in many animation interfaces to make the creation process easier, quicker and the results more convincing. The most prominent example is inverse kinematics. By including inverse kinematics into Creature Teacher, certain animations would potentially be easier to create. One example would be the creation of a walking animation. With the current system, users first animate the upper leg, followed by the lower leg. With inverse kinematics, it would be possible to only grab the foot and guide it along an arc. The basic interaction techniques would remain the same, however, users would benefit from this addition. For the current system in its proof of concept state however, we did not include orthogonal techniques like these. We concentrated on the core interaction of the system for the sake of better validation.

By now, the target group of Creature Teacher are users with few or no animation background, like players of a 3D game. In general, the accuracy of the system as well as of the users' hands is not high enough for professional animating. However, with the inclusion of animation techniques like mentioned above, the system might as well become interesting to professional animators, since they could quickly prototype animations. Different movement styles could be tried out quickly to use the best fitting one for subsequent post-processing steps.

# 8. CONCLUSION

We presented the immersive virtual reality animation system Creature Teacher. The system is used to rapidly create organic cyclic motions for non-humanoid characters without the need for predefined animations and specialized mappings. Our interplay of selection, manipulation and cyclic motion detection allows for fast and easy animation creation while still enabling high expressiveness. We have shown that users with little or no experience in animation were able to quickly create satisfying 3D cycle animations.

# 9. ACKNOWLEDGEMENTS

The authors would like to thank all the users who found many bugs and gave helpful feedback. This work has been supported by the ERC through grant ERC-2010-StG 259550 ("XSHAPE").

# 10. REFERENCES

[1] R. Beimler, G. Bruder, and F. Steinicke. Smurvebox: A smart multi user real time virtual environment for generating character animations. In *Proc. VRIC*, 2013.

[2] M.-W. Chao, C.-H. Lin, J. Assa, and T.-Y. Lee. Human motion retrieval from hand-drawn sketch. *IEEE TVCG*, 18(5):729–740, 2012.

[3] J. Chen, S. Izadi, and A. Fitzgibbon. Kinêtre: Animating the world with the human body. In *Proc. UIST 2012*, pages 435–444, 2012.

[4] J. Davis, M. Agrawala, E. Chuang, Z. Popović, and D. Salesin. A sketching interface for articulated figure animation. In *Proc. SCA 2003*, pages 320–328, 2003.

[5] M. F. Deering. Holosketch: a virtual reality sketching/animation tool. *ACM Trans. Comput.-Hum. Interact.*, 2(3):220–238, 1995.

[6] M. Dontcheva, G. Yngve, and Z. Popović. Layered acting for character animation. In *Proc. Siggraph 2003*, pages 409–416, 2003.

[7] M. Eitsuka and M. Hirakawa. Authoring animations of virtual objects in augmented reality-based 3d space. In *Proc. IIAIAAI 2013*, pages 256–261, 2013.

[8] C. Esposito, W. B. Paley, and J. Ong. Of mice and monkeys: a specialized input device for virtual body animation. In *Proc. I3D 1995*, 1995.

[9] Y. Guiard. Asymmetric division of labor in human skilled bimanual action: The kinematic chain as a model. *Journal of motor behavior*, 19(4):486–517, 1987.

[10] M. Gutierrez, F. Vexo, and D. Thalmann. The mobile animator: interactive character animation in collaborative virtual environments. In *Proc. IEEE VR 2004*, pages 125–284, 2004.

[11] S. Ishigaki, T. White, V. B. Zordan, and C. K. Liu. Performance-based control interface for character animation. *ACM TOG*, 28(3):61:1–61:8, 2009.

[12] A. Jacobson, D. Panozzo, O. Glauser, C. Pradalier, O. Hilliges, and O. Sorkine-Horning. Tangible and modular input device for character articulation. *ACM TOG*, 33(4), 2014.

[13] J. Kim and N. S. Pollard. Direct control of simulated nonhuman characters. *IEEE Comput. Graph. Appl.*, 31(4):56–65, 2011.

[14] S. Kim, X. Zhang, and Y. J. Kim. Haptic puppetry for interactive games. In *Proc. Edutainment*, pages 1292–1302, 2006.

[15] T. Komura and W.-C. Lam. Real-time locomotion control by sensing gloves. *Computer Animation and Virtual Worlds*, 17(5):513–525, 2006.

[16] M. Kostandov, R. Jianu, W. Zhou, and T. Moscovich. Interactive layered character animation in immersive virtual environment. In *Proc. Siggraph 2006 Research Posters*, 2006.

[17] M. Krause, M. Herrlich, L. Schwarten, J. Teichert, and B. Walther-Franks. Multitouch Motion Capturing. In *IEEE Tabletops and Interactive Surfaces 2008*, 2008.

[18] J. Laszlo, M. van de Panne, and E. Fiume. Interactive control for physically-based animation. In *Proc. Siggraph 2000*, pages 201–208, 2000.

[19] J. Leitner and M. Haller. Harpoon selection: Efficient selections for ungrouped content on large pen-based surfaces. In *Proc. UIST 2011*, pages 593–602, 2011.

[20] Q. L. Li, W. D. Geng, T. Yu, X. J. Shen, N. Lau, and G. Yu. Motionmaster: authoring and choreographing kung-fu motions by sketch drawings. In *Proc. SCA 2006*, pages 233–241, 2006.

[21] Z. Luo, I.-M. Chen, S. H. Yeo, C.-C. Lin, and T.-Y. Li. Building hand motion-based character animation: The case of puppetry. In *Proc. CW 2010*, pages 46–52, 2010.

[22] T. Martin and M. Neff. Interactive quadruped animation. In *Motion in Games*, volume 7660 of *Lecture Notes in Computer Science*, pages 208–219. 2012.

[23] N. Numaguchi, A. Nakazawa, T. Shiratori, and J. K. Hodgins. A puppet interface for retrieval of motion capture data. In *Proc. SCA 2011*, pages 157–166, 2011.

[24] S. Oore, D. Terzopoulos, and G. Hinton. A desktop input device and interface for interactive 3d character animation. In *In Proc. Graphics Interface 2002*, pages 133–140, 2002.

[25] N. Osawa and K. Asai. An immersive path editor for keyframe animation using hand direct manipulation and 3d gearbox widgets. In *Proc. IV 2003*, pages 524–529, 2003.

[26] M. Oshita. Multi-touch interface for character motion control using example-based posture synthesis. In *Proc. WSCG 2012*, pages 213–222, 2012.

[27] Y. Seol, C. O'Sullivan, and J. Lee. Creature features: Online motion puppetry for non-human characters. In *Proc. SCA 2013*, pages 213–221, 2013.

[28] H. J. Shin, J. Lee, S. Y. Shin, and M. Gleicher. Computer puppetry: An importance-based approach. *ACM Trans. Graph.*, 20(2):67–94, 2001.

[29] T. Shiratori, M. Mahler, W. Trezevant, and J. K. Hodgins. Expressing animated performances through puppeteering. In *Proc. 3DUI 2013*. IEEE, 2013.

[30] M. Slater, M. Usoh, R. Geeas, and A. Steed. Creating animations using virtual reality thatcherworld: a case study. *Computer Animation*, 0:50, 1995.

[31] P. Song, W. B. Goh, W. Hutama, C.-W. Fu, and X. Liu. A handle bar metaphor for virtual object manipulation with mid-air interaction. In *Proc. CHI 2012*, pages 1297–1306, 2012.

[32] D. J. Sturman. Computer puppetry. *IEEE Computer Graphics and Applications*, 18(1):38–45, 1998.

[33] M. Thorne, D. Burke, and M. van de Panne. Motion doodles: an interface for sketching character motion. In *Proc. SIGGRAPH 2004*, 2004.

[34] A. Vögele, M. Hermann, B. Krüger, and R. Klein. Interactive steering of mesh animations. In *Proc. SCA 2012*, pages 53–58, 2012.

[35] B. Walther-Franks and R. Malaka. An interaction approach to computer animation. *Entertainment Computing*, 5(4):271–283, 2014.

[36] K. Yamane, Y. Ariki, and J. Hodgins. Animating non-humanoid characters with human motion data. In *Proc. SCA 2010*, pages 169–178, 2010.

[37] K. Yamane and Y. Nakamura. Natural motion animation through constraining and deconstraining at will. *Visualization and Computer Graphics, IEEE Transactions on*, 9(3):352–360, 2003.

[38] S. Zhai, W. Buxton, and P. Milgram. The silk cursor: Investigating transparency for 3d target acquisition. In *Proc. CHI 2004*, pages 459–464, 2004.

# NaviChair: Evaluating an Embodied Interface Using a Pointing Task to Navigate Virtual Reality

Alexandra Kitson, Bernhard E. Riecke, Abraham Hashemian, and Carman Neustaedter
School of Interactive Arts and Technology, Simon Fraser University
250 – 13450 102$^{nd}$ Avenue
Surrey, BC, Canada, V3T 0A3
[akitson, ber1, hashemia, carman]@sfu.ca

## ABSTRACT

This research aims to investigate if using a more embodied interface that includes motion cueing can facilitate spatial updating compared to a more traditional non-embodied interface. The ultimate goal is to create a simple, elegant, and effective self-motion control interface. Using a pointing task, we quantify spatial updating in terms of mean pointing error to determine how two modes of locomotion compare: user powered motion cueing (use your body to swivel and tilt a joystick-like interface) and no-motion cueing (traditional joystick). Because the user-powered chair is a more embodied interface providing some minimal motion cueing, we hypothesized it should more effectively support spatial updating and, thus, increase task performance. Results showed, however, the user powered chair did not significantly improve mean pointing performance in a virtual spatial orientation task (i.e., knowing where users are looking in the VE). Exit interviews revealed the control mechanism for the user-powered chair was not as accurate or easy to use as the joystick, although many felt more immersed. We discuss how user feedback can guide the design of more effective user-powered motion cueing to overcome usability issues and realize benefits of motion cueing.

## Categories and Subject Descriptors

H.5.1 [Information interfaces and presentation]: Multimedia Information Systems - *Artificial, augmented, and virtual realities*

## Keywords

Motion cueing; active locomotion; spatial updating; virtual reality; virtual locomotion

## 1. INTRODUCTION

Knowing where we are in a real environment is easy to determine and often automatic. Even when moving short distances with closed eyes, we can remain aware of where different objects are in the surrounding environment. In the case of virtual environments (VE), however, people often become lost and disoriented more easily. Why the discrepancy? And, how can we make navigation through VEs more effective, thus enabling real-world-like performance and ease-of-orientation?

Many researchers believe sensory cues from physical locomotion, such as proprioceptive and vestibular cues, are required to enable

spatial updating - the largely automatized cognitive process that computes the spatial relationship between a person and their surrounding environment as they move based on perceptual information about their own movements [8,13,15,18]. Disorientation often causes unhappiness, anxiety, and discomfort [6]. And, this ultimately results in reduced usefulness, performance, and user acceptance. Being able to successfully orient in VR seems to be essential to completing many tasks, and it appears to be important to minimize sensory conflict to reduce negative side effects. Even though photorealistic immersive stimuli can under certain conditions be sufficient to enable automatic spatial updating when the visual scenery contains well-known landmarks [12], many still fail to update visually simulated self-motions [8]. A large body of literature (see [14] for review) has shown the availability of body-based information during movement in VR enables a better sense of direction compared to only visual information. That is, small physical motions seem to trigger automatic spatial updating and allow participants to more easily navigate in VR. Researchers have found using body rotations can lead to performance improvements in a navigational task compared to visual-only rotations [5,8]. There appears to be a disagreement in the literature as to what the minimum requirements are to enable spatial updating.

One factor to improve spatial updating is embodied, active locomotion (i.e., where users use their own body to move around). Motion cueing is an approach that simulates proprioceptive and vestibular cues as closely as possible when walking is not feasible. Smaller spaces often have constraints that do not allow 1:1 motion, so cheating the senses intelligibly is important in enabling the feeling of moving when actually stationary. Research has found motion cueing in VR can provide means of increasing self-motion or vection [7] (i.e., feeling like you are moving when you are actually not). Similar benefits can be gained using a modified force-feedback manual wheelchair [10] or gaming chair where participants control virtual locomotion by leaning into the direction they want to travel [1,11]. Studies of virtual and real travel have shown positive effects of motion cues on spatial orientation [8].

Motion cueing has been frequently used in industry for driving or flight simulation [2,16]. And, user-powered motion cueing has been shown to facilitate visually-induced vection [4,10,11]. Yet, it has not been determined if motion cueing can also help induce automatic spatial updating, ultimately giving the participant a better and more intuitive sense of orientation in the VE. One ecologically valid spatial updating measure is a pointing task, where participants travel along a pre-determined trajectory and point to previously-seen objects [8,18], and will be used in this study. We assess spatial updating because participants' mental spatial representation will have to be already automatically updated when they arrive at a new location or orientation in order to give a fast, intuitive, and accurate response.

*SUI '15*, August 08 - 09, 2015, Los Angeles, CA, USA
© 2015 ACM. ISBN 978-1-4503-3703-8/15/08…$15.00
DOI: http://dx.doi.org/10.1145/2788940.2788956

This research aims to investigate if using a more embodied interface that includes motion cueing (here: a NaviChair leaning stool interface) can facilitate spatial updating compared to a more traditional non-embodied interface (here: joystick). The ultimate goal is to create a simple, elegant, and effective self-motion control interface. Many VR systems can be very costly, sometimes millions of dollars. Intelligently cheating our senses through small, physical motions could have similar effects as full motion simulators without the cost.

## 2. STUDY METHODOLOGY

The goal was to determine if a more embodied locomotion interface (NaviChair) could help trigger spatial updating and thus increase performance in a virtual orientation task.

### 2.1 Participants and Environment

We recruited 30 (15 female) SFU students with an average age of 22.3 years. Participants had normal or corrected vision and reported they were not prone to motion sickness. Research was conducted under permission of the SFU Research Ethics Board (REB #2012c0022). VE paths were selected to ensure that participants would have to take left or right 60° and 120° turns at regular intervals. The lines of sight were blocked by fog and we removed all the structures and objects from the environment during the pointing tasks. The VE contained no global landmarks or other obvious directional cues. Participants were guided through the VE a female avatar that moved along a pre-defined path. Participants stopped at five different locations and pointed to all six previously memorized objects (cf. 1).

### 2.2 Experimental Design, Stimulus, Apparatus, and Procedure

The experiment uses a within-subject design with two experimental conditions, defined by two locomotion interfaces (cf. 2). (1) User powered motion cueing interface used a swivel seat that acted like a joystick, which we call NaviChair – participants used their own body to move forward, e.g., tilting the chair forward moved yourself in the VE forward, and rotate the chair to rotate themselves in the VE (leaning left/right was disabled to ensure users rotated with the avatar). (2) Non-motion cueing locomotion interface was a stationary chair where participants moved with a normal joystick.

Each participant completed the spatial updating (pointing) task twice – first using NaviChair and then the joystick interface, or vice-versa. The order of interfaces and presentations for two variations of VEs (mirror images) were counter-balanced, creating four distinct experimental groups: NaviChair and VE layout 1 (N=8), NaviChair and VE layout 2 (N=7), joystick and VE layout 1 (N=7), and joystick and VE layout 2 (N=8). In all cases, participants viewed a 2.45 × 1.55m screen non-stereoscopically, which provided approximately 74° by 52° field of view. A single BenQ W1080ST (1920 × 1200). Whenever participants encountered a new location

they stopped and pointed, using a modified joystick, to all six target objects. This allowed us to test how participants' orientation in the environment evolved over time as task difficulty gradually increased.

To ensure sufficient control familiarity, each trial started with a practice run with an open environment. Next, participants were shown the scene with all the embedded objects, were asked to memorize their locations from one fixed vantage point, pointed to each object and were given on-screen feedback of pointing error, which needed to be within +/-23° to continue. Following were two

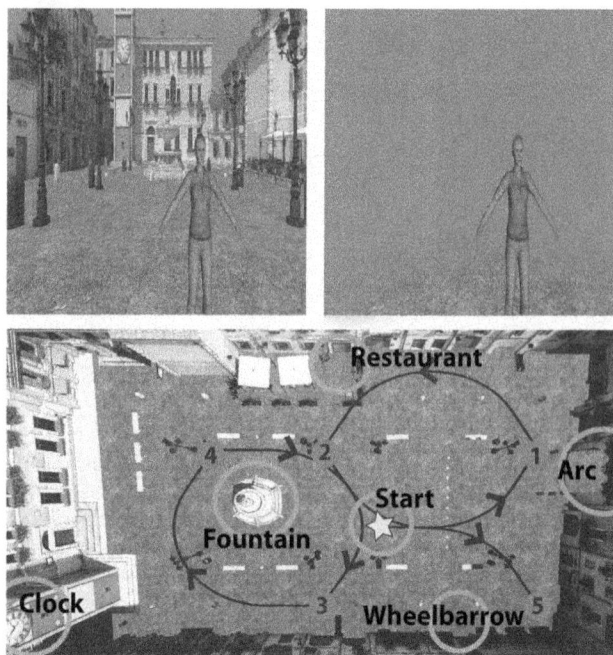

**Figure 1: VE 1st-person POV (top) with (left) and without (right) landmarks, and top-down view (bottom) showing path (black), starting location (star), pointing locations (red dots), and target objects (cyan circles).**

experimental blocks. Between blocks, participants filled out a short demographics questionnaire. Finally, after the second block, we completed a short semi-structured interview.

### 2.3 Data Collection and Analysis

Participants' spatial orientation performance was quantified using *mean absolute pointing error*, i.e., the arithmetic mean of absolute pointing errors for all targets at a given location and measures overall accuracy of the participants. We also assessed motion sickness, self-report orientation ability and task difficulty, and locomotion preference. To test if there was a difference in performance between joystick and NaviChair control, or the two variations of VEs, and if there was an interaction between input device and VE, we performed a within subject, repeated measures 2×2×6 ANOVA. A within subject design was conducted to account for individual differences, which are prevalent in spatial abilities [17]. The independent variables were interface (within), gender (between), and location of objects (within).

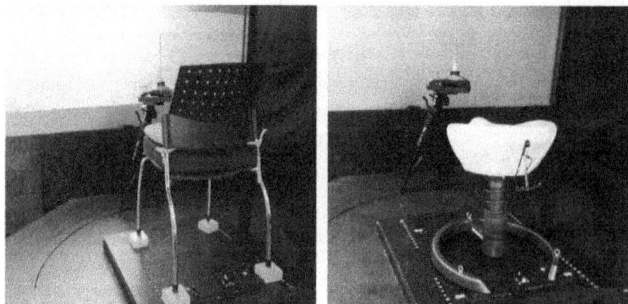

**Figure 2: The locomotion interfaces: no motion cueing with joystick input (left) and motion cueing with NaviChair (swopper chair-based) input (right).**

# 3. RESULTS

## 3.1 Mean Absolute Pointing Error

A significant main effect for interface was found, $F(1, 121) = 17.260$, $p < .001$, $\eta_p^2 = .125$, indicating the joystick interface ($M = 66.66$, $SE = 2.84$) resulted in a lower mean absolute pointing error compared to NaviChair ($M = 80.65$, $SE = 2.59$). The effect size $\eta_p^2$ is medium showing that the effect of interface accounts for 12.5% of the variance in mean absolute pointing error. This main effect was qualified by a significant interaction interface*gender, $F(1, 121) = 4.969$, $p = .028$, $\eta_p^2 = .028$, indicating that the effect of interface was stronger for males than females (**cf. 3**). That is, females had a lower mean absolute error with joystick interface ($M = 74.42$, $SE = 3.81$) compared to NaviChair ($M = 80.90$, $SE = 3.47$), and males had a lower mean absolute error with joystick interface ($M = 58.91$, $SE = 4.21$) compared to NaviChair ($M = 80.39$, $SE = 3.83$). Location showed a significant main effect, $F(4, 121) = 12.138$, $p < .001$, $\eta_p^2 = .286$, indicating that mean absolute pointing error was significantly different depending on the which object location the observer was at (**cf. 3**). Post hoc tests found location 1 had significantly lower mean absolute error than locations 2 ($p < .001$), 3 ($p < .001$) and 4 ($p = .005$), and location 2 had significantly lower mean absolute error than locations 4 ($p = .035$) and 5 ($p = .003$). All other effects, main effects and interactions, were non-significant.

## 3.2 Exit Interview

The majority of participants (21 out of 30) preferred the joystick interface. When asked why they preferred the joystick interface, many participants reported the joystick feeling more accurate, more in control, more familiar to use, mapped proportionally to the movement in the VE, and allowed some to use it as a strategy to remain oriented. Participants who preferred the joystick interface reported NaviChair was uncomfortable to use because of height issues or slipping off the chair, the controls were unfamiliar and hard to learn even after the training phase, NaviChair took a lot more concentration to remain balanced and control their movements, and sensitivity was either too much or too little depending on the participant. There were some participants who found NaviChair to be a more fun and interesting experience, though they ultimately preferred the joystick for familiarity reasons. A minority of participants (9 out of 30) preferred NaviChair for several reasons. Participants reported feeling more engaged with the VE, more oriented, and less motion sick with NaviChair. The main reason participants who preferred NaviChair did not like the joystick was because they felt the joystick was not as immersive. These participants felt as if they were actually moving through the VE with their own bodies, rather than looking at a screen and moving an avatar around.

## 4. DISCUSSION AND CONCLUSIONS

Contrary to our predictions, mean absolute pointing error (**cf. 3**) seems to indicate user powered motion cueing with NaviChair does not help orient participants in a VE, at least for the current methods used. Results show there are different factors having an influence on pointing performance. The interface*gender interaction for mean absolute error shows females on average seem to be worse than males at pointing to previously seen objects in a VE. This result is in keeping with previous research that found males exhibit better way finding performance than females (for a review see [3]). However, males were only significantly better than females with the joystick interface. Our result of the gender effect is inconsistent with a previous study, which found males benefitted from using physical rotations versus visual only rotations where females did not [5]. Our result of females having higher pointing error with the joystick interface compared to males is consistent with females using landmarks (not present in our experimental task) when navigating, and their performance decreases when none are present [9]. Additionally, Waller [17] suggests underlying individual differences in cognitive spatial abilities co-related with gender may explain gender gaps in navigation performance. And Coluccia and Louse [3] hypothesize, based on their literature review, that gender differences in orientation emerge only when tasks require a high load of Visuo-Spatial Working Memory. Here, males would show better orientation performance because of their larger Visuo-Spatial Working Memory span.

This study extends findings on the advantages and disadvantages of user-powered motion cueing for different interfaces including a Gyroxus gaming chair [11], a wheel-chair motion model [10], and the ChairIO gaming interface [1]. In Riecke and Feuereissen's study [11], active control reduced vection occurrence and increased vection onset latencies. Similarly, our study used active control for both NaviChair and joystick interfaces, so the effects of user powered motion cueing may be diminished. It remains to be investigated why and under what conditions active control reduces vection and spatial orientation performance. Moreover, our qualitative results are consistent with Riecke and Feuereissen's who also found that the usability and control issues of the gaming chair might have counteracted the benefit of motion cueing. Based on the insights gained from the current study and prior research (e.g., [1,4,5,11,14,15]), we are planning to study how these usability and control issues could be addressed.

Riecke [10] found that a simple locomotion paradigm like a wheelchair with user powered minimal motion cueing decreased vection onset latency and increased convincingness and vection intensity. While NaviChair did not help with pointing performance, participants did report in the qualitative exit interview that they felt NaviChair to be more immersive and allowed them to feel more a part of the virtual space. So, in terms of convincingness, NaviChair seems to be on the right path though its design needs improvement. Finally, Beckhaus and colleagues [1] designed a similar chair, called ChairIO, as an input device for gaming. They found this interface gives a novel experience for gamers and helped beginners play immediately. Extending these findings, we too found that participants who reported having high 3D game experience also found NaviChair

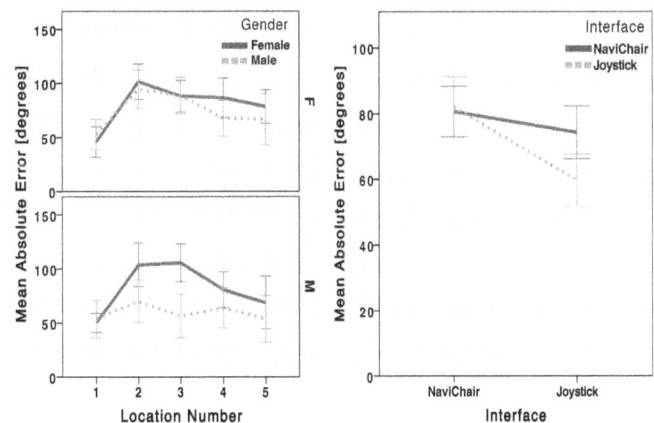

**Figure 3: Mean absolute pointing error (degrees) as a function of location (left) for both females (top) and males (bottom), and gender and interface type (right) with 95% CIs.**

to be a unique experience.

Exit interviews revealed many participants felt more immersed with NaviChair, though they reported better control and accuracy with the joystick. The control mechanism itself could be a contributing factor for why we found the joystick resulted in better pointing performance. NaviChair may have increased path integration errors and cognitive load and, thus, contributed to a worse pointing performance. For example, the need to actively control NaviChair that participants were not familiar with could have indirectly reduced attention to the visual stimulus or changed their viewing and fixation patterns, thus decreasing orientation. Alternatively, participants could have been fully focused on controlling and balancing NaviChair to pay sufficient attention to where they were going, thus increasing both path integration and spatial updating errors. It is feasible NaviChair facilitated automatic spatial updating, in the sense that it was relatively intuitive to remain oriented, but accumulating path integration errors counteracted such potential benefits.

There are several limitations in this study. First, participants are sitting down in both conditions, though they seem to be walking like the avatar in the VE, giving an obvious mismatch between what is real and what is virtual. Second, many of the participants reported in the exit interview they were already very familiar with the joystick, often for gaming, which may bias participants to do better with that mode of locomotion. Third, the design of NaviChair is still in its infancy. Adjustments and testing are an ongoing process in determining the ideal control parameters for the majority of users. Where the traditional joystick has well established control mechanisms, NaviChair still needs improvement. Ideally, the next step in this study will be to refine the controls of NaviChair to make controlling movement easier and fine-tuned to suit the user's needs.

Many factors including gender, location, and interface have an influence on a virtual pointing task. Our results suggest the presence or absence of user powered motion cueing may play a role in one's sense of orientation in VEs. When designing virtual systems, these individual factors should be kept in mind. Moreover, it seems user powered motion cueing with NaviChair in its current form may not be sufficient in helping people remain oriented in VEs. Exit interviews revealed NaviChair was difficult to control and make accurate movements, suggesting the control mechanism itself may have contributed to lower pointing performance. We aim to adjust NaviChair in order to make it as easy to control as a normal joystick.

## 5. ACKNOWLEDGMENTS

NSERC funded this research.

## 6. REFERENCES

1. S. Beckhaus, K. J Blom, and M. Haringer. 2005. A new gaming device and interaction method for a First-Person-Shooter. *Proceedings of the Computer Science and Magic* 2005.

2. Jolie Bell and Stuart C. Grant. 2011. Effects of Motion Cueing on Components of Helicopter Pilot Workload. *Proceedings of the Interservice/Industry Training, Simulation, and Education Conference*. Retrieved February 16, 2015 from http://www.iitsec.org/about/publicationsproceedings/documents/11239_paper.pdf

3. Emanuele Coluccia and Giorgia Louse. 2004. Gender differences in spatial orientation: A review. *Journal of Environmental Psychology* 24, 3, 329–340. http://doi.org/10.1016/j.jenvp.2004.08.006

4. Daniel Feuereissen. 2013. Self-motion illusions (" vection") in Virtual Environments: Do active control and user-generated motion cueing enhance visually induced vection? Retrieved March 25, 2014 from http://summit.sfu.ca/item/13651

5. Timofey Y. Grechkin and Bernhard E. Riecke. 2014. Re-evaluating Benefits of Body-based Rotational Cues for Maintaining Orientation in Virtual Environments: Men Benefit from Real Rotations, Women Don'T. *Proceedings of the ACM Symposium on Applied Perception*, ACM, 99–102. http://doi.org/10.1145/2628257.2628275

6. M. A. Gresty, Sarah Waters, A. Bray, Karen Bunday, and J. F. Golding. 2003. Impairment of spatial cognitive function with preservation of verbal performance during spatial disorientation. *Current Biology* 13, 21, R829–R830. http://doi.org/10.1016/j.cub.2003.10.013

7. L. R. Harris, M. R. Jenkin, D. Zikovitz, et al. 2002. Simulating Self-Motion I: Cues for the Perception of Motion. *Virtual Reality* 6, 2, 75–85. http://doi.org/10.1007/s100550200008

8. Roberta L. Klatzky, Jack M. Loomis, Andrew C. Beall, Sarah S. Chance, and Reginald G. Golledge. 1998. Spatial Updating of Self-Position and Orientation During Real, Imagined, and Virtual Locomotion. *Psychological Science* 9, 4, 293–298. http://doi.org/10.1111/1467-9280.00058

9. Simon Lambrey and Alain Berthoz. 2007. Gender differences in the use of external landmarks versus spatial representations updated by self-motion. *Journal of Integrative Neuroscience* 06, 03, 379–401. http://doi.org/10.1142/S021963520700157X

10. Bernhard E. Riecke. 2006. Simple user-generated motion cueing can enhance self-motion perception (Vection) in virtual reality. *Proceedings of the ACM symposium on Virtual reality software and technology*, ACM, 104–107. http://doi.org/10.1145/1180495.1180517

11. Bernhard E. Riecke and Daniel Feuereissen. 2012. To Move or Not to Move: Can Active Control and User-driven Motion Cueing Enhance Self-motion Perception ("Vection") in Virtual Reality? *Proceedings of the ACM Symposium on Applied Perception*, ACM, 17–24. http://doi.org/10.1145/2338676.2338680

12. Bernhard E Riecke, Markus Von Der Heyde, and Heinrich H Bülthoff. 2005. Visual cues can be sufficient for triggering automatic, reflexlike spatial updating. *ACM Transactions on Applied Perception (TAP)* 2, 183–215. http://doi.org/http://doi.acm.org/10.1145/1077399.1077401

13. John J. Rieser. 1989. Access to knowledge of spatial structure at novel points of observation. *Journal of Experimental Psychology: Learning, Memory, and Cognition* 15, 6, 1157–1165. http://doi.org/10.1037/0278-7393.15.6.1157

14. Roy A. Ruddle. 2013. The Effect of Translational and Rotational Body-Based Information on Navigation. In *Human Walking in Virtual Environments*, Frank Steinicke, Yon Visell, Jennifer Campos and Anatole Lécuyer (eds.). Springer New York, New York, NY, 99–112. Retrieved July 5, 2013 from http://link.springer.com/10.1007/978-1-4419-8432-6_5

15. Roy A. Ruddle and Simon Lessels. 2006. For Efficient Navigational Search, Humans Require Full Physical Movement, but Not a Rich Visual Scene. *Psychological Science* 17, 6, 460–465. http://doi.org/10.1111/j.1467-9280.2006.01728.x

16. Charles H. Scanlon. 1987. *Effect of Motion Cues During Complex Curved Approach and Landing Tasks - A Piloted Simulation Study*.

17. David Waller. 2000. Individual differences in spatial learning from computer-simulated environments. *Journal of Experimental Psychology: Applied* 6, 4, 307–321. http://doi.org/10.1037//1076-898X.6.4.307

18. Ranxiao Frances Wang. 2004. Between reality and imagination: When is spatial updating automatic? *Perception & Psychophysics* 66, 1, 68–76. http://doi.org/10.3758/BF03194862

# Controller-less Interaction Methods for Google Cardboard

Soojeong Yoo
Faculty of Engineering and Information Technologies
The University of Sydney,
NSW, 2006, Australia
soojeong.yoo@sydney.edu.au

Callum Parker
Faculty of Architecture, Design and Planning
The University of Sydney,
NSW, 2006, Australia
cpar9842@uni.sydney.edu.au

## ABSTRACT

Google Cardboard was recently released as Google's attempt at virtual reality (VR) which has made it more accessible, with its low-cost and easy assembly. The purpose of this research is to provide an initial analysis of controller-less interaction and highlight its potential for enabling a truly portable and accessible VR experience.

## Categories and Subject Descriptors

H5.1 [Information interfaces and presentation]: Multimedia Information Systems - Artificial, augmented, and virtual realities.

## Keywords

Virtual Reality; Google Cardboard; Head Mounted Display; Virtual Reality Interaction Techniques

## 1. INTRODUCTION

Smart phone virtual reality, a form of VR that relies on a smart phone's motion sensors to perform head tracking has been gaining popularity recently after Google released their own head mounted display (HMD), called the Google Cardboard [1]. What makes the Cardboard stand out from other HMD's is its inexpensive nature, portability (no cables required) and the growing support on the Android platform due to the SDK available that allows developers to create their own apps with either Unity or native Android. However, a persistent issue is how to interact when fully-immersed in a virtual environment [2]. As the Cardboard is inexpensive and portable, an interaction method should cater for those aspects as well. Therefore, we investigate controller-less interaction methods, using only the Cardboard itself to retain its status as a portable and accessible HMD.

## 2. INTERACTION METHODS

We reviewed 32 Cardboard apps [3] from the Google Cardboard section of the Google Play Store to find the current popular interaction methods being utilized based upon the amount of apps implementing a certain method and rating. After testing the apps, we categorized the interactions based upon the interaction method: (1) Magnetic sliding switch (Fig 1a); (2) Instant Gaze (Fig 1b); (3) Dwelling Gaze (Fig 1c, Fig 1d); (4) Tilt; (5) External controller.

Magnet switch was clearly the most popular interaction method with 16 apps utilizing it (Figure 2). However, it scored on lower on average than the other methods. The apps that used Tilt were a

*SUI '15*, August 08-09, 2015, Los Angeles, CA, USA
ACM 978-1-4503-3703-8/15/08. http://dx.doi.org/10.1145/2788940.2794359

part of the Google Cardboard Demo app, therefore only the score for the demo app was available. External controllers scored lowest.

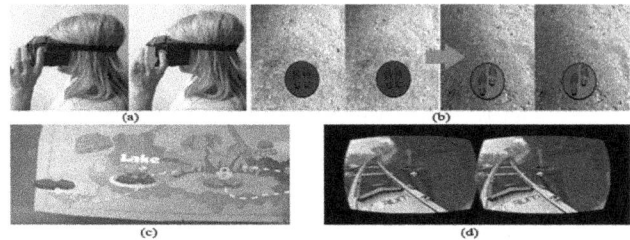

**Figure 1. (a) Magnet sliding switch, (b) Gaze toggle in the Tuscany demo, (c) Gaze menu selection in Froggy VR, (d) Environment interaction using gaze in Roller Coaster VR.**

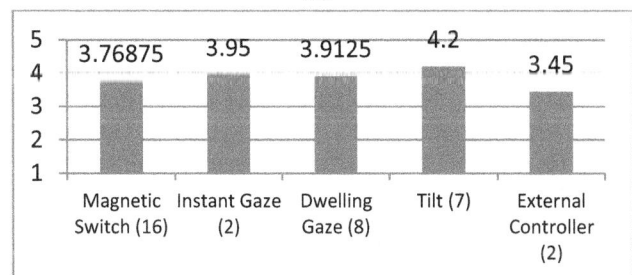

**Figure 2. Average ratings by users on the Google Play store.**

## 3. DISCUSSION AND CONCLUSION

Overall, the Cardboard apps were well received, with an average rating of 3.95 out of 5 stars on the Google Play Store at the time of writing. It demonstrates that there is much potential for this platform and that there is interest in these types of apps.

It is clear that controller-less interaction methods are more popular than external controllers from the sample of apps tested. However, further work is needed with the users themselves to find the preferred method. The inexpensive nature of the Google Cardboard also makes it an ideal immersive platform to be used for education, in a networked, collaborative environment.

## 4. REFERENCES

[1] Google. 2015. Google Cardboard. [online] Available at: https://www.google.com/get/cardboard/ [5 June. 2015].

[2] Oculus. 2015. Best Practices Guide 1st ed. [ebook] Available at: http://static.oculus.com/sdk-downloads/documents/Oculus_Best_Practices_Guide.pdf [5 June. 2015].

[3] Yoo, S. 2015. List of apps reviewed in the study. [online] Available at: http://www.soojeongyoo.com/googlecardboard.html [5 Jun. 2015].

# Differences in Perspective and Software Scaling

Graeme Browning
McMaster University
Hamilton, ON, Canada
brownigh@mcmaster.ca

Robert J. Teather
McMaster University
Hamilton, ON, Canada
teather@mcmaster.ca

Jacques Carette
McMaster University,
Hamilton, ON, Canada
carette@mcmaster.ca

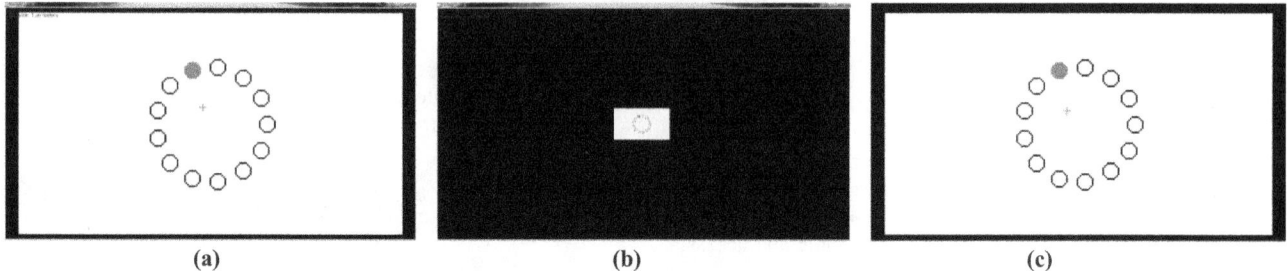

Figure 1. (a) 70" display. (b) 10" display (c) 10" display subject to 700% magnification, yielding same image as 70" display, same quantization, and relative resolution.

## 1. INTRODUCTION

With a greater range in display sizes available than ever before, it is important to understand the effects of scaling content across different-sized displays. We are interested in the effects of viewing distance, which implicitly scales content in isolation from other scale factors (e.g., CD gain or motor scale) due to perspective. This is especially important in spatial applications, since unlike desktop systems, the viewing distance of the user can be highly variable (e.g., standing, or moving) while motor scale is often constant (e.g., absolute 1:1 position, with remote pointing).

The effects of control-display gain have been studied extensively [1, 2]. The effects of visual scale in isolation from CD gain have not been explored in depth [3, 4]. Previous work on visual scale has confounded this with motor scale, for example, changing CD gain with visual scale, hence changing the effective motor task the user performs. We thus present a study comparing distance-based (perspective) scaling with artificial (software-based) scaling. The objective is to assess if visual scale due to viewing distance influences task performance differently than artificially re-sizing content. We isolate this factor by maintaining a constant sized motor space and display resolution.

## 2. USER STUDY

We conducted a study with 12 participants to investigate these issues. The study used a Fitts' pointing task, see Figure 1. We used a 75" TV. In software scale conditions, the task was re-sized in software - Figure 1b depicts a simulated 10" display, while Figure 1a depicts a 70" display. Effective display resolution and motor scale were constant – the same mouse movement would move the cursor the same relative distance on the display. Figure 1c depicts the 10" display magnified to yield the same image as the 70" display. For perspective scale conditions, participants were moved to different distances corresponding to the same scale factors as those used with the software scale methods.

The experiment used a 2x3x3 within-subjects design with the independent variables *scale method* (software, perspective), *visual angle* (24.5°, 21°, 14°, 10.5°, 7°, 3.5°), *block* (1, 2, 3). We report throughput (in bits per second) as the dependent variable.

## 3. RESULTS & CONCLUSIONS

There was a significant interaction between scale method and visual angle ($F_{5,55} = 22.7$, $p < .0001$). See Figure 2. Notably, software scaling at 24.5° was significantly worse ($p < .05$) than all other conditions. The "curvature" of the software scaling line was also significant: both 3.5° and 21° were significantly worse than 14°, 10.5°, and 7°. In contrast, none of the visual angles were significantly different from one another with perspective scaling. Overall, these results suggest a stronger impact of scale with artificial software-based scaling than with perspective scaling.

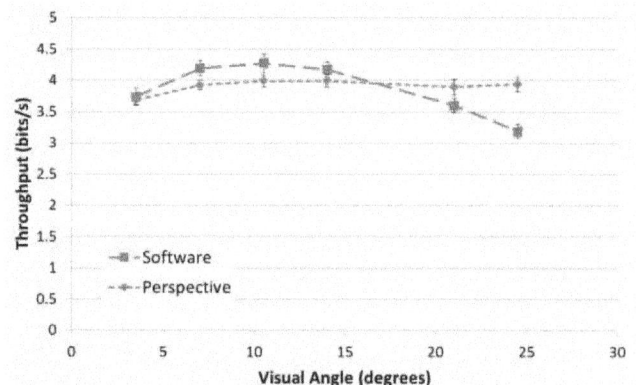

Figure 2. Throughput by scale method and visual angle, averaged over all blocks. Error bars show ±1SD.

## 4. REFERENCES

[1] Casiez, G., Vogel, D., Balakrishnan, R., and Cockburn, A., The impact of CD gain on user performance in pointing tasks, *Human–Computer Interaction*, *23*, 2008, 215-250.

[2] Chapuis, O. and Dragicevic, P., Effects of motor scale, visual scale, and quantization on small target acquisition difficulty, *TOCHI*, *18*, 2011, 1-32.

[3] Hourcade, J. P. and Bullock-Rest, N., How small can you go? Analyzing the effect of visual angle in pointing tasks, *Proc. CHI 2012*, 213-216.

[4] Kovacs, A., Buchanan, J., and Shea, C., Perceptual influences on Fitts' law, *Experimental Brain Research*, *190*, 2008, 99-103.

# Effects of Bezel Size in Large Tiled Display Gaming

Geneva Smith, Robert J. Teather, Joran Lass, Jacques Carette
McMaster University, Hamilton, ON, Canada
{smithgm | teather | lassjw | carette}@mcmaster.ca

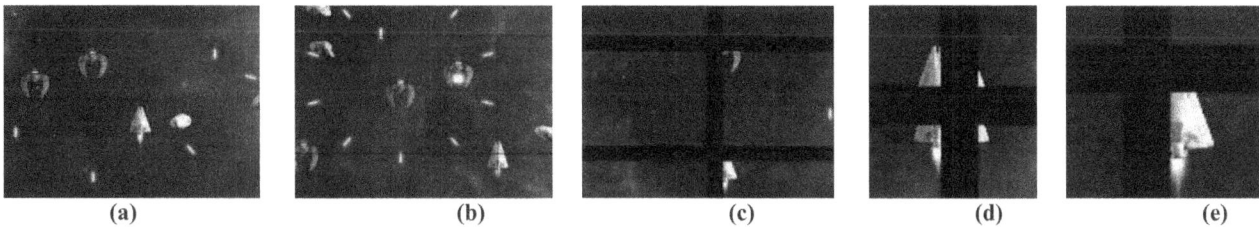

Figure 1. Bezel size/compensation conditions. (a) No bezels. (b) 0.25 cm size, compensation off; (c) 4 cm size, compensation on. (d) Close-up of player ship split by un-compensated bezels. (e) Close-up of player ship occluded by compensated bezels.

## 1. INTRODUCTION

Many spatial UI systems (e.g., VR) rely on large displays. One method of building large high-resolution displays is to use multiple HD monitors as tiles in a single large display. The downside is the presence of monitor borders – bezels – between each tile in such a display. Hardware manufacturers such as NVidia and AMD have developed "bezel compensation" techniques for tiled displays. This treats space behind bezels as part of the coordinate space, hence objects can be occluded behind bezels (Figure 1e). Without bezel compensation, objects break across display borders, and may appear distorted (Figure 1d).

Recent work [1, 2] looked at this problem via static judgment tasks. However games and VR are highly dynamic involving fast-paced reactions and tightly-coupled feedback loops. Previous results may not generalize to interactive scenarios. The effect of bezel compensation is also unclear: consider that "hiding" objects behind bezels could be worse than distorting them!

## 2. USER STUDY

We compared game performance across different simulated bezel sizes in a 3x3 tile configuration. Twelve gamers took part. We used a 3.4 GHz PC with a 75 in. 1080p TV for the display. Participants sat 10 ft. from the screen and played custom game made in Unity 4.5. Bezels (with compensation) were simulated by drawing black bars over the screen. Without compensation, we used multiple cameras with gaps between their viewing volumes to "break" the coordinate space across the bezels. See Figure 1.

Participants played 4 one-minute trials in each condition. The game involved moving the ship to avoid enemies, asteroids, and projectiles. Enemies moved straight down from the top of the screen and fired bullets either straight down or in an outward pattern. Asteroids moved straight down. The player could destroy these with a single shot (increasing their score).

The study used a 6x2x4 within-subjects design. The independent variables were *bezel size* (0, 0.25, 0.5, 1.0, 2.0, 4.0 cm), *bezel compensation* (on, off), and *trial* (1, 2, 3, 4). Bezel size was

counterbalanced with a balanced Latin square. Dependent variables included longest streak duration (in seconds), game score, and the number of times the player died (count) over both all obstacles (enemies, asteroids, bullets) and just bullets.

## 3. RESULTS AND CONCLUSIONS

The main effects for bezel compensation ($F_{1,11} = 2.8$, $p = 0.12$) and bezel size ($F_{5,11} = 0.68$, ns) on score were not significant. Their interaction was also not significant ($F_{5,55} = 0.4$, ns). For longest streak duration, the main effect for bezel compensation ($F_{1,11} = 0.37$, ns) and bezel size ($F_{5,11} = 1.2$, $p = .34$) were not significant, nor was their interaction ($F_{5,55} = 1.2$, $p = .33$)

For player deaths only trial was significant ($F_{3,11} = 3.1$, $p < .05$). We also analyzed how often players were killed by bullets only - the smallest object that could be occluded by bezels. The bezel size/compensation interaction was significant ($F_{5,55} = 2.4$, $p < .05$). Although we expected the largest bezels to have the strongest impact, the worst condition was bezel compensation with 1 cm bezels. See Figure 2.

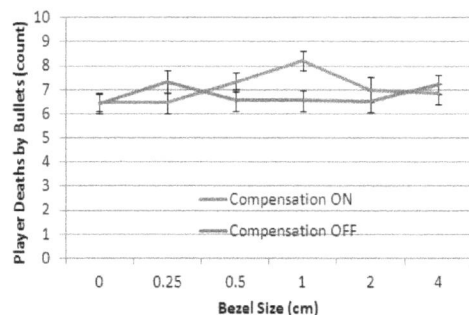

Figure 2. Player deaths due to bullets by bezel size and bezel compensation.

Our current (incomplete) results suggest that the impact of bezel size, or differences due to employing bezel compensation are fairly minimal in games. Future work will focus on different display configurations and using additional participants.

## 4. REFERENCES

[1] Wallace, J. R., Vogel, D., and Lank, E., Effect of bezel presence and width on visual search, *Pervasive Displays 2014*, 118-123.

[2] Wallace, J. R., Vogel, D., and Lank, E., The effect of interior bezel presence and width on magnitude judgement, *Graphics Interface 2014*, 175-182.

SUI '15, August 08-09, 2015, Los Angeles, CA, USA
ACM 978-1-4503-3703-8/15/08.
http://dx.doi.org/10.1145/2788940.2794365

# Exocentric Rendering of "Reality Distortion" User Interface to Illustrate Egocentric Reprojection

Michael Cohen & Tomohiro Oyama
Spatial Media Group, University of Aizu; Aizu-Wakamatsu, Fukushima 965-8580; Japan
{mcohen, m5172115}@u-aizu.ac.jp

## 1. INTRODUCTION

We have been working on "twirling" interfaces, featuring affordances spun in *"padiddle"* or *"poi"* style. The affordances, crafted out of mobile devices (smartphones and tablets) embedded into twirlable toys, sense their orientation and allow "mobile-ambient" individual control of public display, such as a large format screen. Typically one or two users will face such graphical display and twirl their manipulables, whilst a representation of them and their respective toys are projected into a fantasy scene. The projected scene is rendered egocentrically by centering the projection on the avatars as a virtual camera orbits around in an arcing, spin-around "inspection gesture." Besides dorsal, "tethered" viewing perspectives, the projection is intended for frontal, "mirror" perspectives as well and also intermediate camera angles. The fantasy scene is not a totally faithful mapping of the real-life "meatspace" scene, since both avatar handedness and affordance phase are adjusted to flatter frontal views and other camera angles. Environmental lighting is deployed in the user space as a token indicating the relative position of the virtual camera in the fantasy scene relative to the self-identified avatars.

Awareness of virtual camera position and presumed perspective of human users causes supernatural ambidextrous hand-switching and continuous, deliberate distortion of affordance azimuth, parameterized by unwrapped phase of orbiting camera [1]. Readers are encouraged to view a video[1] of an older prototype to appreciate the system, and the accompanying video for a demonstration of the new interface.[2]

## 2. IMPLEMENTATION

But even with the environmental lighting as an indication of subjective viewpoint, such projection can be difficult for users to understand, so we developed an alternate view

[1] http://arts.u-aizu.ac.jp/spatial-media/
mixedreality/Videos/Tworlds2.mp4
[2] http://arts.u-aizu.ac.jp/spatial-media/
mixedreality/Videos/Exocentric_Visualization.mov

*SUI '15* August 08-09, 2015, Los Angeles, CA, USA.
© 2015 ACM. ISBN 978-1-4503-3703-8/15/08.
DOI: http://dx.doi.org/10.1145/2788940.2794357

on the scene. To clarify the reality distortion, a $1^{st}$-order scene display of the pre-warped user space is hereby introduced, logically interpolating between the 0-order user space and the $2^{nd}$-order fantasy scene, featuring an exocentric perspective with basically fixed camera position (except for allowing interocular displacement to accommodate stereoscopic views). We use Alice (v. 3) for both the $1^{st}$- and $2^{nd}$-order renderings, associated by mixed virtuality rigging with affordance-embedded mobile devices through some middleware.

The $1^{st}$-order scene is more like a faithful rendering of the user space, stripped of the fantasy scene elements (setting, costume, props, etc.), but highlighting the virtual-camera-controlled avatar ambidexterity and affordance phase modulation with "ghost" appendages. It features simulation of the orbiting virtual camera, displaying its accumulated phase as a coil, making explicit the unresolved tension ("borrowed" but "unreturned") introduced by the orbit and manifesting as consequent phase perturbation of the projected affordance. Simulation of the environmental lighting is included as well, showing the quadrant-wise determination of the demultiplexed light as the virtual camera sweeps around. The phase coil is portrayed as a helix attached to the orbiting virtual camera, the better to appreciate its unwrapped phase. The height of the camera is fixed (and slightly pointing down) at the height of the avatar head.

## 3. CONCLUSION

The idea of meta-scenes and explicit, objective "full citizen" cameras within scenes is not new. It has been used, for instance, in movie blocking simulations and visualization of computer graphic projections. The research described here applies such ideas to to mixed virtuality environments with fluid perspective. Our prototype is contextualized as a proof-of-concept of mobile-ambient interfaces, using personal devices to control public displays, and supported by the notions of hierarchies of perspective and subject-object relationships.

## 4. REFERENCES

[1] M. Cohen, R. Ranaweera, B. Ryskeldiev, T. Oyama, A. Hashimoto, N. Tsukida, and M. Toshimune. Multimodal mobile-ambient transmedial twirling with environmental lighting to complement fluid perspective with phase-perturbed affordance projection. In *SIGGRAPH Asia Symp. on Mobile Graphics and Interactive Applications*, Shenzhen, China, Dec. 2014.

# Gesture–based Sound Localization and Manipulation

Shashank Ranjan
Department of Computer and Information
Science and Engineering
University of Florida,
Gainesville, Florida

shashankranjan@ufl.edu

Kyla McMullen
Department of Computer and Information
Science and Engineering
University of Florida,
Gainesville, Florida
kyla@cise.ufl.edu

## ABSTRACT

With current advancements in computer vision depth sensing technologies, gestures provide a new means of computer interaction. 3D audio research has gained significant ground in accurately localizing sound in 3D space, but not much work has been conducted relating to modes of user interaction in such applications. In this paper, gestures are used as a more natural way of interacting with 3D spatial audio applications, specifically for the localization and manipulation of sound sources.

## Author Keywords

Kinect; 3D Audio; User Interactions; Sound Localization;

## ACM Classification Keywords

H.5.2 [User Interfaces]: Input devices and strategies, Interaction styles, Auditory (non-speech) feedback

## 1. INTRODUCTION

Gestures as mode of human-computer interaction have gained popularity in recent years with advancement in computer vision and depth sensor technologies. The use of sensors such as Microsoft Kinect in gaming applications have helped increase the general awareness of these devices as well augment the comfort level of their use. Meanwhile, 3D audio applications continue to suffer from lack of intuitive modes for user interaction. Through this work, we show that gestures can be a natural and intuitive method of localizing sound in 3D audio applications. The following sections describe the design and installation of the system, give a brief overview of the demonstration, and give examples of the target audience the system intends to serve.

## 2. SYSTEM DESIGN

### 2.1 Hardware

The system consists of a Microsoft Kinect Sensor for recognizing gestures, a monitor (or any display) for visual feedback, speakers/headphones for audio feedback and a CPU.

### 2.2 Software Design

The system takes hand gestures as input through Kinect sensor and processes them to give 3d-coordinates of the path of the movement. These co-ordinates are then simultaneously transformed to two sets of co-ordinates. One set provides data for changing the position of sound source and the other to change the

*SUI '15*, August 08-09, 2015, Los Angeles, CA, USA
ACM 978-1-4503-3703-8/15/08.
http://dx.doi.org/10.1145/2788940.2794364

on-screen representation of sources. The output of the system is simultaneous visual and audio feedback that gives the impression to the user that he or she is physically moving the sound source.

### 2.3 Installation

The system has been developed to work on Mac OSX operating system version 10.9 and above only.

### 2.4 Commands and Gestures

Table 1 gives all the commands and the respective gestures used in the applications.

**Table1: Commands and gestures to use the application**

| Command | Gestures |
| --- | --- |
| To start/initiate the interaction | Wave |
| To focus on a sound source | Move hand on top of the source |
| To select/grab a source | Push/Grab gesture |
| To unselect/ fix a source | Push/Release gesture |

## 3. EXHIBIT

### 3.1 Stimuli

During the demonstration, users will hear with three distinct instrument tracks separated from a song. The choices of instruments are such that they represent three distinct families of instruments – percussion, string and wind. To reduce distraction to the user, the sounds have to be extracted from same song.

### 3.2 Demonstration

Once the participant is familiarized with interface, he or she will be asked to stand in front of the sensor for a few seconds for calibration. Once the calibration is done, the visual and auditory scene will become active and user can start using the interface. In the scene, three sound sources will be positioned at different locations around the user. Apart from freely moving the sound sources, the user can perform two types of tasks:

1. Moving the source to a target position
2. Moving the source along a given path

## 4. TARGET POPULATION

This system can be helpful for anyone using 3D audio for sound source localization tasks. Music composers and audio engineers can virtually review and correct the placement of instruments before setting up the stage. A director can virtually design the auditory scenes of a play before the performance by simply using gestures. By no means, is an exhaustive list of applications and with further enhancement, the system can serve a variety of interests in the field of 3D audio.

# Making Static Figures Posable: An Interactive Figure Transformation System For Naive Users

Shao-Chi Lee
National Taipei University of Technology
t8820310@ntut.org.tw

Pei-Ying Chiang
National Taipei University of Technology
peiyingc@csie.ntut.edu.tw

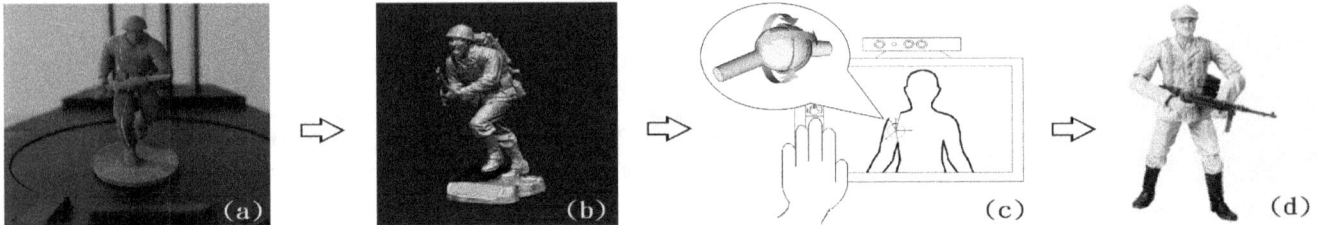

Figure 1: (a)A physical static character figure is scanned. (b)The scanned digital 3D model. (c) Our system develops joints for the 3D model with hand gestures. (d) An articulated action figure can be fabricated with a 3D printer.

## ABSTRACT

We propose a system which can fabricate articulated figures based on static ones. We first scan the static figure to obtain a digital 3D model. The user can then insert joints to this 3D model interactively with hand gestures. Our system will then adjust the position of the joints to match the surrounding geometry and carve the collided area during the rotation inspection process. With our system, a naive user can easily convert and print out a posable, articulated figure.

## Keywords

Articulated Figure; 3D Printing; Fabrication

## 1. INTRODUCTION

Character figures from science fiction movies attract a large following of collectors. Many of those collectable figures are static and are desired to be posable. However, it requires great craftsmanship to convert physical static figures to articulated ones. With advanced geometry processing technology, there is now research on automatic joint creation for digital 3D models. Previous works [1][2] develop new joints in accordance with pre-build skeletons (rigging). Though mature tools such as Maya or 3ds Max provide sophisticated rigging tools, additional training is required for naive users. Our system aims to make a static model posable without the extra rigging training. Users can create joints interactively with pre-defined hand gestures. With our joint-adjustment and carving process, the joints will fit into proper positions automatically.

## 2. SYSTEM OVERVIEW

As illustrated in Figure 1, the process of our system can be described as follows: We first scan the static figure to get a digital 3D model. The user can then create and modify joints on the model with our pre-defined hand gestures. To insert a joint, the user simply points to a desired spot on the model. Our system does the ray-casting following the direction of the finger to the surface of the model. A pair of points on the surface of the model which are passed through by the ray (in and out) will be located. Thus, the joint will be placed at the middle of this pair of surface points. Moreover, by rotating her palm, the user can determine the rotation axis and the maximum rotation degree. The adjacent parts of this joint which collide with each other will be carved accordingly during rotation inspection with CSG [3] technique. Finally, the user can fabricate the articulated figure with a 3D printer.

## 3. REFERENCES

[1] M. Bächer, B. Bickel, D. L. James, and H. Pfister. Fabricating articulated characters from skinned meshes. In *Proceedings of SIGGRAPH 2012*, 2012.

[2] J. Calì, D. A. Calian, C. Amati, R. Kleinberger, A. Steed, J. Kautz, and T. Weyrich. 3d-printing of non-assembly, articulated models. In *Proceedings of SIGGRAPH 2012*, 2012.

[3] D. H. Laidlaw, W. B. Trumbore, and J. F. Hughes. Constructive solid geometry for polyhedral objects. In *Proceedings of SIGGRAPH 1986*, 1986.

*SUI '15 Aug 8–9, 2015, Los Angeles, CCA, USA*
© 2015 Copyright held by the owner/author(s).
ACM ISBN 978-1-4503-3703-8/15/08.
DOI: 10.1145/2788940.2794361

# Modeling Mid-air Gestures With Spherical Coordinates

Darren Guinness, Andrew Seung,
Ashley Dover, G Michael Poor
Dept of Computer Science Baylor University
Waco, TX 76798 USA
{darren_guinness, andrew_seung,
ashley_therriault,
michael_poor}@baylor.edu

Alvin Jude
Ericsson Research
200 Holger Way
San Jose, CA, 95134
alvin.jude.hari.haran@ericsson.com

## ABSTRACT

Generally, touchless mid-air gestural interaction use some form of Cartesian coordinate system within the input space. Most implementations map the input space in 3-D and map it to the 2-D of the monitor for output. In our previous work we showed that modeling the interaction space produces better interaction[1]. In this study, we use the Myo armband to show that a modeled interaction space also benefits devices that use spherical coordinates.

## Keywords

Fitts; Pointing Device; Gestural Interaction; Modeling;

## CCS Concepts

•Human-centered computing → Gestural input;

## 1. INTRODUCTION

Touchless gestural interaction is an interaction style which has seen a sharp increase in interest in recent years. One vein of research has demonstrated that calibrating the user's gestural input space in Cartesian coordinates resulted in a better interaction[1]. In this work, it was hypothesized that improving the existing hyperplane input space to a better model would yield positive results for users. One such method would be to use a spherical coordinate system where the interaction space is essentially one portion of a sphere. However, this model would require the system to measure the length of the forearm and infer the angle of the arm based on the position of the palm. Fortunately, a newer product in the market called the Myo Armband [2] provides the angle of the arms directly. This experiment was designed to evaluate the merits and feasibility of a modeled interaction using spherical coordinates.

## 2. INTERACTION DESIGN

The unmodeled approach was performed with *Global Mouse Control* interaction by Myo's developers, while custom software was written for the modeled approach. Both approaches use the

*SUI '15 Aug 8–9, 2015, Los Angeles, CA, USA*

© 2015 Copyright held by the owner/author(s).

ACM ISBN 978-1-4503-3703-8/15/08..

DOI: http://dx.doi.org/10.1145/2788940.2794356

Myo's Euler angles (pitch, yaw, and roll) but the latter starts with a calibration stage where the user determines their input space. The calibration took 6 seconds, down from 30s in our previous work.

## 3. EXPERIMENTAL DESIGN

8 participants (M=5, F=3) between 19-28 years (mean=23.1) took part in the experiment. They were asked to perform the ISO 9241-9 pointing task using 3 amplitudes {256, 512, 1024} and widths {64, 96, 128} for 9 unique Index of Difficulties ranging from 1.52 to 4.58 bits. All participants used both interactions, with the starting order counterbalanced with a 2x2 Latin square.

## 4. RESULTS

| | Unmodeled | Modeled | $p$ | $d$ |
|---|---|---|---|---|
| **Bivariate Throughput** | 1.56 | **2.22** | <0.05 | 2.40 |
| **Distance** | 2156 | **1056** | <0.05 | 5.45 |
| **Target Entry** | 1.26 | 1.34 | 0.070 | - |
| **Task Axis Change** | 1.80 | 1.67 | 0.120 | - |
| **Movement Dir. Change** | 3.96 | **3.30** | <0.05 | 1.26 |
| **Orthogonal Dir. Change** | 2.74 | **1.49** | <0.05 | 2.20 |
| **Movement Variability** | 90.67 | **30.73** | <0.05 | 5.12 |
| **Movement Error** | 80.41 | **31.92** | <0.05 | 5.24 |
| **Movement Offset** | **-3.54** | 5.86 | <0.05 | 1.25 |
| **Fitts Intercept** | 427.4 | **187.68** | N/A | N/A |
| **Fitts Slope** | 455.16 | **352.09** | N/A | N/A |
| **Fitts $R^2$** | 0.514 | **0.752** | N/A | N/A |

Table 1: **Means of performance and accuracy measures, with statistical ($p$) and practical ($d$) significance of both interactions. Also shown is Fitts's conformance metrics Intercept, Slope and Coefficient of Determination ($R^2$)**

The results in Table 1 shows that a modeled interaction has better performance, accuracy, and conformance to Fitts' law. This demonstrates that modeling the interaction space results in an overall better interaction, even when the input device uses a spherical coordinate system.

## 5. REFERENCES

[1] Jude, A., Poor, G. M., and Guinness, D. Personal space: User defined gesture space for gui interaction. In *CHI '14 Extended Abstracts on Human Factors in Computing Systems*, CHI EA '14, ACM (New York, NY, USA, 2014), 1615–1620.

[2] Thalmic. *Myo Gesture Control Armband*, 2013 (accessed June 6 2015).

# Oncall Piano Sensei: Portable AR Piano Training System

Pei-Ying Chiang
National Taipei University of Technology
peiyingc@csie.ntut.edu.tw

Chung-Hsuan Sun
National Taipei University of Technology
t103598042@ntut.edu.tw

## ABSTRACT

We propose a portable AR piano training system that helps the user to learn piano with affordable cost and no space limitations. The optical music recognition process is first applied so the system can automatically play the melody of a given sheet music. During the performance, the training system indicates which note is playing and which corresponding piano key should be pressed. Our system also detects which keys are pressed and gives sound/visual feedback to correct the user. With no requirement of a physical piano and tutor, our system extends a great range of time and space for someone who wants to learn piano.

## Keywords

Augmented Piano; Optical Music Recognition (OMR);

## 1. INTRODUCTION

There are several limiting factors for people who want to learn piano. One of the main reasons is that people can-not afford them; another is that they do not have enough space. Its physical size and price make it difficult to be available to everyone, not to mention considerable tuition fee. Moreover, even if someone owns a piano, he or she has to go to a specific site to practice. Due to these reasons, people hesitate to start learning piano. There has been some limited research on the projection piano [1][2]. However, they are generally difficult to carry around and not education purpose. Therefore, we propose a portable projection piano training system for people who want to learn piano. The user can practice piano almost anytime and everywhere. The system teaches the user how to play the melody of a given sheet music. The hardware that is required for this system costs much less than the physical piano and it is easy to carry around.

## 2. PROTOTYPE

As illustrated in Fig.1(a), the required hardware of our system includes the following: an external RGB camera cap-

Permission to make digital or hard copies of part or all of this work for personal or classroom use is granted without fee provided that copies are not made or distributed for profit or commercial advantage and that copies bear this notice and the full citation on the first page. Copyrights for third-party components of this work must be honored. For all other uses, contact the owner/author(s).

*SUI '15 Aug 8–9, 2015, Los Angeles, CCA, USA*

© 2015 Copyright held by the owner/author(s).

ACM ISBN 978-1-4503-3703-8/15/08.

DOI: 10.1145/2788940.2794353

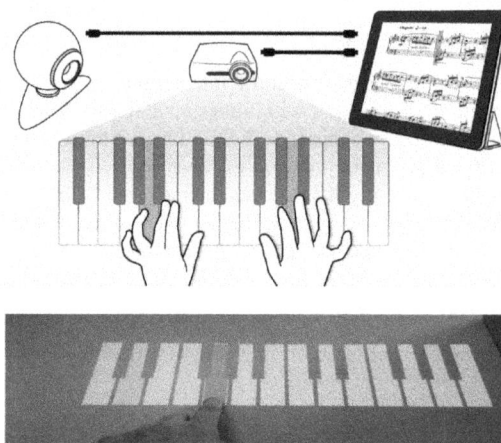

Figure 1: a) The system architecture. b) The projected piano with highlight indicators, as red indicates incorrect.

tures which key is pressed by the user; a portable mini projector displays the piano keyboard and to highlight keys; a tablet does the computation and shows the given sheet music. Our piano system first applies the OMR process to recognize the music notes. The melody can then be automatically played. While playing, the sheet music is showing on the tablet screen and there is a moving indicator highlighting which note(s) is playing. In the meantime, the corresponding key(s) on the projected keyboard will also be highlighted to guide the user as shown in Fig.1(b).

Our prototype can now support two octave keyboards and recognize simple sheet music. We aim to support seven octaves as on a classical piano and be able to recognize intermediate level sheet music. A user interface will also be provided to allow users to adjust preferred practicing tempos.

## 3. REFERENCES

[1] M. Weing, A. Röhlig, K. Rogers, J. Gugenheimer, F. Schaub, B. Könings, E. Rukzio, and M. Weber. P.i.a.n.o.: Enhancing instrument learning via interactive projected augmentation. UbiComp '13 Adjunct.

[2] X. Xiao and H. Ishii. Duet for solo piano: Mirrorfugue for single user playing with recorded performances. CHI EA '11.

# Spatial Audio Feedback for Hand Gestures in Games

Wenjie Wu and Stefan Rank
Drexel University, Philadelphia PA USA
stefan.rank@drexel.edu

## ABSTRACT

We use game prototypes to investigate different audio feedback designs for hand gestures for encouraging immersion. Replacing explicit audio instructions for hand positions and movements with responsive audio feedback, suggestive of interaction methods by using environmental story-related audio cues, leads to measurably higher immersion. We present the design of responsive audio feedback for hand gestures in the context of such a game. The spatial organization of diegetic environmental feedback before, during, and after gesture input is supported by a structured approach towards the design of audio cues.

## CCS Concepts

•**Human-centered computing** → *Pointing devices; Auditory feedback;* Sound-based input / output;

## Keywords

immersion; audio-only; gesture interaction; touchless motion control; responsive feedback.

## 1. GESTURES IN AUDIO-ONLY GAMES

The availability of low-cost gesture detection hardware such as the Leap Motion allows game designers to apply and study the potential of touch-less motion control for more immersive spatial experiences. Norman [1] uses the term gestural interaction to subsume all different forms of motion-based interaction. O'Hara et al. [2] speak about touchless interaction. Here, the context of gestures, their embedding into the narrative of a game, and responsive feedback that reflects the space are particularly important. Audio-only games provide a unique opportunity to study what helps players in forming an inner picture of the environment.

Our approach is to experimentally compare designs of audio feedback that are responsive to hand gestures regarding immersion in gesture-controlled audio-only environments. For an experimental study, two design approaches for responsive

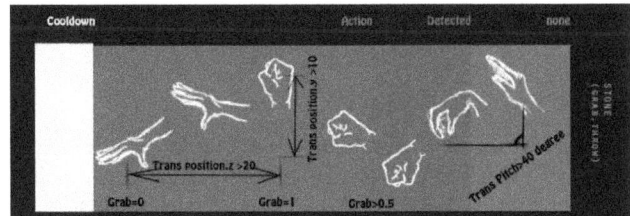

Figure 1: Illustration of a stone-throw gesture.

audio feedback were implemented, combining vocal instructions and non-diegetic audio cues on the one hand and environmental audio cues and diegetic (i.e. story-related) ones on the other.

We consider audio feedback not just as a result of gesture interaction, but as an interactive signal that guides the player while going through the whole process: before, during, and after the gesture sequence. The anticipation principle guides pre-gesture cues, setting up the expectation of an interaction with an object at a certain position, e.g. fish moving in a specific direction. Relative volume changes can further inform the player of the availability of a forthcoming gesture. During a gesture, the attachment of sound sources, such as noisy clothing or a bracelet with bells, can provide immediate feedback of the gesture in-progress. A real-time mapping of hand movement or gesture phases to audio parameters provides an opportunity for enhanced responsiveness that goes beyond replicating natural sounds. Fig. 1 shows the intermediate phases during one of the gestures in our testbed: grabbing and throwing a stone. After a gesture, noticeable positive or negative feedback, e.g. collisions with the virtual environment or more abstract feedback such as a "magic" watch changing its speed, guides further interaction.

These design principles have been successfully evaluated in an experimental setting with 26 subjects, showing a significant improvement in story immersion for the game version that uses the diegetic design.

## 2. REFERENCES

[1] D. Norman. Natural user interfaces are not natural. *Interactions*, 17:6–10, 2010.
[2] K. O'Hara, R. Harper, H. Mentis, A. Sellen, and A. Taylor. On the naturalness of touchless: Putting the 'interaction' back into NUI. *ACM Trans. Comput.-Hum. Interact*, 20.

*SUI 2015, August 8–9, 2015, Los Angeles, CA, USA.*
© 2015 Copyright held by the owner/author(s).
ACM ISBN 978-1-4503-3703-8/15/08.
DOI: http://dx.doi.org/10.1145/2788940.2794363

# TAMGeF: Touch-midAir-Motion Framework for Spatial Input

**Francisco R. Ortega**
Florida International Univeristy
fortega@fiu.edu

**Naphtali D. Rishe**
Florida International Univeristy
ndr@acm.org

**Armando Barreto**
Florida International Univeristy
barretoa@fiu.edu

## CCS Concepts

•**Human-centered computing** → **User interface toolkits**; *Touch screens;*

## Keywords

Input Devices; Framework; User Interfaces

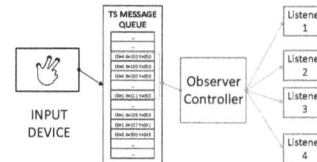

Figure 1: Observer-Queue Controller

## 1. INTRODUCTION

With the explosion of modern input devices, such as multi-touch, vision-based systems (mid-air interaction with devices such as Microsoft Kinect), and inertial navigational systems, the complexity of development has increased. There are different libraries or toolkits that support different features. For example, VRPN[1], which is a C/C++ (primarily C-based) library with socket client/server architecture, provides access to different multiple input devices. Other framework or libraries exist, such as OpenNI that provide vision-based functionality. However, VRPN is meant as the layer between input devices and the developer. We propose a framework that goes further in providing a complete solution. Takala et al. provided a good understanding about the current development challenges for 3D User Interface (3DUI) developers [3]. TAMGeF is based on previous input taxonomies [2], multi-touch interaction framework research (e.g., Mudra and Midas) [1], and our experience accumulated over time. In this paper, we explore two contributions: device abstraction and parallel message handling.

## 2. TAMGeF FOR SPATIAL INPUT

TAMGeF, a modern C++ cross-platform, template-based, multi-threaded framework for spatial input devices, is designed with multiple layers to provide greater flexibility. The primary layers are: (0) input devices; (1) platform core (desktop, web, mobile); (2) gesture recognition; (3) Toolkit modules (plugin, experimentation, task-parallelism, and visualziation); (4) bindings (e.g, Python, Unity, Java, etc.). In this paper, we will discuss part of the lower layer.

We have modified the definition from [2] to a generalized input device: (1) manipulation ($M$) provides the degrees of freedom (DOF) that a device supports. For example, a 6-DOF can be defined as $M = \{Tx, Ty, Tz, Rx, Ry, Rz\}$. (2)

[1]http://www.cs.unc.edu/Research/vrpn/

*SUI '15 August 8–9, 2015, Los Angeles, CA, USA*

© 2015 ACM. ISBN 123-4567-24-567/08/06. . . $15.00

DOI: 10.1145/2788940.2794355

Input Domain ($In$) provides the original device domain. For example, a multi-touch display may provide $X$ and $Y$ values between 0 to the maximum resolution. (3) The resolution function ($Rf$) provides a way to map the input to the output domain. (4) The output domain ($Out$) is the desired result provided by $Rf$. (5) The possible states ($S$) of the device (e.g, down, move, up, idle, cancel, for multi-touch). (6) The possible events $Ev$ that the device may fire. This is related to $S$ but it provides the mechanism to notify listeners. (7) The connection ($Cn$) provides the concrete mechanism to connect the device $D$. Therefore, a device is defined by a 7-tuple: $D = <M, In, Rf, Out, S, Ev, Cn>$.

There are multiple ways to fire an event: callback function, message queue, and observer pattern, among others. They all have drawbacks. In particular, the observer pattern creates problems when working in a multi-threaded environment, as we have experienced and it has been noted by others [1]. While TAMGeF does provide the flexibility to choose the mechanism, we provide some default behaviours. We have proposed a specialized pattern for input devices called **Observer-Queue Controller**, shown in Figure 1. This is an approach to combine a thread-safe message queue, an observer controller, and a set of listeners. This reduces the amount of thread locks and provides a simpler interface.

## 3. CONCLUSION

This paper provided a brief understanding of the lower layer of **TAMGeF** providing the generalization of a device (which can use set-theory to describe it) and a highly-optimized, thread-safe observer-queue controller pattern. We are currently developing this solution at our institution.

## 4. REFERENCES

[1] L. Hoste, B. Dumas, and B. Signer. Mudra: a unified multimodal interaction framework. In *ICMI '11: Proceedings of the 13th international conference on multimodal interfaces*. ACM, Nov. 2011.

[2] J. Mackinlay, S. Card, and G. Robertson. A semantic analysis of the design space of input devices. *Human–Computer Interaction*, 5(2):145–190, 1990.

[3] T. M. Takala, P. Rauhamaa, and T. Takala. Survey of 3DUI applications and development challenges. *3D User Interfaces (3DUI), 2012 IEEE Symposium on*, pages 89–96, 2012.

# Transition Times for Manipulation Tasks in Hybrid Interfaces

Per Bjerre[1], Allan Christensen[1], Simon André Pedersen[1], Andreas Køllund Pedersen[1] and
Wolfgang Stuerzlinger[2]
[1]Department of Architecture, Design, and Media Technology, Aalborg University, Aalborg, Denmark
[2]School of Interactive Arts + Technology, Simon Fraser University, Vancouver, Canada

## Author Keywords
In-air Interaction; Device Transitions; Hybrid User Interfaces.

## 1. INTRODUCTION
In 3D modeling environments, such as Autodesk Maya, users most frequently use 2D input devices, typically the mouse and keyboard, to manipulate objects. While it seems more appropriate to use 3D input for these tasks, previous research on 3D input devices has pointed out several weaknesses, specifically fatigue, lower accuracy, and in some cases a slower interaction speed [3]. Fatigue also becomes a problem when users have to keep their arm suspended in the air for an extended time. Not only is this a problem for the in-air interaction as a main interaction paradigm, the fatigue induced may also cause users to relax the poses needed for gestures, increasing the chances of interpretation errors [3] and decreasing pointing precision [1]. One way to address this is to build hybrid user interfaces that combine the expressiveness of in-air interactions for select operations with the precision achievable by 2D input devices for other interactions.

We investigate a three-device hybrid setup using a keyboard and mouse in combination with the Leap Motion for in-air interactions. We examine the costs associated with transitioning between these interaction devices, and performing 2D manipulation tasks using mouse and Leap Motion.

## 2. METHODS
The study had 31 voluntary participants (five female), with 18 trials per participant (2 devices x 3 manipulation tasks x 3 difficulty levels). The two devices consisted of the Leap Motion and the mouse. For the tasks, they had to rotate, scale or translate an object. In order to perform each manipulation, the participant had to press a key on the keyboard with one hand (typically the non-dominant one) to activate the tool, and then depending on the task, use the mouse or perform a gesture using the Leap Motion with the other (dominant) hand. The main dependent variables in the experiment were the completion time of the primary tasks, and the transition times between the main devices and the alternate devices, including the travel time to and from the devices. We introduced simple alternate tasks in between the core tasks to create situations where participants had to transition between input devices; this ensured that we measured transition time consistently. For the alternate tasks, we used transitions to the keyboard and mouse. The measurements are only for transitions of a single hand; we enforced this by having the users activate a keyboard clutch with the other hand while interacting. There were two types of alternate tasks, one requiring the user to transition to the mouse and the other requiring a transition to the keyboard.

## 3. DISCUSSION
We found that there was a significantly higher transition cost for the in-air device compared to the cost of transitions between keyboard and mouse. Transitions between the Leap Motion and the mouse took 1.26 seconds longer (47% increase), while transitions between the keyboard and the Leap Motion took only an additional 0.48 seconds (16.38% increase). This means that the average transition cost to *and* from the Leap Motion is only 0.87 seconds extra (32% increase). The transitions between keyboard and mouse were comparable to the homing times reported in Card et al.'s work [2]. They found a transition time of 0.4 seconds when transitioning from the keyboard to the mouse or vice versa. In the direct comparison with the mouse, the Leap Motion is slower. However, it is still worthwhile to investigate the kind of role an in-air device can play in a hybrid setup, as the Leap Motion can be used for tasks that are more difficult to perform with the mouse, such as 3D rotations. The findings indicate that the Leap Motion could be used together with the mouse without introducing an overly large transition cost between devices. Thus, for hybrid interfaces the Leap Motion may be an appropriate tool for performing large-scale interactions in the air, while precise fine-tuning is better performed with the mouse. This way few transitions are needed and the impact of longer transition times would be lessened, which also reduces the amount of fatigue arising from prolonged use of in-air interaction devices.

## 4. REFERENCES
[1] Brown, M. A., Stuerzlinger, W., and Filho, E. J. M. 2014. The performance of un-instrumented in-air pointing. In *Proceedings of the 2014 Graphics Interface Conference*, pp. 59-66. ISBN=978-1-4822-6003-8.

[2] Card, S. K., Moran, T. P., and Newell, A. 1980. The Keystroke-level Model for User Performance Time with Interactive Systems. Communications of the ACM, 23 (7), pp. 396-410. DOI= http://doi.acm.org/10.1145/358886.358895.

[3] Sambrooks, L., and Wilkinson, B. 2012. Comparison of gestural, touch, and mouse interaction with Fitts' law. *OzCHI'13*, pp. 119-122. DOI= http://doi.acm.org/10.1145/2541016.2541066.

*SUI '15*, August 08-09, 2015, Los Angeles, CA, USA
ACM 978-1-4503-3703-8/15/08.
http://dx.doi.org/10.1145/2788940.2794358

# Gesture–based Sound Localization and Manipulation

Shashank Ranjan
Department of Computer and Information
Science and Engineering
University of Florida,
Gainesville, Florida

shashankranjan@ufl.edu

Kyla McMullen
Department of Computer and Information
Science and Engineering
University of Florida,
Gainesville, Florida
kyla@cise.ufl.edu

## ABSTRACT
With current advancements in computer vision depth sensing technologies, gestures provide a new means of computer interaction. 3D audio research has gained significant ground in accurately localizing sound in 3D space, but not much work has been conducted relating to modes of user interaction in such applications. In this paper, gestures are used as a more natural way of interacting with 3D spatial audio applications, specifically for the localization and manipulation of sound sources.

## Author Keywords
Kinect; 3D Audio; User Interactions; Sound Localization;

## ACM Classification Keywords
H.5.2 [User Interfaces]: Input devices and strategies, Interaction styles, Auditory (non-speech) feedback

## 1. INTRODUCTION
Gestures as mode of human-computer interaction have gained popularity in recent years with advancement in computer vision and depth sensor technologies. The use of sensors such as Microsoft Kinect in gaming applications have helped increase the general awareness of these devices as well augment the comfort level of their use. Meanwhile, 3D audio applications continue to suffer from lack of intuitive modes for user interaction. Through this work, we show that gestures can be a natural and intuitive method of localizing sound in 3D audio applications. The following sections describe the design and installation of the system, give a brief overview of the demonstration, and give examples of the target audience the system intends to serve.

## 2. SYSTEM DESIGN
### 2.1 Hardware
The system consists of a Microsoft Kinect Sensor for recognizing gestures, a monitor (or any display) for visual feedback, speakers/headphones for audio feedback and a CPU.

### 2.2 Software Design
The system takes hand gestures as input through Kinect sensor and processes them to give 3d-coordinates of the path of the movement. These co-ordinates are then simultaneously transformed to two sets of co-ordinates. One set provides data for changing the position of sound source and the other to change the

*SUI '15*, August 08-09, 2015, Los Angeles, CA, USA
ACM 978-1-4503-3703-8/15/08.
http://dx.doi.org/10.1145/2788940.2794364

on-screen representation of sources. The output of the system is simultaneous visual and audio feedback that gives the impression to the user that he or she is physically moving the sound source.

### 2.3 Installation
The system has been developed to work on Mac OSX operating system version 10.9 and above only.

### 2.4 Commands and Gestures
Table 1 gives all the commands and the respective gestures used in the applications.

**Table1: Commands and gestures to use the application**

| Command | Gestures |
|---|---|
| To start/initiate the interaction | Wave |
| To focus on a sound source | Move hand on top of the source |
| To select/grab a source | Push/Grab gesture |
| To unselect/ fix a source | Push/Release gesture |

## 3. EXHIBIT

### 3.1 Stimuli
During the demonstration, users will hear with three distinct instrument tracks separated from a song. The choices of instruments are such that they represent three distinct families of instruments – percussion, string and wind. To reduce distraction to the user, the sounds have to be extracted from same song.

### 3.2 Demonstration
Once the participant is familiarized with interface, he or she will be asked to stand in front of the sensor for a few seconds for calibration. Once the calibration is done, the visual and auditory scene will become active and user can start using the interface. In the scene, three sound sources will be positioned at different locations around the user. Apart from freely moving the sound sources, the user can perform two types of tasks:

1. Moving the source to a target position
2. Moving the source along a given path

## 4. TARGET POPULATION
This system can be helpful for anyone using 3D audio for sound source localization tasks. Music composers and audio engineers can virtually review and correct the placement of instruments before setting up the stage. A director can virtually design the auditory scenes of a play before the performance by simply using gestures. By no means, is an exhaustive list of applications and with further enhancement, the system can serve a variety of interests in the field of 3D audio.

# HaptoClone (Haptic-Optical Clone): Mid-air Haptic-Optical Human-Human Interaction with Perfect Synchronization

**Yasutoshi Makino**
The Univ. of Tokyo
5-1-5, Kashiwanoha, Kashiwa-shi,
Chiba-ken, Japan
+81-3-5841-6900
yasutoshi_makino@k.u-tokyo.ac.jp

**Yoshikazu Furuyama**
The Univ. of Tokyo
7-3-1, Hongo, Bunkyo-ku, Tokyo,
Japan

furuyama@hapis.k.u-tokyo.ac.jp

**Hiroyuki Shinoda**
The Univ. of Tokyo
5-1-5, Kashiwanoha, Kashiwa-shi,
Chiba-ken, Japan

hiroyuki_shinoda@k.u-tokyo.ac.jp

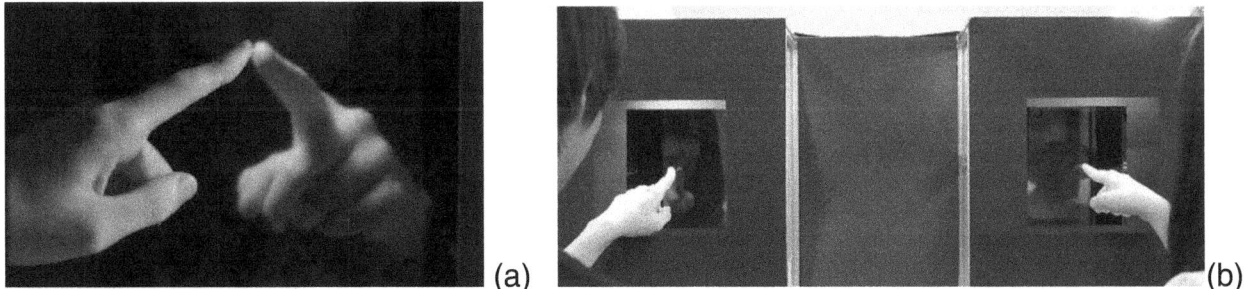

Figure 1. (a) Two people can communicate with cloned image with tactile feedback.
(b) Each side can see and touch the other side's volumetric image in real time.

## ABSTRACT

In this research, we propose a new interactive system that can display haptic and optical clone image in mid-air. We named our system "HaptoClone." Fig. 1 shows how our system works. Our system provides following new experiences. 1) The people facing our system are optically copied to the other side without any time delay by using the Aerial Imaging Plates. 2) A user can see both their own hand and the other's cloned body in the same coordinate. The position and the timing of the clone image is perfectly synchronized to original motion. 3) Tactile feedback can be given when they virtually touch each other. The tactile feedback is given in mid-air by using a phase-controlled ultrasound array. Our system enables users to communicate with each other through haptics in real time with optical clone image.

**Author Keywords**: Volumetric image; Haptic interaction

**ACM Classification Keywords:** H.5.2 User Interfaces (D.2.2, H.1.2, I.3.6): Haptic I/O; H.5.3 Group and Organization Interfaces: Synchronous interaction

## 1. INTRODUCTION

There has been a great deal of research that tried to reproduce volumetric image in mid-air. Some research have used rotating screen to display 3D image [1]. Some have used a concave mirror to replicate real objects [2].

In this research, we developed a system that can display perfectly synchronized volumetric clone image in mid-air with tactile feedback. User can see the other side people without any time delay. The coordinate system of the original one is perfectly copied to the other side. To achieve this, we used the smart optical device "Aerial Imaging Plate" (AIP, ASUKANET Co. Ltd.). The AIP is composed of tiny mirror array. The AIP symmetrically

reflects the light coming from one side to the other. When we use the two AIPs and set them as shown in Fig. 2, the human at A is optically cloned to the position B. As the same way, human standing at B side is copied to the A side simultaneously (Fig. 1 (b)). Based on this technology, two people standing at A and B respectively can see each other through the AIPs in real time.

We also implemented tactile feedback to a cloned image. We use the Airborne Ultrasound Tactile Display (AUTD) system to realize realistic communication with aerial image through touch. The AUTD system, as Monnai et al. used [3], is implemented to our system. By measuring the depth map of users' bodies, the system detect contact to the cloned image to feedback tactile stimuli.

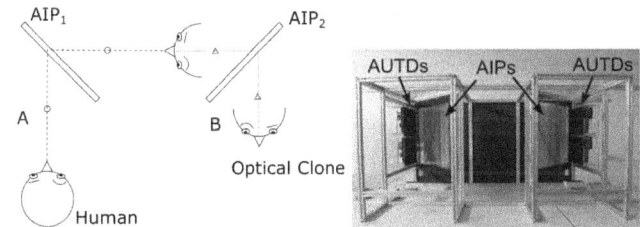

Figure 2. Basic configuration for optical clone.

## 2. PROTOTYPE

Fig. 2 shows our prototype system. Two AIPs are set as shown in the schematic illustration. With this setting, the object at the left side appears to the right side, and vice versa. The AUTDs give tactile feedback onto the aerial copied images.

## ACKNOWLEDGEMENT

This work was supported by JSPS KAKENHI Grant Number 25240032.

## REFERENCES

[1] JONES, A. et al. 2007. Rendering for an interactive 360° light field display. In ACM SIGGRAPH 2007 papers (SIGGRAPH '07). ACM, New York, NY, USA, Article 40.

[2] BUTLER, A. et al. 2011. Vermeer: direct interaction with a 360° viewable 3D display. UIST '11, 569-576.

[3] MONNAI, Y. et al. 2014. HaptoMime: mid-air haptic interaction with a floating virtual screen. UIST '14, 663-66

*SUI 2015*, August 8–9, 2015, Los Angeles, California, USA.
ACM 978-1-4503-3703-8/15/08.   http://dx.doi.org/10.1145/2788940.2794354.

# OpenUIX Demo: A sneak peek at a novel HCI model for AR systems

## [Extended Abstract]

Mikel Salazar
mikel.salazar@deusto.es

Carlos Laorden
claorden@deusto.es

Pablo G. Bringas
pgb@deusto.es

DeustoTech, University of Deusto, Bilbao, Spain

As a result of our research work, we present a demo app that showcases the different interaction techniques that can be implemented using OpenUIX; a novel HCI model that provides the logical mechanisms to easily design Spatial User Interfaces. Thanks to this solution, interaction designers can define widget behaviors that not only take into consideration the physical surroundings of the end users, but also their general context (including their psychological state and any disability they might have). An approach that greatly facilitates the creation and sharing of user experiences adapted to the actual needs and desires of the users (therefore liberating designers from the responsibility of creating *responsive* and *accessible* versions of their user interfaces).

Initially developed as part of a usability study to validate the theoretical foundations of our HCI model, the demo app allows users to evaluate the different interaction techniques in a meaningful way. Although the online version we present in this extended abstract only employs a simplified definition of the interaction space (with just an A3-sized fiducial marker to define the "AR workbench" over which the users can interact), the different use cases it contains offer a comprehensive selection of common tasks (filling forms, object manipulation and gaming), specially designed to gradually introduce users to the new possibilities that three-dimensional UIs offer.

While the current version of the demo app has been developed to work on most Android platforms (version 2.2 and above), due to the relative size of the interaction elements and the estimated duration of the activity (up to 15 minutes), it is highly recommended to employ a tablet equipped with a back handle. For reference, in the lab test of the usability study the experimental platform consisted in a Nexus 10 tablet equipped with a custom-made handle that allowed the participants to hold the device comfortably with one hand (independently of their laterality).

Following the original usability study, the demo app is divided into four different use cases (or interaction scenarios), each one focused on a specific type of interaction technique:

0. *Navigation and System Control:* This use case provides the users with a logical environment that facilitates the navigation between the different interaction contexts and guides them through the associated tasks in the proper sequence. Active throughout the entire execution of the app, this interaction scenario presents the users with a non-spatial virtual environment (commonly referred to as *HUD*) containing several widgets that display instructional information and allows the input of self-reported metric values.

1. *Symbolic Input:* In this interaction scenario, the users are requested to employ spatially-positioned *soft* keyboards to input their personal data and preferences (an information that is also used to modify the appearance and behavior of other widgets). Divided into three separate panels ("Personal Info", "Statistical Data" and "Customization"), each keyboard contains a different key/button layout, adapted to the task at hand.

2. *Object Manipulation:* The goal of this use case is to provide the users with an –AR-based– interaction environment in which they are able to explore the different manipulation techniques at their disposal (translation, rotation and scale). To achieve this goal in a way that could be properly evaluated, the users are asked to recreate an structure using three distinct parts, each requiring a different set of manipulation operations to fit within the delimited construction area.

3. *Selection:* In this final interaction scenario, the users are required to employ different selection techniques (simple, multiple, area) to "destroy" a series of targets before they reach the structure they have built in the previous use case. To further enhance the user experience, the structure displays an "integrity" value that decreases whenever the targets collide with it or the users erroneously perform the selection operation over it. To prevent the value from reaching 0 (and thus, "losing the game"), the users are forced to take advantage of the spatial navigation techniques to select the targets (even when they are occluded by the structure itself).

*SUI '15, August 08-09, 2015, Los Angeles, CA, USA*

© 2015 Copyright held by the owner/author(s).

ACM ISBN ACM 978-1-4503-3703-8/15/08..

DOI: http://dx.doi.org/10.1145/2788940.2794362

# Author Index

www.ingramcontent.com/pod-product-compliance
Lightning Source LLC
Chambersburg PA
CBHW082034230326
41598CB00081B/6511